ARYLAND STATE AND GOVERNMENT: ITS NEW DYNAMICS

MARYLAND

STATE AND GOVERNMENT

Its New Dynamics

By

HARRY BARD, Ed. D., L.L.D.

President, Community College of Baltimore
Instructor, Political Science, Johns Hopkins University

TIDEWATER PUBLISHERS

Cambridge 1974 *Maryland*

Library of Congress Cataloging in Publication Data

Bard, Harry.
Maryland State and Government.

Includes index.
1. Maryland—Politics and government. I. Title.
JK3825 1974.B37 320.4'752 74—22164
ISBN 0—87033—198-1

Printed and Bound in the United States of America

To my mother and father
Fannye and Rubin Bard
who came to this State by choice

and

to my brothers and sisters
who were raised as Marylanders:
Etta, Charles, Sophie, Benjamin, Anne, Ida, Jesse and Lilyan

OTHER BOOKS BY THE AUTHOR

MARYLAND: THE STATE AND ITS GOVERNMENT

MARYLAND TODAY

TEACHERS AND THE COMMUNITY

ACTIVE CITIZENSHIP (Collaborated)

CITIZENSHIP AND GOVERNMENT IN MODERN AMERICA (Collaborated)

CONTENTS

FOREWORD

When I was young my mother lectured me on the value of enthusiasm—the key to charm, love, and success. She would have liked Dr. Harry Bard, the energetic and enthusiastic author of *Maryland, State and Government: Its New Dynamics.* His pursuit of knowledge and his love of people have inspired a life dedicated to teaching at every level of the Maryland educational system.

For reasons mysterious to me, the Maryland academic world has failed to produce a comprehensive book on its state government. Dr. Bard has more than recognized and filled this void; his treatise extends beyond the usual description of the structure of government to its relationship with people.

Dr. Bard is uniquely qualified to write this book. First, he is the author of a number of earlier books on Maryland government, used as texts in secondary schools and colleges as well as for the general public. Second, he is a trained political scientist, having done graduate studies in this field at the University of Maryland, and currently he teaches local and state government at the Johns Hopkins University. Third, he is a practicing political scientist, having served on the Maryland Constitutional Commission, as a delegate to the 1967-68 Maryland Constitutional Convention, as a member of the Baltimore City Charter Revision Commission, and as chairman of the Baltimore City Councilmanic Redistricting Commission on two recent occasions.

Divided into three sections, the book first features people, history, and geography. Ranging then through Maryland's Constitution, its three branches and its local units of government, the middle portion concentrates upon the structure of Maryland government. The final and unique segment devotes itself to a compilation of governmental services for citizens of Maryland.

At a time when public corruption seems pervasive, it is paradoxical that our lives are so dependent upon honesty and efficiency in government. Recent reorganization of Maryland's Executive Branch enables Dr. Bard to give compartmentalized descriptions of the state's programs for its citizens. His diligent presentation rekindles faith in the spirit and the ideals of democracy. If concern for the welfare of citizens is a mark of civilization, Dr. Bard helps us understand Maryland's efforts to achieve this distinction.

WILLIAM S. JAMES
President, Senate of Maryland

PREFACE

The urgencies for rededicating America toward the early dreams of the country whose Bicentennial we are about to celebrate call for a redirection of our treatment of government. Watergate at the national level and the severe shocks of corruption and crisis in confidence at the Maryland county and State levels have brought a great disillusionment about government.

.. Can we bring about a new faith in the democratic ideals?
.. Can we instill in future governmental officials the integrity that is so critically needed?
.. Can we recreate the feelings of the Fathers of the Nation that government is the Servant of the People?
.. Can we restore confidence in Maryland officeholders?
.. Can we eliminate the special interest dominance in local and State politics and establish a new ethic in government?

The author believes that Americans in general and Marylanders in particular must be as creative in putting the Nation and the State back on course in governmental and human relationships as they were in recapturing technological leadership after Sputnik.

The book follows the call of the League of Women Voters of the United States, the National Council for the Social Studies and the American Political Science Association to make the presentation of government more than a mere description of institutions. The author believes that the presentation of government involves investigating political processes and institutions in terms of the human results, the purposes, the changes that are brought and the value systems in which they operate. We must rise above the clichés about democracy and the contradictory images of government and politics. It is more important to have the reader learn how to think about political events than to be able to recite mere descriptive matter.

But one cannot think about political ideas without understandings, generalizations and case studies. The author draws from life situations the troublesome issues with which the Maryland Constitution deals. He outlines the present and new directions for our State courts. He shows the rapid strides taken by Maryland counties in procuring home rule and the tortuous steps yet to be taken. He points to the problems in present plans for metropolitanism and regionalism. He investigates the present legislative processes of the General Assembly and reveals some of the strengths and weaknesses.

It is in the sections on services of government that the author brings exciting new findings. This is the first book to deal descriptively and analytically with the recently created cabinet-level Secretariats for 12 departments of State government. His treatment of where Maryland is going in Secretariat services, such as health, transportation, natural resources, protective and correctional institutions, agriculture, employment and social services, economic and community planning, unveils the streamlined processes under the new structures. He does the same for independent agencies dealing with education, labor and business.

More important, the book gives case studies of how federal, State and local governments collaborate their finances and efforts. These sections are filled with conceptualizations, value studies and analyses. They are consumer-oriented so that the student can have deep understandings and judgment values.

This is also the first Maryland government text to look realistically at our new concerns about treatment of minorities, women, and the elderly. It deals with the recently organized agencies in human relations and points to progress as well as unfinished business. Some important material on black Maryland history is included for the first time in any general book.

The book gives an account of Maryland history, geography and current population trends as background for predictive developments. It shows that Maryland could well point to the beginning of a rebirth in democracy. The thesis is that we start rejuvenating American political institutions close to home in our Maryland towns, counties and in the State. It is a wholesome view held by the author that much that is there is worthwhile and that while there is a good deal that needs undoing, there are great possibilities for accomplishing the task.

It should be remembered that in any book on government, illustrations that give statistics for a particular year are more important in terms of the case study and the example than for the specific figures that are quoted. The reader will have the responsibility for updating the statistics within the framework of the case studies which surround the figures. As indicated earlier, the concepts and generalizations are more important in any understandings of government than are the particular statistics that change from day to day. Nevertheless, statistics are given in this book in order to convey a feeling of the extensiveness of the situation.

The author is indebted to hundreds of Marylanders who encouraged him to write the book and who freely gave time and materials on the subjects of their expertise. He is particularly indebted to Senator William S. James, President of the Maryland Senate, for writing the *Fore-*

word and for his encouragement in terms of the entire manuscript. To Richard W. Parsons of the Baltimore County Public Library, the author will always be grateful for the original stimulation to do a definitive book on Maryland government. He is especially indebted to each and every Secretary at the cabinet-level of State government who gave him time and placed in his hands the latest reports of their departments. This was also true of the department heads of non-cabinet-level standing. He is especially grateful to the staffs of the State departments which made available to him hundreds of photographs from which he selected a large number to include in the book. Foremost among this group were the staff members of the Departments of Economic and Community Development, Transportation, Health and Mental Hygiene, Education, Employment and Social Services, Agriculture, General Services, State Planning, Budget and Fiscal Planning, Public Safety and Correctional Services, and Natural Resources.

* * *

I wish to thank the staffs of the 23 county governments and of Baltimore City for the important data which they placed in my hands. Non-governmental agencies, such as the Maryland Historical Society, were helpful in many ways. In acknowledging the contributions of these agencies, I would like to make it clear that I accept full responsibility for any omissions and for the treatment and point of view.

I salute my wife, Eleanor, for the patience in tolerating and encouraging what yet another book does to planned vacations and family life.

HARRY BARD

Chapter 1
THE PEOPLE OF MARYLAND

Maryland is rich in farmlands, in industrial resources, and in other forms of material wealth; but its greatest resource is the people of the State. The chief characteristics of Maryland's population, as shown by the 1970 U.S. Census, are growth and heterogeneity. In population the State was the 21st in the Union in 1960, when it had 3,100,689 people. In 1970 it moved up to 3,922,399 persons or a 26 percent increase in the ten-year period; thus raising the State to 18th in population. In percentage terms, in fact, Maryland is the fastest growing state east of the Mississippi, except for Florida.

STATE OF MARYLAND

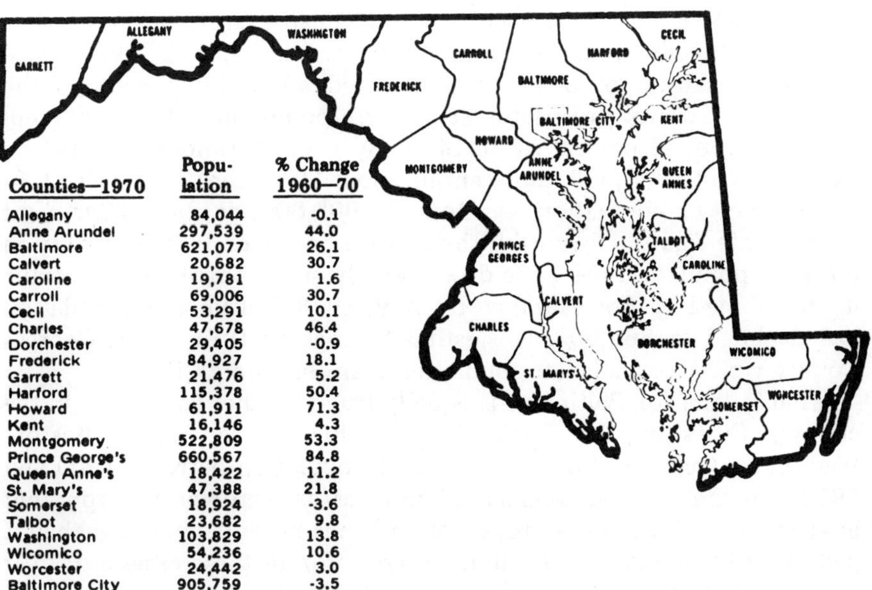

Counties—1970	Population	% Change 1960—70
Allegany	84,044	-0.1
Anne Arundel	297,539	44.0
Baltimore	621,077	26.1
Calvert	20,682	30.7
Caroline	19,781	1.6
Carroll	69,006	30.7
Cecil	53,291	10.1
Charles	47,678	46.4
Dorchester	29,405	-0.9
Frederick	84,927	18.1
Garrett	21,476	5.2
Harford	115,378	50.4
Howard	61,911	71.3
Kent	16,146	4.3
Montgomery	522,809	53.3
Prince George's	660,567	84.8
Queen Anne's	18,422	11.2
St. Mary's	47,388	21.8
Somerset	18,924	-3.6
Talbot	23,682	9.8
Washington	103,829	13.8
Wicomico	54,236	10.6
Worcester	24,442	3.0
Baltimore City	905,759	-3.5

But population growth in Maryland between 1960 and 1970 was uneven. For example, the Eastern Shore's nine counties showed a growth of but 6.1 percent in the ten-year period, while the national capital area, Montgomery and Prince Georges Counties, increased by 69.5 percent. The four westernmost counties had an increase of but 9.9 percent; while the three southernmost counties showed a growth of 32.6 percent. Baltimore City itself actually decreased in population by 3.5 percent; but the five counties in its metropolitan area pushed the whole section up by 14.8 percent.

The heaviest population growth was in the "bedroom" counties adjoining Washington, D.C., with Prince Georges increasing 84.8 percent and becoming the largest county in Maryland with a population of 660,567. The next heaviest growths were in the counties near Baltimore City, with Howard County increasing 71.3 percent, Harford 50.4 percent, Anne Arundel 44 percent, Carroll 30.7 percent and Baltimore County, 26.1 percent.

It was obvious by 1970 that the largest number of Maryland residents lived in suburban communities. Indeed, over one-half the population of the State resided in the two counties surrounding Washington, and the two counties bordering Baltimore City. The importance of the suburban domination could be made clear if the delegations in the General Assembly from these four counties formed a tight bloc to pass legislation favorable to suburbanites.

Baltimore City's Population

Not only did Baltimore City's population decline 3.5 percent between 1960 and 1970; this great city declined sharply in terms of its percentage of the total State numbers. For example, in 1930 Baltimore's population of 804,000 represented about 50 percent of the State total. Twenty years later Baltimore's population of 950,000 represented about 41 percent of the State. By 1960 Baltimore's population had dropped to 939,000, representing about 30 percent of Maryland. In 1970 the city's population was down to 905,000, or about 23 percent of the State figure. Obviously, the relative power of Baltimore City in terms of population has gone down rapidly and probably will continue in that direction. For example, by July, 1973, Baltimore's population had declined to 865,000. It is estimated that by 1981 Prince Georges County would have a larger population than Baltimore City.

What is true for Baltimore is equally true for other large cities in the country. Cities like New York, Chicago, Philadelphia, Detroit, Boston, Washington, and St. Louis have all lost population between 1960 and 1970, but their surrounding suburban areas have grown so sharply that in each case the entire metropolitan area has more people now than it had in 1960. Actually, the suburban areas for all these cities are larger in population than the central city. Thus, when industry or sports promoters study prospective market areas, they ask, "How big is the metropolitan area? Can it support a major league baseball team?" Baltimore's metropolitan area—the city and five nearby counties—in 1970 had 1,803,745 people and the Washington metropolitan area, including the surrounding Maryland and Virginia counties, had 2,800,000.

Race as a Factor

Nearly one of every five Marylanders is a black person. The 1970 Census showed about 3,200,000 residents classified as white. In all, there were 700,000 listed as Negro, 4,200 as Indians, about 3,700 as Japanese, 6,500 as Chinese, 5,100 as Filipinos and 8,000 as of other races.

While the State as a whole has a non-white population (nearly all black) of 18.6 percent, the percentages vary from county to county. In Baltimore the 1970 Census showed that 47 percent of that city's population was black; by 1973 the figure had advanced to 50 percent. The second highest area of black population, in terms of percent of total population, is in Southern Maryland and on the lower Eastern Shore. For example, 37.6 percent of Somerset's, 37.4 percent of Calvert's, 32.9 percent of Worcester's and 31.1 percent of Dorchester's population is black. Western Maryland has the fewest black residents. Garrett County has but 140 black persons, representing but 0.6 percent of its total; and Allegany has but 1.6 percent of blacks. Prince Georges County's blacks number more than 100,000 persons, about 15 percent of the county total.

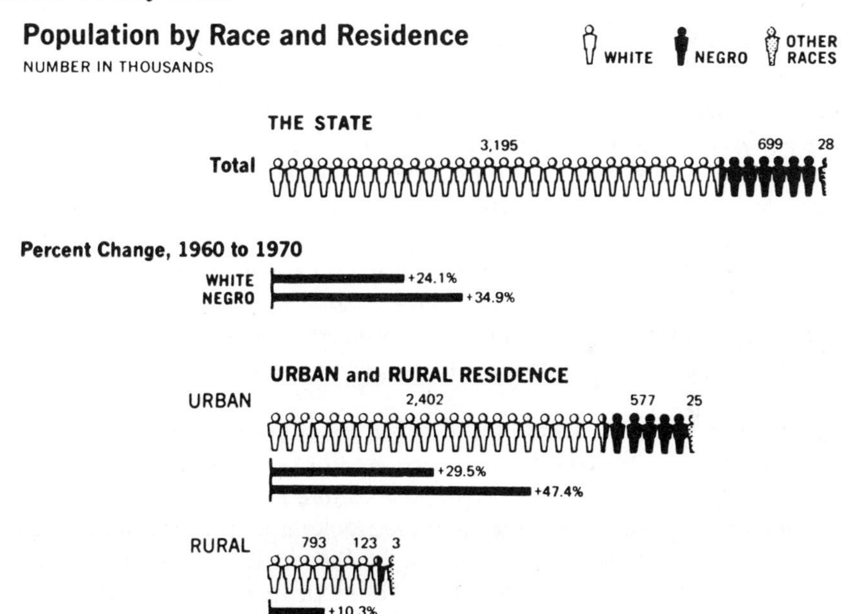

The percentages do not tell the entire story as to race. In places like Baltimore the black population is a much younger group than the white. Many of the younger white citizens have moved out of the city, seeking grass and backyards for their children. So the whites who have remained tend to be beyond child-bearing age. Thus, while in 1973 the populations of whites and blacks were about even, the number of births was greater and deaths lower among the black population. Thus it is obvious that by the 1980's blacks will represent a significant majority of Baltimore's population. Actually, black public school children in Baltimore City now represent over 70 percent of the total school enrollment, and each year brings this figure up. With the voting age now at 18 years, the black voter should soon represent the majority, and the elected officials in the city are likely to reflect this change.

While Baltimore City has more than doubled the percentage of its black population from 23.8 in 1950 to 50 in 1973, the suburban counties surrounding the city have halved their percentages. Thus, Baltimore County's black population, which was 6.7 percent in 1950, dropped to 3.6 in 1970. Anne Arundel had a black population representing 19.2 percent in 1950 and dropped to 11.8 in 1970. True, the total number of black persons increased in those two counties for the 20-year period, but did not approach the total growth.

So, except for some middle-class black citizens who are moving into the suburban counties (not counting Prince Georges, which has had a black increase from 11.8 percent in 1950 to 15 in 1970), the non-white movement in Maryland has been largely to Baltimore. The problem is largely one of housing costs and racial housing patterns. Suburban homes are often far too expensive for blacks on modest or poverty incomes. Add to this the fact that many white families fled from racially integrated neighborhoods in the city and are not inclined to establish them in the suburbs. Thus, some form of subtle housing discrimination exists to keep out those black families that can afford to purchase suburban homes.

One other factor about race is that in the main, where blacks represent a significant part of the population, they tend to live in segregated areas, especially in the inner city of Baltimore where they make up over 90 percent of the population. Yet, in general, some neighborhoods are integrated.

Some way must be found to give full meaning to open housing laws that give people the right to live where they desire and where their incomes permit. Unless this occurs, places like Baltimore City and parts of Prince Georges County will become pockets of poverty with unreasonable burdens of welfare and other problems. The black citizens who have moved to suburban areas like Columbia, in Howard County, have helped destroy the widespread belief that they cannot adjust in an integrated suburban environment. In general, widespread dispersions of various segments of the population will help to give full meaning to the American dream that each man can improve his station.

Incomes and Populations

Relative yearly family incomes reflect a number of factors and are risky to interpret with certainty. Yet they do indicate the median salaries and the nature of housing conditions and costs. The 1970 Census showed that the median annual family income for a Marylander was

$11,063. If he lived in Montgomery County it would be $16,710; if in Howard, $13,472; Prince Georges, $12,450, and Baltimore County, $12,081, with Baltimore City at $8,815. The two westernmost counties and the Eastern Shore counties fall far below the State average, with Somerset last at $5,890.

Income in Maryland is a very good indicator of educational attainment. For example, about 70 percent of all high-school graduates in Montgomery County go on to college. Only 27 percent in this category go on to post-high-school education from Garrett County, and about 35 percent from Baltimore City. It is also true that Montgomery spends about two times as much to educate each elementary and secondary school student as does Somerset. In fact, these disparities have become so important that there are some suits in federal courts to force the State to take over all of public school funding so that each school student would have an equal chance for education no matter where he lives. The question is not an easy one, for if a reasonable floor of support is set, shouldn't so-called wealthy counties have the right to spend for "extra" desires?

State and Federal Aid and Population

Most federal programs are based on population. For example, Maryland's State population is seventeenth in the United States, and when federal revenue-sharing went into effect in 1972, it received more money than all but 16 other states. True, there were other factors, such as poverty in cities, but population was a key factor in distribution of federal monies dealing with pollution, crime, welfare, health, education, and other supports. This was one reason why Baltimore City asked for a recount when the first reports of the 1970 Census indicated there were fewer than 900,000 people there. It is well known that poverty areas tend to show a lower count than probably present, especially if the census is by mail return.

State monies to counties and municipalities for health, education and other services are also distributed with population as a key factor. So it is not sheer pride that causes local and State units to seek accurate counts.

Age and Population

Age counts are important for various reasons as one studies the 1970 Census. To begin with, the numbers from 18 to 64 years of age in Maryland indicate the total possible work force, which is about 2,250,000 persons. But then one must subtract about 275,000 who are from 18 to 21 years old and who represent the college-age group. The nearly 350,000 Marylanders from under one through four years of age tell school authorities that every year about 69,000 new children will be entering first grade—thus we know how many classrooms, teachers, buildings, and funds are needed. The 300,000 Marylanders over 65 indicate that larger numbers of Marylanders are moving into this group. For example, in 1930 those 65 and over represented but 5.9 percent of the total population, in 1970 they were 7.4 percent of the total. Moreover, the older population is not dispersed evenly; for example, this age group represents 10.6 percent of Baltimore City's population and 14.4 of Talbot County's, but only 5.3 of Harford's. Then, too, there is a disparity in race. For example, 14.8 percent of Baltimore's white population is over 65 years of age, but only 5.7 percent of its black population is in that group. These figures indicate enlarged needs for geriatric care, transportation services, housing, and other requirements for aged persons. Of course, businesses, utilities, insurance companies, physicians, hospitals, schools, governmental offices, and other service agents require age counts.

With 18-year-olds eligible to vote, the relation of those over 18 to the total population is important. In all 2,540,000 Marylanders are over 18, with nearly all able to vote, representing 64.8 percent of the total population. Baltimore City has 66.5 percent of its total population over 18 years of age, while Howard has but 61.4 percent; thus, this factor becomes important at election time.

Future Population in Maryland

By 1975 Maryland's population will increase about ten percent over 1970 and reach 4,200,000, while Baltimore City's population will be down to about 850,000. Baltimore County will pick up about 40,000 to reach 660,000. The big jump will be in Prince Georges County, which will increase to about 735,000, and in Montgomery County, which will expand to about 605,000. Anne Arundel will raise its totals to 330,000, Harford will increase to 133,000, and Howard will go up to 95,000. Otherwise, the gains or losses will be slight.

There are two important factors in population increase. First, the "natural increase," which is the difference between births and deaths. For example, of Maryland's increase of 821,000 people between 1960 and 1970, natural increase accounted for 437,000 and new arrivals in the State added 384,000. The latter represented 12.4 percent of the State's 1960 population of 3,100,000. Unfortunately, some local districts had outward migration. For example, Cecil saw a 6.8 percent exodus and Baltimore City lost 12.7 percent, or 120,000 people (mainly whites). Thus even with a natural increase of 86,000 (mainly blacks), the city's population still went down. Howard County had a 53.8 percent influx (largely due to Columbia) and Prince Georges one of 56.1 percent (mainly from Washington, D.C.). Counties that depend on natural increases in population tend to gain in numbers of people, but slowly. Those like Harford, Montgomery, Charles, Anne Arundel, and Carroll, along with Howard and Prince Georges that have heavy influxes as a result of flight from nearby big cities, tend to increase sharply. As we approach the 1980's and 1990's the big question is whether many of the remaining whites and more blacks will leave Baltimore and Washington. As for natural increase, statistics show that birth rates have declined rather sharply in the early 1970's, and while deaths have also decreased, the fall is not as high here. The drop in big families, "the Pill," and planned parenthood will have their effects in the late '70's and '80's.

Marylanders Come from Many Lands

The State has long been a virtual United Nations in that most of its citizens could trace their ancestry—near or far away— to other lands in Europe, Asia, Africa, Latin America, or other continents. The number of foreign born in Maryland have decreased in recent years so that in 1970 only 124,345 persons, or three percent of the total State population, was foreign born. The largest numbers from any single country were about 15,000 from Germany, 11,000 from the United Kingdom, 11,000 from Ireland, 10,000 from Italy, 8,000 from Soviet Russia, 7,000 from Poland, and about 7,000 from Canada. In addition there were about 16,000 born in Asiatic countries and 12,000 in South or Central American countries. When one adds to the foreign born the number of Marylanders with one or two parents of foreign birth, the figures rise appreciably to 329,813 persons, or more than eight percent of the total population. This gives one an indication of the mother tongue of Marylanders. For example, in the 1970 census, about 80,000 native and foreign-born Marylanders gave German as their mother tongue; 52,000 listed Spanish; 50,000, Italian; 46,000, Yiddish; 40,000, Polish, and 39,000, French—though most of these also spoke English. Yet Maryland, as an eastern state, has a very high percentage (87½) of native and foreign born whose native tongue is English.

Maryland, the Home of Many Religions

It is very difficult to acquire accurate statistics on religious affiliations of Marylanders, since the 1970 U.S. Census Report did not record this item. Furthermore, some religious denominations count only those who have formally fulfilled requirements such as baptism or confirmation, while others record all born into the families of those formally or informally related to their faiths. There are at least 800,000 Protestants in Maryland related to these five denominations—United Methodist (250,000), Episcopalian (200,000), various Baptist groups (200,000), three major Lutheran groups (115,000), and Presbyterians (50,000). There are probably as many as 700,000 other Protestants belonging to denominations with smaller affiliations, making about 1,500,000 Protestants in all. The count on Roman Catholics cannot be too accurate because the northern Eastern Shore counties are counted

(L. to r.) The "Freedom of Conscience" Statue in St. Marys City symbolizes religious freedom on which Maryland was founded. (Courtesy Tourist Division, Maryland Department of Economic Development); People of Maryland at the Baltimore City Fair, 1973. (Courtesy Maryland Division of Tourism; Photo by Bob Willis)

as part of the Wilmington diocese figures and the Southern Maryland figures are part of the Washington diocese—yet statistics indicate that there are about 650,000 to 700,000 all told. The figures for Jewish or Hebrew affiliation add up to about 180,000 persons, with the Orthodox group about 50 percent of that and the Conservative and Reform groups about 25 percent each—most persons of that faith living in the Baltimore and Washington metropolitan areas.

(Top, l. to r.) Lloyd Street Synagogue Museum, 1845, Lloyd Street off Baltimore Street, Baltimore. Building commemorates beginning of Hebrew worship in Maryland; Lovely Lane Methodist Church, St. Paul and Twenty-Second Streets, Baltimore, commemorates beginning of Methodism in Maryland. (Courtesy Maryland Historical Trust, Annapolis)

(Bottom, l. to r.) First Unitarian Church, 1819, Charles and Franklin Streets, Baltimore. Structure—beginning of Unitarianism in America. (Maryland Historical Trust); Old Trinity (Episcopal) Church, ca. 1675, Church Creek, Md. (Courtesy Rev. James Valliant)

From its founding in 1634 Maryland had a diversity of religions, though it began then as a haven for persecuted Roman Catholics. In 1649 in an obvious effort to separate church and state in the colony, the freemen passed "An Act Concerning Religion" stating that no person professing to believe in Jesus Christ shall be troubled or molested for or in respect of his religion. In 1664, at the trial of a Jewish physician, Dr. Jacob Lombrozo, the courts extended the State's position to include non-Christians who believed in God. While Maryland's record on religious freedom was blemished many times after these acts, nevertheless, in the matter of freedom of conscience it has been ahead of other places.

"America's oldest church now in active use" is near Church Creek, in Dorchester County. The tiny brick church, Old Trinity, will observe its tercentenary in 1975. Restored in 1960 after almost seven years of meticulous research, Old Trinity is renowned as a gem of restored seventeenth century church architecture. Restoration was made possible by the generosity of Col. and Mrs. Edgar W. Garbisch as a memorial to Mrs. Garbisch's parents, Mr. and Mrs. Walter P. Chrysler.

On July 7, 1806, Bishop John Carroll, a native of Upper Marlboro, Maryland, laid the cornerstone in Baltimore for the first Roman Catholic cathedral in this country, and he became the first archbishop in the United States. George Fox, founder of the Society of Friends, organized the Second Yearly Meeting in America on the West River, in Anne Arundel County, in 1672. The first successful Lutheran Church was built in 1734 by John Casper Stoever in the Monocacy Valley, ten miles south of the present city of Frederick. The first Baptist Church in Maryland was built by Henry Sater at Chestnut Ridge, in Baltimore County, in 1742. Baltimore, too, was the scene of the birth of the Methodist Episcopal Church at a Christmas conference in 1784 held at the Lovely Lane Methodist Chapel, where Reverend Francis Asbury was the preacher. In 1845 the Lloyd Street Synagogue was built to serve more than 200 Baltimore Jews who had prayed above a grocery for the previous 15 years; this is the third oldest American Hebrew place of worship. Unitarianism had its beginnings in 1820 with the Baltimore church that still stands at Charles and Franklin Streets. The Seventh Day Adventists since 1904 have had their world headquarters in Takoma Park, Maryland. The Pipe Creek Church, built in 1803 near New Windsor in Carroll County, is one of the older Church of the Brethren houses of worship in this country. The priests at the large Greek Orthodox Church at Maryland Avenue and Preston Street in Baltimore, conduct services for a sizeable Greek (Eastern Orthodcx) community that has worshipped together since about 1900.

Maryland Represents Mobility in Population

Practically every other Marylander who was born in this country came from another state; the total of such migrants is 45.8 percent. The largest numbers, 19.5 percent, came from the South; then 13.4 percent from the Northeast, 5.5 percent from the North Central States, only 1.9 percent from the West and 5.5 percent not giving state of birth. Thirty-seven and a half percent of the native American black population in Maryland came from other states. The importance of net migration into the State is made clear by the fact that while Maryland increased by 821,710 people between 1960 and 1970 or by 26.5 percent, only 436,870, or 14.1 percent, was due to natural increase (difference between births and deaths). As much as 12.4 percent of the increase, or 384,840, was due to net migration into the State over migration out.

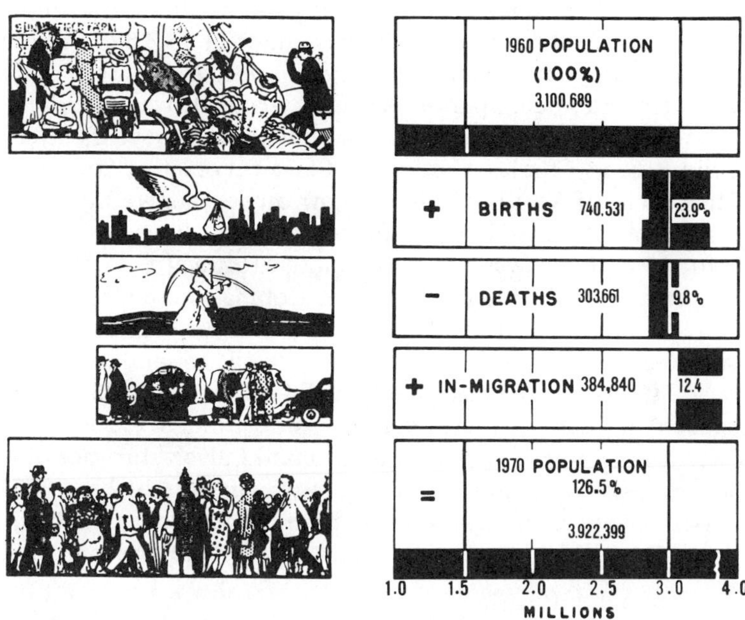

Chapter 2

THE HISTORY OF MARYLAND

George Calvert, to whom King James I gave the title Lord Baltimore, originally established a colony in Newfoundland in 1623. Known as Avalon, this colony was planned largely as a refuge for Roman Catholics, who were then being persecuted in England. It was abandoned six years later because of the unfavorable climate. A few years after Avalon's failure, King Charles I promised Calvert a tract of land north of the settled areas of Virgina. This the new owner named *Mary Land* in honor of Henrietta Maria, the King's wife. On June 20, 1632, the charter for Mary Land was formally granted to Cecil Calvert, George's son, who had inherited his father's title. Hoping to interest Protestants as well as Roman Catholics in his father's ambitious project to establish a colony where religious tolerance should prevail, he sent out two ships, the *Ark* and the *Dove*, from England on November 23, 1633. More than 200 persons of high and low degree, some Roman Catholic, others Protestant, were aboard. So, too, was Leonard Calvert, brother of Cecil, who became first governor of the colony. On March 25, 1634, the colonists disembarked on St. Clements Island in the Potomac River near Chesapeake Bay. This date is celebrated as Maryland Day or Founders' Day.

Maryland as a Colony

In 1634 the first settlement, St. Marys City, became the colonial capital. It remained so for 60 years; then the seat of government was removed to Annapolis. Fifteen years after the first settlement, Maryland set an example for the rest of the world when her Assembly passed the "Act Concerning Religion" (Toleration Act) in 1649. Maryland's history was colored by the English Civil War of the 1640's, and by the numerous wars which the mother country waged with France in both Europe and America during the 18th century. Difficulties with neighboring colonies claimed much of Maryland's attention during the colonial period. Boundary disputes with Pennsylvania were in part settled by a survey made between 1763 and 1767 by Charles Mason and Jeremiah Dixon, two English mathematicians. The Mason-Dixon Line later was regarded as a line of demarcation between free and slave states.

Maryland's Part in Favoring Independence

Maryland was one of the eight colonies to send representatives to the Stamp Act Congress that met in New York. Soon after the First Continental Congress (1774), the Maryland counties sent representatives to a convention of their own that met in Annapolis and there made plans for organizing a militia. The colony had seven representatives at the Second Continental Congress (1775). Foremost of these was Thomas Johnson, Jr., who later became first governor of independent Maryland. At the meeting of this Congress a year later, four Maryland representatives—Charles Carroll of Carrollton, Samuel Chase, William Paca, and Thomas Stone—signed the Declaration of Independence.

Maryland during the Revolution

Marylanders played an important part during the Revolutionary War both as soldiers and as staunch patriots who combated the activities of Loyalists (English sympathizers). Alongside Massachusetts troops, Maryland soldiers helped drive the British from Boston. Led by Major Mordecai Gist, Marylanders took part in covering Washington's retreat from Long Island. The valiant fighting of the Maryland Line, as the State Militia was then called, in this and subsequent engagements, including Yorktown, won for Maryland the nickname Old Line State.

First Maryland State House, St. Marys. (Courtesy Division of Tourism. Photo by Bob Willis)

Maryland under the Confederation

Because Maryland feared the power of states that held claims to western territory, she refused to sign the Articles of Confederation until the land question was satisfactorily settled. Virginia, New York, and other states eventually gave up their claims and proposed that the lands become the common possession of the whole nation. It is evident that Maryland's attitude in this situation was partly instrumental in establishing a land policy for the Northwest Territory. This is considered a key event in American history.

Maryland and the Constitution

Sensing that the Articles of Confederation were inadequate, Maryland proposed that representatives from states bordering Chesapeake Bay and the Delaware and Susquehanna Rivers meet at Annapolis and there discuss the taxation of imports. Virginia suggested that all states be invited. At Annapolis, in 1786, representatives of the five participating states agreed that all states should convene at a later meeting in Philadelphia. Thus, in 1787, the Constitutional Convention came into being.

At the Constitutional Convention, Maryland was represented by Luther Martin, John Francis Mercer, James McHenry, Daniel of St. Thomas Jenifer, and Daniel Carroll. The last three signed the document in its final form. When the document was submitted to the states, Maryland was seventh to ratify the Constitution.

Maryland in the War of 1812

Baltimore City, already a fairly large town, experienced a boom during the Napoleonic Wars. Privateers in vessels known as "Baltimore Clippers" did a thriving business. They suffered one bitter experience in 1807, however, when the frigate *Chesapeake* was attacked by a British ship just outside Chesapeake Bay. The assault on the *Chesapeake* was followed by other British attacks on American ships; these attacks, together with other factors, led the United States to declare war on England in 1812.

The Battle of Baltimore

After marching into Washington and burning the Capitol, on August 24, 1814, British forces were moved up Chesapeake Bay with the aim of invading Baltimore City. Enemy frigates anchored off North Point, and invading troops marched toward the city. Led by Generals Samuel Smith and John Stricker, Americans forced the British to retreat to the ships from which they had come. Because of this victory, Marylanders now celebrate September 12, Defenders' Day, as a legal holiday.

The Star-Spangled Banner

While British troops were storming Baltimore City by land from the north, enemy ships were attacking the city from the south, at Fort McHenry. On the morning of September 13, 1814, the British started their bombardment of the city. For 25 trying hours the shelling continued; on several occasions British victory seemed possible. But the defenders of the fort, commanded by Lieutenant Colonel George Armistead, succeeded in throwing back the repeated British assaults, and on the morning of September 14 the American flag was still flying over battered but unbeaten Fort McHenry.

An involuntary spectator present at this decisive action was Francis Scott Key, a young Maryland lawyer. Key was on an American truce ship that had been forced to accompany the British fleet up the Bay; the lawyer had received permission from the enemy to fulfill arrangements for the release of a friend, who was being held prisoner. Detained by the British, Key spent the night aboard ship. The sight of our flag still waving in the early morning hours inspired him to write *The Star-Spangled Banner*, our national anthem. Shortly after the battle of Baltimore the war came to an end.

(L. to r.) The *Constellation*, shown anchored in Baltimore, was one of the first American naval vessels; Antietam, Hagerstown (Photo: R.L. Braun)

Maryland in the War between the States

The first blood shed during the Civil War was spilled in the streets of Baltimore City. There, on April 19, 1861, the Sixth Massachusetts Regiment was marching from one railway station to another. Claiming that they had been assaulted by a small crowd of Southern sympathizers, the soldiers fired into the mob. It has never yet been clearly determined who was at fault, but when the fracas was over, twelve citizens, among them some innocent bystanders, and four of the soldiers, were dead.

The news of this affray spread rapidly and far. When James Ryder Randall, a Marylander who was then teaching school in faraway Louisiana, heard of the incident, in a spirit of passion he wrote the verses of *Maryland, My Maryland*, the State anthem.

While the Maryland General Assembly was in session at Frederick (Annapolis had been occupied by federal troops), General Ben F. But-

(Top) Fort McHenry and the American flag at the time of the War of 1812. (Courtesy Division of Tourism. Photo by Bob Willis)

(Bottom) *First Blood.* The 6th Massachusetts Regiment fighting their way through Baltimore, April 19, 1861. (Courtesy Maryland Historical Society)

ler, with Union forces, took possession of Federal Hill, overlooking Baltimore harbor, on May 13, 1861. Thereafter secessionist uprisings quieted down.

Though Maryland supplied troops to both the North and the South, the State remained loyal to the Union throughout the conflict. On September 6, 1862, Confederate troops led by General Robert E. Lee invaded Maryland. The Battle of Antietam Creek, just south of Hagerstown, was fought on the following September 17. In the summer of 1863 General Lee again marched through the State on his way to Gettysburg. The third and final invasion of Maryland took place in July, 1864, when Confederate forces, under General Jubal A. Early, captured Hagerstown and threatened Baltimore City.

Maryland during the Reconstruction Period

During the decade that followed the Civil War, Baltimore City experienced a tremendous commercial and industrial boom, in which, of course, much of the State also shared. In that period the Pennsylvania Railroad Company began to be a strong competitor of the older Baltimore & Ohio. During this period, too, a number of Maryland industrialists, notably Johns Hopkins and Enoch Pratt, made fortunes that they later left for the promotion of philanthropic enterprises in the state. In October 1876, the Johns Hopkins University was founded. Later bequests of Enoch Pratt led to the establishment of free public libraries in Baltimore City.

Maryland in World War I

Maryland soldiers with the Rainbow Division were among the first to go overseas in World War I. After fighting successfully on the Western Front, in 1917-18, many men remained as part of the Army of Occupation. Of the 65,000 Marylanders serving in our Armed Forces, 1,752 men and ten nurses gave up their lives. At home the State's citizens subscribed heavily to all war loans. Women gave freely of their time and effort in the work of the Red Cross and other agencies.

Maryland in World War II

About 250,000 Marylanders, or one in every eight residents, served in the Armed Forces during the war period from 1941 to 1945. Almost 4,500 of these gave up their lives during this conflict.

Marylanders served in many units and in all parts of the world. A brief account of the 29th Division illustrates the State's military role. The 29th, made up of men from Maryland and other nearby states, was active in the D-Day assault, landing on the Normandy shores of France on June 6, 1944. This glorious "Blue and Gray Division" played a leading role in the defeat of the Germans at Brest, where men of the 29th captured 13,000 prisoners. Their later battles took them into

Germany itself. Hospital units from the staffs of Johns Hopkins and the University of Maryland served in the Far East, while an unattached medical unit was active in the European campaigns, including the Battle of the Bulge.

Army installations in Maryland included ordnance testing at Aberdeen Proving Ground and the chemical center at Edgewood Arsenal, both in Harford County, the Adjutant General's School at Fort Washington and Andrews Air Force Base, both in Prince Georges County; the biological warfare experimentation center at Camp Detrick in Frederick County; the center for foreign language interpreters and counterintelligence at Camp Ritchie in Washington County; Fort George C. Meade in Anne Arundel County, and the Curtis Bay Ordnance Depot and the Holabird Signal Depot in the Baltimore area.

Naval installations in the State included the David W. Taylor Model Test Basin and the National Naval Medical Center in Montgomery County; the Naval Air Test Center in St. Marys County; the Naval Powder Factory in Charles County; the Naval Training Center at Bainbridge in Cecil County; numerous naval establishments including the United States Naval Academy in the Annapolis area, which made up the Severn River Naval Command; and a naval communications center, dispensary, magazine, and storehouse in the Baltimore area.

As the reports of Maryland's War Records Division make clear, the State's civil and industrial efforts were as admirable as her military exploits. Working round the clock, Maryland's farmers, with 30 percent less labor than in prewar days, produced 40 percent more food. With management and labor cooperating closely, the State's factories, mills, and shipyards filled government contracts totaling more than $5.5 billion between 1940 and 1950. Airplanes, ships, guns, and many other types of military equipment were represented in this huge sum. On the home front, war bond drives were oversubscribed, citizens participated in civilian defense activities, and school children helped the war effort through scrap drives, Red Cross campaigns, and other programs.

Maryland in the Korean War

In the 37 months of the Korean conflict between June, 1950 and July, 1953, about 340 Marylanders lost their lives and about 1,300 were wounded. This war, as others before it, showed that Marylanders of different racial, religious, and social backgrounds were ready to stand together to defeat any common enemy.

Maryland since 1950

The State concentrated on political, social, and economic progress in the period following World War II. The most exciting developments were those in the social field. Starting with the 1954 Supreme Court public-school desegregation decision, a whole host of civil rights for black citizens came into being. Foremost was the breaking up in 1954 of the separate public schools for Negro and white students, which had existed since public education began in Maryland in the 1820's. The State had comparatively few problems in integrating the schools—though by 1974 there were still many public student bodies practically all white or all black. The '50's and '60's brought open housing laws and equal job opportunity laws. While 1974 found much unfinished business in treatment of black citizens, the number of black elected executives, legislators and judges had increased sharply in Maryland. Moreover, it was obvious that not only the elementary schools, but former all-white colleges and universities in the State were increasingly becoming racially integrated—though "at too slow a pace," said the U. S. Civil Rights Commission.

Politically, there were a number of important reforms. In 1967 a Constitutional Convention was called to revise the 100-year-old Maryland Constitution. This body recommended a document that would have reformed all branches of State government, but the people voted it down in a special election in 1968. However, after that date many of its recommendations were adopted separately by the General Assembly and became the laws of the State. For example, the administrative offices were streamlined in the late '60's and early '70's so that instead of 140 different departments, there were to be 12 Secretaries forming a Governor's cabinet with each representing a highly important area, such as transportation, health, and natural resources. Each Secretary was a well qualified specialist in his field and was given great power to issue regulatory pronouncements within the powers granted by the legislature. Other recently adopted reforms by the Legislature that came out of the ill-fated 1967-68 Constitutional Convention were: creation of the office of Lieutenant Governor, creating lay and professional nominating committees for the purpose of recommending judicial appointments to the Governor, the establishment of Statewide property assessment evaluations, protection of civil liberties, the creation of single-member senatorial districts, lowering the voting age, the expansion of opportunities for home rule by counties, greater educational opportunities for young and old, and protection in the fields of consumer purchases and natural resources.

Cultural, Social and Industrial Changes

The 25-year period after 1950 saw great expansion of opportunities in education. All of the 16 public community colleges in the State started after 1945 and most after 1955, yet by 1973 about 55,000 students were studying in these schools, full or part-time. In 1973 more than 25,000 pupils were in seven public four-year colleges and 45,000 more at the various campuses of the University of Maryland.

The 25-year period also saw great expansion in urban development. Baltimore's Charles Center changed the face of the downtown area at a cost of $180,000,000 and the City's Inner Harbor development was well under way to be fully completed at a cost of $486,300,000, including a $21,000,000 World Trade Center.

Federal government operations spilled over into Montgomery and Prince Georges Counties with large establishments devoted to research and administration in many fields. Private research and development operations also expanded, especially in the Maryland counties adjoining Washington and Baltimore.

It was a period, too, of sports development with major league baseball, football, hockey, soccer and basketball servicing the State with exciting teams in Baltimore and Washington.

The most controversial subject of the period was the Viet Nam conflict and American participation from 1960 to 1973. Maryland, like other states, contributed thousands of men and women who fought in this hapless war. Here, too, the State was divided between those who favored and were against the war. All were glad to see it end.

Communications developed to exciting heights in that 25-year period. Color television became available through two or three major commercial outlets servicing most of the State. Maryland Public Broadcasting, Inc., a public educational TV project formed in the 1960's, operated in conjunction with the Maryland State Department of Education and covered the entire State.

It was a period of suburban development encouraged by freeways, expressways, and beltways leading in and out of Baltimore (which also had a Harbor Tunnel) and Washington. Indeed, 1974 found each of these cities moving swiftly toward completion of mass transit subway passenger service, permitting even larger and faster traffic within their metropolitan areas. In 1973 the second span of the Bay Bridge was completed, making it easier for Marylanders to reach the Atlantic beaches—and causing rapid housing development in the Ocean City area.

Rapid expansion of suburban roadways caused much of the retail trade that was carried out in the central areas of large and small towns to be moved to the outskirts where better parking facilities were available. Numerous suburban industrial parks also were established, thus causing the central cities—large ones like Baltimore and smaller ones like Cumberland—to actually lose population.

As indicated elsewhere, manufacturing and agriculture held their own, with some slight drop in the 1960's. But it was the services that increased sharply in this period, moving to 22.9 percent of the total labor force. Between 1958 and 1968 the number of service establishments in the State jumped from 13,000 to more than 17,000, including facilities such as auto repair, laundry, tourism (including motels), recreational, legal, health, and educational. It all adds up to more than 256,000 people employed in services in Maryland.

With all the development in Maryland, like elsewhere, the quarter century between 1950 and 1974 found racial riots in Baltimore, Cambridge, Frederick, and other towns. Charges of political scandals in Baltimore and Anne Arundel Counties were foremost in 1974. The approach of 1975 found all Marylanders with the hope that both the national stain of Watergate and the sad resignation of Vice President Spiro T. Agnew, as a result of charges of bribery and tax evasion when he was Baltimore County Executive, Governor of Maryland, and holder of the nation's second highest post, would act as a catharsis that might bring major changes in the way democracy was operating.

Certainly, as the last quarter of the 20th century was approaching, all voices in Maryland and throughout the Nation sought to bring greater effectiveness to American democracy. Reform in politics, rethinking about materialistic objectives, new concerns about ecology and our physical environment and perhaps most important of all, greater respect for fellow man could emerge from the crucible of the 1970's. The Declaration of Independence is a living document, and the bicentennial year—1976—might well be a time when a rededication to its principles will have been accomplished.

(Top) The Great Falls of the Potomac in Maryland near the boundary of the District of Columbia. The river pours through a long passage of rocks, making a display of white racing water that is famous. (Bottom) Point Lookout, St. Marys County. (Photo by Richard Weeks)

Chapter 3

THE GEOGRAPHY OF MARYLAND

Physical Features of the State

Forty-second in size among the States of the Union, Maryland has a total area of 12,303 square miles. Of this area, 9,874 square miles are land, 703 are inland water; and 1,726 square miles of the Chesapeake Bay are in the State. Chesapeake Bay, the State's chief body of water, measures 195 miles in length and varies in width from about 20 miles at the Maryland-Virginia line to three miles at its narrowest upper reaches. From east to west the extreme width of the State is 240 miles; its extreme length from north to south is 125 miles. At one point, in the western part of the State, the northern boundary is separated from the southern by a distance of barely 1 and 1/2 miles.

There is great diversity in Maryland's topography and natural resources. Traveling through the State from east to west, from the Atlantic Ocean to the Allegheny Mountains, one passes through the low coastal plain of the Eastern Shore, across the Chesapeake Bay, over the rolling Piedmont section of Central Maryland, and into the forests and mountains of Western Maryland. In few states could such a short ride offer so much variety in physical features.

Physiographic Regions. The three physiographic regions into which Maryland is divided affect both the characteristics and the work of the people who inhabit them. These regions are described below.

1. The Appalachian Region extends from the western limits of the State to the border of the Piedmont Plateau in the central part. The Appalachian Region consists of a series of parallel mountain ranges that have a mean elevation of about 2,500 feet, though some of the peaks reach more than 3,000 feet. The largest valley of the region is Hagerstown Valley; here Hagerstown, Maryland's third largest incorporated city, is located. The Appalachian Range covers the geographic area known as Western Maryland.

2. The Piedmont Plateau extends from the eastern limits of the Appalachian Region to an irregular line that runs southward from Elkton as far as Washington, by way of Baltimore City and Laurel. This line is known as the Fall Line because waterfalls are found in most of the streams at the point where they pass over the easternmost ledges of the Piedmont Plateau to make their way through the soft soil of the Coastal Plain in the eastern and southern parts of the State. The Fall Line had much to do with the origin and early development of several Maryland cities. The Piedmont Plateau consists of low undulating hills that reach as high as 800 feet. It covers the area known as Central Maryland.

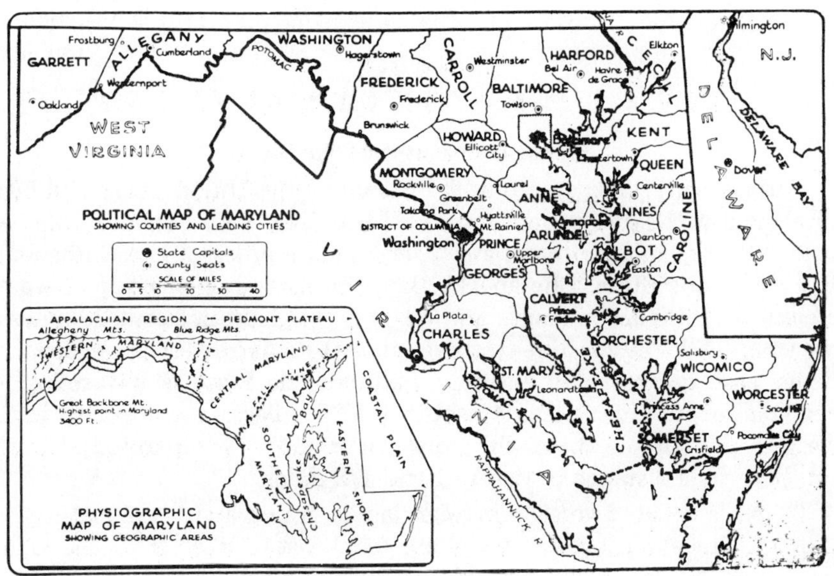

3. The Coastal Plain extends from the Fall Line eastward to Delaware and the Atlantic Ocean, southward to the limits of the State. The Coastal Plain, broad and low, has an altitude of some 300 feet along its western edge. From such a height it gradually slants downward toward its southeastern extremity till it reaches a point where it is only a few feet above sea level. Chesapeake Bay divides this region into two large geographic areas: the Eastern Shore and the Western Shore. The Western Shore really includes the western part of the Coastal Plain, the Piedmont Plateau, and the Appalachian Region. Geographically, the southern part of the Western Shore is designated Southern Maryland.

Climate. Variety of physiographic regions and the existence of a large water area (Chesapeake Bay) create marked differences of climate within Maryland. Maryland lies midway between the rigorous climate of the North and the mild climate of the South. In the eastern and southern parts, there are mild winters and hot summers. The more elevated western parts have cold winters and cool summers. The mean minimum temperatures in January vary from 32° F. on the southern borders of the Eastern Shore to 20° in western Garrett County. The mean maximum temperatures in July vary from 86° in Central Maryland to 80° in the western part of the State. The mean annual precipitation ranges from 36 inches to 48 inches, according to locality. In most parts of the State the rainfall is 40 inches or more, which is sufficient for the needs of agriculture.

Minerals and Forests

Maryland's Mineral Wealth. Minerals have long played an important role in Maryland's progress. In 1970 the State produced more than 16 million short tons of stone valued at $32.8 million; 13 million of sand and gravel, $20.4 million; 1.6 million of bituminous coal, $8 million; 1.1 million of clays, $1.4 million; 4,000 of peat, $47,000, and 813 million cubic feet of natural gas, $200,000. These, plus unitemized minerals valued at $25.2 million, added up to a total of $88.4 million for the State's 1970 mineral production.

It is important to note that the coal production, confined to Allegany and Garrett Counties, in 1907 had reached a peak production of 5,500,000 short tons. The decline, however, seems to have levelled off.

Forests and Lumber. The lumber and other forest-product industries draw raw material from about 2,900,000 acres of woodland in Maryland; representing 47 percent of the State's land area. The live saw timber and growing stock are largely shortleaf and loblolly pine and various Eastern hardwoods, such as the oaks, yellow poplar, hickory, sweet gum, maple, beech, and gum. Hundreds of sawmills, scattered throughout the State, offer employment to thousands. Maple syrup and sugar products in Garrett County and rayon and plastic materials in Allegany County create related industries.

Chesapeake Bay

With an area of 1,726 square miles in Maryland (1,511 more in Virginia), the Bay represents Maryland's richest resource. It has two outlets to the Atlantic Ocean, one through Delaware Bay via the Chesapeake and Delaware Canal, the other between the Virginia Capes. It is the Bay's shipping possibilities that raised the deepwater Port of Baltimore to its present potential. As early as the period after the War of 1812 it brought the Baltimore clipper ships to fame and currently affords a lane for ships to that port from all over the world. From a commercial point of view, the Bay provides thousands of Marylanders with gainful employment in the seafood industry. To thousands more it offers the recreational joys of boating and fishing.

Fish and Seafood. A study of the seafood yield brings to mind H. L. Mencken's description of the Bay as an "immense protein factory." About 17,000,000 fish—mainly menhaden, rock (striped bass), alewives, white perch, and shad—worth about $2. million were caught in the Bay in 1970. More than 26.5 million crabs, worth nearly $3 million, were harvested, as were more than 15 million oysters, worth $9 million, and more than 20 million clams worth $4 million. In an average year, the Chesapeake yields seafood products with a retail value of more than $75 million. Harvesting the more than 40 salable species in the Bay gives work to 9,700 watermen who operate more than 7,200 vessels and provide work for an additional 4,500 people employed in Maryland's 275 seafood processing plants.

Like so many of our natural resources, the Bay is in danger. Tributaries like the Susquehanna River pour mine acids, raw sewage, and other pollutants into the great inland sea. As one result, 30,000 acres of once flourishing oyster beds were closed recently when health authorities found the presence of infectious disease. Fortunately, the Board of Natural Resources and the State Health and Mental Hygiene Department have taken necessary precautions to combat this degradation of Maryland's greatest asset.

Agriculture in Maryland

The 1970 Census showed 21,480 Marylanders engaged in agriculture out of a total State labor force of 1,538,766, which means that farm workers constitute but 1.4 percent of the total. In 1940 agricultural workers constituted 10 percent of the labor force. Thus Maryland steadily becomes less agrarian and more industrial. While farmers in Maryland are a mere handful compared to industrial and professional workers, agriculture-related work provides 190,000 jobs.

Farms still represent slightly more than half the State's land area and number about 19,000. The average size of a Maryland farm is 176 acres. Total 1972 cash receipts from sales of all farm commodities were $412.9 million ($9.5 million government subsidy might be added).

(L. to r., top to bottom) Stripping tobacco in St. Marys County. Soybeans represent an increasingly important Maryland crop, ranking third in dollar value (about $20 million annually) behind corn and tobacco; the broiler industry, on the Eastern Shore is Maryland's top agricultural industry. Production exceeds 180,000,000 annually. (Photos: Maryland Department of Agriculture)

While farms decrease in number, the size of each is increasing, and so is the yield. For example, on a dairy farm 20 years ago, the average herd size was about 26 cows; today it is more than 60 and the investment is $2,500 per cow. With twice-daily milking and high standards of nutrition, management, and sanitation, milk yield per cow is at an all-time high. The great problem is lack of adequate labor, and Maryland farmers are turning to machines that efficiently harvest such crops as corn, tomatoes, cucumbers, and to a lesser degree, tobacco.

In terms of cash yield, livestock and livestock products are Maryland's No. 1 farm commodity. The yield in 1969 was $265 million. This includes broiler chickens, a leading industry on the Eastern Shore, which alone brought in $113 million. The yield from horticultural and forest products that same year was about $111 million. Not far behind in 1969 was the dairy industry, bringing in $96 million. Field crops, including vegetables, fruits, nuts, and berries, yielded about $95 million. Income from tobacco in 1969 was $22 million.

An interesting recent development in Maryland agriculture is the "no-till" farming process. The earth is not plowed. A winter cover crop (rye or barley) is harvested and the stubble sprayed with chemicals to reduce it to an organic mulch. A onceover with a planter deposits the seeds in this preparation, and nothing more is done until the crop is

Corn is Maryland's leading field crop, with most of the harvest utilized for grain feed. (Maryland Department of Agriculture)

harvested. Using this method, farmers produce corn and soybeans crops equal to or better than those cultivated in the conventional manner.

The Maryland Farm Bureau, an independent, non-governmental organization representing 10,000 farmers, arranges for much marketing and negotiating with fruit and vegetable processors. The Maryland Agricultural Marketing Association is a cooperative for many Eastern Shore farms. The University of Maryland, its College of Agriculture, and the university's Agricultural Experiment Station, as well as various federal agencies, assist in improving farm practices. Especially helpful to Maryland farmers is the National Agricultural Research Center of the U. S. Department of Agriculture, at Beltsville in Prince Georges County.

In 1972 a State Secretary of Agriculture was added to the Governor's cabinet, thus giving more status to the farm image. (A separate chapter on this operation is found in this book).

Blacksmith, Carroll County Farm Museum. (Maryland Division of Tourism. Photo by Bob Willis)

Industrial Development in Maryland

From the founding in 1634 through much of the 1700's, the State's economy was largely agricultural, with tobacco as the main product. Soon iron works started, in 1715, and shortly after that the manufacture of woolen and linen products joined flour mills in operation. Shortly after 1776, card and nail factories joined tanneries as business enterprises. In the first half of the 19th century agriculture, commerce, and shipping became the leading industries.

Today there are more than 3,400 manufacturing firms in Maryland. The 1970 Census showed that 299,352 Marylanders or about 20 percent of the total labor force, were employed in manufacturing. The chief characteristic of these firms is industrial and agricultural diversification. Here are a few categories, mainly in the Baltimore area, with some sample firms:

Food and related products (Schluderberg-Kurdle, Goetze, National Brewery; Campbell Soup and Green Giant in Salisbury; Maryland Cup Corp.)

Electrical equipment (Westinghouse; Western Electric and Black & Decker; Frederick Electronics; C.G.R. Medical Corp.).

Pharmaceuticals and chemical goods (McKesson, W. R. Grace-Davis Division; Carroll; Hynson, Westcott & Dunning; Merck, Sharp & Dohme; Allied Chemical and Noxell).

Clothing and mills (Worsted-Tex; Misty Harbor Co.; Londontown; Lebow; Sagner's; Grief; Schoeneman Men's Clothing; Bata Shoe Co.; Mt. Vernon Mills).

Shipping and automotive equipment (Bethlehem Steel Corp.; General Motors; Maryland Shipping and Drydock Co.).

Aircraft (Fairchild; Martin-Marietta).

Automobiles (General Motors assembly plant in Baltimore; Mack Truck in Hagerstown; Kelly-Springfield Tire Co. in Cumberland).

Governmental services (Social Security; Aberdeen Proving Ground; National Institutes of Health).

Glass and aluminum (Carr-Lowry Glass Co.; Maryland Glass Co.; Pittsburgh Plate in Cumberland; Eastalco Aluminum Co.).

Steel and other metal materials (Arundel Co.; General Refractories; American Smelting & Refining; Armco Steel; American Can; Continental Can; Crown Cork & Seal Co.).

Printing (Craftsman Press in Bladensburg; Waverly Press; Lord Baltimore Press Division of International Paper Co.; National Plate Grainers, Inc.).

Publishing (Williams and Wilkins).

Research (Hydronautics in Howard County; Kodak; Xerox, Gillette Research Inst.; I.B.M.; InterRand and Comsat in Montgomery County and Goddard Space Flight Center and Patuxent Wildlife Research Center in Prince Georges County).

Maryland's technological development showed a 13.2 percent increase in value added by manufacture between 1967 and 1971. Food and related products represented Maryland's leading manufacturing industry in employment and value during 1971. During 1972 manufacturing produced $19,800,000,000 in Maryland in terms of wages and salaries and proprietors' incomes. Actually the State's largest payrolls are in government and in the wholesale and retail trades. During the eight-year period between January 1, 1965, and December 31, 1972, 438 new manufacturing industries were started in Maryland.

Research and development in various Maryland biological sciences, chemicals, electronics, aircraft, and communications industries employed more than 140,000 persons in 500 firms. For example, the cyclotron at the University of Maryland and research equipment at the Johns Hopkins University, including its Applied Physics Laboratory in Howard County, deal with energy conversion, laser experiments, solid state, and materials science, and biomedical research. Indeed the Baltimore-Washington corridor is probably the second "brain center" in the country, with New York first.

Since the first stone of the Baltimore & Ohio Railroad was laid in Baltimore on July 4, 1828, the B. & O. has played an important role in the historical and industrial development of the State. In recent years the railroad has kept pace with modern requirements and inaugurated trailer-on-flat car (piggyback) service, tying in with the Baltimore port's container ships. In 1963 the B. & O. affiliated with the Chesapeake and Ohio Railroad, with the merged group becoming known as the Chessie System.

Chapter 4

THE CONSTITUTION OF MARYLAND

During the last few decades the federal government has played such an important role in our lives that some of us may have come to consider the State government of secondary importance. Yet the fact is that the State regulates a wide area of our everyday activities—ranging all the way from the lowest age at which we may marry to the highest speed at which we may drive an automobile. The State government protects us from disease by enacting and enforcing pure food and drug laws; it provides funds for schools, hospitals, and highways; it safeguards our property and our very lives by defining and setting penalties for criminal offenses. All these rights and responsibilities of the State are derived from its Constitution and are determined by the needs of the people. For, in a democratic country such as ours, the State government, like the federal government, is the servant of the people.

History of Our State Constitutions. The present Constitution of Maryland, the fundamental and supreme law of the State, was framed and adopted in the year 1867. This is the fourth Constitution to be in effect since the colonial charter was renounced.

Maryland's first Constitution was adopted on November 10, 1776, shortly after the State had issued its own Declaration of Independence from Great Britain (July 6,1776). As the years passed, this Constitution became outmoded and obsolete, especially since the 1830 and '40's marked reforms all over the world, so a second was framed and adopted on July 5, 1851. The third Constitution was adopted on October 12, 1864. Changed conditions resulting from the Civil War had made a new fundamental law necessary. The period of reconstruction that followed the war seemed to call for additional revisions; accordingly, a fourth Constitution was adopted on September 18, 1867. Despite an attempt to write a proposed new one in 1968, the fourth document is still the law of the State.

People and Their Representatives Can Amend the State Constitution. As Article IV makes clear, the Constitution of Maryland may be amended two ways as: First, piecemeal, with each amendment embraced in a separate bill, an omnibus bill can embrace a number of changes that deal with the same subject or could bring together a series of amendments for the purpose of removing or correcting provisions that are obsolete, invalid, unconstitutional, or duplicative. The proposed amendment would have to be passed by three-fifths of all the members elected to each of the two houses of the General Assembly and then passed by a majority of the voters voting on that item. About 200 amendments have already been made to the 1867 Constitution in this manner. Second, the voters get an opportunity to call a Constitutional Convention every 20 years. If the voters choose to have a convention—the next opportunity will be 1990—the legislature must provide for the election of delegates to such a convention at the next general election. The number of delegates from each county and district is to be the same as the total in the House of Delegates and Senate. After the convention revises the current Constitution or rewrites a totally new one, it must submit the new document to the voters and win their approval before it becomes the law of the State.

The last time a Maryland convention was called was in 1967, and a new Constitution was submitted to the people in 1968. Though it included some important changes, the document was submitted in one vote only—take it all or none. It lost, though as this book's chapter on history shows, many of its reforms have since been adopted.

The U. S. Constitution is the supreme law of the land, and State constitutions may also be changed by new federal constitutional changes. For example, the 26th Amendment of the federal Constitution was changed in 1962 to give the right to vote to those 18 years of age or older; the Maryland Constitution accepted this revision. Earlier, the federal 15th and 19th Amendments forced voting rights for black and female citizens upon the State.

Courts Can Change Meanings of the State Constitution. For example, the United States Supreme Court decision in the 1961 case of *Torcaso v. Watkins,* (367 U.S. 488.81 S. Ct 1680 1961) ruled that any religious tests (including a required belief in God) such as those requisites in Article 37 of the Maryland Constitution's Declaration of Rights were not in line with the U.S. Constitution's Article VI, nor in conformance with the 1st and 14th Amendments in the federal document. Torcaso had been appointed a notary public and was denied his commission because he refused to declare a "belief in the existence of God".

In the 1966 case of *Schowgurow v. Maryland,* (213 A. 24 475), the Maryland Court of Appeals ruled in favor of Schowgurow, who claimed that he, as a Buddhist convicted of homicide, was judged unfairly by jury members who had to declare their belief in God. The Court ruled that on the basis of the Torcaso decision, by the highest court of the land, the Schowgurow trial was invalid and Article 39 of the Maryland Constitution's Declaration of Rights was unconstitutional.

The Attorney General Interprets Constitutional Questions. The Maryland Attorney General often rules on the constitutionality of a debated question. For example, in 1972 when 18-year-olds were given the right to vote, he was asked whether students at the University of Maryland could participate in the local elections at College Park and whether that city could be their voting place at all elections. He ruled that if a person declared this to be his domicile and registered there, as well as not registering elsewhere, there was no reason why College Park could not be home base of these student voters. The Attorney General always asks "What was the *intent* of the framers of the Constitution?"

Characteristics of a Good Constitution

A good constitution displays these characteristics:

1. *It Seeks to Keep the State a Significant Part of the Federal System.* The United States is a federal government with many powers shared between national and state governments. Moreover, the 10th Amendment to the U. S. Constitution makes it clear that powers not delegated to the national government are reserved to the states or to the people. Thus the state constitution should reflect these requirements. For example, crime is largely a responsibility of the states; therefore, their constitutions should establish a structure for firm and dependable judicial systems.

2. *It Creates a Sense of Stability.* The relationships of individuals to the government and of parts of the structure to other parts must be made clear so that citizens and agencies know where they stand. For example, if the constitution declares that the accused may request a trial by jury, laws should not be passed to take away this right.

3. *It Is Flexible and Contemporary.* The right to vote under the first two Maryland Constitutions was limited to white males over 21 years of age. Democracy is an expanding concept, and when the nation developed it was evident that the electorate should also mean people of color, and women. Indeed, further flexibility in 1972 expanded the concept to mean all citizens over 18 years of age. Proper wording of a constitutional concept permits flexibility in interpretation by courts which seek to mete out justice in changing times. For example, the U. S. Supreme Court recently ruled that capital punishment was really a form of "cruel and unusual pains and penalties" (words of Maryland Constitution) and therefore could not be used.

Constitutions need to reflect the times in which they exist. The accused have long had the constitutional right to refuse to give evidence against themselves in criminal cases. To bring this up to date, constitutions should provide safeguards against wiretapping and other forms of electronic devices. Times change and constitutions which, for example, forbid the mentally sick from voting ignore completely the new medical practices which, through chemotherapy, analysis, and electric shock, often cure the emotionally ill in short order. Constitutional revisions acknowledging that we are a mobile society provide for absentee voting.

4. *It Is Primarily Concerned with Fundamentals.* A constitution should be comparatively brief and deal with broad fundamentals. *Statutory law*, passed by legislative bodies, should pick up the fundamental ideas and present the specifics. For example, the constitution might make it clear that the State has the responsibility for supporting public

education. But the actual structural pattern, such as the establishment of boards of education, and the amount of money to be given each local school system should be established by *statutory laws* passed by the legislature. Indeed, even the legislature will want to leave the passage of yet smaller details, *e.g.*, what constitutes passing student grades and the individual school calendar, to the various school boards that have the power to pass *regulatory laws.*

Functions of a Constitution

1. *Protects the Citizenry in the Exercise of Its Civil Liberties.* All state constitutions (and the federal as well) seek to protect the public from undue oppressions by the government. Historically, these fears go back to times when governments were despotic, arbitrary, autocratic, and monarchial. This is why *bills of rights* are included in these documents to assure freedom of speech, press, and religion, and to make certain that no one shall be deprived of life, liberty, or property without *due process.* A constitution is a compact between the populace and the government and it should make it clear that government is the servant of the people.

2. *Defines the Powers and Structures of the More Important and Permanent Governmental Bodies.* All constitutions should define the way the executive officers are elected and the extent of their powers. For example, what are the Governor's powers in case of riot? Which administrative officers does he have the right to appoint? What are his budgetary powers? The same would apply to the judiciary and the legislative branches. Since county and municipal governments (especially Baltimore City) are so important in Maryland, and are permanent bodies, they, too, should be given State Constitutional powers. In other states where townships and villages are key political units, they would be constitutionally established.

3. *Provides Methods for Changing the Constitution.* As described earlier in this chapter, the people of Maryland have the final voice in changing the Constitution. Statutory laws may be changed by the very legislative bodies that create them (though the people may ask for a referendum under certain circumstances). Regulatory laws, passed by agencies created by legislative bodies, may be changed by administrative bodies, such as school boards, though a dissatisfied public can take such decisions to court. But constitutional provisions can be changed, added, or deleted only by the final authority of the people.

The Three Essential Parts of the Constitution

The Constitution of Maryland consists of three essential parts: The Declaration of Rights, the Frame of Government and the Amendment Articles.

1. *The Declaration of Rights.* The 46 articles of the Constitution's

Declaration of Rights guarantee what Americans understand to be the "rights of man". Article I deals with the concept that government is derived from the people. The second article asserts the supreme authority of the Constitution of the United States. Article V recognizes our English and colonial heritage by guaranteeing certain rights that were established while Maryland was under the rule of England and the Lord Proprietor. Other articles deal with the right of freedom of speech, of the press, and of assembly; with the right to petition; with protection against cruel and unusual punishments; and with the right to a speedy and public trial by jury. Still other articles prescribe the subordination of military power to civil authority, the right to freedom of worship, and additional rights. Encouragement of education is the subject of another article. Article 46 deals with equality of rights for men and women.

2. *The Frame of Government: State and Local Governments.* The Frame of Government sets forth the way in which government is actually to be carried on; it also prescribes how various parts of the governmental machinery are to be operated. Article I defines who is eligible to vote and prescribes the manner of holding elections. Articles II, III, and IV deal with the conduct of the executive, legislative, and judicial departments. The duties and responsibilities of certain officeholders, among them the Attorney General and the State Treasurer, and the functions of the General Assembly, with respect to educational and military affairs, are set forth in Articles V to X. The government of Baltimore City is dealt with in Article XI as are the questions of county and municipal home rule. Article XII is concerned with the work of the Board of Public Works, while Article XIII describes the procedure to be followed in forming a new county.

3. *Amendments, Referenda, Quadrennial Elections, and Various Other Miscellaneous Affairs Are Treated in Articles XIV to XVII.* A summary of the content of these seventeen articles shows clearly that they are often concerned with Maryland's code of laws as well as with the structure of the State's government and that thus the document can be shortened to conform with guidelines for a good constitution.

Relationships between the Federal and State Government

From the beginnings of our country the relationships between the nation and the state have been in debate. The United States is a federal government with a compact existing between the nation and the state; with the United States Constitution having some powers *delegated* to the former, others *reserved* to the latter, and yet others *shared* by both. Despite this general agreement the federal government has increasingly moved into spheres of operations reserved for the states for years. For example, the operation of the public schools was by agreement the responsibility of the states. Yet in 1954 the federal court stepped in to enforce racial integration, claiming this right to act under the 15th Amendment to the United States Constitution. Moreover, in the 1950's Congress passed a number of acts, such as the National Defense Education Act giving federal financial support to elementary and secondary studies in science, technology, mathematics, and foreign languages. The federal government felt that America's security was based, in part at least, on the education of our people.

So the federal government in the 20th century has taken over more power in the fields of public welfare, recreation, health, conservation, transportation, education, safety, crime, and a whole host of services formerly believed to be within the realm reserved for the states. With states having varying financial abilities to carry out these services, citizens were treated well or meagerly according to the state they lived in. When the federal government established grants-in-aid for practically all public services administered by states, most people were pleased to see it come for it tended to even out the amount of services citizens would receive. Moreover, the states were glad to be relieved of these expenditures. For example, for Maryland alone in fiscal 1974, of a total State budget of about $2.5 billion, the federal contribution was $507.8 million, or more than 20 percent of the total.

Thus, by the time the 1970's came along, the federal government was entrenched in practically all services to people. Many recognized that with federal grants came more federal control. Was the price for federal grants too high? Would it destroy the balance between state and federal control? Most Americans wanted a wider application of rights, such as health care and education. But they recognized that every decision that expanded the U. S. Constitution so that it covers more rights, protects more, and gives more to individuals is a decision that centralizes power in Washington.

In the 1970's there came into being a group of political thinkers who refer to themselves as the New Federalists. They believe that the decision as to which government—federal, state or local—should handle a service would be determined by which delivers most fairness with the least offensiveness. For example, under this philosophy, the federal government would be responsible for establishing the rates to pay welfare recipients and send them the checks rather than have the states in charge. On the other hand, manpower training would be gradually turned over to the states and local political units since they would be more responsive in meeting face to face with those citizens having the problems.

All through this book there are references to services carried out by the State of Maryland and federal government in consort. It will be interesting to note whether the mutuality can continue through the last quarter of the 20th century.

(Top) Edwin White's painting of Washington resigning his commission hangs in the State House in Annapolis, on view to the public. (Maryland Department of Economic and Community Development); (Bottom) Maryland State House, built 1772-1779 and oldest in the Nation still in legislative use; Capitol of the United States, Nov. 26, 1783—Aug. 13, 1784. Here, General Washington resigned his commission as Commander-in-Chief of the Continental Army before the Continental Congress, Dec. 23, 1783; on Jan. 14, 1784, Congress ratified the Treaty of Paris to end the Revolutionary War and, May 7, 1784, appointed Thomas Jefferson Minister Plenipotentiary; from here, Sept. 14, 1786, the Annapolis Convention issued the call to the states that led to the Constitutional Convention. (A Registered National Landmark, Maryland Historical Society. Photo by Bob Willis)

Chapter 5

ELECTIONS AND THE ELECTION PROCESS

In 1973 the charges of federal violations in the Presidential election of 1972, especially the burglary of Democratic National Committee Headquarters (the "Watergate affair"), brought indictments against top Republican figures and finally caused President Richard M. Nixon to resign as head of the government. Moreover, that same year, Spiro T. Agnew was charged with bribery and extortion while he had been executive of Baltimore County, Governor of Maryland (1967-69), and Vice President. The charges led to his resignation, simultaneously with his plea of no contest to a charge of income-tax evasion. There was a general outcry for election reforms that would bring honesty in politics and government, and a general feeling that the very fibers of American democracy were being destroyed at the highest levels of national and state government.

The United States Constitution Affects Election Laws. How are our election laws and procedures determined and how might they be improved? As made clear earlier, the United States Constitution takes precedence over all state constitutions. Numerous federal Constitutional amendments affect voting procedures. For example, the First Amendment restricts the power of Congress so that it cannot make laws prohibiting the right of the people peaceably to petition the government for a redress of grievances. The 12th Amendment requires the President and Vice President to run together as one ticket. The 15th Amendment assures the right of the black male to vote. The 17th Amendment makes certain the popular election of United States senators. The 19th Amendment gives women the right to vote. The 22nd Amendment limits the Presidential period to two terms. The 24th Amendment prohibits the use of the poll tax or other tax by states in the election of federal officeholders. The 25th Amendment deals with the procedures for replacing the President and Vice President in case of removal, death, or resignation. (The body of the Constitution itself, Article II, indicates how the President and Vice President are elected.) The 26th Amendment gives 18-year-olds the right to vote.

The U. S. Courts Determine Election Procedures. Various actions of the United States courts, especially the Supreme Court, have affected state voting procedures. For example, in *Baker v. Carr* (369 U. S. 186-1962), the Supreme Court ruled that Tennessee had violated the 14th Amendment's guarantees of "equal protection of the laws" by not reapportioning its legislative body so that one person's vote would count approximately as much as another's and so that state aid to local units would be based more fairly on the number of people in that unit, rather than the amount of legislators in a malapportioned body. This 1962 ruling served to force Maryland to reapportion and redistrict its boundary lines for representation in the General Assembly and in local lawmaking bodies, such as the Baltimore City Council.

The U. S. Congress Determines Election Procedures. Though election laws fall primarily under the "reserved powers" of states (see U. S. Constitution—10th Amendment), nevertheless, the power of the national government to regulate elections of federal office-holders and its power to enforce constitutional amendments, as in *Baker v. Carr*, give Congress much leeway in this area. For example, in 1965 Congress passed the Voting Rights Act, which invalidated literacy tests in states that used this as a method of keeping out many black voters. In 1973, following the Watergate investigations, Congress passed a bill limiting the amount anyone could contribute in a presidential election. There was much talk then of having candidates procure all their campaign funds from governmental sources so that elections would not be bought. As a result, in 1973 Congress introduced, but failed to pass, a bill that called for financing all federal elections, starting in 1976, with tax dollars from the federal treasury. Covered were presidential primary and general elections and general elections for House and Senate seats.

The Maryland Constitution is a Prime Source of Voting Procedures. In addition to describing the powers of officeholders, the State Constitution prescribes election laws. The Maryland Constitution is filled with philosophy and procedures on this subject. For example, Article 7 of the Declaration of Rights declares that "the right of the People to participate in the Legislature is the best security of liberty and the foundation of all free government." In the body of the Constitution, Article I deals with the elective franchise and gives the residency and age requirements for voting, and sets up a policy toward absentee voting, change of voting place, registration of voters, ineligible citizens, methods of taking oath of office, and punishments for violators. Articles II, III, and IV deal with requirements for holding offices in the executive, legislative and judicial departments and the establishment of election districts as they relate to the General Assembly and the court system. Articles V and VI deal with requirements for the election of the Attorney General, State's Attorneys, the Comptroller, and the Treasurer. Articles VII and XI deal with election of county and municipal officers. Article XIV deals with amending the Constitution. Article XVI deals with the highly important concept of the referendum and Article XVII sets the terms of office for all State and county officers elected by voters (except certain judges) to four years.

Especially important is the delegation by the State Constitution to the General Assembly of authority to "pass laws necessary for the preservation of the purity of elections" and "to regulate by law, not inconsistent with this Constitution, all matters which relate to the judges of election, time, place and manner of holding elections in this State and of making returns."

The Old Senate Chamber was first used in 1779 and continued in use until the new Chamber opened in 1905. (Maryland Department of Economic and Community Development)

Direct Legislation: The Referendum

In the 1930's there was a search for election reforms all over the country, especially to find a way to give citizens the right to control decisions. Three reforms held the spotlight:

1. The Initiative, which gave citizens the right, through petitions, to get legislation started, without waiting for bills to be passed by the legislators;

2. The Recall, which permitted citizens the right, through petitions, to vote on whether or not an officeholder should finish out his term of office and

3. The Referendum, which permitted citizens, by petition, to halt the affect of a bill passed by the legislature.

Maryland has but one of those three—the *referendum.* The referendum privilege is described in the Maryland Constitution (Article XVI) and states that petitions for referenda dealing with statewide issues must be signed by at least three percent of the qualified voters of the

State of Maryland, calculated upon the number of votes cast for the Governor at the previous election. The further restriction is that not more than one-half of those signatures can come from any one county (or Baltimore City). If the issue is one of a local public law, rather than statewide, then ten percent of the qualified voters of that county (or Baltimore City) must sign.

If at least one more than half of the required number of signatures to the petition are affixed before June 1st (when all but emergency bills are scheduled to become laws) then the bill's date of effectiveness is held off. If the remaining half of the signatures are produced within another 30 days, then the passed bill is held off completely until the voters have an opportunity at the next general election to pass judgment on whether they want the bill or not. Two types of bills are excepted from the operation of the referendum. First, appropriation bills (except in certain rare cases), and second, bills dealing with spirituous liquors. Most cases of referenda have dealt with local issues, but some are of statewide import, such as the referendum on the ballot in 1972 concerned with public support for non-public school financing. The voters turned down this State aid proposal.

The General Assembly Passes Election Laws

As in the cases of other areas, *e.g.* education, the State Constitution sets forth the broader policies and it is up to the Legislature to establish and change from time to time the more specific statutory laws. Laws dealing with any one subject, as elections, are codified under one article of the very large Maryland Code which, unlike the Constitution, consists of many volumes. The Election Code is set forth mainly in Article 33, though there are portions of other articles that affect voting laws. For example, the Criminal Code (Article 27) has a section dealing with fines for placing election posters in improper places.

Article 33 deals with the State and local Boards of Election Supervisors. The State Administrative Board of Election Laws consists of five members, headed by an administrator, all appointed by the Governor, and having power over fulfilling election laws. Its office is in Annapolis and all those who file for Congress, Statewide offices, or a position involving more than one county have to file there. The board is also responsible for compiling local election returns from the various county boards, and collating them into State totals. It also has the responsibility of meeting with the county board members and educating them in State requirements.

Each county and Baltimore City has its own board of supervisors of elections. Each of these boards has three members, two from the *majority* party (that of the Governor) and one from the *minority* party. The Governor appoints, subject to State Senate approval (or House approval where there is no State Senator from that county, *e.g.*, Kent) these three from recommendations given to him by the members of the State Central Committees (Republican and Democratic) from the counties (or Baltimore City) where the vacancies exist. The local boards have a great deal of power in determining voting places (subject to State law), judges of elections, fulltime registrars handling registration of voters and absentee voting, preparing ballots and voting machines, challenging procedures and registration, and judging fraudulent election practices. The local election boards can determine the nature of registration procedures. In 1974 the Baltimore City Board of Supervisors of Elections initiated voter registration by mail, with the necessary forms distributed by volunteers at booths located throughout the city. The local elections boards also have jurisdiction when one files for an office that applies to but one county (or Baltimore City). Many people believed that the fulltime staff of election boards should come under civil service and merit systems, and so in 1973 this happened.

Certificate of Candidacy. Those who file for office must do so 30 days before the date of the primary election except for special elections when shorter periods are allotted. Fees for running for office vary from $290 for those who seek to become Governor or U. S. Senator to $100 for those running for Congress to $50 for those aspiring to the State Senate to $10 for those seeking to become members of State Central Committees. As is evident, the certification fees are small enough to tempt many, including some who run for publicity alone.

Registration and Voting Requirements. All those who desire to vote in Maryland must register at the offices of the local Board of Supervisors of Elections. To vote, one must be a citizen, 18 years or older, a resident of the State for 30 days preceding the election, and living in the county where he votes. At registration time one declares whether he is a Republican, Democrat, member of a minority party, or independent, officially labeled "Declined". Maryland has *permanent* and *continuous* registration.

Primary Elections and Nominations by Petition. There are three ways to get one's name on the general election ballot. The first, and most popular, is to file for office and to run in the primary elections held by the Republican and Democratic parties in September previous to the general elections held on the first Tuesday following the first Monday of November. Maryland has *closed* primaries, which means that only registered Democrats can vote for candidates of that party, and the same applies to Republicans. In Maryland, unlike those states that have open primaries, those registered as Independents ("Declined") cannot vote in any primaries. Those who are successful candidates in the primaries are sanctioned by their party's State Central Committee and become the official nominees of the Republican and Democratic parties, which then seek to get these people elected in the general election. Primaries are held in Maryland for all local, State and federal offices.

Indeed, the State also holds Presidential Preferential Primaries previous to the National Nominating Conventions. At this time, Maryland delegates to the Conventions are elected, having run as attached to a particular candidate or unattached. The successful delegate must vote for the Presidential candidate who won in the district where they were running—at least until it is evident that he cannot win at the Convention.

One registered as an Independent can get himself nominated and thus become a candidate in the general election through *petition*. The petition candidate needs to file for candidacy and pay his fees just as though he were running in the primaries. He then must secure petition signatures, previous to the primaries, to the amount of not less than three percent of the eligible voters for the office for which such nomination is sought. No person may sign more than one petition and the forms, procured from the Board of Supervisors of Elections, must have all signatures validated. This is a hard road by which to be nominated and thus it is rarely used. But when one succeeds, his name does get on the ballot at the general election.

The third way to get one's name on the ballot is by selection through the *convention* process. The Maryland Election Code makes it clear that "Any party may elect and hold a meeting or convention." It further states that "The State convention of any party shall nominate . . . . . candidates for presidential electors/of the party in such manner as the convention determines." Thus the nominees for Presidential electors of all parties are not selected by the voters, some are chosen by convention. In the general election of 1970 the American Party ran candidates in two Maryland Congressional districts and also candidates for a U. S. Senate seat and for Governor and Lieutenant Governor—all selected by their party convention. In 1972 the American Party had fewer than the 10 percent of total registered votes that would have permitted them to have primaries, but the Attorney General ruled that their candidates for President and Vice President could get on the Maryland general election ballot for 1972 since they were selected by convention. The Attorney General further ruled that the American Party had a right to select its nominees for Maryland's Presidential electors at a State party convention.

General Elections. Presidential general elections are held in even years every four years, with the next ones in 1976 and 1980. Members of the U. S. House of Representatives, who hold office for only two years, are also elected then. In every other Presidential election, one of the two U. S. Senators from Maryland, who hold office for six years, also runs. Each Congressman is elected from his own district, and there are eight in the State. The U. S. Senators are elected Statewide.

Gubernatorial general elections are held in even years other than those used for Presidential elections. Here all Statewide officers—Governor, Lieutenant Governor, Attorney General, Comptroller, members of the General Assembly, and county officials are elected for four years. So are the eight Congressmen elected for two years. So are the judges who hold office for four or fifteen years, depending on their posts. In every other gubernatorial election a U. S. Senator is elected.

Mayoralty general elections are usually held every other odd year in Maryland. This is especially true for Baltimore City, where the Mayor, the President of the City Council, and the Comptroller are elected citywide and the members of the City Council by districts. Smaller cities may have elections more frequently than every four years.

Of course, each general election also gives the voters opportunities to amend the State Constitution or their city charters, and to vote on referenda.

Employers must give employees time off to vote, but may insist on seeing receipts evidencing proof of voting.

Fair Election Practices. Perhaps the most important section of the Election Code is that known as the Fair Election Practices. This section seeks to bring about reforms in election campaigns. It requires that every candidate in a primary or general election appoint a treasurer who would be in charge of contributions and disbursements and make his records available to the related Board of Supervisors of Elections. It places limits on funds which candidates may spend on their own campaigns, and limits contributions by any individual, not running for office himself, to the campaigns of others. This section, however, has many loopholes. For example, an individual may not contribute more than $2,500 to any campaign, but he can always have his wife or his children each contribute that amount. The section sets up various penalties (mainly $1,000 fines) for those offering, accepting, or soliciting bribes, for those making contributions other than to a bonafide treasurer, for those coercing employees, and for those issuing improper campaign literature.

The section has all the so-called safeguards, but the 1970 Maryland Presidential campaign indicated that there were numerous violations that went unpunished. Indeed, there were so many violations that a cry went up to put "teeth" in this section. For example, there was general agreement that those who profit from State contracts, especially such as engineering and building contractors who receive jobs without closed competitive bids, not be allowed to contribute any funds to campaigns. Some members of the Legislature believe that there should be a campaign expenditure limit based on number of voters eligible to participate in that portion of the election. Others say only public funds raised by taxes should be used in any election.

In 1974 the Legislature passed a number of election campaign reforms. One bill requires those who do more than $10,000 yearly worth of business with the State government to report contributions of more than $100 to political candidates. Another bill limits all cash contributions to $100. An additional bill establishes the beginning of partial public financing (though not effective until 1978) whereby nominees of both major parties in general elections would get $3.00 of public funds for every $1.00 privately raised if running for Statewide office. Candidates for local offices would get $2.00 of public funds for every $1.00 privately raised. There would be a limit for campaign spending for each job, based on a formula that considers the population in the area where the candidate is running for office. Thus, for example, the ceiling for campaign spending for Governor would be $400,000; for State Senator, $8,400; for Delegate, $4,200; for Mayor of Baltimore, $64,000, and for Baltimore City Councilman, $3,500.

When campaign chests run over one million dollars for gubernatorial candidates and when only the rich or those heavily supported by funds can possibly hope to win, the prospect of "bought elections" becomes great. The years ahead will find new and stronger election laws.

Absentee Voting. Maryland has liberal absentee-voting laws. People who are sick (hospitalized or at home), out of town, or in the military are given the right to vote by absentee ballot. Absentee ballots should be procured from the elections board at least seven days before the election. An emergency absentee ballot form, properly signed by a licensed physician, can be secured up to the very day of the election. Absentee voting applies to all elections of candidates and all questions on ballots, including State, federal, and county offices and for Baltimore City, and municipal elections elsewhere in Maryland. If an absentee voter marks his ballot and sends it in before election, but dies before election day, it is not counted.

Political Parties. The Election Code makes it clear that political parties have governmental responsibilities. Article 33 requires that political parties in Maryland have written constitutions and bylaws which describe their governing structures and the way the party meetings are operated. Political parties in this State operate as in other parts of the country, governed more by unwritten rules than by constitutions. Though the days of ward and city or county bosses are long gone, power is still difficult to identify and harder to take away from long-established sources.

State Central Committees. The Election Code and the party constitutions both recognize the importance of State Central Committees. These are established at the county level (in Baltimore City there is one State Central Committee in each legislative district) with each Committee having as many members as there are delegates in the House of Delegates from that area. The members of the State Central Committees are elected by the voters, for a four-year period, during the gubernatorial primary elections. In this way only registered Democrats vote for those running as Democratic State Central Committee members—the same applies to Republicans.

Theoretically, in the county and Baltimore City districts, State Central Committee members discuss political campaigns, endorse party candidates in the general elections, and select precinct and other election officers. Actually they have three main tasks: (a.) To nominate replacements for members of the General Assembly who die, resign, or are forced to leave office. The Governor is required to accept their nominations. (b.) To nominate the majority party (two) or the minority party (one) members for the local election boards. The Governor usually accepts their choices. (c.) To meet with other local State Central Committees of their party at Statewide Central Committee conventions which select state representation for National Committeemen and Committeewomen and which drafts party constitutions, and selects some delegates (in addition to the delegates who must be elected) to the National Nominating Conventions.

State Courts Affect Voting Laws. The election laws are so complex that very often cases are taken to State courts where judges rule on controversies. For example, in 1972 the Maryland Court of Appeals ruled that Ms Mary E. Stuart had the right to register and vote under her maiden name rather than that of her husband, which was Austell. Earlier, the Howard County Board of Supervisors of Elections had removed Ms Stuart's name from their voter rolls since she refused to register under the name of Austell. Interestingly enough, the Maryland Court of Appeals overruled the Howard County Circuit Court in this case since the latter had supported the position of its county election board. In this case as in hundreds of election cases that reach State courts—a large number recently on the validity of reapportionment and redistricting—the effect of the court decision is that of establishing new laws.

Attorney General Rulings. The Attorney General of Maryland rules on many of the fine points in election laws. He is officially the advisor to local election boards and to the State Administrator of Election Laws. For example, in recent years he ruled that (1) any person who will become 18 years of age on or prior to the day of the general election, if otherwise entitled to register, may register to vote while still 17 years old and may actually vote in the primaries while still seventeen, providing he becomes 18 years on or before the date of the general election. (2) He also ruled that anyone waiting in line at the time the polls are due to close shall be permitted to vote. (3) He further ruled, in 1972, that durational residence necessary for voting, such as Maryland's former six-month requirement, drew lines which are not permissible under the equal-protection clause of the 14th Amendment of the U. S. Constitution.

Chapter 6

THE GOVERNOR AND ADMINISTRATIVE OFFICES

The history of the Maryland governorship represents a complete cycle—the movement of an office from great privilege to one holding little power then to its current position, one best described as "effective executive power." In the earliest colonial period (1634-42), the Governor was appointed by the Lord Proprietor, Cecilius Calvert, and was given widespread power in respect to initiating legislation, personally conducting many of the court sessions, and, at the same time, being the chief administrator. He virtually had the power of a king.

At the opening of the American Revolution and under the first Maryland Constitution (1776), the powers of the Governor were markedly diminished and he was elected by the joint ballot of both Houses of the Legislature to serve for one-year terms. In Maryland he had no veto power in these early days of the Republic, and the Governorship was viewed cautiously by Americans who did not want a strong executive, having just rid themselves of an autocratic king. For more than half a century in America, state governors were completely overshadowed by their legislatures. In fact, under the Constitution of 1851, the State was divided into three Gubernatorial districts: The Eastern Shore, Southern Maryland and Baltimore City, and Western Maryland, and each was to take a turn in providing a Governor.

After the Civil War there came a general distrust of the Legislature, and the Governor was increasingly given more power. The big turn took place under Governor Albert C. Ritchie, who held office for 15 years (1920-1935) and during his four terms consolidated his powers, such as those related to appointments and leadership of the Democratic Party in Maryland. He crowned his glory by being given power over finances, especially with the establishment of the so-called Governor's Budget whereby he determined appropriations to different departments and, in a sense, the raising of necessary revenue. Then, too, under Ritchie and under later Maryland chief executives, the Governor's role as chairman of the three-member Board of Public Works gave him great authority in the awarding of small and large contracts. Under Governor Spiro T. Agnew (1967-69) a move was initiated to merge about 200 State administrative boards under 12 executive Secretaries, to be appointed by the chief executive and to be directly responsible to him. These offices came into existence under Governor Marvin Mandel (1969-19-) and thus, along with the other powers recently added, established the office of the chief State administrator with more strength than it had ever had at any previous time under the Republic.

Term of Office and Salary

In Maryland the Governor holds office for four years and is eligible for two consecutive popular elective terms. Besides his annual salary of $25,000 (in 1973), the Governor has the use of the official mansion in Annapolis and is given an expense account and personal staff. He is not

Government House, Annapolis, Md.

allowed to receive profits from any other office. The Legislature in 1974 passed a bill to raise the Governor's salary to $40,000, subject to passage of the Constitutional amendment by the voters.

The Lieutenant Governor

Maryland had a Lieutenant Governor under the 1864 Constitution, but the public's dismay over acts of those in power during the Civil War led them to abolish this office, under the 1867 Constitution. The resignation of Governor Agnew in 1969 to become Vice President of the United States and the fact that the State Constitution did not require another Statewide elected officer to succeed him led a demand for reinstating the Lieutenant Governorship in 1970. The Constitution calls for the Governor and Lieutenant Governor to run together, as holds true for the President and Vice President. In this way the election assures that they will be of the same political party. In Maryland the Lieutenant Governor has only the duties delegated to him by the Governor. Like the Governor, he must be at least 30 years of age and a resident and voter in the State for five years immediately preceding his election.

Election and Successors and Impeachment

The Governor is elected, along with the Lieutenant Governor, State Comptroller and Attorney General, as well as members of the General Assembly, in even years other than those used for Presidential elections. If the Governor dies or leaves office, he is succeeded for the rest of his term by the Lieutenant Governor. If both leave at the same time, the General Assembly selects a person to fill the Governor's term; until the Legislature can do this, the President of the Senate serves as Acting Governor. The Lieutenant Governor also serves as Acting Governor when the Governor notifies him in writing that the chief executive is temporarily unable to perform the duties of his office. The General Assembly by the affirmative vote of three-fifths of all its members may declare the Governor or the Lieutenant Governor unable, because of physical or mental disability, to perform his duties.

The General Assembly may provide by law for the impeachment of the Governor and Lieutenant Governor. Proceedings start in the House of Delegates, where a majority of all elected must pass on the impeachment. Trial, if voted, then moves to the State Senate, where conviction can take place only if two-thirds of all elected members of that body concur.

Powers of the Maryland Governor

As Chief Executive of the State, the Governor's responsibilities imply that his job is to see that all laws are properly executed or carried out. In this regard the Secretaries of these 12 major departments are his key administrative officers: Health and Mental Hygiene, Natural Resources, Economic and Community Development, State Planning, Licensing and Regulation, Personnel, Public Safety and Correctional Services, Employment and Social Services, General Services, Transportation, Budget and Fiscal Planning, and Agriculture. In addition there are agencies without overall Secretaries—for example, the numerous educational boards whose officers—including the State Superintendent of Schools—advise the Governor. Moreover, as chairman of the powerful Board of Public Works, the Governor virtually controls the awarding of contracts and purchases by the State.

It is not usually recognized that the Governor has many legislative powers. For example, his right to veto bills gives him much force in legislation. Then, too, his State of the State address before each legislative session calls attention to the need for passage of certain bills. Actually, the Governor's aides often lobby openly for support of his suggested legislation. If the Chief Executive happens also to be the titular head of the party in power, he can use this added influence to support his legislative wishes. Most important of the Governor's power sources is the budget. Most bills have price tags attached to the legislation, thus whoever controls the budget has much clout in passing bills. Finally, the Governor has the power of appointment for many jobs, and he can trade off part of his Greenbag (list of appointments) for support of his bills.

As for the judicial powers of the Governor, it is he who in nearly all cases makes the initial appointments of judges. It is the Governor who appoints the lay members of judicial nominating commissions who, along with lawyer members, make recommendations of a slate from which he makes his judicial appointments. The Chief Executive appoints members of various quasi-judicial commissions, such as members of the Workmen's Compensation Commission who hear accident cases and adjudicate claims for compensation arising under the law.

As the Maryland Constitution makes clear, the Governor is the "Commander-in-Chief of the land and naval forces of the State; and he may call out the Militia to repel invasions, suppress insurrections, and enforce the execution of the Laws." On numerous occasions in the 1960's and early 1970's the Governor did call out the Militia at the time of college campus riots. The State Militia was largely responsible for quelling the disorders in Baltimore City in 1968.

The Legislature has the privilege of giving the Governor emergency powers, as it did in a special session in November, 1973. The question of potential energy shortages was so serious that the General Assembly gave him extraordinary powers including those to reduce speed limits on State roads, to force oil companies to submit accounts of fuel supplies and needs, to declare priority fuel ratings to hospitals and schools, and to establish Statewide closing hours for all businesses. The Governor was further granted authority to suspend any State or local law—including a modification of State air pollution standards—to meet the energy crisis. In order to keep a check on the Governor's powers the Legislature insisted that his emergency measures be approved by its Committee on Administrative, Executive, and Legislative Review. The General Assembly further set a deadline for these powers to be reviewed in March, 1974, (when they would be in session) for the purpose of determining the need for time extension.

All these powers make it obvious that the Governor is the key figure in State government. Legislators, appointive officials, and the public at large look to him for leadership in carrying on the State's business and solving problems.

Powers of the Governor

I. EXECUTIVE POWERS	I. RESTRICTIONS
(a) The Governor appoints all civil and military officers of the State whose selection is not otherwise provided for. There are several hundred such appointive officials, including members of the Council on Higher Education and the Public Service Commission, including its General Counsel and People's Counsel. The Governor also has power to remove any such officials.	(a) Appointments made by the Governor, with special exceptions, are subject to approval by the Senate. Unlike the practice in the United States Government, the Treasurer, the Comptroller, and the Attorney General are not appointed by the Governor. Most civil employees obtain their positions through the State's merit system.
(b) The Governor supervises the work of the 12 key agencies with Secretaries as heads.	(b) Although the Governor appoints these Secretaries, the functions of the departments in question are usually prescribed either by the State Constitution or by statutes, and the chief administrative officers are given powers not easily challenged by the Governor. Furthermore, the appointments of the Secretaries must be approved by the State Senate.
(c) In case of an emergency, the Governor may call out the militia for the purpose of suppressing insurrection or enforcing the laws.	(c) Unless the Legislature gives its consent, the Governor may not take personal command of the militia.
(d) The Governor is responsible for the State Budget. This is a plan in which proposed expenditures and estimated revenues are set forth for a certain fiscal period.	(d) Before a Budget may be put into effect, it must be approved by the General Assembly. The Assembly can cut expenditures proposed for many items.
II. LEGISLATIVE POWERS	**II. RESTRICTIONS**
(a) The Governor may initiate legislation by submitting so-called administration bills during a regular session, or during a special session that he has called.	(a) The amount of influence any Governor can bring to bear in order to cause the passage of proposed legislation depends upon his political relationships with the General Assembly.
(b) The Governor can veto any bill passed by the General Assembly.	(b) The General Assembly can override the Governor's veto by a three-fifths vote.

III. JUDICIAL POWERS	III. RESTRICTIONS
(a) The Governor appoints virtually all judges when vacancies occur.	(a) All such appointments must be approved by the Senate. The Governor's appointments must be made from a roster presented by a nominating commission. The appointed judges, in many cases, must run for office after the initial appointment.
(b) The Governor appoints members of so-called quasi-judicial boards. One such board is the Workmen's Compensation Commission.	(b) The functions of all such boards are usually prescribed by law and the appointments must be approved by the Senate.
(c) The Governor may grant reprieves from death sentences. He may also remit fines and forfeitures.	(c) He must explain to either House of the General Assembly, when required, the reasons which influenced his decisions.

The Governor's Cabinet

Perhaps the most important growth in the Governor's powers in recent years has been in the administrative area. In 1970 the Assembly approved the Governor's plan to combine and merge operations of about 200 departments into a number of Secretariats. All of these Secretaries meet regularly with the Governor at cabinet sessions.

Each Secretary has the virtual power of a regulatory body and in some respects authority equivalent to that of statutory law, with the added advantage of being able to act at a moment's notice. For example, on a number of occasions the Secretary of Health and Mental Hygiene has closed nursing homes that have violated sanitary laws and stopped home building in areas of the State where there was improper drainage and sewerage. The Secretary of Transportation ordered a pedestrian and bicycle overpass bridge built across U. S. Route 29 in order to link the east and west sides of Columbia and thus tie the community together and help avoid accidents. These decisions ultimately are made on one man's judgment, though all Secretaries seek the best guidance before taking drastic actions. Moreover, each Secretariat has a Board of Review and/or advisory commissions which help to set policy and have appeal power to overrule the Secretary.

All Secretaries are appointed by the Governor, with the consent of the State Senate. He also has the power of removal. The strength of the Governor's Cabinet determines the success of his administration.

By 1974 these were the twelve Departments headed by Secretaries:

1. Health and Mental Hygiene
2. Natural Resources
3. Economic and Community Development
4. State Planning

5. Licensing and Regulation
6. Personnel
7. Public Safety and Correctional Services
8. Employment and Social Services
9. General Services
10. Transportation
11. Agriculture
12. Budget and Fiscal Planning

Since there are comparatively fewer people to monitor under the cabinet arrangements, this gives the Governor more administrative power. Communication can exist with these 12 persons almost daily. The consolidation of many departments into 12 Secretariats means that there can be savings in management, avoidance of duplication, and better articulation of governmental services. Perhaps most important of all is the fixing of responsibility.

Some Marylanders believe that the consolidation has meant a loss of creative power by formerly independent departments, *e.g.*, the State Roads Commission. Yet proper coordination does not submerge any agency; it merely integrates its contributions with the total efforts.

The Independent Agencies

In addition to the 12 Cabinet Departments, there are a large number of independent agencies. The greatest number are those related to education, and many political scientists and government officials believe that they will ultimately all be merged into a comprehensive Cabinet level Secretaryship. Other independent agencies are related to fields of planning, law, aging, military affairs, workmen's compensation, human relations, finance, and transportation. These are more likely to remain independent agencies, for no "umbrella" seems to cover them. Some might be absorbed among the present 12 Cabinet Departments.

Chapter 7

THE STATE LEGISLATURE AND THE LEGISLATIVE PROCESSES

The State Legislature is viewed by most political scientists as the focal point of all State governmental activities. A strong legislative body sets the tone for all State activities. It has to respond to the will of the people and if the members of the State Legislature are strong and if that body acts responsibly, then governmental activities in the other branches, *viz.*, the executive and judicial, will seek to measure up to the established standards. Legislators represent the people, and thus their views cannot be too far ahead or behind.

General Assembly of Maryland: A Bicameral Body

The official title of the State legislative body is the General Assembly of Maryland. Like all other state legislatures in the United States (but one, Nebraska) the Maryland Legislature has two distinct branches; a Senate and a House of Delegates. Some political scientists believe that a unicameral body such as Nebraska's can be more efficient, more economical and timesaving. Those who believe in a bicameral body claim that there are checks and balances under this plan and that unnecessary or harmful legislation is less likely to be passed.

The United States and Maryland Constitutions Place Limitations upon State Legislatures

Article I, Section 8 of the United States Constitution makes it clear that only Congress can establish rules of naturalization, coin money, establish post offices, declare war, regulate commerce with foreign nations, and carry out other responsibilities listed in the powers delegated to the federal government.

The Maryland Constitution places certain restrictions upon the Legislature. For example, no member of Congress or person holding any civil or military office under the United States government can also be a Maryland legislator. Not until 1974 could a clergyman hold office in the General Assembly. It prohibits the General Assembly from enacting laws authorizing private property to be taken for public use without just compensation as agreed upon between the parties or awarded by a jury. One of the most controversial restrictions is that prohibiting the Legislature from increasing the executive Budget, though it can decrease it. (Thus the "power of the purse" is with the Governor.) The Legislature cannot authorize a lottery grant except one operated by and for the benefit of the State. The General Assembly cannot pass laws suspending the privilege of the writ of *habeas corpus.* Since the State Constitution goes into specific discussion of the structure and the procedures of the Legislature, the age and residence requirements for holding office, and the length of the sessions, in a sense all of this describes what cannot be done as well as what is in order.

The Maryland Constitution Gives Widespread Powers to the Legislature

Actually, the State Constitution grants many more powers to the Legislature than it enforces restrictions. It is important to understand that every constitutional belief or law brings a whole host of powers to the Legislature. Sometimes the Maryland Constitution expressly states these powers. For example, Article 7 of Declaration of Rights states that "elections ought to be free and frequent." In Article 3, Section 42, the Constitution specifically gives the General Assembly the power to "pass laws necessary for the preservation of the elections." Out of these expressions of responsibility the Legislature has passed literally hundreds of laws related to operating elections; as described in this book's chapter on the subject, these are known as *statutory laws* codified in the Elections Code. At other times such as in the case of public health, welfare, and recreation, the right of the Legislature to pass laws in these areas grows out of such implied powers conferred by the Constitution "that the Legislature ought to encourage . . . . the general melioration of the condition of the People."

In general the following are duties and responsibilities of the Senate and the House of Delegates:

1. To pass laws necessary for the welfare of Maryland's citizens.
2. To pass public laws for counties and special taxing areas.
3. To decide the manner in which State funds are to be spent.
4. To supervise the State's administrative agencies.
5. To propose amendments to the State constitution.

The Legislature is instrumental in integrating public demands with public policy.

Sessions of the General Assembly

The Maryland Legislature has a yearly 90-day session, starting on the second Wednesday of January. It may extend its session beyond the 90-day calendar, but not exceeding an additional 30 days, by resolution concurred in by a three-fifths vote of the membership in each House. The Governor may call a special session whenever he feels it is important. When he does, it cannot last longer than 30 days and may be as short as one day.

A number of state legislatures (including New York, Pennsylvania and New Jersey) are on *continuous session,* which means that there are no limitations on length of regular sessions. The advantages of such sessions are (1) they discourage careless and hurried passage of bills in the closing days of sessions that are limited, (2) legislators see their task as a full-time job and (3) there are fewer bills starting from scratch each year, as is required when important legislation does not get through all three readings due to lack of time. On the other hand, the limited sessions with a specific number of working days permits many capable people who hold other full-time jobs as lawyers, farmers, businessmen, and skilled workers to hold office in the Legislature and still be able to devote the remaining nine months of the year to their professional tasks.

Maryland takes a middle position and extends the regular sessions when necessary by special sessions and arranges for the Legislative Council, a portion of the General Assembly, to meet in the summer and fall months preparing suggested items for the next regular session of the Legislature.

Qualifications, Elections and Terms of Office, Vacancies

A member of either House must have resided in Maryland at least three years before the election and the last year in the district where he runs. Candidates for the House of Delegates must be at least 21 years of age and those for the Senate at least 25 years at time of the election. Legislators in both Houses are elected by districts for four-year terms at the Gubernatorial Elections. This differs from many states, where members of the lower House serve for but two-year terms. In case of vacancy, members of the State Central Committee from the district and party concerned nominate to the Governor a person to fill out the term.

Membership of the Senate and the House of Delegates

Until a major reapportionment and redistricting of both Houses which became effective for the election of 1974, the State Senate had 43 members and there were 142 Delegates. As a result of a Constitutional Amendment, approved by the voters in 1972, this was changed, effective with the election in 1974, to 47 Senators and 141 Delegates. The figures were determined so that there would be a one to three ratio between the upper and lower Houses. Moreover, they were part of a broad plan to have single-member Senatorial districts throughout the State. For example, before 1974 each of the six legislative districts in Baltimore City had two Senators, now each of the eleven has one. Then, too, some of the Senatorial districts have been subdivided into three Delegate subdistricts, thus providing single-member Delegate districts. However, other Senatorial districts, such as those in Baltimore City, have kept the Delegates in multiple-member boundaries that are coterminous with those for Senators. Thus, in Baltimore, a voter will vote for one Senator and three Delegates. The advantage of a single-member district is that the citizen knows whom to contact and the legislator serves a smaller number of constituents in a smaller geographical area that is more likely to be homogeneous in population and to have unique problems. Campaigning is cheaper and easier. On the other hand, the multi-member district is larger and less likely to be parochial.

The one criticism pointed at the 1974 membership arrangement is that a total membership of 188 is too large to function smoothly. Many political scientists favor a maximum of 75. On the other hand a small Senate means that many counties will not have a separate Senator representing them. This was true for a few small counties before 1974. Because the two Houses are based on reapportionment due to changes in population as reflected by the 1970 Census, the smaller the membership the more the counties cannot be represented by a separate legislator in each House. Actually, in 1974, for the first time in modern years, very small counties like Talbot and Garrett may not even have a separate Delegate. On the basis of one Delegate for every 16,000 people (Kent's population), it would be necessary to have a House of Delegates of about 260 members. So in 1975 some Senators and some Delegates will serve voters in more than one county.

Reapportionment After Every U. S. Decennial Census

The Maryland Constitution calls for the Legislature to have a plan for reapportionment and redistricting every ten years, after the Census is taken. If the Legislature fails to produce a plan that is acceptable to itself in time to take effect at the election following the Census, then the Governor's plan must be accepted. Either plan may be taken to court—as was true in 1973—if any citizen believes that it does not conform with the "one man, one vote concept" under the Supreme Court's decision discussed in Chapter 5. In 1974 Baltimore City lost representation in the Legislature because it declined in population between 1960 and 1970. On the other hand, Prince Georges County saw a massive population growth and thus increased in representation.

Composition of 47 Legislative (Senatorial) Districts by Counties

(Each Senatorial District is entitled to one Senator and three Delegates)

1. Garrett (all) and Allegany (part) make up district 1 and share its Senator; with the Delegate subdistricts having one shared and two to Allegany.
2. Allegany (part) and Washington (part) make up district 2 and share its Senator; with one Delegate subdistrict shared and the other two allocated to Washington.
3. Washington (part) and Frederick (part) make up district 3 and share its Senator; with one Delegate subdistrict to Washington and two Delegates in a shared subdistrict.
4. Frederick (part) and Carrol (part) make up district 4 and share its Senator; with one Delegate subdistrict to Frederick and two Delegates in a shared subdistrict.

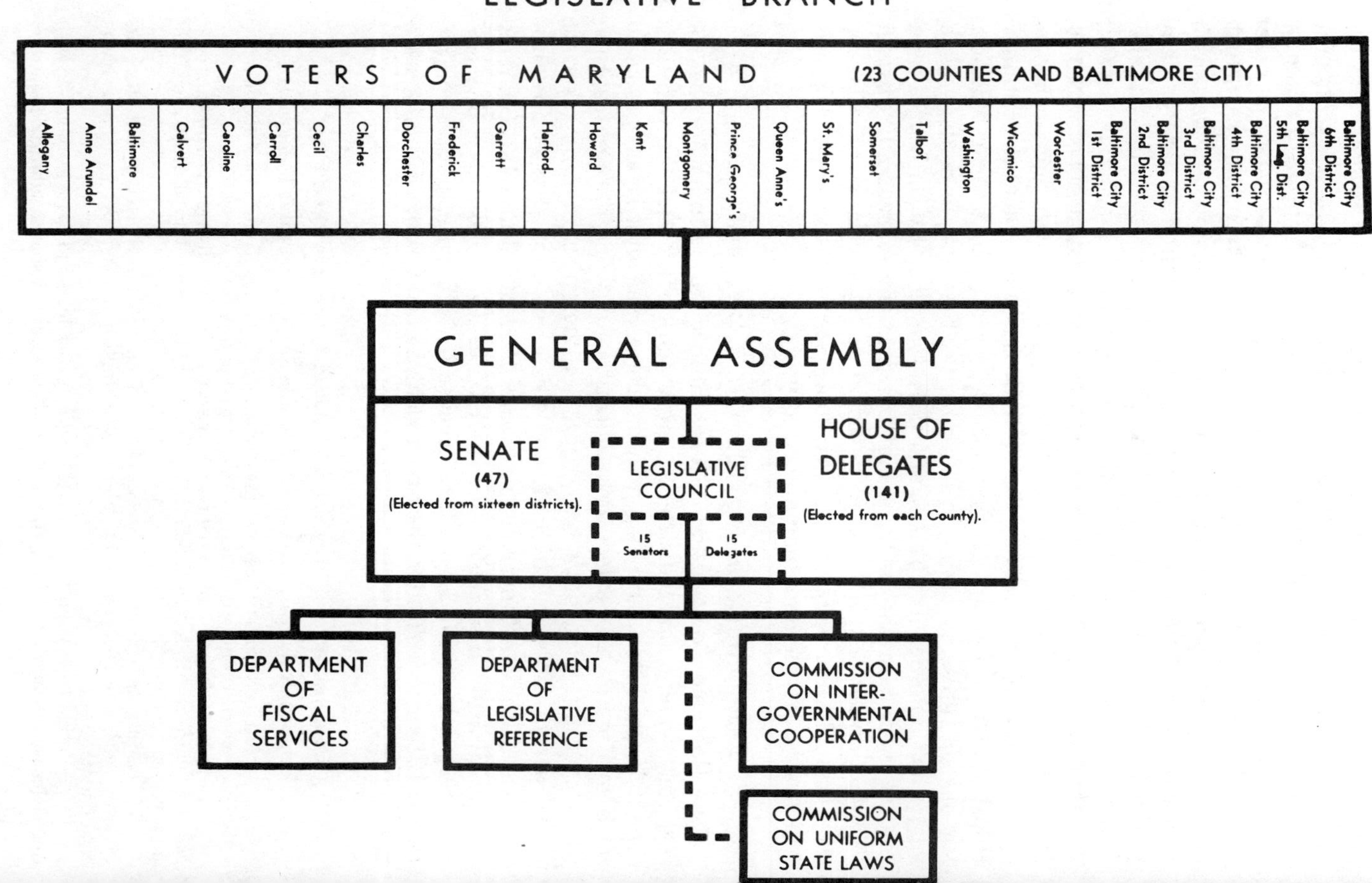
LEGISLATIVE BRANCH
VOTERS OF MARYLAND (23 COUNTIES AND BALTIMORE CITY)
Allegany
Anne Arundel
Baltimore
Calvert
Caroline
Carroll
Cecil
Charles
Dorchester
Frederick
Garrett
Harford
Howard
Kent
Montgomery
Prince George's
Queen Anne's
St. Mary's
Somerset
Talbot
Washington
Wicomico
Worcester
Baltimore City 1st District
Baltimore City 2nd District
Baltimore City 3rd District
Baltimore City 4th District
Baltimore City 5th Leg. Dist.
Baltimore City 6th District
GENERAL ASSEMBLY
SENATE (47) (Elected from sixteen districts).
LEGISLATIVE COUNCIL
15 Senators
15 Delegates
HOUSE OF DELEGATES (141) (Elected from each County).
DEPARTMENT OF FISCAL SERVICES
DEPARTMENT OF LEGISLATIVE REFERENCE
COMMISSION ON INTER-GOVERNMENTAL COOPERATION
COMMISSION ON UNIFORM STATE LAWS

* 5. Carroll (part), Harford (part), and Baltimore County (part) make up district 5 and share its Senator; with one Delegate subdistrict to Harford and two Delegates in a three-county shared at-large district.

6. Harford (part not in district 5) makes up district 6 and gets that Senator with the three Delegates elected at large.

7. Baltimore County alone (other than its parts in district 5) makes up districts 7, 8, 9, 10, 11, 12, and 13, and gets their seven Senators; each of these seven Senatorial districts has three Delegates elected at large in their districts—21 Delegates in all.

8. Howard (all) and Montgomery (part) make up district 14 and share its Senator; with two Delegates allocated to Howard and one in a shared subdistrict.

9. Montgomery (other than its parts in district 14) makes up districts 15, 16, 17, 18, 19, and 20, thus getting six Senators; and the accompanying 18 Delegates with all but three elected at large in their Senatorial districts.

10. Prince Georges (all but the parts in district 28) makes up districts 21, 22, 23, 24, 25, 26, and 27, thus getting seven Senators and the accompanying 21 Delegates, with three elected at large in each Senatorial district.

11. Charles (part) and Prince Georges (part) make up district 28 and share its Senator; with the three shared Delegates elected at large.

12. St. Marys (all) and Charles (part) make up district 29 and share its Senator; with the three shared Delegates elected at large.

13. Calvert (all) and Anne Arundel (part) make up district 30 and share its Senator; with one Delegate shared and the other two allocated to Anne Arundel.

14. Anne Arundel (all but parts in district 30) makes up districts 31, 32 and 33, thus getting three Senators and nine Delegates, three elected at large in each Senatorial district.

* 15. Cecil (all), Kent (all), and Queen Annes (all) make up district 34 and have a three-way shared Senator; with the three shared Delegates elected at large.

* 16. Caroline (all), Talbot (all), Dorchester (all), and Wicomico (part) make up district 35 and have a four-way shared Senator; with the three shared Delegates elected at large.

* 17. Worcester (all) and Wicomico (part) and Somerset (all) make up district 36 and have a three-way shared Senator; with the three shared Delegates at large.

18. Baltimore City (all) makes up districts 37, 38, 39, 40, 41, 42, 43, 44, 45, 46 and 47, thus getting eleven Senators; with the accompanying thirty-three Delegates, three running in each subdistrict at large.

Composition of General Assembly after Gubernatorial Election in 1974—total 47 Senators and 141 Delegates.

Organization of the Senate and the House of Delegates

The reapportionment of 1974 created a Senate with 47 members, with most counties (and Baltimore City) represented by one or more, but with the smaller counties sharing a Senator. The President of the Senate is elected by members of that body; usually the choice is made by a caucus of members of the majority party.

By the 1974 reapportionment the House of Delegates has 171 members, with nearly all counties and Baltimore City having one or more Delegates. The presiding officer, the Speaker, is elected by members of that body and is usually the choice of a majority-party caucus.

*Note: In any legislative district which contains more than two counties or parts of more than two counties and where Delegates are to be elected at large by the voters of the entire district, no county, or part of a county, shall have more than one Delegate residing in it.

The choice of officers is the first order of business at the opening of each yearly session of the State Legislature. In addition to the presiding officers, the caucuses held by the political parties determine who shall be the majority and minority floor leaders. The majority party in caucus also selects committee chairmen. Seniority is not necessarily the basis for being selected for one of these posts. Numerous factors, such as prestige in the party, member preference, geographical distribution, ability and support by the Governor, all count.

Salaries and Compensation

Members of the General Assembly received $11,000 a year (1973), higher than some states pay, but much lower than that in other states such as California ($21,200), Michigan, New York ($23,200) and Pennsylvania. The latter states, however, have continuous sessions. The President of the Senate and the Speaker of the House of Delegates each receives an additional $2,000 salary. Delegates also get an expense allowance of $3,500 for clerical assistance; Senators get $5,000. There is also a per diem allowance (hotel and meals) with a maximum of $25 per day and a mileage allowance if the per diem is not used. The State also contributes to a pension plan for those who have served at least eight years. No extra pay is given for service during summer and winter months when the Legislative Council meets, nor for attendance at special sessions. The General Assembly Compensation Commission recommends changes in salaries and the Legislature may accept, reduce, or reject, but not increase the amounts. In 1974 the Commission recommended that the salary of legislators be increased to $12,500 a year and the Legislature that year approved the change, to go into effect in 1975.

Legislative Committees

The casual visitor to either chamber of the General Assembly will be unaware of the tremendous amount of work that goes on behind the scenes. The bulk of the Legislature's work is carried on in committee rooms, rather than in the two chambers. This work is done by committees, of which there are five kinds.

1. *Standing Committees* deal with issues that have much the same character during each session of the Legislature. Members hold their places on these committees throughout an entire session.

2. *Select Committees* are appointed by the presiding officer for the purpose of dealing with some special matter, usually an issue that pertains to the affairs of a single county, or a small group of counties. In the House of Delegates, the select committee is largely composed entirely of representatives from the county affected by the bill. In the Senate the committee may include one or more Senators from bordering counties. The group is likely to be dominated, however, by the

Senator whose county is affected by the bill. These committees are very important, since the Legislature generally feels that it owes the local delegates the "courtesy" of doing what they recommend.

3. *Joint Conference Committees* are organized whenever the two houses are in disagreement about a particular bill. Members are drawn from both Houses of the General Assembly. Usually a compromise bill is drawn up by a conference committee, and is then submitted to both Houses. The report of a conference committee must be accepted or rejected without amendment. During any legislative session, many joint conference committees are appointed.

4. *Committee as a Whole*—this term designates the action of either legislative body in organizing the total membership into one committee for a brief time in order to discuss some issue. Such action, though seldom taken, is used when one of the Houses wants to act hurriedly on a bill. The House saves time by calling itself a committee; this procedure makes it unnecessary to recommit the bill under discussion to a standing committee or to a new committee. Since no minutes are kept during a meeting of this sort, members may feel more free than usual to discuss the matters at issue. Moreover, this procedure permits the Legislature to hear comments from citizens and governmental officials, whereas in a regular session only the members may speak.

5. *Joint Budget Committees*—the House Appropriations Committee and the Senate Finance Committee comprise the Joint Budget Committee in order to hear State departmental agency budget presentations simultaneously. This procedure saves time and assures both committees of hearing identical testimony. There are also four joint committees on appropriations which hear specific departmental budgets. Members of both the Senate and House finance committees serve thereon. They are Health and Education, Human and Natural Resources, Public Safety and Transportation and Capital Budget. The Joint Budget Committee makes recommendations to both Houses on the Operating and Capital Budget Bills as to amendments (*i.e.* reductions).

Opening of the General Assembly

The first step at each annual meeting of the General Assembly is the choice of officers. Following the election of a *pro tempore* (temporary) President of the Senate and Speaker of the House of Delegates, permanent officers are selected for these posts. Having administered the oath of office to members and having selected so-called "desk officers," each presiding officer appoints a minority and majority floor leader. Actually, each of these has already been designated at a caucus of members of his political party. Following these preliminary formalities, the General Assembly begins to hold meetings, all of which are open to the public. On rare occasions, one or the other House may hold a private or so-called executive session.

(Top) President of the Senate, Senator William S. James of Harford County, presides over the Maryland State Senate at 1974 Legislature session. Note clerks and officers of the Senate at the long desk below the speaker's table. State senators are seated at the desks facing the speaker. (Bottom) Speaker of the House of Delegates, John H. Briscoe, delegate from St. Marys County, presides at the open session of 1974 Legislature. Note that delegates' desks face the speaker. The electric voting board is to the right of the delegates and the visitors' gallery is shown above the speaker.

Powers of the President and Speaker

In addition to presiding, the President of the Senate and the Speaker of the House of Delegates have many other important powers. Each presiding officer has power to choose between two or more members who may at the same instant rise to speak. This so-called power of recognition gives a presiding officer the right to permit some members to speak and at the same time to deprive others of that privilege. Utilizing this power, he may, for example, forestall action on a bill by referring it to a committee, and by not recognizing a member who has risen for the purpose of suggesting that some other action be taken on the bill. The President of the Senate has the privilege of the first speech during any discussion of action to be taken on a bill; in consequence, he may be able to influence other subsequent speakers. The presiding officer of each House has the right to vote on all bills. He also has power to appoint members of the various committees in his branch of the General Assembly. This power is perhaps the most important of all those held by the presiding officer.

The Origin of a Bill

Any bill may originate in either the Senate or the House of Delegates. The one restriction is that a bill must be introduced before the last 35 calendar days of the 90-day session, unless agreed to by a two-thirds vote of the members in the House where it was introduced. These days are required for printing the bill, for discussing it in committees, for readings, for hearings, and for other necessary procedures through which a bill must pass in each House.

Drafting a Bill

Any Delegate or Senator who draws up a bill may either work independently or enlist the aid of the Department of Legislative Reference.

A bill may be introduced by a single member; jointly, by two or more members acting in concert; or by the entire delegation of representatives from any one county or from a legislative district in Baltimore City. The person who submits a bill is known as the sponsor, and may add the words *by request* after his signature on the bill. This indicates that he does not necessarily favor passage of the measure, but is only offering it at the request of a constituent in the county or district he represents. The Constitution requires that the title of a bill indicate the nature of its contents, and that a bill deal only with the subject indicated by its title.

How a Bill Becomes a Law

Before a bill can be approved by the General Assembly, it must go through three readings in each House. Passage of a bill requires that a majority of the members of each chamber vote in favor of it. The bill then goes to the Governor for his signature, in which case it becomes law.

If either House rejects a bill or takes other unfavorable action on it, the bill is said to be killed. As we have seen, in case the two Houses fail to agree upon amendments either may have proposed, they usually appoint a joint conference committee to draw up a bill that will be regarded with favor by both chambers. If the Governor vetoes a bill that has been passed by the General Assembly, the members may override his veto by means of a three-fifths majority.

In 1950 the Constitution was amended so that bills vetoed after adjournment must be submitted by the Governor to the next legislative session and become the first order of business.

Governor Marvin Mandel, with Senator William F. James (l.) and Delegate Thomas H. Lowe (r.), signs Senate Bill 18 bringing proprietary nursing homes under State Certification of Need Program. Maryland's CON legislation requires all hospitals and health-related institutions to obtain certification of the need for new or modified buildings or changes in services.

When Does a Bill Become a Law?

Laws passed by the General Assembly become effective on the first day of June following the session in which the bill was passed. Exceptions to this rule are sometimes made, but they must be noted explicitly in the bill itself. A bill may be passed as an emergency measure, in which case it needs three-fifths of the total number of members in each House, and it becomes a law immediately after getting the Governor's approval.

HOW A BILL BECOMES A LAW IN THE MARYLAND GENERAL ASSEMBLY

IDEA OR NEED	You—or any citizen—may request a member of the legislature to introduce a Bill for you.
DRAFTING OF BILL	By the Dept. of Legislative Reference which prepares most bills for introduction.
PUT IN "HOPPER"	Bill is introduced only by a member of Legislature. He takes it to Chief Clerk's office, where it is given a number. (Ex., HB5—House Bill 5; SB5—Senate Bill 5)
FIRST READING	By title only, done by Reading Clerk. Must be introduced before the last 35 calendar days of a 90-day session, unless allowed by 2/3 vote of all members.
PROPER COMMITTEE TIME FOR ANY POLITICAL PRESSURE!!	Presiding Officer (House—the Speaker; Senate—the President) refers Bill to proper Committee at once. A hearing is held, if requested (open to public). The committee may pass it as is—reject it entirely—amend it—take no action. This "pigeonhole" kills a Bill, but it may be forced out to floor on petition of 3 Senators (if in Senate) or 15 Delegates (if in House). The fate of a Bill is usually decided in Committee.
SECOND READING DEBATE	If reported "out" by Committee, Bill is read again by title only, and is open for debate and vote on Committee's report (favorable or unfavorable). The Bill itself may be substituted for unfavorable report and voted directly. The Bill may be amended on the floor.
THIRD READING VOTE	Must be on a separate day; if pressed for time, vote of 2/3 majority may suspend rules. After 3rd reading, and debate, vote is taken by roll call.
SECOND CHAMBER SAME PATTERN	If passes both Houses, goes to Governor. If amended in 2nd House, must return to 1st for adoption of amendment. If amendment not accepted, a joint conference committee works out a compromise, which must pass both Houses to go on to the Governor.
GOVERNOR	Signs a Bill and it becomes Law on June 1st or July 1st after session, sooner if passed as an emergency bill by 3/5 vote. If a Bill is vetoed after adjournment it becomes first order of business at following session unless there is a new General Assembly that is meeting after a Gubernatorial election. All vetoed Bills may be passed over the Governor's veto by a 3/5 vote of all members of both Houses.

A RESOLUTION goes through same process, but is *not* a Law. It is a request or expression of the will of the Assembly. (Numbered HR-5 or SR-5 or if a joint request, HJR-5 or SJR-5).

A CONSTITUTIONAL AMENDMENT is a Bill which must pass by 3/5 vote of both Houses. It must be passed by a majority of voters at next General Election.

Budget Bills

The annual State Budget is now almost $3 billion and its passage represents the most important task that is carried out by the General Assembly. Indeed, bills having financial components cannot be passed early in the session until the Budget is first approved because the commitment of funds could have an adverse effect upon the Budget.

The Governor delivers the Budget to the presiding officer of each House within the first five days of the session. The Legislature cannot increase items in the current operating Budget (it can with the capital improvement funds). It cannot decrease estimates for the judicial branch, nor may it cut items concerning the State debt service, or those items in the public school system mandated by law, or public salaries specified in the Constitution. Actually it is also difficult, though possible, to cut items where federal matching funds go to the State providing Maryland contributes a share, *e.g.*, many of aspects of education, health, welfare, protection of natural resources, mass transportation, and protection from crime.

Hearings are held by the joint Senate Finance and House Appropriations Committees of both Houses on each section of the budget. Administrative heads are questioned on subjects ranging from broad policies to live items. (Actually, many of the hearings also take place when the Legislature is not in session and these two standing committees carry out their year-round reviews). In a sense, the final budgetary approvals for a department, *e.g.*, education, determine the program; thus the Legislature, in a sense, can be making administrative decisions. On the other hand, the hearings force the administrative heads to justify the value of their requests.

The Capital Improvement Budget is submitted separately, but at the same time as the Current Operating Budget. The Legislature can increase capital items. Hearings are also held on this Budget. Because capital funds are financed through bond purchases, no debts may be authorized by the Legislature unless taxes are provided to pay the interest and discharge the principal on bonds.

Supplemental budgets may also be passed by the Legislature when submitted by the Governor after the annual Budget is approved. Supplemental budgets can be passed only if the necessary funds are provided in revenues.

Standing Committees

After a bill is introduced and read for the first time, it is assigned to a committee by the presiding officer. Usually, the assignment is made on the basis of subject matter. Sometimes there are two or more committees to which a bill might be appropriately referred, and the choice rests with the presiding officer.

Number and Workload in the Senate. The Senate has eight standing committees. Five of them deal with subjects that are self-explanatory and are not involved with processing bills: Rules, Organization and Procedure; Investigation; Executive Nominations; Ethics; Entertainment.

The three major committees in the Senate are Finance, Judicial Proceedings, and Economic Affairs. Every Senator is a member of one of these three committees, which carry the workload of the Senate.

The Senate makes no provision in its rules that the minority party have representation on each committee, but in practice it is so arranged that each party is given proportionate representation.

House of Delegates

The House of Delegates has six committees that carry out the major workload in that body: Appropriations; Constitution and Administrative Law; Economic Matters; Environmental Matters; Judiciary; Ways and Means. Every Delegate serves on one of these six committees. The rules of the House of Delegates require that minority representation on each committee shall be in proportion to that party's membership in the House (presently one Republican to six Democrats). In addition to the six major committees, the House of Delegates, like the Senate, has committees not involved with processing bills.

Joint Committee on Ethics and Disclosure

To police itself the General Assembly established its own Ethics Committee to ensure that public office not be used for private gain other than compensation provided by law. The rules make it clear that personal interest impairs a legislator's independence when he or she acquires a direct financial interest, benefits financially from a close economic association with the firm affected or with the lobbyist for the enterprise, or solicits or accepts gifts or loans from persons affected.

Legislators need to disclose their interests, and when in doubt about conflict of interests, seek advisory opinions.

In 1973 a State Disclosure Law was enacted requiring legislators and key appointed and elected officeholders to submit annual reports of financial and land holdings. In this way it would be evident if support of certain bills represented conflict of interest. State officeholders must reveal publicly any land they hold, any interest in corporations or in any company doing $10,000 or more worth of State business annually. All statements must be filed for public view. Officials who disobey the law could be held in contempt of court and also have their salaries cut off. In 1974 there was a movement to extend disclosure to county and municipal officeholders.

Lobbies and Pressure Groups

All legislative agents, or lobbyists, working at Annapolis for different kinds of private or public agencies related to almost every phase of life—business, health, industry, recreation, education, civic activities, and transportation—must register with the Secretary of State at each session and account for their expenses and salaries, if any. Legislators are subject to many pressures by lobbyists. On the other hand, paid and unpaid legislative agents educate the legislators on different points of view of controversial subjects and may serve valuable purposes.

The Legislative Council and the Standing Committees

The Legislative Council meets fairly regularly between Assembly sessions. It is made up of 15 members of the House of Delegates and 15 members of the Senate. They deal with practically every subject dealt with by the General Assembly, and carry on research and hold public hearings on important issues. The Legislature often assigns them topics for study. The Legislative Council does not have the power to pass bills, but it does prepare bills for introduction at the opening of each session so that the General Assembly does not start from scratch. Most of the bills prepared for favorable introduction are usually passed by the Legislature.

The standing committees of both Houses also meet periodically between sessions and they, too, carry out research and conduct hearings. They work intimately with the Legislative Council during the between-session periods, which usually run from May through November.

The Department of Fiscal Services

Between legislative sessions, the Department of Fiscal Services studies the Budget, which represents the most single important issue dealt with at each session. It determines whether expenditures are in conformance with the Legislature's desires; and thus its staff workers attend hearings by the Finance Committee of the Senate and the Appropriations Committee of the House of Delegates. It also carries out research, not necessarily related to the Budget, on subjects such as taxes, finances, and other fiscal matters affecting the State.

Chapter 8

THE JUDICIARY AND THE JUDICIAL PROCESSES

At no other time in the history of our country has there been as much concern about the need for reform of the judicial machinery of government. Every segment concerned—the legal profession, the public, the defendants, and the jurists themselves—say we must put more meaning behind our belief in "equal justice under the law." Most American institutions rest upon respect for the law—and this cannot be achieved without an effective and impartial judicial system.

Sources of Law

As has been made clear in earlier chapters, *the law* covers a multitude of requirements. The sources of our laws are identifiable. To begin with, there are the constitutional laws—those embodied in the United States and Maryland Constitutions. Though seldom amended, they are continually subject to new interpretations.

Then there are the federal, State, and local statutes passed by elected members of legislative bodies and subject to change by these same bodies. The Maryland Annotated Code consists of many volumes and contains laws about health, education, elections, crime, zoning, planning—virtually every subject under the sun. Violations of the State Criminal Code, for example, bring punishments clearly identifiable, though subject to some flexibility in decisions by State courts. The Code represents statutory laws.

Constitutional and statutory laws are continually subject to interpretation by the courts. Thus, when a federal court says that a defendant is entitled to a lawyer, Maryland needs to set up a public defender system. When a Maryland court rules that members of a jury need not take an oath of belief in God, this State Constitutional requirement is changed. So courts really establish what might be called "decision laws."

Much of the law is not precisely written down in terms of required responses or punishments. For example, laws dealing with one person's responsibility toward another—as when a man enters your home or place of business and meets with an accident due to your careless arrangement of hazardous equipment—are not normally written out in statutes. Each accident in such situations differs from virtually every other one that might take place. Therefore, the legal responsibility can only be determined by what some judge in the past ruled in closely related situations. Thus, over hundreds of years a whole body of common law has come into existence based on customs and court decisions.

Most civil cases, such as lawsuits involving personal property damage or injury to body, are settled through common law decisions. Indeed, the Maryland Constitution recognizes the fact that state inhabitants "are entitled to the Common Law of England," which goes back hundreds of years before the United States was organized.

Then, too, there are some civil disagreements that are not covered by either statutory or common laws. These litigations often have right on both sides. For example, if there is a divorce and children are involved who should have their custody? Perhaps the equitable solution is to give each parent custody at different times. Equity involves the carrying out of justice according to the principles of ethics, the fair thing to do. In such cases precedents are not as clear-cut as they are in common law. Then, too, cases in equity are concerned with seeking relief from a threatened act, rather than an accomplished one.

Rules of Law

In general, except for specialized rules, such as those applied by the military or in maritime cases, the rules of law might be divided into two categories: (1) criminal law and (2) civil law. Criminal laws are rules dealing with acts injurious to the public welfare. For example, treason is the most serious form of a federal criminal act. The more serious State criminal acts are called *felonies*, such as murder, manslaughter, arson, burglary, rape, and larceny. Minor criminal acts, such as disturbing the peace and panhandling, are known as *misdemeanors*.

Civil law rules are concerned with individuals, and while violations do not necessarily bring injury or threat to the public at large, they are still subject to decision by public courts. Among the more common civil law cases that reach adjudication are those concerned with property, torts (wrongs to individuals, such as slander, libel, and damage), contract and other business operation suits, and domestic relations.

Many cases involve elements of both criminal and civil law. For example, let us say your automobile is hit by a speeding car. You suffer bodily injury and your car is wrecked. The offender is charged under criminal law with violating statutory rules on speeding. You are also likely to sue him for damages under civil law.

Due Process of Law

The American concept of justice includes numerous protective measures for those charged with violations of the law and, on the other hand, the public at large. For example, the concept of *habeas corpus* requires that the defendant know the charges. The concept of a fair trial involves *due process*, which requires that proper steps be taken, such as indictments (or presentments) and convictions before sentence is issued. The right of appeal is another important step in due process, as is the right to select jury trial in all cases but misdemeanors.

The United States Constitution and the Maryland Courts

The federal Constitution contains many safeguards against despotic government and inhumane treatment of citizens. The pages of history are filled with the stories of rulers who performed indignities, and the pledge of our Nation was that government would be the servant of the people, not the other way around. For example, the Fifth Amendment makes it clear that no person can be held for a crime unless there is a presentment or indictment by a Grand Jury (except in times of war or public danger); nor can there be double jeopardy; nor can one be compelled to be witness against himself, nor can one be deprived of life, liberty, or property without due process of law.

In the Sixth Amendment speedy and public trial are guaranteed a citizen, as is the right to be confronted with the witnesses against him. In the Seventh Amendment the right of jury trial in suits at common law are guaranteed. The Seventh Amendment also prohibits excessive bail and fines, and cruel and unusual punishment. In the Fourteenth Amendment the federal government prohibits any state from making or enforcing any law which abridges the privileges or immunities of American citizens, and it reinforces the right of all under "the equal protection of the laws."

The Maryland Constitution and the Maryland Courts

The State Constitution in its Declaration of Rights virtually restates the federal document's protections under due process. For example, Article 16 is much like the federal Seventh Amendment. Article 17 clearly states the principle of no *ex post facto* law.

Article IV of the main body of the Maryland Constitution describes how judges are selected, their terms of office, how they may be removed, how the four-tier system of State courts operates, how the Orphans' Court operates, and how court officers are elected and operate.

Article V describes the work of the Attorney General and the State's Attorneys.

The Maryland Statutory Laws and the Courts

The Legislature is granted power under the State Constitution to establish intermediate courts of appeal—and it has done so. It is given numerous powers to pass laws dealing with procedure. The Criminal Code written by the Legislature establishes a system of fines and punishments used by the courts.

The Maryland Four-Tier Court System

By 1973 Maryland practically completed its long-time program of establishing a four-tier State court system, which brought about a number of reforms in a heretofore complicated court system with many

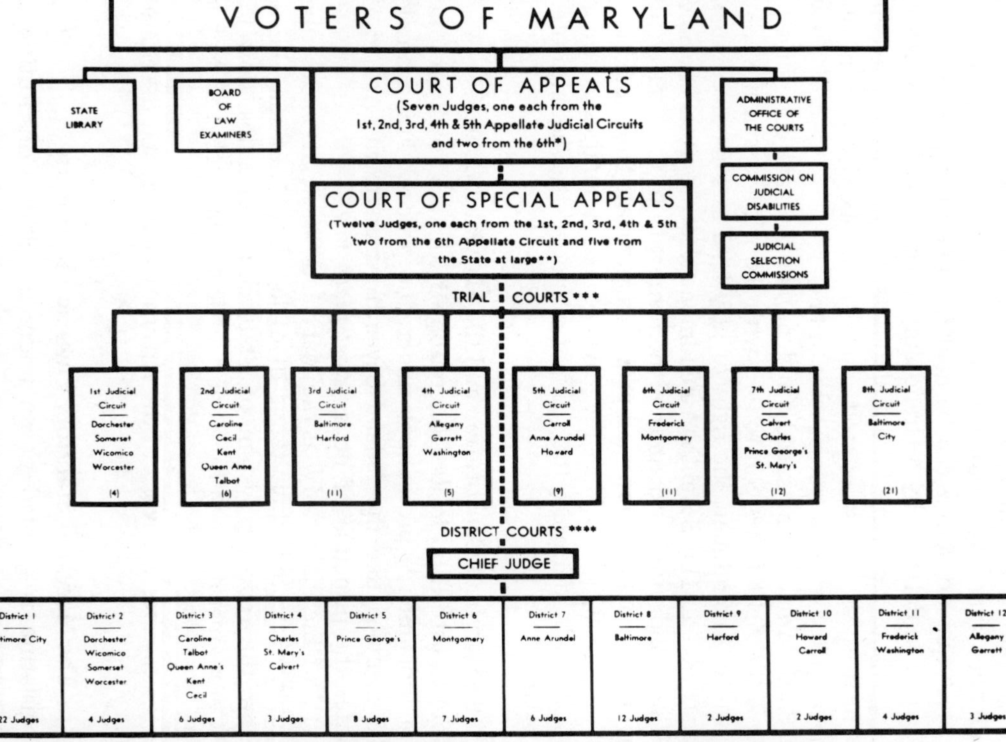

* The Judges of the Court of Appeals are elected by the voters of their respective Appellate Judicial Circuits for fifteen-year terms. The Circuits are: 1st—Caroline, Cecil, Dorchester, Kent, Queen Anne's, Somerset Talbot, Wicomico, Worcester; 2nd—Baltimore, Harford; 3rd—Allegany, Frederick, Garrett, Montgomery, Washington; 4th—Calvert, Charles, Prince George's, St. Mary's; 5th—Anne Arundel, Carroll, Howard; 6th—Baltimore City.

** The Judges of the Court of Special Appeals are also elected by the voters of their Appellate Judicial Circuits for fifteen-year terms. Those representing the State at large are elected Statewide.

*** The Judges of the First, Second and Eighth Judicial Circuits are elected by the electorate of the entire circuits; the Judges of the Third, Fourth, Fifth, Sixth and Seventh deficiencies. To begin with, the lowest courts, where misdemeanors and traffic cases were tried, differed from county to county; as late as 1960 many judges in these courts were not even trained as lawyers. These lowest courts were not courts of records and there was no tight supervision of them at the State level. Actually they were financed at the local level.

The trial courts, at the intermediate level, were somewhat better structured and conducted in the 1960's, and did have judges trained as lawyers. However, judges were originally appointed by the Governor without the chief executive receiving strong recommendations for his selections, except for recommendations by the local and State bar associations. Moreover, a year or so after their appointments by the Governor, judges had to run for office in open election, spending much money and time and risking loss of their new jobs after they had already given up law practice to move to the bench. Many capable persons rejected judicial appointments that might leave them "out on a limb."

As for the highest court, the Maryland Court of Appeals, its work has always been concerned mainly with cases that have already been heard in lower courts. Increasingly its case load became overbearing as the State grew larger and as more and more people properly took advantage of their right of appeal. In 1966 the Maryland Constitution was amended to create an intermediate appeals court in order to take some of the burden off the Court of Appeals. The Legislature was then empowered to implement this Constitutional requirement by statutory laws. This it did by creating the Court of Special Appeals whose jurisdiction was limited to hearing primarily criminal cases, except where death sentence was imposed, and such trials would still go to the Court of Appeals. In 1970 jurisdiction of the Court of Special Appeals was widened to include numerous civil matters, but not all. Even by 1970 the whole issue of appeals cases needed review if the Court of Appeals were to do what its primary task should be, namely, to build up a body of "decisional law" in Maryland, as the Supreme Court does for the country.

This was the picture throughout much of the 1960's and fortunately some reforms started by groups in the last part of that decade improved these situations. For example, the judicial recommendations of the 1967-68 Constitutional Conventions, including the establishment of a four-tier State court system, had much influence in what was to happen in the early 1970's.

Below is a description of the courts as they now exist in the 1970's. It is evident that many reforms have taken place, but some further changes are in order. The four-tier system includes a District Court system at the lowest tier, trial courts known officially as Circuit Courts in the middle tier, and two appeals courts at the top—the Court of Special Appeals and, at the very apex, the Court of Appeals.

The District Courts

These courts were created by a Constitutional Amendment passed in 1969 and implemented by Legislative law in 1970. The system was begun in 1971 and provided for a Statewide 79-judge structure in 12 districts. While judges are assigned to certain districts, under this unified system they may be moved around by the Chief Judge if case loads are very heavy in certain places, or if there are vacancies or illness. The State pays all the expenses and all of the 79 judges use Statewide laws in their decisions.

District Courts have jurisdiction in all civil cases up to $5,000 and jurisdiction in all misdemeanors, as well as in the case of five felonies dealing with such issues as bad checks, shoplifting, thefts up to $500, false pretense, some forms of larceny, and receiving stolen goods. They also have jurisdiction over traffic and motor cases. All cases heard are nonjury cases—in other words, settled by the assigned judge. The assignment of some felony cases to the District Courts by the legislature in 1971 has done much to lower the heavy load of the trial courts where they were before.

Appeals from decisions in the District Courts go to the next level of the four-tier system, namely, the trial courts. In the 23 counties they would go to the related Circuit Court. In Baltimore City the appeals in traffic and criminal cases would go to the Criminal Court and the civil cases would go to the Baltimore City Court—both of these courts are part of the City's 8th Circuit Court system, more popularly known as the Baltimore Supreme Bench.

District Court judges are nominated by judicial commissions made up of lay persons appointed by the Governor and he selects the appointee, subject to approval of the State Senate. The judges serve for ten years and must be reappointed by the Governor unless they are charged with incompetence or violations of the law. They serve full time at salaries of $30,085 a year.

Under the judges are 160 district Commissioners. The Commissioner usually meets the offender first after he has been brought in by the police officer. The Commissioner determines pretrial release and whether the suspect is eligible for bail; he also issues warrants and summonses. In sum, the commissioner prepares the case for the judge.

Since the District Courts have been reorganized the whole system of justice has been improved in the lowest courts. Maryland is now but one of a few states in which every litigated case is settled by a judge who is a full-time professional, trained as a lawyer.

Since most people who get in trouble have their day in court at these lowest levels in such cases as traffic violations, reform here is especially important. Many believe that traffic cases, particularly parking violations, ought not be heard by District Court judges but by Commissioners in this Court. Others believe such cases should be heard by hearing officers attached to an administrative body such as the Motor Vehicle Department.

The Circuit Courts

The Circuit Courts are where the serious criminal and civil cases are heard. These are courts of record, so that testimony can be reviewed and appeals made. In most states they are referred to as trial courts.

The eight Circuit Courts have original jurisdiction in all criminal and civil cases, except those of less seriousness which are, as noted earlier, assigned to the District Courts. While these 80 or so judges are assigned to Circuit Court districts which, except for Baltimore City, embrace two or more counties, they may be moved around by the Administrative Office of the Courts if situations such as illness or vacancies require such changes.

Because of Baltimore City's large population, it is in a separate judicial circuit, the eighth. Because there are so many cases to be tried in the city, there are special sections of the trial court system. For example, there are two Criminal Court sections dealing with serious offenses as murder, arson, burglary and rape. Attached to these Criminal Court sections is the Juvenile Court, which hears cases of young persons, except for very serious offenses that might be referred directly to the Criminal Court proper. Domestic and family relations cases, which are normally thought of as *cases in equity* are heard in the two Circuit Court sections—(not to be confused with the title 8th Judicial Circuit, which refers to the total Supreme Bench). The Superior Court section hears appeals from the Employment Security Board, which is an administrative office. The Court of Common Pleas is commonly referred to as the "marriage license court," since it performs all civil marriages. The Baltimore City Court hears appeal cases of a civil nature from the lower District Court. While the jurisdictions noted above for the various sections of the Baltimore Supreme Bench are exclusive, nevertheless it is important to recognize that in some cases there are shared jurisdictions. For example, the sections that house the Court of Common Pleas, Baltimore City Court, and the Superior Court are civil-law courts and they share jurisdiction in contracts and in torts involving amounts exceeding $5,000.

In addition to the judges the Circuit Courts have other officers. For example, there are *masters* who are usually assigned to *cases in equity* such as family and domestic relations, divorce proceedings, and sometimes juvenile disputes. These masters carry out pretrial discussions with the persons concerned and make their findings available to the judges in the equity courts. In most cases, their recommendations are

Court of Special Appeals of Maryland; (Seated, l. to r.) Judges Charles E. Moylan, Jr., James C. Morton, Jr., Charles E. Orth, Jr., C. Awdry Thompson and Jerrold V. Powers. (Standing, l. to r.) Judges Alfred L. Scandan (Ret.), Richard P. Gilbert, J. DeWeese Carter (Ret.), W. Albert Menchine and Rita C. Davidson. Two were added in the 1974 legislative session. (Photo by Whelan of Annapolis, Inc.)

Court of Appeals of Maryland as of Jan. 1, 1974; (l. to r.) J. Dudley Digges, Frederick J. Singley, Jr., Wilson K. Barnes (resigned as of 1/31/74; seat now vacant), Chief Judge Robert C. Murphy, William J. McWilliams (retired 1/7/74; seat filled 1/7/84 by appointment of John C. Eldridge), Marvin H. Smith, Irving A. Levine. (Photo by M. E. Warren, Annapolis)

followed. Thus in a sense, they carry out the work which in some states is done in officially labeled domestic relations courts.

All Circuit Court judges throughout the State are nominated by Judicial Selection Commissions. There are eight such commissions, one for each of the circuits. Each commission is made up of lay persons from the district concerned, selected by the Governor, and lawyers chosen by the attorneys who work in that district. Bar associations and individual citizens may make recommendations to a Commission which submits its nominations to the Governor for the final word on selection, subject to approval by the State Senate.

After serving until the next election (for at least one year), Governor-selected Circuit Court judges must run for election in their districts. They may enter their names in both primaries so that if, for example, they lose in the Republican primary and win in the Democratic, they may still have their name on the ballot at the general election. Anyone meeting the requirements—legal background—may run against these candidates even though he has not first been appointed by the Governor to serve until the election. The advantage is usually to the candidate who has served in office for he runs as a "sitting judge."

The term of office is 15 years and judges may serve until they are 70 years of age. The State pays Circuit Court judges $35,500 a year, plus pension privileges.

The Court of Special Appeals

This court was first established in 1966 to take some of the burdens off the highest court, the Court of Appeals. It was first given jurisdiction in criminal cases only, and in 1970 received limited jurisdiction in some civil cases. In 1973 the Court's jurisdiction was extended to permit it to handle all appeals cases from the trial courts, effective January 1, 1975.

The Court of Special Appeals has twelve judges, one from each of the first five circuits, two from the sixth circuit (Baltimore City), and five at large. The Governor appoints the judges from nominations submitted by a Statewide committee made up of lawyers (selected by attorneys) and lay persons selected by the Governor. The State Senate must confirm the Governor's appointments. Within a year or so—at the next election—the judges are required to run for office in the districts in which they serve (or at large, if they so serve) for their 15-year terms. The candidates may cross-file in the Republican and Democratic primaries and then enter the general election.

Judges of this court receive annual salaries of $37,500 and are eligible for a pension. They may serve until 70 years of age.

The Court of Appeals

This is the highest court in the State, though appeals from its rulings may be taken as high as the United States Supreme Court. Starting with 1975, it becomes a "pure *certiorari* court" handling only cases of importance, thus establishing "decision law" as does the Supreme Court for the nation.

The Court has seven judges, one from each of the first five appellate circuits (the same boundaries as those for the Court of Special Appeals) and two from the Sixth Circuit, Baltimore City. They serve their 15-year term through the same procedure as the Court of Special Appeals. While they are assigned to districts, they may be moved around. Their salaries are $40,000, with pensions for services which may last until they are 70 years of age.

The Orphans' Courts

Existing outside the four-tier State court system in Maryland are the Orphans' Courts, one in each county (Montgomery and Harford have special arrangements) and Baltimore City. Each Court has three judges, chosen at Gubernatorial Elections for four-year terms. Vacancies are filled by the Governor, with State Senate confirmation.

The Orphans' Court is involved in cases dealing with wills and other testamentary matters related to the deceased. Much of the work of the Court is carried out by the Register of Wills, who is elected for a four-year term at the same time as the judges of the Orphans' Court.

Unlike the courts in the four-tier system, each county and Baltimore City pays the expenses. Actually many people believe that the Orphans' Court should be abolished and its responsibilities made a part of the duties of the State District Courts, or possibly, be absorbed by the trial (Judicial Circuit) courts.

Other Judicial Offices

The Administrative Office of the Courts examines the dockets of the courts in terms of needs for assistance and recommends these to the Chief Judge of the Court of Appeals, compiles statistics and recommends policies for improvement of the courts.

The Commission on Judicial Disabilities is made up of seven members appointed by the Governor. Four of the seven are judges representing the Appellate Courts, the Circuit Courts (including Baltimore City's Supreme Bench), and the District Courts. Two are lawyers and one is a lay person. The Commission investigates improper actions and incapacities of judges. It may, upon proper cause, and after hearing witnesses, recommend that any judge in the four-tier system or the Orphans' Court be censured or removed from his job by the Court of Appeals.

The Commission was established by Constitutional amendment in 1966 and implemented by Legislative law in 1967. A few serious cases of improper actions by judges motivated the move, and the wisdom of having such a body has been proven by cases heard since its establishment. The conduct of judges must be exemplary.

The State Board of Law Examiners, with three members, is appointed by the Judges of the Court of Appeals. It conducts examinations for admission to the Bar and passes upon petitions of attorneys from other states desiring admission.

The Attorney General is a constitutionally-designated position. As directed in Article V of the Maryland Constitution, the Attorney General:

1. Represents the State in all cases in the Maryland Court of Appeals or the United States Supreme Court.

2. Gives his opinion in writing whenever required by the General Assembly, the Governor, Comptroller, Treasurer, or any State's Attorney on any legal matter.

3. Responds to the request of the Governor or General Assembly to aid any State's Attorney in prosecuting any suit brought by the State.

4. Prosecutes and defends any suit which the Governor or the General Assembly directs.

Under Article 32-A of the Maryland Code, the statutory law gives the Attorney General the general charge, supervision, and direction of the legal business of the State and the representation of State boards and departments which carry out activities in health, education, welfare, protection of natural resources, and other activities. Regulatory bodies and administrative State officers are continually asking for opinions as to meanings of laws affecting their work. The staff of the Attorney General is present at all sessions of the General Assembly to check on legality of bills.

A comparatively new department in the Attorney General's office is the Division of Consumer Protection. It is concerned with the control and regulation of fraud and false advertising. The 1974 Legislature gave this division the power to issue cease and desist orders, to make rules governing consumer protection and to set up a consumer council advisory board.

The Attorney General is elected Statewide for a four-year term at the Gubernatorial Election period and may be reelected without restriction. The Governor fills a vacancy in the office if it occurs before the term expires.

The State's Attorneys

Each county and Baltimore City has a State's Attorney who, with his staff, is charged with prosecuting violators of the law in the various courts. These officers, seeking indictments and convictions where they are applicable, determine the nature of law and order in their geographical areas. Each State's Attorney works with grand juries in his county to ferret out criminal and other illegal actions.

The State's Attorney is elected for a four-year period at the time of the Gubernatorial Elections. It is a Constitutionally established position. Some legislators believe that State's Attorneys should be removed from the risks of the election process and that the State should establish public prosecutors, instead, who would be appointed by boards of trustees. In this way the State's Attorneys would be free of political promises.

Court Officers. Each court has administrative officers, such as bailiffs and clerks who are increasingly being placed on civil service. In addition, each county and Baltimore City has a sheriff who is largely an official who sees to it that court orders, such as seizure and sale of property in order to satisfy a judgment, are carried out. The Sheriff is a constitutionally established office and his election calls for a four-year term. Clerks of the eight Judicial Circuits are also elected for four-year terms at the time of Gubernatorial Elections.

The Jury System

Origin of the Jury System. Maryland's jury system, like that in other states, stems from the nation's British traditions. As far back as the 11th century, the English rulers sought to further justice by giving the people themselves a voice in determining whether their neighbors had committed offenses against the law. Modified and improved since that time, the jury system was brought to Maryland during the colonial period.

The system calls for two types of juries: the *grand* jury and the *petit* or *trial* jury. In Maryland the 23 counties and Baltimore City summon citizens to serve regularly on both kinds of juries. While some states are now giving less attention to the jury system than in the past, in Maryland its popularity or usefulness has never been seriously challenged. The criticism is especially strong of the grand jury with the belief that money and time would be saved if the State's Attorney merely presented the charges instead of a grand jury indicting.

The Grand Jury

To make up a grand jury, each county and Baltimore City select, by lot, 23 persons. One of their number is designated as a foreman. This group makes up the grand jury for a period of from four to six months. In more densely populated areas, such as Baltimore City, the grand jury serves every work day; in other places, the body meets only a few days a week. While they serve, the members of the jury are paid a small fee.

Indictment Function. In Maryland a grand jury has two major functions. First, it hears charges presented by the State's Attorney against persons who have been arrested and are accused of violating criminal laws. The jury decides, from the hearing and from other investigations, whether or not to indict the accused—that is, to accuse him formally of law violation and bring him to trial. The grand jury may also submit a *presentment* (accusation) against any person *whom they, of their own knowledge, believe to have violated the criminal laws of the State.* It is important to note that in the case of an indictment or a presentment, the accused has not yet been found guilty. It is not the task of the grand jury either to try the case or to pass judgment on the guilt or innocence of the accused.

Clearly, the power of indictment is of great importance. Upon the grand jury rests the responsibility of deciding whether an accused person is to be released or brought up for trial. In some states the grand jury is not empowered to make this decision. Instead, it is made by the judge of the criminal court or by the prosecutor. In this case, the accused is said to be *presented by information.* In Maryland, only in certain special cases are arrested persons presented by information rather than indicted by the grand jury.

Investigatory Function. The second function of the grand jury is to investigate any activity that concerns the welfare of the county or its citizens. Some students of public affairs consider this function to be even more important than indictment. Note that it enables a nonpolitical group of citizens to look into the school system, the county jail, the health and welfare departments, and other institutions and conditions that affect the day-to-day life of the community. The purpose is primarily to discover the existence or nonexistence of a violation of the criminal law, not to censure individuals or agencies for actions that may be debatable but legal.

The value and effectiveness of these investigations depend, of course, upon the caliber of the people who make up the grand juries. In some counties grand jurors' associations have been formed so that citizens who have served on these bodies can utilize their knowledge and experience to aid the county.

The Petit Jury

After the accused has been indicted by the grand jury or his case has come up through information, he then goes to trial. The defendant in a criminal or civil suit coming before a Circuit Court may choose to be tried by a judge alone or by a judge and jury.

If the defendant chooses a jury trial, the case is heard by a *petit jury,* made up of twelve citizens, who base their decision on the facts presented by the prosecuting and defending attorneys.* In criminal cases, the verdict—either to *acquit* or to *convict* the defendant—must be agreed upon by all twelve jurors. It is important to remember that petit

*In criminal cases, juries are judges of the law as well as of the facts. Since 1950, the presiding judge can give such a jury advisory opinions on the law involved. In common law (civil) cases, juries are judges only of the facts, not of the law.

juries do not impose the sentence; this is done by the judge. The jury merely decides whether or not the accused is guilty, as charged.

Jurors are selected by lot, to ensure that the jury represents a cross section of the citizenry. Federal courts have voided cases tried by juries not representative of the public at large.

The twelve persons selected for a petit jury serve for a period of a few weeks. During this time, they usually hear a number of cases. In Baltimore City, they serve every work day; in most counties, they are usually on call for service throughout the week. Like members of the grand jury, they are paid by the county or Baltimore City for their services.

Throughout much of the country, jury trials are now used less often than in the past; in some states, indeed, they are scarcely used at all. Maryland, however, still relies on them quite heavily. Some judicial authorities believe that petit juries should be smaller (six persons) in civil cases; others that a unanimous decision not be required in criminal cases. It is, therefore, of the greatest importance that all citizens understand their obligations under the jury system, and serve willingly and conscientiously whenever their names are drawn. The citizen who tries to avoid jury duty on the grounds that he is "too busy to serve" is failing in one of his basic responsibilities to his community and his state. Such a citizen certainly has no cause for complaint if the administration of justice is not as efficient as he would like it to be.

The Maryland Public Defender Law and Legal Aid Societies

In 1972, due to federal court decisions such as the 1966 Miranda case stating that all those charged as offenders were entitled to proper legal defense at preliminary hearings, the Maryland General Assembly passed the Public Defender Law. This provides for legal defense of the needy defendant through a full-time staff and hired private attorneys to serve on panels from which public defender counsels are drawn. The Public Defender may also use the services of volunteer workers. He may enter into contracts with private and public organizations. The system is headed by a Board of Trustees, which sets policies, and by advisory committees for the various districts which have the same boundaries as the District Courts.

The Legal Aid Bureau of Baltimore operates in the entire city metropolitan area. It is a private non-profit organization that is not concerned so much with defending people charged with crimes as it is with supplying them with free legal aid related to such problems as wage claims, bankruptcy, welfare and consumer problems, landlord—tenant difficulties, divorce, custody and guardianship, and workmen's and veterans compensation.

Court Reforms. It is obvious that Maryland court structure and procedure has changed radically recently, and for the better. Yet the State has some way to go to make justice more even-handed, to break the backlog of cases in civil, criminal, and appeals courts. There is a need to speed up the work and efficiency of the State's Attorneys in preparation of cases, and to improve the effectiveness of jury operations.

Fundamentally, the judges are the most important persons, and unless the best qualified hold office, the people are in trouble. Many jurists believe that judges should not be made to run for office, but should be reappointed if worthy, or at least should run against their own record rather than against opponents who have never served. Actually, judges in the District Courts do not run for second terms; they are appointed.

Recent studies show that only small percentages of those indicted are convicted; thus it seems that cases should not be brought to trial unless there is reasonable evidence of guilt. Then, too, the whole question of what is a criminal act needs review. For example, some people feel that acts that concern individuals alone and have little bearing on the State, such as card playing or homosexual relations, should not be subject to punishment. Others disagree. The answers are not clear.

Chapter 9

COUNTY GOVERNMENT

In Maryland the county is the most important political subdivision. Except for incorporated cities, towns, villages, and special-tax districts, it is the only agency of local government. Note that Maryland counties are not subdivided into townships, as in some other states.

From the very beginning of the State's history, in 1634, the county played an important role. Unlike the more northern colonial settlements, Maryland's farmland was more level and lent itself to large plantations, especially for the growth of tobacco. While the New England soil was rocky and population was more tightly knit in villages, Maryland's people were spread out. Actually, the county system became

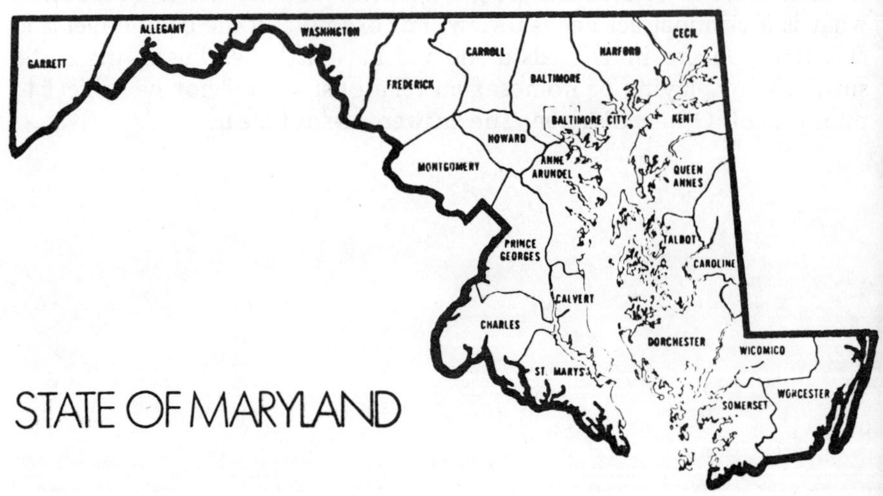

fixed in all states south of the Mason-Dixon Line. Thus to this day, when you ask a Marylander where he lives, he is more likely to name his county rather than his town. If you ask a teacher, health officer, or social worker where she works, she will name the county, for she is on that payroll. (Since Baltimore City operates as though it were a county, one must think of that political unit in that context while reading this chapter.) In New England the orientation would be toward the town rather than the county government, which is minimized. It is this long tradition of county importance which is not easily understood by those who come to Maryland from other states. The 23 counties (and Baltimore City acting as a 24th unit) are very important in this State.

The single exception to this scheme of local government is Baltimore

City. It belongs to no county and has itself carried on the functions of county government since 1851, at which time it withdrew from Baltimore County.

Functions of the County

The modern county serves a dual function. First, it acts as an agent of the State government in the administration of State functions. Next, it is an instrument of local self-government.

As an agent of the State government, the county is called upon to do a number of things. (1) It administers State laws and tries violators of them. (2) It carries out elections for Statewide offices and for its own representatives in the General Assembly. (3) It collects taxes that go to the State. (4) It enrolls units for the State Militia and for civil defense activities. (5) It enforces Statewide regulations having to do with such matters as agriculture, education, health, public welfare, and travel on the highways and in the air.

As an instrument of local government the county performs the following main functions: (1) It provides help to the needy. (2) It administers its own county regulations having to do with education, health, public order, police protection, public facilities for transportation, and public housing. (3) It assesses and collects taxes to be used for county purposes.

The Pattern of County Government

One basic point about county government in Maryland is that it cannot be divided into the conventional pattern of legislative, executive, and judicial branches.

Many county laws are usually made by the General Assembly. In actual practice, a given county's representatives in the two Houses of the Legislature determine the laws for that county. Members usually submit bills for their counties, and they are always appointed to the numerous local committees that recommend action on such bills. Since these recommendations are customarily accepted by the General Assembly, it is clear that each county's legislative representatives are, in effect, its lawmakers. This is especially true for those counties that do not have home rule. Eight counties now have home rule, and fewer local bills are passed in the Legislature for this group.

The Governor has the right to veto bills relating to a county's affairs, just as he can veto any other bills passed by the General Assembly. This obviously gives the Governor some direct control over government in counties where there is no home rule.

Since crimes are regarded as offenses against the State, rather than against the county in which they were committed, there is really no county judicial system. However, there are county ordinances, such as those involving motor vehicles and the sale of liquor. Violations of these ordinances are almost all of a relatively minor nature.

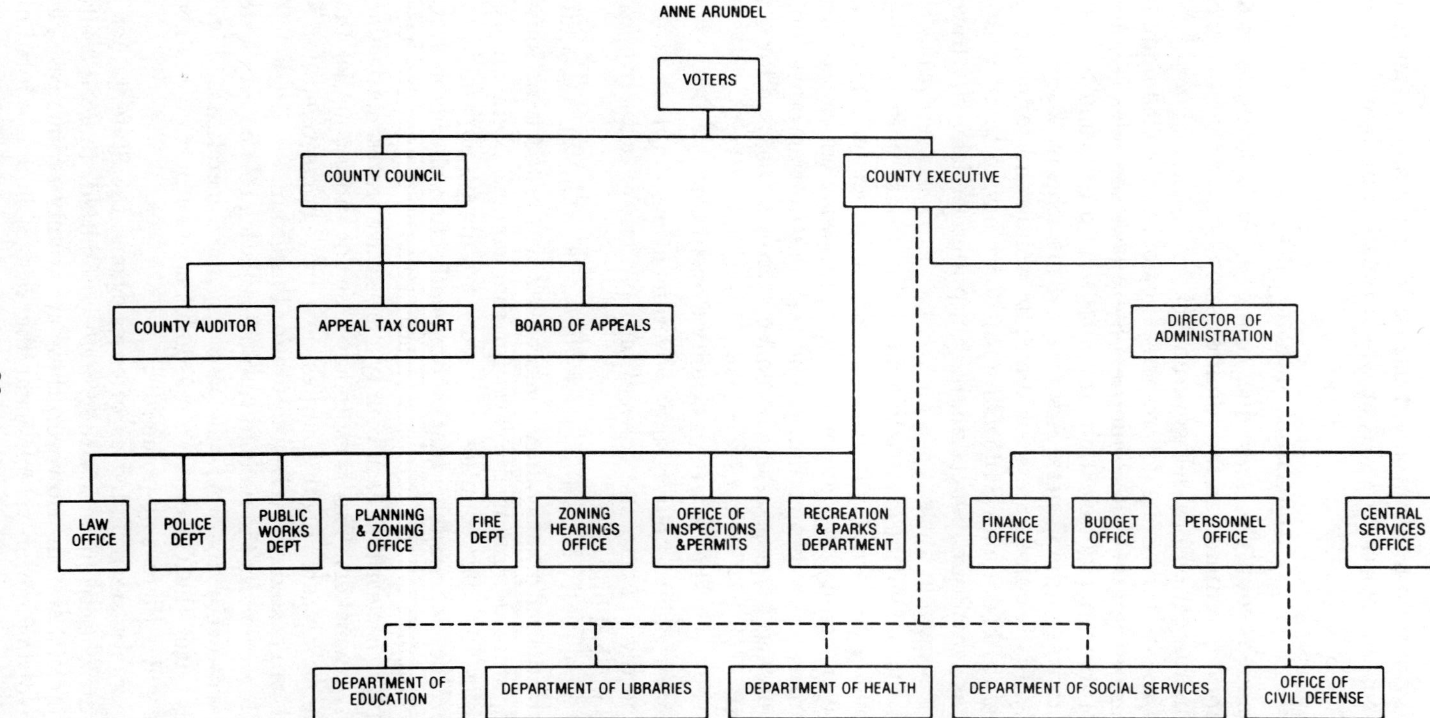
GENERAL ORGANIZATION OF COUNTY DEPARTMENTS UNDER CHARTER
ANNE ARUNDEL
VOTERS
COUNTY COUNCIL
COUNTY EXECUTIVE
COUNTY AUDITOR
APPEAL TAX COURT
BOARD OF APPEALS
DIRECTOR OF ADMINISTRATION
LAW OFFICE
POLICE DEPT
PUBLIC WORKS DEPT
PLANNING & ZONING OFFICE
FIRE DEPT
ZONING HEARINGS OFFICE
OFFICE OF INSPECTIONS &PERMITS
RECREATION & PARKS DEPARTMENT
FINANCE OFFICE
BUDGET OFFICE
PERSONNEL OFFICE
CENTRAL SERVICES OFFICE
DEPARTMENT OF EDUCATION
DEPARTMENT OF LIBRARIES
DEPARTMENT OF HEALTH
DEPARTMENT OF SOCIAL SERVICES
OFFICE OF CIVIL DEFENSE
Departments under State control in whole or in part.
County Departments.

There is considerable overlapping between State and county jurisdiction in education, health, and other fields of public welfare. Although the county has been set up in Maryland as an independent unit of local self-government, the fact is that the State retains considerable supervisory powers over certain functions to ensure that the counties do their jobs properly. Education is a prominent example of this. In some cases, the State may go so far as to exercise direct control; this is done in certain counties, for example, with respect to the repair of roads.

The Maryland Constitution and County Government

Home Rule. Article XI-A in the State Constitution deals with how a county may secure home rule, thus enabling its local legislative body to pass bills which affect only this political unit. Eight counties (Anne Arundel, Baltimore, Harford, Howard, Montgomery, Prince Georges, Talbot, and Wicomico) and Baltimore City have availed themselves of this opportunity. It is evident that home rule is especially valuable for the larger counties, though some smaller ones like Talbot have selected this form of government.

To obtain home rule there must first be a petition signed by at least five percent of the county's registered voters or by 10,000 voters, whichever group is smaller. At that point the county commissioners may appoint a board to write a new charter. A county charter is the organic law of that political unit much as the State Constitution is for the larger political unit. The county charter and the State Constitution are not open to change except by the vote of the people.

Once a charter board is appointed (or in some cases elected), this body has one year to draft its proposed new charter. The newly-written document must be advertised in a county newspaper with general circulation not later than 30 days or earlier than 90 days before the election. If a majority of the votes on this issue indicate approval, then the new charter becomes a law. On the same ballot giving voters the opportunity to accept or reject the new charter, there appears the names of the possible new officeholders, subject to support of the charter plan.

Every home-rule charter must provide for a legislative body, to be known as the County Council, and for executive and administrative officers. In 1972 Article XI-A was amended to permit county councilmen to be elected by district or at large. The charter also spells out the new county government's powers.

Home rule does not permit the counties complete leeway in powers. To illustrate, the County Council cannot vote local political unit exemption from a Statewide or public general law which deals, for example, with equal-opportunity employment or inspection of milk. In the latter case they could, of course, add to that Statewide law by requiring that milk containers be dated when sold in stores and not be handled five days after a specified sale date. Then, too, the State has reserved certain local powers that affect only that county. For example, Baltimore City, acting as a county, cannot place any local bond issues on its own city elections ballot until given permission of the General Assembly. Thus, it is not complete home rule that is granted.

Code Counties. One way for a county to get some semblance of home rule, but not the fuller autonomy under Article XI-A, is to become a code county. The procedure here is to act under Article XI-F of the Maryland Constitution. This merely requires that two-thirds of the county commissioners pass a resolution that the local unit become a code county. The resolution is then submitted to the voters of that county and, if approved, the desirable action takes place on the thirtieth day after the election. Councils do not replace the commissioners in code counties as they do in home-rule counties. The actions of code county commissioners in amending, repealing, or passing laws are subject to referenda created by petitions signed by five percent of the voters. A number of other limitations are placed on code counties; for example, their powers are classified in terms of four groupings based on population. Code counties do not have the strong powers that home-rule counties have on local tax issues. No wonder, then, that only Kent has elected to become a code county.

New Counties. Article XIII provides for the establishment of new counties. The voters of the newly established county and those from the county, or counties, to be dismembered must give their permission. Furthermore, the new county must contain at least 400 square miles and a population of not less than 10,000.

The Proposed Maryland Constitution of 1968 and County Government

All over America there is a search for the reform of county government. Such changes were proposed by the 1968 Maryland Constitutional Convention. In essence it gave each county home rule. Furthermore, the Convention suggested that the General Assembly be given the power to establish, merge, or dissolve multi-county governmental units and that there might be popularly elected representatives of regional governments so organized. Then, too, the 1968 proposed Constitution suggested that these multi-county regional governments be given taxing powers. Unfortunately for the 1968 Convention, many Marylanders feared that regional government would destroy the powers of the counties and thus the voters turned down the proposed Constitution.

The State Legislature and County Government

The Maryland Constitution empowers the General Assembly to pass laws dealing with county government. To begin with, more than 25 percent of the bills passed by the Legislature deal with one county only and are thus referred originally to *select committees* made up of the

Senators or Delegates from the county affected and also representatives from nearby counties if the county affected does not have enough representation for a committee of three. The Assembly generally follows the recommendation of the select committees on the basis of *legislative courtesy*, namely, "We'll approve your local recommendation

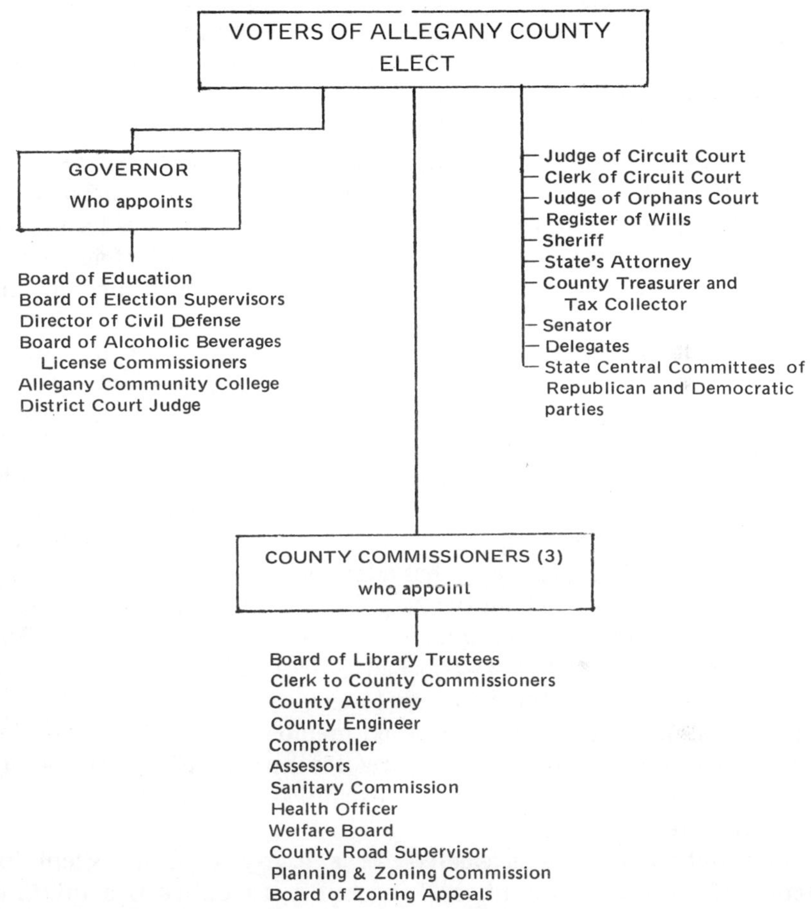

and you'd better do the same for us." As more home-rule counties come into being, the need for local legislation to be passed by the General Assembly is diminished.

The Maryland Constitution gives the Legislature power over the granting of county charters. It also gives the Legislature the power to implement the rights to counties under Articles XI-A, XI-F, and XIII.

Commissioner Counties

Most of the counties in Maryland, namely 14 of the 23 (not counting Baltimore City), have refused to become home-rule or code counties.

They have kept the older county commissioner form of government. The commissioners vary in numbers from three to eight and are elected for four-year terms by the voters of the county during Gubernatorial elections. From among their own numbers they select one person to act as president of the board of county commissioners.

The commissioners are the most important officers of the county and carry out both executive and limited legislative functions from their offices at the county seat. Their meetings are open to the public, and citizen hearings are held frequently.

Clerk of the Commissioners' Board. The board of county commissioners appoints a clerk, or secretary, who is responsible for keeping full minutes of meetings of this body and accounts of all financial transactions. Every year, after the annual assessments and levies have been made up, the clerk uses this information to prepare a list of all county residents who are subject to taxation. The tax list, which includes the name of the taxpayer, a description of his property, its assessed valuation, and the rate of tax payable on it, is turned over to the county treasurer.

The Home Rule Counties

The eight home-rule counties and Baltimore City have three things in common. Each has a chief county executive (in Baltimore City called a mayor) and a legislative body known as the County Council, elected for a four-year term. Then, too, each has administrative divisions headed by persons appointed by the county executive or by his first assistant, who is most often known as the chief county administrative officer. The County Councils are charter-established offices and these local officers, while not full time on their jobs, meet regularly in open session to pass county laws. When a council has seven members, and such is true for most home-rule counties, at least four votes must be affirmative before a bill is passed. A veto by a county executive may be overriden by a two-thirds vote.

The county executive is elected for a four-year term, except for Talbot and Wicomico Counties. The county executive is a full-time officer having veto power over laws passed by the County Council. The chief county administrative officer is appointed by the county executive and is usually a person who has had experience in public administration. He is responsible for integrating the administrative operations. He is often a person who can work well with both major political parties and may stay on whether the county executive is a Democrat or Republican. In Talbot and Wicomico Counties the County Council carries out both administrative and legislative powers. The council appoints an administrator.

A number of administrative departments are common to all of the larger home-rule counties, such as Anne Arundel, Baltimore, Montgomery, and Prince Georges, and are present to a lesser degree in Harford, Howard, Talbot, and Wicomico. These are:

1. Police and fire departments protecting life and property.

2. Human resources and community development departments dealing with human relations, programs for the aging, veterans affairs, community renewal activities, and youth action commissions.

3. Department of hospitals dealing with health care and drug and alcoholic rehabilitation.

4. Department of economic development charged with bringing in desirable new industry and commerce and preparing in-depth studies of the fiscal and social climates.

5. Office of law, headed by a county attorney or solicitor appointed by the county executive or council and acting as a legal advisor to the executive, the council, and to all agencies receiving or disbursing county funds. It also represents the county in zoning and condemnation activities.

6. Office of central services, carrying out purchases from paper clips to computers and supervising all county property.

7. Office of personnel which recruits, tests, and classifies new employees and conducts in-service programs, as well as establishes civil service and merit hiring and promotional guidelines.

8. Office of finance manages tax collection, disbursements, and bond sales.

9. Office of budget and programming has overall responsibilities for preparing the budget, which in Montgomery County, for the fiscal year 1973-74, was $354,000,000 for current operating expenditures and another $115,800,000 for capital appropriations.

10. There are also departments unique to some of the home-rule counties—for example, Montgomery has an office of landlord-tenant affairs seeking to advise both sides and settle cases out of court. Montgomery also has an office of consumer affairs that investigates questionable practices and seeks to settle disagreements amicably.

Other County Officers

Some offices are common to all 23 counties—commissioner and home rule—and they are described below:

County Treasurer. Every four years the voters of commissioner counties elect a treasurer, who must, among other duties, bill and collect all State and county taxes and all other monies due the county. He appoints clerks and deputies to assist him in his many activities. The county treasurer makes out taxpayers' bills and forwards them. He gives notice when discounts are offered and when interest is due on unpaid taxes. He has custody of money received until the county comptroller requests a transfer of funds to the proper recipient. In home-rule counties the treasurer is part of the department of finance and is an appointive office.

County Auditor. The board of county commissioners, or the county executive in home-rule counties, is empowered to appoint a county auditor. In home-rule counties, like Prince Georges, he is appointed by the council. The chief duties of this official include the following: (1) He audits all demands for money made upon the county; that is, he checks to make sure that the demand is proper, and sees that it is duly met. (2) He prescribes the system of record keeping used by each office of the county government. (3) He assists the county treasurer and the clerk of the board of county commissioners in preparing the annual budget and the tax bills. (4) He makes a complete financial survey of every agency using county money.

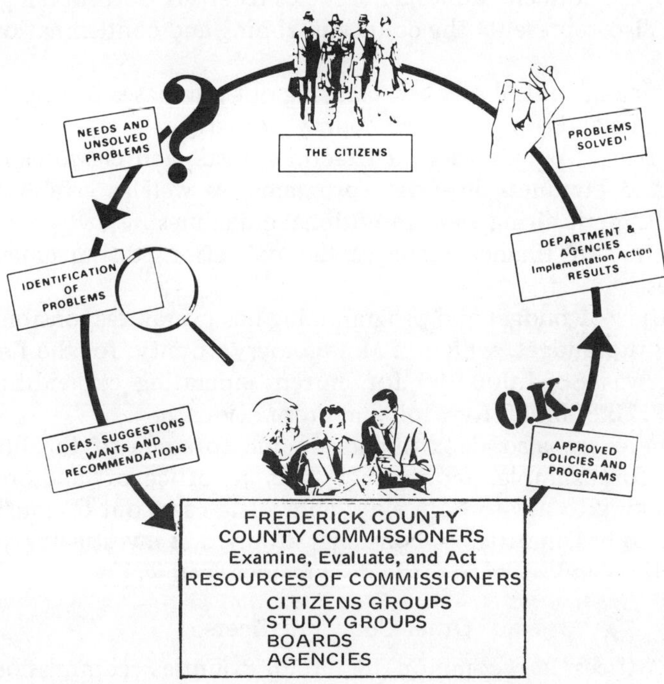

In the larger counties like Baltimore County, the work of the county auditor is a part of a department of audits and disbursements. This agency has been created because of the unusually large number of financial transactions in which these counties engage. In general, the involved job of auditing the financial affairs of Maryland counties is well conducted.

County Attorney. Appointed by the board of county commissioners in commissioner counties and in home-rule counties by the county executives, the administrative officers, or the councils, the attorney heads the law departments of his county and advises the county government on legal cases.

Purchasing Agent. Some counties centralize their purchases of materials. This saves money, especially where purchases involve "general supplies," such as automobiles, typewriters, and stationery, which are used by all types of agencies. Some county agencies, however, need their own particular supplies, not usable elsewhere; this is true, for example, of educational, health, and library services. Because of such

GOVERNMENTAL ORGANIZATION OF BALTIMORE COUNTY

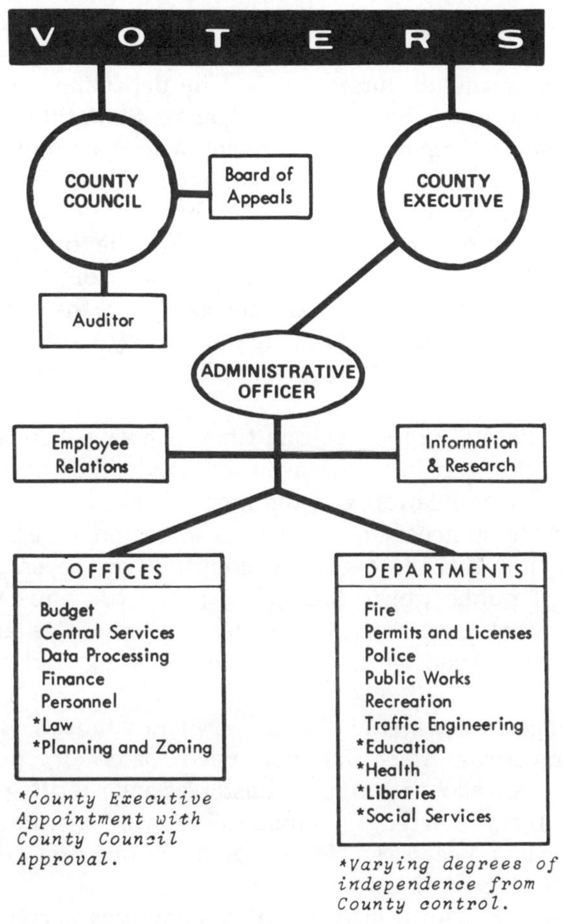

AGENCIES NOT DIRECTLY CONTROLLED BY CHARTER:

Board of Supervisors of Elections	County Surveyor	Register of Wills
Board of Liquor License Commissioners	Cooperative Extension Service	State's Attorney
Supervisor of Assessments	County Judicial System - Circuit Court	County Sheriff
Appeal Tax Court	Orphans' Court	Trial Magistrates
Baltimore County Revenue Authority	Clerk of Circuit Court	People's Court

specialized requirements, some counties prefer to have purchases made by divisions.

Where centralization of purchases—in whole or in part—is in effect, this responsibility is placed in the hands of a special purchasing agent. The official in charge of this work usually has other duties as well. For example, in Baltimore County and in Prince Georges County purchasing is handled by the office of central services. In Montgomery County, the chief administrative officer carries out the duties.

County Finance Departments. In the interests of efficiency and economy, most counties in Maryland have set up departments of finance. For example, in Montgomery County this department is the custodian of all county monies, securities, and insurance policies; it also collects taxes and invests and disburses funds. The department of finance in Prince Georges County handled a budget of $283,000,000 in 1973.

County Highway Engineer. This official, who is appointed for a term of four years by the board of commissioners, controls construction of county roads that do not form part of either State or federal highway systems. The county engineer contracts for the purchase of road-building materials, employs the labor needed, and organizes the actual work of construction. In some Maryland counties, the engineer is also responsible for the proper maintenance of county roads. In about half of the counties of the State, however, upkeep of county roads is supervised by the State.

Director of Public Works. At one time highways were virtually the only public works activity undertaken by Maryland counties. However, the expansion of population and the increasingly complex patterns of living have made it necessary to devote attention to other forms of public works. For this reason, some counties have recently organized departments of public works, headed by a director who oversees such activities as street cleaning, trash collection, sewerage and drainage systems, street and road lighting, traffic engineering, and building construction.

County Police Departments. When Maryland counties consisted very largely of rural areas, there was little need for county police departments. Forty years ago, the county constables and sheriffs could handle almost all problems related to public safety, with assistance from the State Police when necessary. In the urban population centers, town police forces took care of law enforcement.

Today, however, significantly populated counties, such as Baltimore, Howard, Montgomery, Prince Georges, and Anne Arundel, have organized county police departments that carry on programs similar to those of large city police forces. In 1973 the Prince Georges police department had a police force of 156 men and women. Wherever established, these county police forces cooperate with police departments of incorporated communities and with the Maryland State Police. Some of the less populated counties still have law enforcement agencies headed by sheriffs.

Other County Officials. In every county there are additional offices which are concerned with elections, education, agriculture, recreation, library service, health, and public welfare. The responsibilities and activities of the superintendents and directors of these departments are set forth in chapters dealing with their particular fields. These offices are as much related to State operations as they are to county activities, and thus their funds come from both political units.

Numerous county officials carry on work related to court procedure. The activities of the sheriff, the State's attorney, clerk of the circuit court, register of wills, and the numerous judges have been discussed in the chapter on judicial affairs. The work of the bailiff and the court crier, though not as important as that of the other officials, helps to keep court procedure orderly and efficient.

In the area of special services, some counties employ, among other officials, building and electrical inspectors, supervisors of weights and measures, and taxicab inspectors. In addition, many counties have special attorneys who are assigned to assist the commissioners with legal matters. Counties that permit the commercial sale of alcoholic beverages have special boards of liquor licenses, while those counties which distribute alcoholic beverages only through county dispensaries have liquor control boards.

The County Seat

Usually the county seat is the leading city or town of the county. This is in every sense the "nerve center" of the county's affairs. Here is the courthouse in which court sessions are held and in which the county commissioners and other officials and boards have their offices. The jail, too, is ordinarily located in the county seat. In the same town one also finds other county buildings, if such are necessary (see map p. 24).

Intercounty Cooperation

Ways must be found to facilitate intercounty arrangements. Much that is good along these lines has already taken place. For example, since 1927 the Maryland National Park and Planning Commission has developed long-range land use and zoning master plans, overseen the parkland, and administered recreation programs for Montgomery and Prince Georges Counties. The Washington Suburban Sanitary Commission, a non-profit governmental utility, supplies water and sanitary sewerage systems for Montgomery and Prince Georges. The Baltimore and Washington areas have transit systems servicing these metropolitan areas—each covering a number of local units—with mass transit. Actually, the new Washington Metro Plan will serve that city as well as counties in Maryland and Virginia. The Maryland Port Administration ties together the harbor waterways and trade requirements for the Port of Baltimore which includes Baltimore City, Anne Arundel and Baltimore Counties. Both the Baltimore and the Washington areas have regional planning boards working to integrate the economic requirements of those heavily populated metropolitan centers. Other regional planning councils seek to coordinate requirements of the Eastern Shore and the western counties.

Reform of County Government

Throughout the country, much criticism has recently been directed at the existing forms of county government. Some observers have gone so far as to suggest that the county system of government be abolished. Others, equally well informed, advocate keeping the county as a political subdivision, but with drastic reforms to increase efficiency and cut costs.

One important factor working against further reform of Maryland counties is the lack of complete home rule. As has already been pointed out, the present administrators of most of Maryland's counties can do little to modernize county government because the General Assembly exercises "remote control" over the affairs of 14 counties—those without home rule. A step toward remedying this situation was taken by the State Legislature as early as 1915, when it amended Maryland's Constitution so as to permit home rule for any county or for Baltimore City. By 1974 only eight counties and Baltimore City have availed themselves of this opportunity, and one county has gone halfway under the code form.

More intercounty cooperation is needed. Maryland will move slowly, if at all, in developing new intercounty formal governmental units, or in merging counties. But more regional arrangements must come into being. Rivers, roads, the Chesapeake Bay, and other resources do not recognize county boundaries.

The Maryland Association of Counties can be a source for accelerated cooperative ventures and for the establishment of efficiency and fiscal responsibility. There is much that is good in the county system that Maryland has had since its beginnings. While some states have sought to combine their hundreds of political units, made up largely of small towns or tax districts, Maryland has had the good fortune to have to work with but 24 units, the 23 counties and Baltimore City.

Yet another problem faced by counties is that caused by too rapid growth. For example, in 1973 Carroll County found that when new single families moved there in significant numbers, the demands on services were such that there was a net loss to the county of $280 a year for each family unit coming there. The added costs of such services as roads, schools, police, and fire protection were far above the funds recovered through additional taxes. The way out seems to be to assess a developer $200 or more for each dwelling unit he builds. The losses may thus be recouped by either zoning large land areas for industrial and commercial growth or establishing county building fees. The larger and wealthier counties have enough in assets to absorb such temporary losses; the smaller counties do not have the working capital.

A difficult problem continually faced by Maryland counties is its fiscal responsibilities to the State. The counties, and Baltimore City, share costs with the State of Maryland for many services such as education, health, and social welfare. This has been a long-held principle in Maryland. In many cases such as education, the claim is that the State has the responsibility to see that the services are not uneven among counties. This was how the State was won over to support full State funding for school construction. Now many Marylanders would like to have full State funding for current operating costs of schools and for other services such as hospital care of the indigent, court ordered commitments, State-mandated tax credits to the elderly, and the cost of housing State agencies in county-owned buildings. The State has objected to this takeover, indicating that it would be very costly.

Despite the high cost of State takeover for full funding of hospital care for the indigent, the 1974 Legislature voted to move more rapidly toward just such action, thus relieving the counties of costs in the millions of dollars.

Counting full State funding for schools, the cost would run into hundreds of millions, and the State says it would have to take over some present forms of revenue now received by the counties if it had to do so. The State argues that the counties ultimately would be no better off fiscally and that they would lose their contact with the services since they were not financial contributors. The Maryland Association of Counties says most of these functions (perhaps excluding education) are State programs and therefore should be paid at that level. It is true that in seeking to solve their financial plight the counties might lose their traditional responsibilities to make certain that key services to citizens are carried out at the grass roots level.

One important advantage of the Maryland county system is that when the federal government shares grant-in-aid programs such as those dealing with education and health and natural resources, the county system is a good arrangement for distribution of such funds. The same advantage holds true when federal money is set aside for revenue-sharing projects. Those states that do not have a strong county system like Maryland work under handicaps in dealing with distribution of federal assistance; they usually have too many political units entitled to portions of the national allotments.

Chapter 10

LOCAL AND METROPOLITAN GOVERNMENT

Local Government

A municipality comes into being when the residents of a particular locality are convinced that their needs and problems differ markedly from those of the rest of the county. Ordinarily, this will happen only after the locality in question has experienced a sizable increase in population. As a result, the people are no longer satisfied with county services in such fields as health, welfare, and education. They feel that concentration of population in a small area calls for supplementary services—for example, street lighting, garbage collection, and sewage disposal. To meet these special needs, the usual procedure is to organize a municipal government.

How and Whether to Organize a Municipality

The Maryland Constitution in Article XI-E establishes the broad concept that municipalities shall have the right to establish charters, under the laws passed by the General Assembly, and that these cities and towns can pass ordinances that are uniquely related to their local needs. Previous to 1953 the requests for municipal charters came rather rapidly in the 20th century as population growth was accelerated, especially in Prince Georges and Montgomery Counties. The leaders of proposed towns could then go directly to the Legislature and seek a charter.

In 1953 all this was changed when the Legislature revised Article 23-A of the Annotated Code of Maryland so that each county governing body was to be the final authority to approve or veto any proposal for municipal incorporation. As a result, not a single municipal incorporation has taken place since 1953. The new route has proved too tortuous for communities desiring incorporation to try it. For example, Columbia, a planned community in Howard County that came into being after 1953, has established village councils that operate outside of charter powers, since the town is not incorporated. Yet, Columbia has a population much larger than many incorporated communities. Silver Spring, in Montgomery County, is another example of a heavily populated suburban center—nearly 80,000 persons—that is not incorporated.

Indeed, no community in Baltimore or Howard Counties is incorporated. The citizens either prefer to have their towns remain unincorporated because they can possibly save additional taxes or they are satisfied with the services the county governments give them. It must be recognized that at one time pockets of suburban development in rural counties felt that unless they provided their unique needs, such as garbage collection, police and fire protection and street lighting, they would not procure these services. Now that many Maryland counties are in heavily urbanized metropolitan areas, the county commissioners (or the county councils and executives where there is home rule) give full attention to populated areas.

Basic services are often available to significantly populated areas through regional arrangements such as the Washington Suburban Sanitary Commission and the Maryland-National Capital Park and Planning Commission, which serve Montgomery and Prince Georges Counties. Furthermore. some of these needs can be purchased more cheaply from nearby incorporated communities rather than supplying them by newly created governments under a charter. For example, the citizens of Towson and Timonium, as well as other Baltimore County unincorporated communities, are buying their filtered water from Baltimore City. Then, too, the General Assembly will often give a county permission to provide certain services, at charge, to an urban section that has special requirements. For example, Anne Arundel appoints additional policemen for Glen Burnie; Baltimore County builds sidewalks for Towson; Montgomery and Prince Georges Counties collect garbage for some unincorporated communities.

The question is thus raised as to whether Maryland has not entered a new period when town and county have virtually merged. Still, the 151 incorporated communities would respond that there is yet a great need for establishing municipalities. Actually, this affirmative response is endorsed by the federal government, which gives cities financial support for various activities such as manpower planning (the Baltimore City area was given $7,900,000 for fiscal 1974) and community development.

The Charter. The charter prescribes territorial boundaries for the municipality, the rights of self-government in that area, the form of governmental organization, and sometimes a maximum local tax rate. After a charter has been granted, the people of the community vote on its acceptance or rejection. If the community votes for acceptance, the town or city becomes a corporate body, an "artificial person" which may sue or be sued in the courts. Municipalities, it is to be noted, do not possess any sovereign power; all their authority is granted by the State. The Legislature can modify or revoke a municipality's charter at any time. In actual practice, however, the State has seldom taken such drastic action against any incorporated community.

A charter holds somewhat the same relationship to the people of an incorporated community that the State Constitution holds to the citizens of Maryland. Neither of these documents can be changed without the approval of the people at an election—they are both organic laws. On the other hand, the relationship of the municipalities to the State is somewhat different from that of the counties to Maryland. Municipalities are organized by volunteer groups that obtain permission to incorporate from their counties and from the Legislature. In a sense they operate as business corporations. Counties are organized by the State. Maryland would have the right to step in, along with the county authorities, to straighten out any municipality that defaulted on its debt principal or interest or that had excessive tax delinquencies.

Kinds of Incorporated Communities. The term "municipal government" refers to government in the smallest administrative unit of our State—the city, town, or village. Maryland has no townships, which in many states are the rural units that make up a county. There was a time, however, when the counties of Maryland were divided into rural subdivisions known as hundreds; the term and idea were of English origin. Maryland abolished the hundreds in 1821, but the term survives in some areas—for example, "Bay Hundred" on the Eastern Shore.

Besides Baltimore City, the State has 150 incorporated cities, towns, and villages. Maryland municipalities vary in size from Highland Beach, with a population of 6 (in 1970), to Baltimore, with a population of 905,759. Maryland makes no legal distinction between city, town, and village, though in nearly all cases cities are the largest municipalities and villages the smallest.

Most of the incorporated communities have banded together to form the Maryland Municipal League, with offices in Annapolis. The League acts as a clearing house for governmental ideas and works for more municipal home rule. It assists municipalities in research and staffing problems and has established exchange of ideas dealing with such practical problems as sewage, water supply and taxing procedures. It is a nonprofit private group that also lobbies for municipalities at the time the Legislature meets.

Major Incorporated Municipalities

Baltimore City. Baltimore City is the leading industrial center of the State and its largest city. There are numerous reasons for this. First, the city's location near the head of Chesapeake Bay makes it a center for foreign trade. Waterborne shipping can be carried farther inland here than at any other point on the eastern coast of the United States. Located on the Fall Line, the city began early in its history to make use of the water power developed there; this greatly stimulated industrial growth. Strategic location at a site where favorable highways cross the country from north to south brought about Baltimore City's prominence in domestic trade. Proximity to important sources of raw materials and to large markets was also distinctly helpful. In 1970 some 905,759 people lived within the corporate boundaries of Baltimore City; the entire metropolitan area had a population of 2,070,670. Baltimore has a Mayor-Council form of government.

One of the most unusual and most beautiful household sights in Baltimore City is the row after row of white marble steps. They are kept polished and cleaned by housewives as part of their pride in the city and their homes. (Photo by Bob Willis)

Rockville, Montgomery County. Next in size to Baltimore, Rockville s the largest city in Maryland with a 1970 population of 41,564. The ity (also the county seat) has a Council-Manager form of government vith the Mayor and four councilmen elected at large by a nonpartisan ote for two-year terms. These five persons appoint a professionally rained city manager, responsible to them. He carries out the Council's olicies, as well as acting as personnel officer and supervisor of all dministrative and departmental activities.

Rockville has a campus of the Montgomery Community College in its nidst. There are about 400 commercial, professional, and retail business firms in the city. Among these are U.S. Radiological Health Center, O.C.R. (Operations of Control Data), Hydrospace, Xerox, and Gillette Research Institute (chemistry). Near the city are the Atomic Energy Commission and the National Bureau of Standards of the federal government, IBM, Fairchild Technology, COMSAT (aerospace), and the National Geographic Society's membership center.

Hagerstown, Washington County. Hagerstown is the county seat of Washington County and the third largest city in the State, with a 1970 population of 35,826. The city has a number of clothing manufacturers, the larger ones being Fennel, Dorbee and the Hagerstown Shoe Co. The largest employer is Mack Truck, Inc. which produces truck engines and employs nearly 4,000 people. An aircraft division of Fairchild Industries, Inc. employs about 1,000 persons. The Pangborn Division of the Carborundum Company makes industrial machinery and employs 800. The Hagerstown Junior College serves the entire county. The city has a Mayor-Council form of government.

Bowie, Prince Georges County. Bowie is the fourth largest city in Maryland, with a 1970 population of 35,028. It is the fastest growing city in the State and possibly the nation. In 1960 the population of Bowie was estimated at but 1,072. Purchase of the historic Belair estate and its development into residential homes by Levitt and Sons, Inc. brought the rapid development. The city is a bedroom area for many who work in nearby Washington. Bowie State College is located there as is one of the nation's leading racetracks.

Since 1963 Bowie has operated under a Council-Manager form of government. The Mayor and six Councilmen are elected citywide on a nonpartisan basis for two-year terms. Five of the six Councilmen run as representatives of as many election districts; the sixth may come from any district. The Mayor serves as chairman of the Council. The Council appoints a professional City Manager, who appoints department heads and the City Treasurer. The Council also appoints a City Attorney and committee members.

Cumberland. With its population of 29,724, Cumberland, county seat of Allegany County, is Maryland's fifth largest city. It lies in the western part of the Appalachian Region, in a valley on the upper reaches of the Potomac River. Founded as early as 1750, Cumberland remained little more than a settlement until 1811. In that year, the federal government appropriated money for building a road that was to start at Cumberland and run westward from there to the Mississippi River. The road, first to be federally financed, made a city of this rural hamlet. Known first as the National Road, it later became part of U.S. Route 40, stretching from Atlantic City to San Francisco.

Next to Baltimore City, Cumberland is the State's most important railroad center; it has access to three railway systems and is the site of a large repair shop belonging to the B&O-C&O Railroad. The municipal ity owns and operates an airport. In addition to having excellent transportation facilities, the city lies in the midst of huge resources of lumber and coal. Since Cumberland is at the heart of a rich farming and mining area, it is an excellent market for products either manufactured or merchandised locally. The leading industrial plants include the Kelly-Springfield Tire Company, the Celanese (fiber) Company, Pittsburgh Plate Glass Industries, Allegany Ballistics Laboratory, and the B&O-C&O Railroad.

Cumberland has a City-Commissioner form of government. The Allegany Community College in the city serves the entire county.

United States Naval Academy, Annapolis. Midshipmen here prepare for the regularly scheduled dress parades which are open to the public Wednesdays, 3:30 PM in Spring and Fall, weather permitting. In the background is the chapel which houses the crypt of John Paul Jones. (Photo by Bob Willis)

Annapolis. This quaint capital of Maryland and Anne Arundel County seat is situated on the Severn River. It combines the old charm of colonial homes and historic St. John's College with the up-to-the minute activities of the United States Naval Academy. In 1950, its population was 10,047, but a large annexation of territory in 1951 brought it to a total of 29,592 persons in 1970 and made it Maryland's sixth city in size. Manufacturing plants at Annapolis engage in making concrete products, paints, building and repairing boats, and packing seafood. As the State capital and county seat, it is the center of numerous governmental activities, federal, State, and local.

Annapolis has a Mayor-Council form of government. The Mayor is elected at large as is one alderman with seven other aldermen elected from wards. The Mayor and aldermen perform both legislative and administrative functions. The Mayor has no veto powers.

College Park, Prince Georges County. With 26,156 population, College Park is the State's seventh largest city as well as home campus of the University of Maryland. Its inhabitants are largely employed in activities of the university or businesses serving the college, though many commute to work in Washington. However, there is some significant industry in the town itself—for example, the Amecom Division of Litton Systems, Inc., which manufactures electronic equipment and mine detectors, is located there. Nearby are a number of Prince Georges County industrial centers which are zoned for and include light or heavy industry, such as, the Beltsville Industrial Center and the federal government's agricultural, naval, and space-flight research centers. Wilbur and Orville Wright taught many to fly at the College Park airport, the nation's first, which was built in 1908. College Park has a Council-Manager form of government.

Frederick. Frederick is the county seat of Frederick County and the eighth largest city in the State, with a population of 23,641. Hood College, a private women's school with a national reputation, and Frederick Community College are located in the city. Many Frederick residents work at Eastalco Aluminum Company's plant at nearby Buckeystown. Other industries include Frederick Electronics and Sagner's, a well-known clothing manufacturer. The city is in the midst of a large dairying area; the county is famous for sending over $20 million worth of milk to Baltimore and Washington annually. Frederick has a Mayor-Council form of government, with five aldermen.

Takoma Park. Situated just outside Washington, the city of Takoma Park spreads over two counties, Montgomery and Prince Georges. It has its own police department, and one of the campuses of the Montgomery Community College is located within its boundaries. Largely a bedroom for the nation's capital, its 1970 population was 18,455 and it was the ninth largest city in Maryland. The municipality has a Mayor-Council form of government, though many of its affairs are under the jurisdiction of a city administrator.

Salisbury. Salisbury is the county seat of Wicomico County and, with a population of 15,252, the tenth largest city in the State, and the largest on the Eastern Shore. It has a Mayor-Council form of government with five councilmen and an executive secretary handles many of the management problems.

More than 1,100 work at its chief industry, A.W. Perdue, Inc., which processes broiler chickens and feeds. A Campbell Soup Company plant and Dresser Industries, producing service-station pumps, employ more than 900 and 600 respectively. The Green Giant Company and Manhattan Shirt Company each employs 500. Marine resources of fish, crabs, clams, and oysters give employment and fun to thousands of natives

Aerial view of downtown Salisbury.

(Top) Baltimore from Federal Hill. The Hill commemorates Maryland's ratification of the U.S. Constitution. (Photo by Bob Willis) (Bottom) Baltimore's City Hall and War Memorial Plaza.

and visitors. Salisbury State College serves the Eastern Shore and other parts of the State.

Unincorporated Communities

Maryland is unique in that some of its most heavily populated communities cannot be called cities since they are unincorporated. All of these communities are in the densely populated suburban counties surrounding Baltimore and Washington. It is important to note that the figures here are from the 1970 U.S. Census areas so labelled, not the county district areas which often have the same names but may be larger or smaller in area. There is a long tradition in Maryland for communities to maintain allegiance to county governments rather than incorporate. For example, Baltimore County and Howard County have no incorporated communities. Thus, in Baltimore County unincorporated communities are Dundalk with more than 85,000 persons, Towson with 78,000, Catonsville with 55,000, Essex with 38,000, Parkville and Randallstown with about 34,000 each; Woodlawn—Woodmore with 29,000, Arbutus with 22,000, Rosedale and Middle River with about 20,000 each; Lansdowne—Baltimore Heights with 17,000, Reisterstown with 14,000, and Pikesville and Lutherville—Timonium with about 25,000 each. In Anne Arundel County, Glen Burnie has about 39,000, Severna Park 16,400, and Brooklyn 14,000. Columbia in Howard County is growing so rapidly that its population probably will pass 100,000 by 1990. In Prince Georges County there are Chillum with more than 35,000, Suitland with upward of 30,000, Hillcrest Heights with 24,000, and Camp Springs with 23,000. In Montgomery County there are Silver Spring with more than 77,000, Wheaton with 66,000-plus, Bethesda with more than 71,000, and Chevy Chase with more than 16,000. Eliminate Baltimore City, and it is clear that in Maryland the unincorporated communities have larger populations than the so-called cities.

Forms of Municipal Government in Maryland

Virtually every form of municipal government that is popular in the United States can be found in Maryland. Indeed, if one studies the governmental structures of this State's incorporated communities, he understands, through case study, how cities operate throughout the country. Below is a description of five different patterns:

1. The strong Mayor-Council form of government is in operation in Baltimore City. Here a Mayor is elected citywide for four years and is the chief executive of the city, having general supervision over all municipal officers and agencies. He appoints administrative officers of the city who head departments and many board members, with Council approval required.

Eighteen members of the City Council are elected by districts—three of them from each of six districts—and one, the President, city-

(Top) Somers Cove Marina, Crisfield, Md. Location of the National Hard Crab Derby. (Bottom) Chestertown, Kent County, Md.

wide. The Council passes ordinances under home-rule power and the Mayor has power of veto which may be overridden by a three-fourths Council vote. Most very large cities in the United States have the strong Mayor-Council form of government.

2. The weak Mayor-Council form of government is represented by Hagerstown and is more characteristic of Maryland's municipalities than any other form. Hagerstown is governed by a Mayor and five Councilmen, all elected for terms of four years. The Mayor is elected by the city as a whole and one Councilman is elected from each of the five wards. The Mayor presides over the Council and he does not have distinct responsibilities as the chief executive, though he appoints some of the city officials. The Council passes ordinances dealing with upkeep of streets, buildings, and markets and with purely local affairs. Annapolis is another example of a weak Mayor-Council government.

3. The Town-Commissioner form of government has long been in existence in small incorporated communities in Maryland. The governing body consists of three to five town commissioners elected for one-year terms in some places like Perryville, and for two-year terms in other places like Aberdeen. In some small towns like Barton, Berlin, and Sharpsburg, the voters also elect a Mayor, called the burgess, in a few places, particularly in Frederick County. In many of these small towns like Denton, Elkton, Galestown, Thurmont, Aberdeen. Betterton, Poolesville, Centreville, and Oxford, the chief executive is president of the town commission. The town commissioners pass ordinances required to govern the municipality. These might deal with town property, care of streets, regulation of traffic, and health measures. They also levy taxes for the support of the town's activities and appoint town officeholders, such as the clerk and treasurer.

4. The start of the City-Commissioner form of government in this country is usually credited to Galveston, Texas, in 1901, though other cities had tried it out earlier. After a hurricane and flood devastated Galveston, a new charter was written placing the Mayor and commissioners in one body that had both legislative and executive powers. Thus the elected commissioners, together with the Mayor, made the laws and carried them out. Each one of the five commissioners was assigned a different department, such as finance, public works, or public safety, to supervise. So policy-making and execution were placed under the same people and responsibility could be fixed.

Cumberland does not have a pure City-Commissioner form of government, but is close enough in structure to act as a model. The Mayor is elected at large and serves with four Councilmen elected at large on a nonpartisan basis, with all also being commissioners. Each heads one of the administrative departments of the city—police and fire, streets and public property, water and sanitation, and finance and revenue. The Mayor is not the chief executive and he does not have veto powers, nor can he interfere with any commissioner's power, though the Council as a whole can. The Mayor, who is also president of the Council, has a vote on legislation. Frostburg, also in Allegany County, has patterned its local governmental structure after its sister city.

5. The Council-Manager form of municipal government received its start in this country in Staunton, Virginia, in 1908, but really became famous after Dayton, Ohio, used it in 1914 to meet the sudden problems of a devastating flood.

At least 12 Maryland incorporated communities have adopted this form. Seven are in Prince Georges County: Bowie, Capital Heights, Cheverly, College Park, Greenbelt, New Carrollton, and Seat Pleasant. Two are in Montgomery County: Gaithersburg and Rockville. Then there are La Plata in Charles County, Pocomoke City in Worcester County, and Princess Anne in Somerset County. All of these municipalities have elected councils consisting of about five members, one of whom is named a mayor largely for ceremonial requirements. The Council hires in turn a town (city) manager, who is a trained public administrator, to run the day-to-day operations of the government. He is usually also given the authority to appoint needed town employees. The manager is not a politician, but an expert in municipal affairs, thus he can stay on the job though political party power changes. Greenbelt, a town built by the federal government in 1935, was the first community in Maryland to adopt this form of municipal government, in 1937.

The Government of Baltimore City

Baltimore City's Unique Status. Because of its vastly superior size, its many-sided industrial and commercial activity, and the character of its population, Baltimore City must meet problems of local government that are quite different from those confronting any other municipality in the State. This unique status is clearly reflected in the governmental devices that have been developed to serve the needs of Baltimore's nearly one million residents.

Baltimore City operates as though it were, at the same time, a municipality, a county, and an autonomous state within a State. As a municipality, it has a city charter and the accompanying power to make certain laws for itself, much as do Hagerstown, Cumberland, and other Maryland towns. Since Baltimore City, unlike any other municipality in Maryland, is not in any county, it also operates as though it were the State's "24th county." It has separate health, education, and public welfare departments, just as do the 23 counties. But Baltimore City has more self-government than any of Maryland's counties. For example, although county offices of education are under the direct supervision of the Maryland State Department of Education, this agency has limited authority over Baltimore's schools. Though county school and community college board members are appointed by the Governor, Baltimore City's school and community college boards are selected by the Mayor of that city.

MUNICIPAL ORGANIZATION - CITY OF BALTIMORE

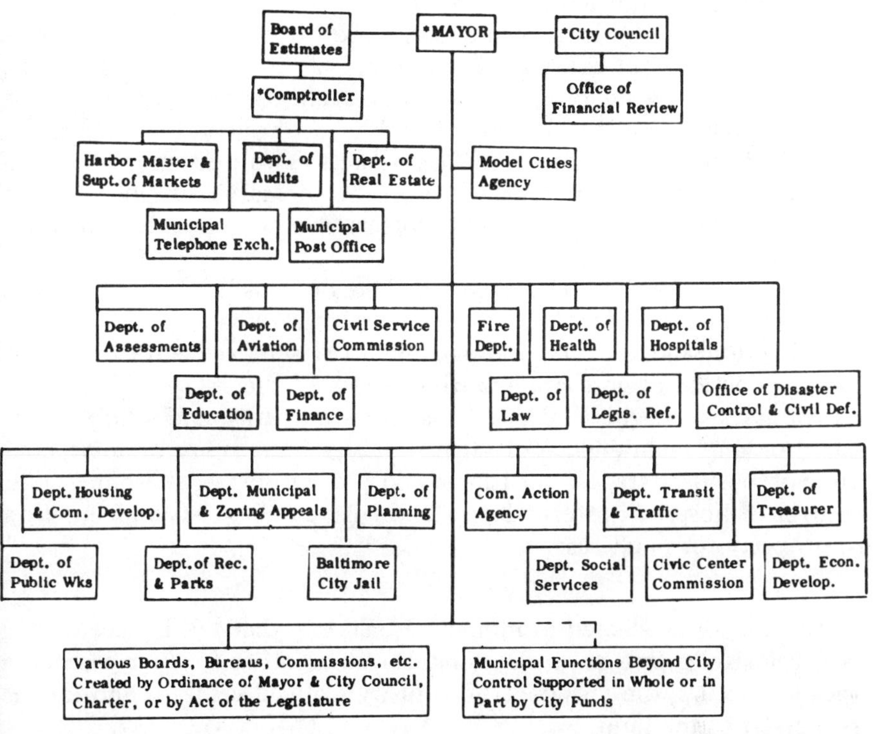

*Elected Officials

Charter and Home Rule. Baltimore became an incorporated city in 1797. Between that date and 1898, few radical changes were made in the city's charter. In that century, however, many events occurred which had far-reaching effects on the city's government. In 1851, for example, Baltimore City left Baltimore County and became an independent community, which it has been ever since.

Recognizing the need for important changes, the Mayor and City Council in 1897 appointed a commission to draw up a revised charter for Baltimore. In 1898 a charter containing many important changes was approved. Among other things, it strengthened the appointive powers of the Mayor, required the appointment of experts in departments where professional knowledge and skill were needed, and fixed the responsibilities of public officials. So effective was the 1898 Charter that it was used as the basis for the Home-Rule Charter of 1918. This document was drawn up in order to give Baltimore City the home rule permitted by the Maryland Constitution. The only other significant change introduced by the 1918 Charter was a merit system for choosing city employees. The 1918 City Charter has undergone major revisions in 1946 and 1964, as well as numerous amendments, in general strengthening the power of the Mayor.

The home-rule clause permits Baltimore City to amend its charter and its laws without the State's sanction. Baltimore City is, of course, subject to Statewide general laws, and there are many purely local matters over which the General Assembly still has control. In spite of these limitations, Baltimore City has home rule to a far greater degree than any other unit of local government in Maryland. As we have already noted, however, similar privileges may be extended to other cities in the future.

Powers of the City Government. The officials of Baltimore have charter power to control and regulate activities such as the following: Construction and use of buildings; use of streets; vehicles offered for hire; protection against fire and disease; use of the Patapsco River and its tributaries; weights and measures; libraries, parks, and schools; construction and maintenance of sewer, drainage, and water systems; conduct of business trades, vocations, and professions; establishment and control of hospitals, reformatories, and jails; purchase or condemnation of property for public use.

The Mayor of Baltimore City

The Mayor is elected in municipal balloting that takes place during odd years following State elections. He holds office for four years. If a vacancy occurs, the President of the City Council succeeds him for the remainder of the term.

Qualifications and Salary. The Mayor must be more than 25 years of age, must be a citizen of the United States, and must have been a resident of Baltimore City for at least ten years preceding his election. The Mayor's annual salary is $35,000.

Duties and Powers. The Mayor's chief duty is to see that city ordinances are properly carried out. To fulfill this responsibility, he is authorized to appoint hundreds of administrative officers. The efficiency of Baltimore's government, in the last analysis, depends on the caliber of the men whom the Mayor names to key administrative posts. Some of the more important boards and bureaus whose members are appointed by the Mayor include those with authority over education, fire protection, health planning, public welfare, human relations, recreation, municipal music, and libraries. For reasons that go back to pre-Civil War days when Baltimore was known as "Mobtown," the police department is under the Governor though the city pays the costs. The Mayor is an *ex officio* member of each of these boards (that is, he serves on them by virtue of his office as Mayor), and he exercises broad supervisory powers over them.

The Mayor also has a number of powers related to lawmaking. Since he is usually the political leader of the dominant party or faction in the City Council, his views naturally carry much weight with municipal legislators. The Mayor can veto ordinances passed by the Council, although that body can override any veto by a three-fourths majority. Special sessions of the Council may be called by the Mayor when he deems it necessary.

The City Comptroller

The City Comptroller is elected for a four-year term. His department has general supervision over all municipal accounting. He is a member of the Department of Finance and the Board of Estimates. He appoints and supervises the work of the City Auditor. He is also head of the department of real estate which acquires, sells, and disposes of city property. He is in charge of the city markets, including the historic Lexington Market. His salary is $22,500.

The City Treasurer. The Treasurer is appointed by the Mayor after each municipal election, and serves for four years. He is president of the board of finance (including the Mayor, Comptroller and two lay persons), which is responsible for issuing and selling city bonds. He is custodian of all monies and securities belonging to the city.

Other City Officeholders

The city's chief legal officer is the City Solicitor, appointed by the Mayor. He supplies legal advice to the Mayor, the City Council, and the many municipal boards and departments. Whenever the General Assembly is in session, this official is particularly active in drafting laws that affect Baltimore City. He heads the city's law department and represents Baltimore City when suits are filed against it. He is also a member of the Board of Estimates. The City Solicitor's salary is $35,000.

The Department of Public Works. One of the most important agencies in the government of Baltimore City is the Department of Public Works. Its Director has jurisdiction over the work of all the bureaus in his department. He is appointed by the Mayor for a four-year term and serves on the Board of Estimates.

Each of the different bureaus described below is directed by an engineer, or by a chief, who is appointed by the Mayor with the consent of the City Council. Most of the staff workers are appointed through Baltimore City's merit system. The Department is organized into six major bureaus:

1. The bureau of engineering coordinates the work of the divisions of water, waste water, highways, utility construction and surveys and records.

2. The bureau of consumer services coordinates the activities of the divisions of applications and licenses, customer accounts and services—related to changes in private and business structures—and communications with the public.

3. The bureau of utility operations has charge of the divisions of highway maintenance, utilities and sanitation, and all operations of water and waste water.

4. The bureau of inspection coordinates the work of public building inspection and tests.

5. The bureau of general services carries out services related to building operations and maintenance and motor vehicle and mechanical shops.

6. The bureau of markets and comfort stations takes care of the historic and newer markets owned and leased by the City, including the famous Lexington Market Authority and the New Marsh Wholesale Market Authority.

The City Council

The lawmaking body of Baltimore City is known as the City Council. Membership in the Council is an honored and responsible position.

Composition of the Council. Before 1923 the city's legislative body consisted of two branches; now it is a unicameral, or one-branch, assembly. The City Council includes 19 members who are chosen by the voters every four years. The President of the Council is elected by a citywide vote. The other 18 members represent six councilmanic districts, each of which elects three Councilmen. From among their own members the Councilmen themselves select one to act as Vice President of the Council.

Qualifications and Salary. In order to become a City Councilman, a person must be 21 years of age or older. He must have been a resident of Baltimore City for at least two years prior to his election. The President of the City Council is paid an annual salary of $22,500; the Vice President is paid $13,000, and each of the other councilmen $12,000. The members usually also have private occupations and other sources of income.

Meetings and Powers. The Charter indicates that the City Council should begin its annual meeting on the Thursday after the third Monday in December and continue in session for as long a period as may be necessary for the proper conduct of the city's affairs. Actually the Council starts annually in September, holding regular sessions until the municipal budget is passed in May or early June; then the Council recesses for the summer. In recent years committees have met throughout the summer. Meetings are held in the Council Chamber of the City Hall and are open to the public. Most meetings take place on Monday evenings.

The most important function of the City Council is to pass ordnances for the government of Baltimore City. Sometimes seemingly trifling matters, such as changes in street names, business permits, and dedication of special events, take up much of the Council's time. In spite of this, the Council enacts many important measures dealing with the health, safety, and general well-being of the people of Baltimore. The Council also has the right to cut the city's budget, after it has been prepared by the Board of Estimates, and thus to lower the tax rate, which is determined by the budget. The Council cannot raise the operating budget after it is received from the Board of Estimates.

How a Bill Becomes an Ordinance. A bill must pass three readings in the Council, on three separate days, before it becomes an ordinance. The first of these consists merely of a reading of the bill's title, followed by a referral of the bill to any one of several committees. These committees will often hold public hearings if the bill in question seems important enough to warrant doing so. At the second reading, the committee submits its report and a vote is taken to determine future action. At the third reading the Council finally votes on whether or not the bill is to become a city ordinance. The individual votes of Councilmen are recorded only on the final reading of the bill.

Board of Estimates. The Board of Estimates is one of the more important bodies in the Baltimore City government. It meets once a week to carry out its functions. The Board awards contracts on bids for capital improvements and for large purchases and outlays by the City. It determines how much each municipal department of government can spend for annual operating expenses, subject to approval by the City Council. It also has an important role in determining the annual tax rate. Thus, while it is not a lawmaking group, this body has very important administrative powers.

The Board of Estimates is composed of the President of the City Council, who acts as chairman of the board; the Mayor, the Director of Public Works, the City Comptroller, and the City Solicitor. Since the Mayor appoints two of the five, counting his own vote he holds the majority in his hands.

Sick Urban Cities

The problems of the two large cities that directly affect the State of Maryland, Washington and Baltimore, have become increasingly troublesome. In the cases of both cities the flight of white middle-class populations to nearby Maryland counties has had a dual disturbing effect. First, much in tax dollars is lost, especially as the residential exodus is accompanied by industrial and governmental flight. The tax bases of American cities have not been very secure in recent years, since there is so much dependence on property taxes. When large numbers of taxpayers leave the city and are replaced by older indigent citizens and by poverty-stricken persons (in both cases partially exempt from prop-

The world-famous Baltimore Symphony Orchestra. (Photo by M.E. Warren)

erty tax requirements—and with justice), the urban centers lose much of the needed fiscal support. Second, while the tax base dwindles the service requirements rise, since poverty, among white and black people, brings greater needs for improvement in health, education, welfare, police and fire protection, and other facilities. So the costs of government increase in heavily populated cities like Baltimore and Washington, while the numbers left in these cities who can afford to pay taxes dwindle. Thus, those who do remain in these cities, and can afford to pay property taxes, are required to carry a heavier proportion of the total burden than do those who live in the surrounding counties. This causes even more of the cities' capable taxpayers to join the migration to the counties. The vicious circle persists.

Cities like Baltimore have made heroic efforts to stave off what ultimately could lead to bankruptcy. Baltimore has rebuilt its downtown areas, such as Charles Center and the Inner Harbor, so that new business and commercial enterprises bring higher assessable property bases. New apartment houses in the inner city have brought some people back to Baltimore. Completion of the Inner Harbor development (expected in the 1980's) and a mass transit subway system should promote further vitality.

Further, the federal government has given financial assistance to all big cities in terms of revenue-sharing funds that amount to millions of dollars and grants-in-aid dealing with problems of welfare, transportation, education, health, and police protection. The State, too, recognizes that Baltimore City has special financial needs in Maryland. The 1974 Legislature added $15 million in State aid to Baltimore, upgrading school assistance, taking over more hospital care costs, and freeing Open Space funds for city park use. This aid lopped some 45 cents off the projected Baltimore property tax.

Moreover, Baltimore has sought to improve its governmental services so that the public will find the city offering unusual opportunities in cultural, recreational, and educational pursuits. The hope, for example, is that as schools improve in Baltimore more people will be prepared for gainful employment and higher standards of living, and thus welfare payrolls will be smaller and the pool of taxpaying citizens will be enlarged. Most people agree that if any city in the United States can prove that large urban centers are economically viable and still rewarding, Baltimore might be the model.

Metropolitanism, a Way Out

More and more people are becoming convinced that we can no longer think in terms of the big city apart from the surrounding suburban area. For example, while practically every large city in the country, including Baltimore, lost population between 1960 and 1970, the suburban areas surrounding the metropolises gained in numbers of residents. The two

Maryland counties—Montgomery and Prince Georges—adjoining the District of Columbia ballooned from 698,323 in 1960 to 1,183,376 in 1970. The Baltimore metropolitan area, which includes the City and Baltimore, Anne Arundel, Carroll, Harford, and Howard Counties, had 1,803,745 people in 1960 and 2,070,670 in 1970.

It is evident that all political units in this region have much more in common than their unique county requirements. Each day many who live in Baltimore City travel over county roads to their places of employment and thousands who live in the counties use city highways to get to work. The suburban dependence upon Baltimore's economy is also evident for those who don't work there. For example, the Baltimore port's operations service the entire metropolitan region, and if anything were to happen to them, the counties would suffer immeasurably. Sports centers in Baltimore provide enthusiasts with major-league baseball, football, tennis, soccer, and ice hockey. The Baltimore Symphony, the City's art museums, the local civic opera and dance facilities offer cultural activities to the entire metropolitan area. The City's Zoo in Druid Hill Park offers fun and education to all. Johns Hopkins University, Morgan State College, Loyola and Notre Dame Colleges, Coppin State, the University of Baltimore, the University of Maryland's professional schools, and the Community College of Baltimore service the entire metropolitan area, not just the City.

The well-being of any part of the Baltimore metropolitan region affects its other parts. Poverty or poor health in the City will ultimately affect the nearby counties. The same would hold true for Washington and its metropolitan region which includes the surrounding Maryland and Virginia counties.

Ways of Cooperating to Solve Regional Problems

Annexation. When an urban population finds its surrounding area involved in similar problems it can seek to bring it into its boundaries through annexation. For example, at numerous times in its history, Baltimore City annexed adjacent land, the last time in 1918 when it added 52 square miles and about 75,000 people from Baltimore County. Realistically, the possibility of the City annexing land from Baltimore or Anne Arundel Counties, which adjoin its borders, no longer holds today. In 1955, Article 23-A of the Maryland Code tightened annexation provisions, requiring petitions from both political units involved and, finally, a majority vote. As a result of the 1955 law, recent annexations that have taken place have been small in land area—less than one-quarter square mile—and have occurred only where an urban fringe has developed adjacent to or surrounding a municipality.

Mergers. The Maryland Municipal League has gone on record as recommending the merging of two small or middle-sized communities that adjoin each other. This becomes difficult if each is in a differen county. It does save funds in cases of providing water and sanitation services, as well as police and fire protection.

The Intergovernmental Service Contact. This is the most widely utilized system of urban-suburban cooperation. For example, the Washington Metropolitan Transit Commission will serve that city and surrounding Maryland and Virginia counties with mass transportation. All political units involved are represented in the venture.

Intergovernmental cooperation can take several forms, such as Baltimore City selling filtered water to Baltimore Countians. Baltimore City and Baltimore County are seeking common ventures in the incineration of trash and garbage. The Washington Suburban Transit Commission arranges joint efforts in transportation for Montgomery and Prince Georges Counties, as the Maryland National Park and Planning Commission does for the same counties in its field.

Intergovernmental ventures can also take place by establishing a corporate entity authorized for one or more specific services in a prescribed area. The Washington Suburban Sanitary Commission is a good example of an authority that provides water, sewage removal, trash collection, and related services to Montgomery and Prince Georges Countians. The Maryland Port Administration, serving the Baltimore area, is another illustration.

Regional Planning Councils. For some years regional planning councils in both the Washington and Baltimore areas have sought to plan on a wide front. The councils believe that it is good for Baltimore City and Baltimore County to cooperate in water usage and it is well for Prince Georges and Montgomery Counties to set up a separate authority to serve them as the Washington Suburban Sanitary Commission. But, say the councils, intergovernmental cooperation that embraces but two counties and deals with but one or two services of government (sewage and water) does not go far enough. For example, the Regional Planning Council for Metropolitan Baltimore includes representatives from the neighboring five counties and the City, as well as a significant fulltime staff. Its first five-year update of the general development plan for the area, in 1972, included a very broad range of factors affecting the quality of life. The update gave attention to the Council's longtime traditional recommendations dealing with open space, transportation and water, sewers, and solid waste disposal. But, for the first time, the update dealt with such major concerns as natural and manmade environment, economy and manpower, housing, health, safety, justice, education, and libraries. For example, the Council suggested stronger cooperative ventures and possibly merger of the efforts of the different community colleges in the region.

The Metropolitan Washington Council of Governments, popularly known as COG, operates for that area along the same lines as the Baltimore regional groups, covering the same concerns.

The Regional Council for the Baltimore area recommended recently that much attention be given to coordinating its work with its sister agency in Washington, calling attention to mutual growth interests meeting at many points in Maryland.

Constitutional and Legislative Encouragements. In some states there have been constitutional changes encouraging metropolitanism and regional government. The proposed 1968 Maryland Constitution gave counties the right by law to create new municipal corporations and other units of local government. It also gave the General Assembly the right by law to establish multicounty governmental units and arrange for popularly elected regional governments to embrace all or part of two or more counties. The Legislature was further given the power to grant to these intergovernmental authorities the right to impose service charges, borrow money, and collect taxes imposed by the General Assembly. Since the 1968 proposal failed, none of this became effective.

Such newly created regional governments have been initiated in other parts of the country. For example, Miami and Dade County (Florida) still exist separately for many purposes, but they have merged into a joint city-county venture known as Miami-Dade regional government, which services such activities as public higher education.

The advantage of constitutional provisions on regional cooperation is that they might speed up such ventures. Yet Maryland voters, fearing damage to the more informal cooperative efforts, turned down the proposed 1968 Constitution.

Whichever of the processes described above, as well as others, are used, the important thing is that Marylanders must recognize that county and city boundary lines no longer fully determine economic and social needs. Regionalism, even that which cuts across state lines (as for example, the new hospital regions established by the federal government), must be given attention if we are to solve some of our more acute domestic problems.

Chapter 11

DEPARTMENT OF HEALTH AND MENTAL HYGIENE

In 1969 Maryland restructured its services in public health and mental hygiene through some far-reaching steps. A significant number of what had been separate health and mental hygiene agencies were brought together under a cabinet-level Secretary to head a newly created Department of Health and Mental Hygiene. This was not just an integration of formerly separate health services, but rather an attempt to establish a new structure that would give full meaning to many frontier concepts of health. For example, in recent years there has been a growing feeling that institutionalized care of the indigent aged, the emotionally disturbed, the severely mentally handicapped, and the unmanageable young, is the wrong approach. Yet Maryland has held on to hospitals and other institutions for the care of such persons.

The new Department was pledged to establish community treatment centers, inpatient and outpatient care, extended care facilities, half- and quarter-way hospitalization, and other decentralized approaches; and to emphasize consumer involvement, foster care, and cooperative programs such as joint school and State health educational ventures. Moreover, the Department was to take a hard look at single-purpose institutions. For example, some of the State health institutions had been established to cure particular illnesses which were no longer as prevalent as in the past or which no longer required specialized quarters. By way of illustration, Mt. Wilson State Hospital was established many years ago for the cure of chronic respiratory diseases. As the number of tuberculosis cases declined, excess bed space increased at Mt. Wilson while there were serious shortages for other patients, such as those needing geriatric care. It was evident in 1969 that while some facilities were not operating at optimum, others were so overcrowded that serious problems accrued. Placing all health and mental-hygiene facilities under one department would permit the establishment of more comprehensive care facilities and encourage more economical operations.

In 1971 the new Department opened its doors. For a time there were some challenges to the whole concept of coordinating and integrating public-health services. Each of the smaller divisions had cherished its independence and its ability to report directly to the Governor and the General Assembly. Then, too, there was the honest fear that the specialized competencies of former department, bureau, and division heads might be ignored or completely forgotten since the new department covered so many agencies. Furthermore, the early 1970's found some with the belief that too much power was concentrated in one person, the Secretary of Health and Mental Hygiene.

While it is still too early to judge with finality, the general feeling is that the promises of the new Department are being fulfilled. At least there is a strong belief that the earlier health agencies had not brought to large numbers the hopes that new findings in medicine would bring better health care. Perhaps this new way will bring meaning to the concept of good health as a right of all, rather than a privilege for those few who can afford it.

Board of Review

The Department's board of review consists of seven members appointed by the Governor, with the approval of the State Senate, for three-year terms. Four represent the general public and three the various fields under the Department of Health and Mental Hygiene. The Board makes recommendations about operations to the Secretary. It also hears and determines appeals from decisions of the Secretary or from any of the agencies in the Department.

Comprehensive Health Planning Agency

The Comprehensive Health Planning Agency is the hub of the Department. It is here that the broad objectives are set forth and the long-range planning takes place. It is this organ of the Department that needs to address itself to such a dichotomy in health care which recognizes on one hand the medical, scientific, and technological advances in the extension of life. On the other hand, it is still true that millions of poor people lack essential health services; there are still many substandard hospitals and nursing homes; and there exists to this day shortages in the field of health care workers from physicians to technicians.

The federal government recognized this dichotomy when Congress passed the Partnership in Health Act in 1966. This Act authorized the Surgeon General of the United States to make federal grants to any state whose health-planning concepts were in agreement with the national objectives. In 1968 the Maryland General Assembly passed such a bill and as a result, the State Advisory Council on Comprehensive Health Planning came into being. In 1969 the Council was placed under the newly established Secretary of Health and Mental Hygiene as one of its agencies.

The Agency follows federal and State requirements in respect to its operations. The Advisory Council (the policy-making organ) of the Agency is made up of about 40 members. Most of them are not health workers, but *consumers*, active as homemakers and in community, civic, and governmental pursuits. The so-called *producer* members represent hospitals, nursing homes, physicians, dentists, nurses, veterinarians, pharmacists, and health-care teaching institutions. The Agency, representing the staff workers, recognizes that the Advisory Council is not a rubber stamp for its ideas.

The Agency has been given broad powers by the Legislature so that, for example, it passes judgment on new health-care proposals under the 1970 Health Facility Certification of Need bill. Under this State law no hospital or nonprofit health-related institution may be established or may modify its existing services unless it conforms to the health-facilities plan for the State. In 1972 the law was amended to include all profit-making nursing homes under the certification program.

In order to reach grass-roots decisions, the Agency has established regional counterparts of its own structure. These are known as area-wide agencies, which are also eligible for federal ($200,000 in 1973) and State funds for community health-planning projects. They assist institutions in their areas to further health programs, provide research, review and comment upon local applications for health grants and proposals, and administer the State's health facilities certification legislation for that area. The areas cover Western Maryland, the lower Eastern Shore, metropolitan Baltimore, and other parts of the State.

The Agency, though young, has many accomplishments to its credit. For example, it established a Health Services Cost Review Commission, regulates rates of hospitals and in the future may cover nursing homes and other health institutions. It brought about expansion of the Department's Environmental Health Administration. It developed guidelines for the conduct of the new theory of health-maintenance organizations (HMO's). It expanded opportunities for those, like medics, who had health-care experiences in the armed services, to use their skills in civilian life. It established a State Health Data Committee and a Center for Health Statistics. Maryland is a pioneer state in comprehensive health planning.

Office of Program Services

The Office of Program Services, through its 10 programs, might be referred to as the central system of the Department of Health and Mental Hygiene. From this Office fan out services that thousands of Marylanders require: the addict, the emotionally disturbed and the mentally ill, the young offender, the aged who are poor, and the sick who are indigent. But the Office also prevents illnesses, ensures pure air and water, coordinates county health programs, and offers laboratory testing.

Drug Abuse (Alcohol) Administration. The 1970's found drug addiction one of the most serious ailments of our times, especially its effect upon the young. Until the Department establishes community health centers with capabilities to meet the total health needs of a neighborhood or town, the DAA plans to carry out numerous direct services. These include a center for drug emergencies, so that individual and family crises can be met and medical and psychiatric care provided. Detoxification services are given for those who can profit, on an outpatient or inpatient level. Medical treatment, including methadone substitutes, is offered where patients agree. Laboratory tests are given to those who seek analysis. Individual guidance, group therapy, and family counseling are available. Under another program, correct information about drugs and referral offices to treat addicts is disseminated. A plan has been established to provide detoxification services to all inmates in correctional institutions. A variety of temporary living arrangements is available to those drug addicts who can profit from halfway houses, therapeutic communities, and other group living experiences.

One in eleven of the 83 percent of Marylanders over 21 years of age who consume alcohol is a heavy drinker. Alcoholism is a factor in more than half of all traffic deaths. The Alcoholism Control Law of 1968 contends that the criminal law approach is an ineffective deterrent. It recommends, instead, treatment and rehabilitation services for alcoholics and families, alcohol education, public information, and evaluation and research.

Mental Health Administration. The 1970's could be a turning point in the treatment of Maryland's mentally ill and emotionally disturbed. Previous to the mid-1960's a person assigned to a Maryland mental hospital saw this as a possibly terminal decision and that he might remain there the rest of his life. True, the period of illness was shortened by chemotherapy, analysis, and other treatments. Yet even Maryland laws such as those on voting took rights away from the mentally ill forever. Understandably, few were willing to admit the possibility of mental illness and submit to treatment.

Major changes in the treatment of the mentally ill started with the Congressional Acts of 1963 and 1964 setting aside federal funds to states which would prepare plans to eliminate custodial care (except for the few) and substitute "the open warmth of community concern." Key administrators in the former Maryland Department of Mental Hygiene had established a few earlier community centers before the experimental federal Act.

In response to the federal incentive, Maryland's General Assembly in 1966 passed the Community Mental Health Services Act. It spelled out the requirements for State and local authorities to establish a network of community-based mental health services. The theory of community services (replacing in large part the older institutional hospitals which dotted the State) is that near home, persons with emotional and mental disturbances would have readier access to evaluation, advice, and, if necessary, treatment. Good as the State mental hospitals were, for some there was still the stigma of being institutionalized for long periods of time.

Seven mental-health regions have been established to serve different areas of the State, such as the upper and lower Eastern Shore, Western Maryland, Baltimore City, and metropolitan Baltimore. Each regional office plans certain services such as mental-health care for the aged or aid to children.

In 1973 the five public mental institutions previously known as State Hospitals—Crownsville, Spring Grove, Springfield, Eastern Shore, and Clifton T. Perkins—were given new names: Hospital Centers. Though they were to continue to serve the smaller number of acutely ill patients who needed prolonged hospitalization, they were also to become more comprehensive in coverage. For example, Spring Grove Hospital Center has set aside one cottage as an inpatient unit for the Southwestern Community Mental Health Center of Baltimore County. Springfield operates a day-care center for Carroll County.

The community approach to mental health requires larger allocations in budgets. Fortunately, the federal government contributes heavily for capital construction and planning, but more State funds will need to be forthcoming. Then, too, a greater manpower pool in psychiatrists, psychologists, and mental-health technicians will be needed. Also needed are accreditation and certification regulations. Perhaps most important is the educational task of informing people about the possibilities for large numbers of citizens to profit.

The Legislature in 1973 passed a series of bills that might be referred to as "the right to treatment." One Act requires insurance companies, for the first time, to include mental health benefits in all health policies. Since about 70 percent of Maryland's population is covered by health policies, the effects will be widespread. A second Act permits the mentally ill to select, under either commercial or nonprofit insurance, either physicians or certified psychologists for treatment. This will have the effect of increasing the pool of available health personnel. The third bill widens the coverage of nonprofit insurance companies to include those that service Montgomery and Prince Georges Counties, the only two local units not embraced in the territory of the Maryland Blue Cross-Blue Shield.

The Mental Retardation Administration. Of all health and mental hygiene programs due for change, those at Maryland institutions for the mentally retarded are most likely to be radically reformed. For too many years the institutions for mentally retarded included seclusion rooms with locked doors and little for patients to look forward to except death. For the first 23 years of its existence, starting with its founding in 1889, the Rosewood State Hospital was known as the Asylum for the Feeble-Minded of the State of Maryland. That title alone indicates the hopelessness conveyed. In the 1940's and early 1950's a series of grand jury and newspaper investigations led to some reforms. More important, the late 1950's brought research indicating that behavior modification was possible for many who had been previously condemned. The National Association for Retarded Children promoted its credo that "Retarded children and adults are first and foremost human beings. Like all human beings, they possess certain basic rights, among which is the right to be treated with dignity."

The Department of Health and Mental Hygiene organized the Mental Retardation Administration to bring reform on a number of fronts such as:

Counseling to reduce the percentage of retarded births by encouraging regular medical examinations and recognizing genetic factors.

Advice to families on care, feeding, and behavior modification.

Establishment of regional centers as coordinators of comprehensive care and services for the retarded within their communities.

Financing of programs encouraging mental retardates to develop skills.

Establishment of day-care centers so that young retardates could live in their homes and receive training in toilet skills at the centers.

Building of bridges to public and private school classes for the trainable.

Offering pre-vocational programs for teenage retardates to prepare them for sheltered workshops.

Continuing residential care for smaller numbers of retardates who must be treated through institutional short- or long-term care—but doing so in regional establishments close to retardates' homes.

Use of residential or group homes, in neighborhood settings, to house small numbers of retardates.

With the new view in mind, in 1973 the Department moved toward decreasing the population of all of the State retardate institutions: Rosewood, Henryton, and Great Oaks. Indeed, the hope was to close Rosewood by 1980. Meanwhile the three hospitals were to move toward more comprehensive treatment, to be known as Centers, and by all means to eliminate the hopelessness that previously permeated Rosewood and Henryton. Great Oaks, opened in 1970, never went through the early period of treating retardates. From its beginnings it has offered comprehensive care, both in the residential and community settings, to non-ambulatory and partially ambulatory cases.

The Juvenile Services Administration. About 40,000 young Marylanders (age six to eighteen) are brought to the attention of the Juvenile Services Administration each year. Urban juvenile offenses usually include thefts, assault, and property destruction. In the suburban and rural areas juvenile problems are more likely to involve self-destructive acts such as drug abuse, unacceptable sexual behavior, or refusal to conform to family or community standards.

The important philosophical change in the treatment of the juvenile offender lies in the current conviction that juvenile anti-social or deviant behavior is symptomatic of underlying emotional, psychological, and social problems which can be treated in health and mental hygiene programs rather than through corrective or custodial programs.

A twelve-member Advisory Board of Juvenile Services, each member serving a three-year term, reports in a consultatory capacity to the director.

Of all the cases referred to Juvenile Services, 75 percent come from police departments and the remainder from social agencies, schools, and parents. The key Maryland juvenile-services legislation, passed in 1969 as a result of the new philosophy, requires that a preliminary inquiry be conducted whenever a complaint is filed in order to determine whether the case should come before the Juvenile Court or whether it can be handled without court action. The Juvenile Services Administration has staff workers assigned to the trial courts. The workers determine whether complaints should be dismissed, handled informally by the staff worker, handled informally by the staff worker, or sent to the courts. Informal handling might involve staff referral of cases to the State Department of Employment and Social Services for jobs, to public departments of education for school placement, to private religious groups for assistance, or to the local community health centers. Fully two-fifths of all cases do not reach the courts.

If a petition by the staff members notes that the juvenile offender is in need of supervision or dependent or neglected, he is referred to the Department of Employment and Social Services, which makes arrangements for institutional or foster-care attention. If the cases indicate mental retardation or emotional disturbance, they are referred to the two offices of the Department of Health and Mental Hygiene discussed earlier in this chapter. If the juvenile offender has multiple problems he is not referred outside the department, though his case receives consultant help.

The 1969 Maryland law on juvenile offenders requires that before a youngster may be adjudicated legally as a delinquent, allegations must be proved "beyond reasonable doubt." Federal court decisions give the alleged juvenile offender the right to legal defense. Of those brought to Juvenile Court, about one-third (more than 5,000) are placed on probation. The probation worker develops a close association with the offender, his school, employer, and social, health and child-welfare agencies which can contribute to his rehabilitation. The probation worker draws on his knowledge of abnormal behavior, of child development, of the significance of family relationships, and of cultural and environmental influences. In the probation worker's decision-making, he must balance the protection of the interests of society with the urge to help the offender develop acceptable patterns of community living.

Those who are tried and not placed on probation are assigned to one of the Administration's 11 institutional facilities, to private institutions or group homes where care is purchased for them, or to institutional community groups (now few in number but growing) operated by the Administration.

At the Montrose School for Girls in Baltimore County (one of the eleven public institutions), which handles girls from 13 through 18, vocational education is offered for job placement. Boys of about the same ages are sent to the Maryland Training School in Baltimore County, which also stresses vocational training. Boys' Village in Prince Georges County handles somewhat younger boys and gives emphasis to academic and pre-vocational training. Victor Cullen School in Frederick County is being phased out as a juvenile-offender institution and will handle mental retardation cases in the future. The Maryland Children's Center in Baltimore County evaluates juvenile offenders with special problems—male and female—through its detention diagnostic facility. Only 20 percent of the 1,000 cases evaluated annually are committed to institutions.

Five boys' forestry camps are located in Allegany and Garrett Counties. Each accommodates about 35 boys, 16 or 17 years of age, who work on soil conservation, grounds beautification, and fire control projects.

Studies show that a considerable number of boys and girls now institutionalized could benefit by living in group homes (operated by the Juvenile Services Administration) in the community, under adult supervision, going to school or work daily. Three such homes are now in existence in Baltimore City, and the emphasis here is on normal family living. The Administration also purchases care in some private group homes.

The juvenile services field stresses the fact that three key points must be followed. First, most so-called juvenile offenders belong in group homes or with their parents. Second, those who must be institutionalized should be evaluated regularly and individually tailored changes instituted to bring about progress. Third, preventive services must be stressed; for example, the Youth Service Bureaus, such as the tri-county one (Calvert, Charles and St. Marys) where youngsters in trouble receive assistance before cases become acute.

Aged and Chronically Ill Services. About 300,000 Marylanders are 65 years of age or over. More than 53,000 of that number are past 80. In 1930 those 65 and older represented but 5.9 percent of the population; in 1970 they were 7.4 percent. In Talbot County this age group represents 14.4 percent. The older citizens are a significant part of the total population.

The federal Older Americans Act of 1965 was a turning point in the treatment of citizens 65 years and over. Social Security and its accompanying federal old-age survivors and disability benefits came in 1935, and later Medicare was added to provide economic and health security. In recent years it has been evident that the older citizen is neglected; that he is put on the shelf while still having much to offer. When he gets sick, he is likely to be institutionalized and forgotten even by members of his family. The 1965 Act dealt with these and other problems of the older citizens. The White House Conference on Aging in 1971 broadened the view about the needs of those over 65, dealing with income, manpower for servicing the aging, education, gerontology and health care, employment, spiritual well-being, transportation, housing, nutrition, and social and recreational services. The Older Americans Act was amended in the early 1970's to expand federal grants to states to include community programs and nutritional assistance for the aging. (In 1973 Maryland received a $1,300,000 federal grant to supply 3,000 meals a day to needy elderly.) The stimulus of the federal laws and the accompanying financial aid to states encouraged Maryland to expand its programs for the aged. In 1974 a large percentage of the State's lottery profit was supposedly so earmarked. Fifty-six percent of all aged live alone or with non-relatives and of that group more than half are below the poverty level. As inflation grows, those with fixed incomes have decreasing purchasing power whether it be in food, housing, health care, or paying debts such as mortgages. Thus standards in all these areas decline as dollar value shrinks.

The most serious problem of the aging is health care. About 15,000 older Marylanders are in the State's 200 nursing homes at any one time. A special Governor's Commission on Nursing Homes, which was appointed after 36 older persons lost their lives in a tragic incident in a Baltimore nursing home in 1970, recommended that a separate Maryland Office on Aging be created to begin remedial actions including the following:

Carry out federally funded programs under the Older Americans Act.

Establish and operate a pre-retirement and retirement information and referral service for the aged, providing counseling and follow-up in the areas of health, social services, recreation, education, housing, nutrition, and legal services.

Assist in the development of alternative choices for the aged through the planning and delivery of community and home-based services, as well as innovative programs for institutionally-based services. Such planning should do much to minimize use of nursing-home and institutional mental-hospital care—two sources causing great concerns.

Develop funding for Statewide geriatric screening and evaluation centers.

Evaluate, analyze, and make policy recommendations to the

Governor, Legislature, and State agencies in the long-term care area including social, medical, nursing, and recreational services.

Conduct public hearings with the power to subpoena witnesses and examine records.

Create a better payment mechanism for community services in order that home health care may become a genuine alternative for a sick or disabled person. For example, payment of homemaker services for those not on public assistance.

Establish a Senior Citizens Advocacy and an Interdepartmental Committee on Aging. The former would deal with problems of individuals—the latter with making certain that problems of the aging affected by services such as social welfare, education, and transportation would be dealt with in a coordinated way through the cooperative efforts of the responsible State departments.

These recommendations should have far-reaching effects and will take years to accomplish. For example, the early 1970's found large numbers of older persons still being dumped into geriatric wards of State mental hospitals. The proposed expansion of geriatric screening and evaluation centers would make certain that the mental hospitals did not become a first rather than a last resort. Yet there must be some place to place the elderly individual being discharged from the hospital into the community. The substandard nursing home is not much better than an inappropriate mental hospital. Nor are the large, undifferentiated, domiciliary homes; nor are apartments without services.

The Department of Health and Mental Hygiene handled in 1973 the most serious problems of the aging—health services. The nursing homes were licensed by the Department and it operated the State hospitals for the chronically sick and the mentally ill. But the local and State departments of social services had the responsibilities of home care. Indeed, the Baltimore City and the Baltimore County Departments of Social Services experimented successfully with the idea of placing older indigent persons who have some physical or mental disabilities (but can still take care of their personal needs) in private homes. The Departments paid the foster families for the food and shelter. Other financial needs were taken care of by medical-assistance programs.

In 1974 the Governor followed the recommendations of the Commission on Nursing Homes and set up a special agency on health and the aged.

It is important to note that there is a Maryland Commission on Aging that is concerned with problems other than health or social services. This Commission is a separate agency under the Governor, but not at the cabinet level. (See Chapter 14 for separate discussion.)

Medical Care Programs Administration. As early as 1945 it became evident that federal medical-care programs could not meet the health requirements of growing numbers of aged and younger chronically ill who could not afford examinations by physicians, drug bills, and hospital or nursing home attention. Maryland was one of the first states to establish a State medical care program in 1945.

The State medical care program is under the Department of Health and Mental Hygiene. It administers Medicaid, which is not to be confused with Medicare, a federal program. Medicaid is financed jointly by federal, State and local funds, though Maryland contributes by far the greatest portion. Anyone who is on public assistance qualifies for Medicaid, as do others with low yearly income and few assets. The county (or Baltimore City) public social-services department must first approve applicants as being medically indigent, which does not mean that they are necessarily poor. The Medical Care Programs Administration then takes over through local health departments, which arrange for participating doctors, osteopaths, druggists, dentists, podiatrists, optometrists, opticians, hospitals, nursing homes, and laboratories to be approved for services and to be paid by scheduled fees. Skilled nursing-home care and home nursing visits are also approved. In certain cases prosthetic appliances and ambulance services are covered. Coverage is allowed as supplemental to health insurance if the need is cleared. Where Medicare pays most of the physicians' fees, Medicaid may pick up the rest of the bill.

There are some cases where the State will seek to recover some of the Medicaid funds it has paid out. For example, if after litigation insurance or lawsuit claims bring the plaintiff money for medical fees, Maryland will have to be repaid. If the recipient of Medicaid dies and leaves no spouse, nor children under 21 years of age, nor blind or disabled children of any age, and yet the estate claims property at death—then Maryland will claim some or all the money from the sale of a house or from life insurance.

Appeals from such decisions may be made to the Medical Care Programs Administration or to local health or social-services departments.

The Medicaid program in Maryland has increasingly taken a larger share of the State's budget. In fiscal 1974 the allotment was for $187 million. Though more State funds have been made available in recent years, the needs grow more rapidly than the allotments. Medicaid is often required to meet the needs of indigent sick who cannot get financial assistance anywhere else. If a general federal program of health insurance, such as that debated by Congress for many years, were in existence, then stopgap programs such as Medicaid might not be necessary.

Environmental Health Administration. The growing emphasis on ecology has emphasized the fact that the environment in which we live may be hazardous to our health. In the early days of health departments in Maryland, the main environmental activities were to make certain that cities had pure water for drinking and bathing and that sewage was handled so that there would be no epidemics of typhoid and cholera. Later, pure food and milk became concerns of these departments.

Our industrial society and its mass production have brought pollution of land, air, and water. So present-day environmental health activities include control of air quality and water pollution, solid wastes disposal, radiation hazards, noise abatement, food, drugs, housing, and industrial hygiene along with treating earlier recognized problems.

The Bureau of Air Control Quality under the Environmental Health Administration seeks to enforce Maryland's Air Quality Control Act of 1970. In cooperation with local health departments, the aim is to bring all pollution sources into compliance with pollutant-emission regulations. For example, industrial business and hospital enterprises must file their compliance plans for air-pollution control and abatement schedules. Local health departments have enforced bans against excessive smoke emission, dust nuisances, odor problems, and open burning.

The federal government, in the field of air quality as in so many other areas, has set up guidelines that encourage support through financial aid. For example, the federal Clean Air Act of 1970 set a target date of 1977 for implementing plans to curb industrial and motor-vehicle emissions. In 1973 the federal government criticized the air quality in Baltimore City and suggested improvements in transportation control strategies, including: exclusive bus and car-pool lanes on major routes from outlying areas to downtown—thus giving preference to multiple riders. It also suggested limiting size and number of cars in parking lots—thus decreasing emissions. The federal Environmental Protection Agency polices the Act and requires states to conform. A further illustration would be Maryland's new laws governing the emissions of nitrogen oxides from industrial smokestacks. Another example would be the Maryland Power Plant Siting Act, which necessitates air-quality safeguards as a requirement for approval of future power-plant sites. In 1971 Baltimore City changed its equipment for monitoring its air to conform with EPA standards.

As for water, Maryland is more fortunate than many states in that quantity is high due to rainfall, rivers and wells. But supply is still hard put to meet demand, and water pollution further endangers the quantity and quality of water.

More than 85 percent of the State's population uses community water supplies and disposes of its sewage through State-approved treatment facilities subject to regular inspection. Where inhabitants depend upon private water and sewerage systems, installations are inspected by local health-department personnel and the Administration's Division of General Sanitation.

Municipalities and counties submit 10-year water and sewerage plans to the Administration to review for adequacy and to process for federal and State construction grants.

Shellfish are checked for bacteriological surveys, and fishing may be rohibited until bacteria counts go down. Beaches are protected for athers by water tests along shorelines. Construction plans for public ools must be approved.

Garbage and trash collections are studied by the Administration's ivision of Solid Wastes. Studies are made to encourage recycling of the rash and the use of both trash and garbage as licensed landfill. Open urning dumps are being displaced by modern incinerators.

Officials of 13 states tour Allegany County pilot project of Solid Wastes Division, ederally funded to demonstrate successful conversion of abandoned strip mine into sanitary landfill for solid wastes disposal.

The Division of Food Control inspects milk and various foods, as ell as food-processing plants and food-handling establishments.

Much attention currently is being given to nuclear power plants. The ivision of Radiation Control has been approved by the federal Atomic nergy Commission to conduct on-site surveillance at the nuclear plant ow being built at Calvert Cliffs by the Baltimore Gas & Electric Comany.

Industrial plants cooperate to prevent occupational hazards to orkers due to airborne contaminants such as dust, fumes, and gases. hey check excessive noise, heat, or humidity. Excessive noise has become an increasing problem, and findings indicate that it can lead to loss of hearing, migraine headaches, ulcers, persistent tensions, and even high blood pressure and heart problems. A number of county governments and Baltimore City have recently passed anti-noise ordinances.

Environmental health laws require continual inspection, and only as the consumers or the public (for whom a special bureau exists in the Administration) understand the laws can they thus be enforced. Even then conflicts arise, expressed as "force all pollutant old cars off the roads and thus bring personal problems," or "drill offshore of Maryland's coast for oil and resolve energy shortages—and yet bring more pollution." For example, in 1973 the Department of Health and Mental Hygiene took the courageous stand of saying all building plans must be stopped along the Reisterstown—Randallstown—Pikesville corridor in Baltimore County because of the daily overflow of more than a million gallons of raw sewage into the Gwynns Falls watershed that services this area. Housing projects were delayed in counties such as Montgomery because of lack of sewerage facilities. The secretary of the department who made the decisions recognized that overloaded sewerage pipes posed a serious health hazard. Some builders and prospective home owners were very disturbed, but the moratoriums held. The answers are not easy when economic development runs counter to health requirements.

Preventive Medicine Administration. This service which includes staff specialists in pediatrics, obstetrics, epidemiology, dentistry, and veterinary medicine, has long been a part of the Department of Health and Mental Hygiene. Maternal and child-care services are provided through local health departments. Nutritionists operating through local health departments service programs related to preventive, curative, and rehabilitative requirements.

The Division of Communicable Diseases reviews weekly reports from private physicians on 47 different diseases and conducts epidemiological studies during outbreaks such as those of influenza. The Division sends its data to the U.S. Public Health Service Center for Disease Control in Atlanta, Georgia, where federal studies are made and assistance is given to states.

The 1963 federal Vaccination Assistance Act made funds available to states that were combating poliomyelitis, measles, and other children's diseases. These funds have enabled Maryland to make a concentrated attack on diseases like measles, which could cause blindness, deafness, and mental retardation. More than 600,000 Maryland school children were given rubella vaccine between 1969 and 1971, thus cutting down on a chain of transmission that could damage yet-unborn fetuses in pregnant mothers.

Tuberculin testing takes place in all schools. The Division's recent attacks have been against venereal diseases, which remain the most

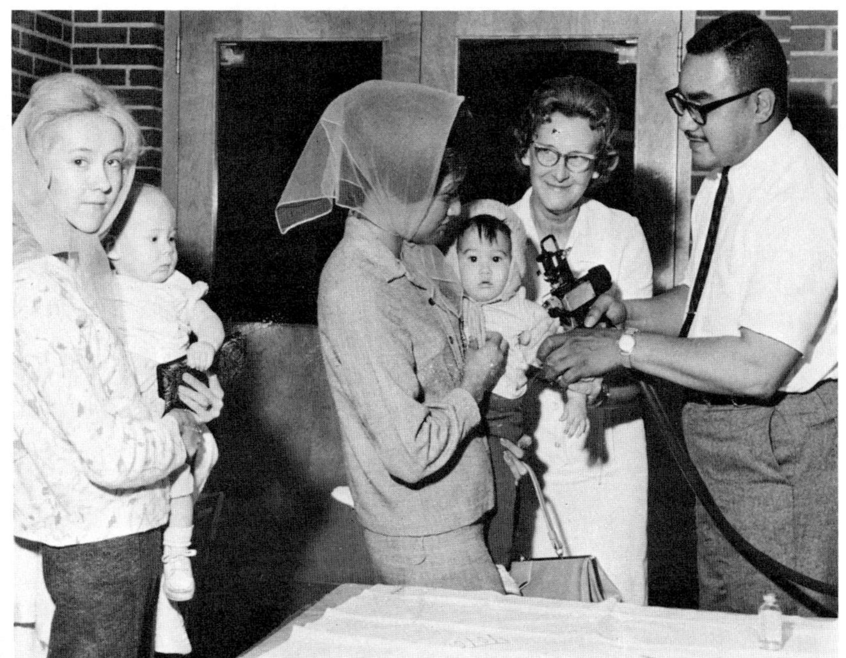

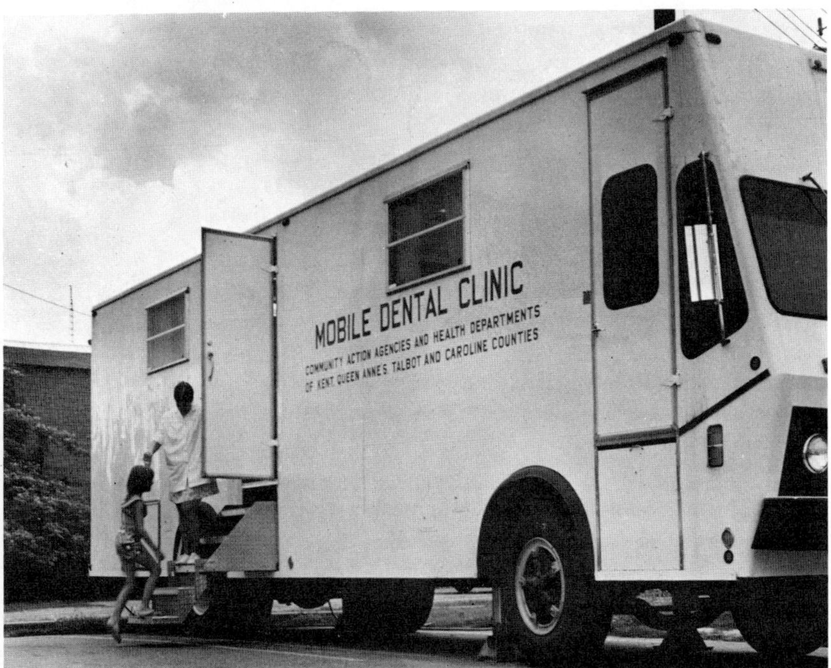

(Top) Physician injects pre-school youngster during mass rubella immunization conducted in centers set up in schools throughout Baltimore City. (Bottom) Innovative dentistry-on-wheels concept brings dental services to children throughout Caroline, Kent, Queen Annes and Talbot counties. (Maryland Department of Health and Mental Hygiene)

difficult hard-core public-health problem in Maryland. In 1970 alone about 15,000 cases of gonorrhea were reported—possibly four times as many were not reported. About one-third of the reported cases are among teenagers and young children. Social problems, disability, heart disease, blindness, and even death may result. The Division carries out informational and clinical treatment in cooperation with local health departments.

Laboratories and Research Administration. The State maintains laboratories in Baltimore and its branches in the local health departments to service physicians, hospitals, dairy plants, public water suppliers, and even federal agencies such as the Food and Drug Administration. About 300 laboratory workers test approximately 2,300 specimens each working day.

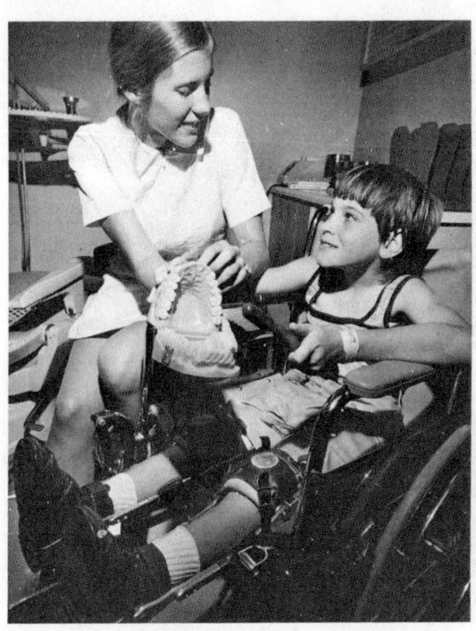

(L. to r.) Extending the dentist's care, a young patient is instructed in proper use of the toothbrush and the importance of careful cleaning. Special supportive braces help the youngster to cope with spinal defect; each morning the mailman brings an enormous pile of specimen containers which must be opened, carefully sorted and routed to appropriate laboratory units. (Maryland Department of Health and Mental Hygiene)

In the microbiology laboratory, cultures are grown from specimens taken from ear, nose, blood, and other sources. Specimens are examined for typhoid fever, diarrheal diseases, intestinal parasites, venereal ailments, and viral diseases. In conjunction with the veterinary medicine program, testing takes place for zoonotic diseases. Checks are made on rabies. Expectant mothers are checked for RH factors, rubella, and other harmful symptoms. Tests are made for sickle cell anemia, lead poisoning, and cervical cancer, as well as for air and water quality.

Local Health Services Administration. As has become apparent from reading this chapter many of the activities carried out under the Department's Office of Medical Care Program Services are operated through the 24 local health departments. Each county and Baltimore City has its special problems, but they also have many health and mental-hygiene problems in common. For example, the Prince Georges County Health Department in its preventive program makes thousands of chest x-rays and diabetes screening examinations. Montgomery County's Health Department has an exciting family-life and sex-education planning project. Frederick County's Health Department has established community consultation services in mental health with a "hot line" telephone tied in with drug and alcohol addiction. Baltimore City's Health Department has a unique noise-abatement program.

The Licensing Agencies

Until the Department of Health and Mental Hygiene was created in 1969, dozens of licensing boards related to health care operated independently. Now they operate under general guidelines. Each board still has its own specific requirements for bringing people into the profession or for carrying out its activities, but all are under the general supervision of the Secretary. Each board consists largely of professionals appointed by the Governor after nominations from professional societies.

There are boards for examining prospective professional practitioners, such as podiatrists, chiropractors, dentists, nurses, optometrists, funeral directors and embalmers, physicians, physical therapists, veterinary physicians, psychologists, pharmacists, sanitarians, osteopaths, and nursing home administrators. Then there are boards on health and legal medical services such as hospital construction, air quality, anatomical bodies for hospitals and schools of medicine, hospital licensing, post-mortem examining, radiation control, bedding examination, health service cost reviews, school health, physical fitness, medical discipline, kidney disease, and hospital authorities. All of these boards were established by the Legislature, which reviews their operations from time to time. But the Department now has the authority to make changes in terms of standards, consumer representation, and other crucial issues. The major concern is that these boards not become self perpetuating in their views.

The Future

In the first five years of its operations, the Department of Health and Mental Hygiene accomplished much that could not have been done under previous structures, but it was also true that there were still many unresolved problems.

Most people accept the fact that some form of national health insurance is certain to come to the United States. The big debate in this area is what form will it take. On virtually the last day of 1973, December 29, President Nixon signed the Health Maintenance Organization Act, which authorized spending $373 million to 1978 to help set up and evaluate those community arrangements in which subscribers pay a predetermined flat fee monthly or yearly, and in return are entitled to basic health-care services as they need them.

Under such an arrangement the new law contains a financial incentive to keep subscribers healthy; thus preventive medicine is stressed. The Act nullifies any state law requiring approval of a medical society before a health maintenance organization is established.

Columbia in Howard County has an interesting H.M.O. established in cooperation with Johns Hopkins Hospital. Other health maintenance organizations are likely to be established in different parts of Maryland now that the federal H.M.O. Act has been signed.

However, this Act cannot delay the long-time debate as to the nature of the national health insurance plan that is likely to emerge for all Americans in the 1970's. Good health is still far too costly and evasive—a solution must be found.

Chapter 12

EMPLOYMENT AND SOCIAL SERVICES

The federal Social Security Act of 1935 marked a radical change in the way Americans looked at fellow citizens in financial trouble. The plight of millions in this country during the Great Depression of the 1930's led the federal government to deal with two problems:

Aiding those in need as soon as possible by creating temporary welfare and work-relief programs, reopening closed banks, and re-establishing confidence in the economic structure.

Creating structures designed to prevent a recurrence of economic panic and depression—or at least render them less devastating. These safeguards were to be erected under programs such as unemployment insurance, bank-deposit guarantees, public housing, public social-service programs, collective bargaining, and a host of social security and allied programs. Financing would be federal, but administration would be at State levels.

For many years following 1935 these federal efforts were supported by state laws all over the country including those of the Maryland General Assembly. Two important related programs established in Maryland have, at different times and in different places, been both roundly applauded and criticized. These are the employment-security operations (particularly unemployment insurance) and social services (earlier known as public welfare).

The Department of Employment and Social Services

For nearly 35 years these two services were administered by separate State agencies, with significant federal financial assistance. In 1970 these two functions (along with other State-related operations such as those in the fields of economic and equal opportunity, human relations, veterans problems, and manpower needs) were placed in the newly created Department of Employment and Social Services under a cabinet-level Secretary. It was hoped that the new structure would bring about a coordinated and strongly directed attack on problems of economic need, poverty, unequal economic opportunity, and related matters.

In its general objective the new Department sought to enable the persons served to become self-sustaining and economically independent whenever possible. It is recognized that temporary situations, caused by unemployment, illness, poor housing, family problems, poverty, lack of educational attainment, racial and other prejudices, and numerous disadvantages that are often beyond the control of individuals, require emergency and sustained assistance. But the hope is that new jobs will replace old ones, that increased schooling and occupational training will move people out of poverty, that medical aid will help rebuild bodies, that public housing and rental assistance will insure decent living, that counseling will heal family strife, and that stringent laws will bring about equal-opportunity employment.

Of course, the remedies are not easily found. Often, for example, deep-seated problems of society, such as racial prejudice, must be solved before the real solutions come about. It is unrealistic to expect the Department to solve all personal and societal problems. In some areas the Department will be a caretaker until broader solutions come about. For example, until private developers find it profitable to build homes for low-income groups, public housing cannot contract its operations. Moreover, there will always be some who will need longtime care. The goal is not to eliminate all unemployment, nor all poverty (though that might be the wish), but to keep the numbers affected at a minimum and to make life secure and self-respectful for all, even in the days when they receive governmental assistance. The goal is also to make certain that in the effort to aid the needy individuals, assistance is adequate yet cases are carefully screened for validity and programs are administered economically and with accountability.

Board of Review

The Legislature in 1970 created a Board of Review consisting of seven members, four representing the public and three with knowledge in one or more fields covered by the Department. The members serve for three-year terms. The Board acts in an advisory capacity and also as an appeal agency with respect to decisions made by members of the Department or by the staffs of the local social-service departments in the 23 counties and Baltimore City.

Program Planning and Evaluation

Many important activities of the Department exist apart from the two key programs of (1) social services and (2) employment security and economic opportunity. These activities fall under broad categories related to federal employment programs, community leadership, and legal services, and are under the Department of Employment and Social Services.

SERVE (Service Employment for Recipients Who Volunteer Employment) was begun in 1972 with federal funds as a project to provide jobs as social and human service aides to 350 heads of households receiving public assistance. The Legislature provided matching State funds to employ 350 additional persons from the same grouping in similar jobs. The rationale was that thus 700 persons would go off public-assistance rolls and at the same time assist State and local agencies in the expansion of their human services. It is true that taking 700 families off the Maryland welfare rolls from the category of aid to families with dependent children, which had in 1972 a total of 55,000 family units, is not a major contribution. Yet the SERVE project can be indicative that welfare rolls can be cut down.

Three Federally Funded Programs in the 1970's. First, a specialized staff was provided to assist the Department in furthering the new federal regulations concerning separation of services to welfare clients from financial assistance programs; and arranging for purchase of such services as well as monitoring and evaluating the results. The second program initiated a special information service to enable governmental officials to understand public-assistance and social-service programs at State and local levels. A third program provides in-depth counseling, job training, and placement for 2,000 offenders, aiming to reintegrate them into community life.

The Maryland Legal Services Program. The program operates in Baltimore under purchase of services from Legal Aid, Inc., and in the counties under the Judicare Plan. The goal is to provide competent legal services to persons who lack the money to employ an attorney to assist in needed civil legal services. Included are nonvoluntary, nonsupport, and paternity cases, thus possibly favorably affecting the charges which might otherwise fall on public assistance budgets. The State has the requirement to provide legal assistance in criminal and juvenile matters under the Public Defender Law (*see* Chapter 8).

Office of Childhood Development. With financial assistance from the federal government, the State administers a comprehensive plan for child development and the day-care programs of the local (23 counties and Baltimore City) departments of social services.

Social Services Administration

Four important forces affect seriously the activities carried out by the Department's Social Services Administration. First, the fact that so many persons with problems are involved; there were about 265,000 persons on State public welfare rolls in 1972.

Second, the fact that the public seems to think that more welfare recipients should work. Actually less than one percent of all welfare recipients, or 2,000, are able-bodied employable males who are temporarily out of jobs. The aged, blind, or disabled add up to 42,000. Mothers with dependent children and with no supporting husbands add up to 58,000 more. The largest single group of persons on the rolls, 163,000, consists of children.

Third, the fact that the recipients or welfare clients do not receive enough funds to meet their needs at a time of rapidly rising prices. In 1973 the maximum grant of $200 per month for a family of four was hardly enough to purchase food, rent, clothing, utilities, household needs, furnishings, personal care, and insurance requirements. In 1974

Department of Employment and Social Services

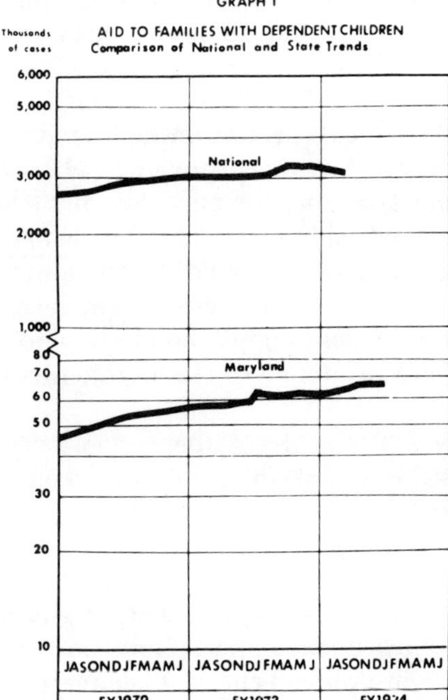

Department of Employment and Social Services

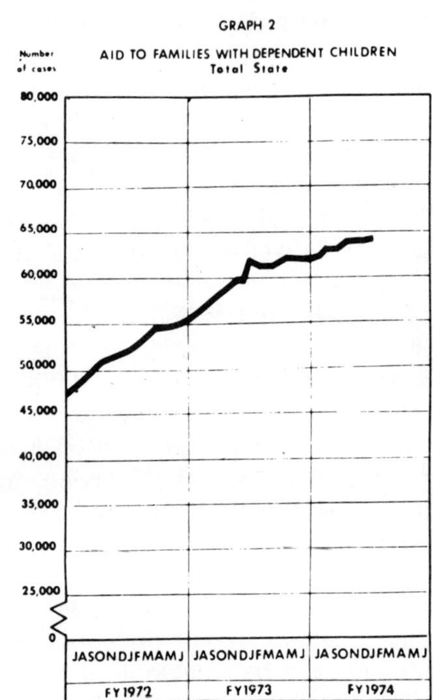

Department of Employment and Social Services

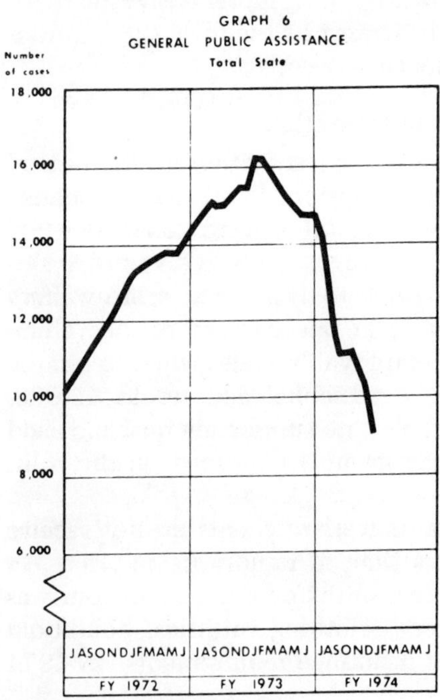

Department of Employment and Social Services

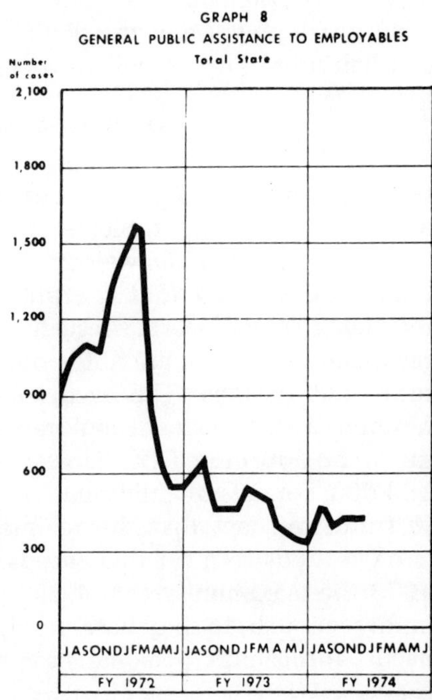

all State welfare rates were raised by 13 percent in order to keep up with living costs, but further rises in prices meant requirements were still unmet. In recent years increased recipient concerns have been supported by client groups such as welfare rights organizations and legal aid bureaus.

Fourth, the inability to depend upon long-range federal support. Congress and the federal administration have long debated such plans as guaranteed annual wages, family support plans, and other alternatives to current public-assistance programs. The one clear decision, in the early 1970's, was that public welfare should be so administered that social services would be separated from public assistance, and the federal government was to fund completely the public-assistance components. Advice and service were to accompany a check to the client only when he requested them.

Stalemates between the Congress and the Presidency have postponed final decisions. Meanwhile, federal appropriations have been decreased for social services but increased for direct payments to clients in terms of checks for public assistance, while the guidelines are more stringent.

Moreover, federal allotments for the social service components are no longer open-ended, but rather determined by the allocated state share of a national budgetary ceiling. In Maryland this meant that no matter how needs might increase in numbers of persons assisted or in kinds of services, only $48.5 million in federal funds was available in fiscal 1974 for the service category.

The Social Services Activities

While 265,000 persons were receiving assistance or income maintenance in 1972, only 20 percent were requesting or eligible for services. The rest were merely getting the checks due them.

Services to Families with Children. With the separation of social services from income maintenance (or public assistance), local departments have sought to find new ways of aiding communities. Some of these methods include decentralizing service offices and creating outreach stations in public housing projects and in areas remote from transportation. The social worker now is more likely to ask the client what help he feels he needs and where he believes there might be sources of assistance. Then the worker might refer the client to additional sources such as those dealing with homemaker services, day-care assistance, low-income housing possibilities, and job-referral agencies. In this way each individual client is guided to help himself first and then to make use of the numerous public and private assistance programs that exist largely outside the formal structure of the department's Social Services Administration.

Among the many who receive the social-service assistance to families with children are mothers whose husbands are ill, incapacitated, or dead. The services are available to all families receiving public assistance and are mandatory to those having an unemployed male or employable children over 18 years old and not in school. The latter requirement is but one indication of many that the local social-service departments insist that where there are employment possibilities, these be explored before public-assistance funds are distributed to clients.

Protective Services. The Social Services Administration in recent years has given much attention to child abuse and neglect. Under the State law social workers, physicians, nurses, and school personnel must report suspected child abuse to their local social services departments and to their State's attorneys.

Single Parent Service. This service is largely used by young, unmarried, or abandoned mothers or pregnant girls who seek adoption services, public assistance, medical aid, and family-planning advice. A small number seek abortion counseling. Unfortunately, the Service has not been successful in reaching single fathers who are left with children.

Services to Adults. Those adults who have social and health problems and are public-assistance recipients receive family and individual counseling and self-care and self-support services. Homemaker services are available to indigent aged, blind, and disabled. One of the more exciting experiments in this area is the foster-care programs for the aged carried out in Baltimore City and Baltimore County.

Intermediate Care. While in 1972 the administration of intermediate care was moved to the State Department of Health and Mental Hygiene, the Social Services Administration continues to hold responsibility for eligibility and for social services of clients. The program is for those eligible for medical assistance who, because of physical or mental incapacitation, indicate needs below that of skilled nursing attention but above the level of mere domiciliary care. Such intermediate care may take place in licensed nursing homes or in approved private homes handling but one or two intermediate-care patients and thus not requiring licenses.

Vocational Rehabilitation Services. This program is for public assistance clients who need vocational rehabilitation. It is carried out jointly with the Vocational Rehabilitation Division of the State Department of Education.

Homemaker Service. This is a rapidly growing agency seeking to keep social-service clients in their home environments so that the adults will not be institutionalized and the children not be placed in foster-care homes. The Service provides homemakers who help the needy families to create healthful home environments and to receive community services. This Service is especially important to those who are acutely or chronically ill, are incapacitated by emotional or mental illness, or lack of knowledge of child care and nutritional and home care skills as well as home management. It is also available to non-social-service recipients who are only medically indigent and receive Medicaid funds. In this respect the Service cooperates with the Department of Health and Mental Hygiene.

Foster Care. In 1972 about 10,500 children in Maryland were receiving foster care. These were children who could not return to their own homes or be adopted, and thus were placed in permanent foster homes. To facilitate exchange of ideas, some local social service agencies have established foster-parent associations, and a Statewide steering committee was organized. Problems arise from a shortage of foster homes for the older and troubled youngster and a lack of funds to pay foster parents reasonable rates.

Adoption. Adoption service was given to 2,359 children during fiscal 1972. Of this number, 413 were placed for adoption and 93 with adoptive families who receive a subsidy. Some of the problems are the availability of attorneys' services to local departments (especially to facilitate guardianship actions) and the need for uniform legislation governing licensing and relinquishment.

Licensing of 24-hour Child Care Facilities. In 1972 there were 10 child-placing agencies, 20 institutions, and nine group homes licensed for 24-hour care of children. The homes serve youths between the ages of 13 and 18 years who have experienced numerous unsuccessful placements in foster homes or have problems requiring individualized services and adult supervision.

Food Stamp Program. In 1972 there were 73,721 households comprising 225,150 individuals participating in the food stamp program. The group was larger than usual because of flooding conditions in large areas of the State, including Baltimore City. Ordinarily more than 80 percent of the recipients of food stamps are on public assistance. Some 18 to 20 percent of recipients are hardship cases whose family incomes are not low enough to qualify them for public assistance, but still so marginal that when one considers their low liquid assets, they qualify for food stamps. Participants pay from one-third to one-half the value of the food stamps, though on rare occasions, as was true in the case of the 1972 flood victims, free stamps are distributed. The project is an important way of assuring that needy people eat nutritious food.

Medical Assistance Programs. The local departments of social services certify applicants for Medicaid, which is administered by the Department of Health and Mental Hygiene. All persons receiving public assistance are judged as eligible for medical assistance. However, many who do not need (or desire) public assistance funds find that they cannot cope financially with bills that accrue from illnesses. These persons are judged to be medically indigent and thus eligible for Medicaid. In 1972 the State eligibility list for medical assistance covered 387,000 persons.

The Major Public Assistance Programs

About 265,000 persons in Maryland receive funds from the major public-assistance programs, if one includes the Supplemental Security Income program operated and funded by the federal government and the two major public assistance programs, Aid to Families with Dependent Children and General Public Assistance to Employable operated by the State.

The number of persons on public assistance varies in different parts of the State. In 1971 for example, Baltimore City had 136,655, or about 15 percent of its population, receiving public or welfare assistance. These high figures are true for all large cities all over the United States and reflect the poverty of the metropolis. On the other hand, Baltimore County had about one percent, as did Howard County; while Harford, Carroll, and Anne Arundel each had about two percent of their population on the major public assistance programs.

The State public assistance programs all have clearcut guidelines that equate income, size of family, need, type of disability, family assets, and special factors in determining needs. Need for all programs considers food, clothing, shelter, household maintenance, insurance premiums, personal care, school supplies, and other basics. Applications are made to the local social service departments in the 23 counties and Baltimore City. Professional social service workers determine the amount of assistance given to clients by applying the State formula for grants.

The State Public Assistance Programs

Aid to Families with Dependent Children. AFDC is by far the largest State public assistance program. In 1972 it aided 55,652 families, or about 190,000 persons. The program was funded for $102.6 million, with the federal government contributing 48.43 percent, the State 45.09 percent, the local governments 2.37 percent, and private funds (relatives) 4.11 percent. The federal government is expected ultimately to take over this program.

AFDC provides financial assistance to parents on behalf of dependent Maryland children who are under age 18 (or 21 if attending school) and are without parental support by reason of death, illness, incapacity, unemployment, or absence of father. They must be living with a close relative and in a family home meeting standards of care and health. In 1973 the maximum monthly allowance for an average family of four (mother and three children) was $200, or $2,400 a year. This represents only 59 percent of the $4,038 per year the State itself says a welfare family needs to subsist. In 1974 the allotments were increased by 13 percent, but prices also rose.

General Public Assistance to Employable. The GPA-E program is for those who live in parts of Maryland that recognize the need to grant temporary assistance to able-bodied persons who are not eligible for required funds from other sources, such as unemployment insurance and aid under other public assistance programs. Only nine local political units recognize this program. In 1972 the monthly average on GPA-E was 1,072 families, or about 12,000 families for the year. The total funding was $1.2 million. The State contributed 48.43 percent, local units 51.50 percent, and private contributions (relatives) came to .07 percent. The federal government does not contribute to this program.

An assortment of social services such as day care, homemaker, home management, work experience for parents, and special education for children are also provided where needed.

Supplemental Security Income for the Aged, Blind and Disabled

In 1974 a major change took place in the whole concept of public assistance. Previous to that year the federal government contributed the highest percentage of the funding for the four major State public assistance programs, with the State and local governments adding their shares. The chief criticism of the tri-governmental funding centered around the fact that needy families, under the same circumstances, received a far greater allotment in funds if they lived in a northern state like New York than if they lived in a southern state like Mississippi. Since these were state programs, the money received by clients differed from state to state.

In 1974 this principle was changed under SSI (Supplementary Security Income for the aged, blind and disabled). SSI established a national ceiling for all states for three public assistance programs (old age assistance, public assistance to the needy blind, and aid to the permanently and totally disabled) that formerly were administered by the 50 states and were now to be administered under SSI by the federal government, through local offices of the Social Security Administration.

The new SSI federal law will, of course, save the State millions of dollars in that Maryland will not need to contribute to the funding of the public assistance components of these three programs. Some of the funds that will be saved by Maryland can be used to offer greater support for the social services that will still be provided by the State and local departments to clients who were on State rolls for both public assistance and social services before 1974 and those new to SSI.

Hopefully, some of the State savings might also go toward having Maryland absorb all local (county and Baltimore City) funding of remaining State programs, especially Aid for Families with Dependent Children (AFDC). For some time the counties have asked the State to take over the costs of social service programs. Actually, under the so-called James (Senator William James, Harford County) Formula, the State has arranged for local contributions for social services to be absorbed gradually until 1976, and completely by then. Even after 1976 there might still be some local contributions toward such programs for the poor as Community Action and Manpower projects.

The question many ask is: Shouldn't all local social service departments (including Baltimore City's) then be controlled directly by the State, which would be the full funding agent? Some say full financing by Maryland but not State control; for grass-roots decisions are vital and the local advisory boards would go out of existence if the State directly ran and made the decisions for the local departments.

In 1973 local contributions to social services were governed by the James Formula whereby counties (and Baltimore City) contribute in terms of assessable property. In December, 1973 a Governor's commission recommended that the State assume all the costs and that the State have more control. The 1974 Legislature moved further in this direction by placing the personnel of the Baltimore City Department of Social Services effective July 1, 1975, under the State control.

Another question asked as a result of the SSI program: Does this mean that the federal government will ultimately take over the costs and the operations of the remaining public assistance programs, such as Aid for Families with Dependent Children (toward which it now contributes a major share of funding) and perhaps even General Public Assistance, toward which it currently contributes nothing? The answer probably is "yes," since the trend in the social service field is to establish a "national floor" for the public assistance components so that everybody in the same circumstances will receive the same size check no matter where he lives in the United States. The only way that can happen is to let the federal government operate all the public assistance programs.

As for the services, such as counseling, child care, and home care and management, these might still differ from one locality to another in terms of unique circumstances.

How Supplemental Security Income Operates

First, it is important not to confuse SSI with Social Security. The restrictions herein noted for SSI do *not* apply to Social Security. Second, it is to be noted that the new federal program, SSI, replaces the earlier State programs listed as Old Age Assistance, Public Assistance to the Needy Blind, and Aid to the Permanently and Totally Disabled. Fortunately, all records for clients of these programs kept by the State and local departments of social services were turned over to the federal Social Security offices; thus no time was lost in arranging for payments to those eligible in 1974. Clients did not need to refile their claims.

The aim of SSI is to provide aid so that everyone who is 65 years of age or blind or disabled (irrespective of age) will at least have a basic cash income.

Supplemental security income is paid to people 65 or over who have very little money coming in and not much in savings or other assets. The same holds true for blind and disabled of all ages who need this help.

	SUPPLEMENTAL SECURITY INCOME FOR THE AGED, BLIND, AND DISABLED
GOALS:	*a design for dignity to answer the needs caused by vast changes in society*
A MORE ADEQUATE INCOME A NEW SECURITY	the greatest amount for those with greatest need no dunning of relatives for support assist people who want to retain homes
EQUITY & FAIRNESS FOR EVERYONE	a uniform payment & eligibility standard for everyone, everywhere—a floor on which to build
CASH PAYMENTS TO THE POOR THEMSELVES	the dignity of decision cash, instead of services
MOTIVATE TO MEANINGFUL ACTIVITY	to assist those who wish to work
HELP FOR HANDICAPPED CHILDREN	payments to the blind or disabled may be made regardless of age
	Part of a comprehensive strategy to help the AGED, BLIND & DISABLED

STATE-FEDERAL PARTNERSHIP
...each to do what it can do best

STATE: Governors and Legislatures retain decision

- to supplement the Federal payment for new recipients
- to keep or add services

and continue:

- to provide social services
- to make disability determinations
- to offer vocational rehabilitation employment services

FEDERAL:

- makes cash payments

For people with no other income the maximum federal payments are $140 per month for one person and $210 for a married couple. Moreover, there is a "disregard" factor of $20 a month which one may make as income (other than earnings) from other sources, such as rent. This amount of $140 a month is a good deal better than one would have received under the earlier State Old Age Assistance (OAA) program, which would have given him but $96 a month.

Cash, money in bank, stocks, government bonds, and other liquid assets cannot be more than $1,500 for an individual or $2,250 for a couple. Money in the bank is counted as an asset. Personal effects, insurance policies, household goods, and a home do not count as assets. A car may or may not affect eligibility.

The fact that one receives a Social Security check does not necessarily rule him or her out. If the amount of the check is less than $140 a month, one might still receive some SSI benefits.

There is a more liberal policy on earnings than on other income. A recipient of SSI funds may still earn as much as $65 a month without having it count against him. Any earnings above that will have one-half of the totals count as deductions from the $140 a month.

Apart from earnings (and a $20 a month disregard factor in other income), money received from pensions, workmen's compensation, annuities, gifts, and Social Security will tend to diminish SSI benefits.

The Local Departments of Social Service

It is important to note that the operative Maryland programs of social services are the local departments. Each of the 24 units has its own unique problems and each has its own advisory board. For example, in Montgomery County only one percent of its population receive public assistance, while in Baltimore City the figure is about 15 percent. Thus the Baltimore City Social Services Department has decentralized its work; plans call for 19 centers to be established throughout the city. Clients are bringing more problems to the neighborhood clinics and waiting less time than they did before decentralization. In turn, social workers are playing a more intimate role in community projects that aim at self-improvement.

The Baltimore City Department experimented with a rent-supplement contribution to needy families who were not in public housing and not on public assistance. The program might be regarded as offering indigent support in housing much as such aid is given to the medically indigent. The average support was about $21 a month with one-time only payments of $30 to have utilities turned back on, up to $125 for furniture, and up to $25 for moving. A limited number were aided.

The State and the local social services departments are conscious of public criticism. Fiscal management and audits are regularly employed so that the undeserving are not getting assistance checks. The State Department of Employment and Social Services has quality control audits and these services are available to local departments. In 1972 the Baltimore City Department of Social Services used quality control to pick up clients who abused the public assistance programs. Fiscal management procedures and audits further improved business practices and helped to make certain that the right people received assistance and the right amounts. With all these precautions, a self study by the Administration in 1973 showed that a sampling of 1,200 welfare cases Statewide, 14.7 percent of the recipients were ineligible and 28.5 percent were getting too much.

Employment Security Administration

The Employment Security Administration represents the second large program of the 1970 newly created Department of Employment and Social Services headed by a Secretary with Cabinet rank. The rationale for putting employment and social services together in one department comes from the belief that job services and unemployment insurance will cut down on welfare rolls. The Administration is headed by an Executive Director appointed by the Secretary.

Unemployment insurance is not a welfare program. The insurance contributions paid to unemployed workers come from funds paid by employers. They should be looked upon as any other form of insurance, such as sickness insurance, which one receives because he paid for protection at an earlier time when he was well. Though supported in part by federal funds toward administrative charges, this is, nevertheless, a State activity. Nor should unemployment insurance be mistaken for programs such as Supplemental Security Income or Medicare, which are federal activities.

About 40 years ago, the federal Social Security Act of 1935 included the concept of unemployment insurance after the Depression made it clear that loss of jobs by millions was the major cause of economic failure. In 1936, the Maryland General Assembly passed the Unemployment Compensation Law and noted the following resolution in order to make the State eligible for federal funds: "Economic insecurity due to unemployment is a serious menace to the health, morals, and welfare of the people of this state. . . ." Shortly after unemployment insurance became effective it was evident that a strong program of employment services needed to be initiated so that the jobless could get other positions.

Advisory Councils. The Governor appoints a State advisory council and the Executive Director of the Administration appoints members of local advisory councils made up of representatives of the public, employers, and employees.

State's Labor Force. In 1972 the State's work force averaged 1,599,500 persons. In that same year the average monthly Statewide unemployment of 80,900 represented 5.2 percent of the labor force. In recent years the State unemployment rate has been as low as about 4.0 percent. The Maryland labor picture in 1972 was somewhat uneven, reflecting recent long-time trends. For example, though the Baltimore Metropolitan Area is where more than half of the State's work force is employed, that section of Maryland showed a job growth of less than one percent in 1972 over 1971. For every five additional Maryland workers employed during the year, only one received a job in the Baltimore area. Moreover, the Baltimore area averaged an unemployed rate of 5.6 percent in 1972, though the overall State rate was 5.2 percent. Allegany, Calvert, Queen Annes, and Carroll Counties also showed unemployment problems in 1972, but there was some improvement in 1973.

Unemployment Payments. Initial Maryland claims for unemployment compensation, the first filed at the beginning of a period of unemployment, rose from 210,513 in 1971 to 241,606 in 1972. Net benefit payments under the regular State program in 1972 amounted to about $86.1 million compared to $63.6 million in 1971. In 1972 the maximum weekly benefit was $78 and the average check was $60.13. The average duration of benefit payments was 13.2 weeks in fiscal 1972 and but 12.7 weeks in 1971. In 1974 the Legislature hiked the maximum weekly benefit to $89.

In 1971 about 25 percent of all claimants exhausted their full 26-week entitlement under the regular program (eligible for more under the extended benefits) and only 20.7 percent in 1972—thus showing how the employment picture changes from year to year. Yet the situation was so bad in 1972 that an additional $8.9 million was paid to claimants who exhausted regular benefits and qualified for additional payments under the federal-State system of "extended benefits," funded on a 50 percent State and 50 percent federal basis.

Over $9 million was paid in regular and extended benefits programs under two permanent federal projects—Unemployment Compensation for Ex-Servicemen and Unemployment Compensation for Federal Employees.

Contributions. The law requires that the employer pay contributions at the standard rate of 2.7 percent of his total wages, minus adjustments made due to experience rating. If an employer's record is good in such labor relations as layoffs and forced vacations, then his experience rating is especially high. In 1972 out of 60,562 employers, as many as 27,949 (or 46.1 percent) were paying but 0.1 percent experience rating unemployment insurance on their payrolls. On the other hand, as many as 3,055 firms (5.0 percent) paid 3.6 percent on payrolls. Minimum experience rating goes up (0.7 percent in 1974) as fund balance goes down.

Payments. Payments to claimants are determined after claims are filed and there has been registration for work. A formula based on past salary determines how much is paid, with benefits varying from $10 a week to $89.

An additional dependents' allowance of $3 a week for each dependent child under 16 years up to a maximum of four children is permitted, providing totals are not beyond the maximum ($89 in 1974). Partial benefits are permitted for partial unemployment. The maximum length of payments, under normal circumstances, is 26 weeks. However, in periods of high unemployment, an additional 13 weeks of extended benefits may be paid.

Reasons for Denial or Delay in Benefits. A claimant does *not qualify* for unemployment insurance payments when:

a. He is unable or unavailable for full-time work.

b. He left work voluntarily without good cause.

c. He has been discharged for misconduct connected with work.

d. He failed, without good cause, to apply for or accept suitable work.

e. He is physically unable to continue employment.

f. His unemployment is due to stoppage based on labor dispute.

g. He is receiving unemployment benefits from another state or the federal government.

h. He applies for benefits in a second year and has not earned enough to qualify.

i. He has not followed instructions about filing claims.

j. He is engaged in self-employment.

k. He is not looking for work.

Penalties. Claimants are subject to fines and even imprisonment if they fail to report all wages earned during any period in which they claim benefits. This includes odd job earnings, pensions, workmen's compensation payments, and any vacation, dismissal, or holiday payments by a previous employer.

Appeal Rights. After receipt of notice of denial or reduction of claims, claimants may file with the appeals division of the administration, then to the Board of Appeals (a three-man board appointed by the Secretary of the department) and finally to the trial courts in Maryland. In 1972 the division heard 6,500 appeals and the board processed 936 cases.

Employment Service Division

It is the responsibility of the Employment Service Division to seek out employment opportunities for those in need of jobs and to explore and initiate job training and work projects that will provide new opportunities for fruitful labor. The more jobs there are, the less need there will be for unemployment insurance.

Below are some of the projects carried out by the Employment Service Division:

The Statewide Job Bank. This is a computer assisted job inventory and control process which are listed in a daily Job Bank book (actually microfiche film) and permits those in need of employment ready access to job information. The control unit operates so that there are no multiple referrals to one job opening. A large number of public and non-profit employment agencies have access to the data. Individuals may use the data by appearing at the central office in Baltimore or at

(Top) After an applicant has made his job choices, he meets with a Job Bank interviewer who insures that all job requirements are met before arranging an appointment for the applicant. (Bottom) The nucleus of the Job Bank's busy self-service area is approximately 100 GAF 7511 microfiche readers; about 90 are used by the applicants, as shown here, and the remaining readers are used by the interviewers.

branch offices in the counties. Individuals are free to use the bank as a self-service means of procuring jobs.

Urban Federal Job Programs. At different times the Employment Service Division has cooperated with federal programs seeking to widen employment opportunities in urban areas, particularly Baltimore City. For example, the Division has the responsibility for the Work Incentive Program (WIN), which provides counseling, training, supportive services, and job placement to employable public assistance recipients and is funded largely by federal funds. In recent years the Division has cooperated with the Baltimore Concentrated Employment Service (CEP), which operates through Community Action Agencies designated throughout the country by the federal government to alleviate poverty in urban areas by coordinating job opportunities, especially for the hard-core unemployed. The Employment Service community worker aids the graduates of CEP programs with his personal and occupational problems. Veterans returning from Vietnam presented a special problem. The federal government by Executive Order 11598 required all companies awarded federal contracts to list job openings with the local Employment Service Office. Priority referrals are given to veterans.

Yet another group of unemployed workers receiving special attention during recent years were the scientists, engineers, and technicians who lost their jobs because of cutbacks in defense efforts. Grants are provided to this group for job search, relocation expenses, and retraining. Part of the task is carried out by self-help, with professional engineers helping each other to find jobs.

The Rural Manpower Services seek to provide residents of rural areas with training and job opportunities. A mobile service unit is available for those not near a local Employment Service office. The service also helps place migrant workers.

The Employer Services Functions. Staff members of the division visit employers to encourage them to develop more job opportunities, participate in job analysis, job restructuring and job modification.

Maryland Office of Economic Opportunity

MOEO is in existence to provide technical assistance to 14 Community Action programs in the State and to further the activities of programs funded under the federal Economic Opportunity Act. In a sense, this agency deals with the underlying causes of unemployment and poverty while the Divisions on Unemployment Insurance and Employment Service deal directly with these problems.

State Technical Assistance Program. STAP is federally funded for the purpose of providing long-term, on-sight special technical assistance to rural Community Action agencies in the areas of economic development, manpower, and housing.

Optional Jobs Program (OJP). This program is operated by MOEO as a manpower training activity. Under the general sponsorship of the U.S. Department of Labor in 1972, this program trained 1,000 disadvantaged persons in the Maryland counties and helped them find jobs.

The Local Employment Service Offices

These offices are located in the counties and carry out grass-roots requirements. For example, in Allegany County the service encourages the local branch of the National Alliance of Businessmen (funded under the federal Manpower Development and Training Act) to hire and train a fair share of financially poor persons and Vietnam veterans. In Allegany, Washington, and Frederick Counties, the WIN program, with $174,000 of federal funds in 1972, provided work experience and vocational training for 431 public assistance recipients. Each county surveys its own labor market and new possibilities for employment. Community economic inventories are available from each county office.

The Human Services Agencies

Attached to the Department of Employment and Social Services are a number of commissions with human-service motifs that exist with autonomy and with their advisory committees. Some were established by statutory actions of the Legislature, motivated by federal programs and funding, as, for example, the Veterans Commission and the Commission on the Status of Women. Others were established by Executive Order of the Governor, as, for example, the Youth Advisory Council and the Commission on Concerns of Spanish-Speaking People.

The Maryland Veterans Commission services the State's military veterans who make up 588,000 persons or 15 percent of the total population; with their families this would be 62 percent. During fiscal 1972 about 100,000 claims were processed involving more than $13 million. Claims and counsel involve applications for pensions or compensation, admission to Veterans Administration hospitals, advice on G.I. insurance benefits, educational assistance to war orphans, on-the-job training, and higher educational privileges.

The Maryland Commission on the Status of Women assists in the enforcement of State and federal equal-opportunity laws. The Commission is particularly active in working with federal authorities to see that equal opportunity laws regarding hiring, placement, promotion, and salaries are fulfilled by employers, especially as they pertain to women.

For example, the federal Equal Pay Act of 1963 requires that there be equal pay for comparable work regardless of sex. While 33 million women in America represent about two-fifths of the national labor force, they seldom get the high-paying jobs. According to the U.S. Department of Labor, in 1970 the median yearly earnings for women were $5,323, or 59.4 percent of $8,966 for men. Some counties and Baltimore City also have Human Relations Commissions to enforce local ordinances dealing with rights for women.

The Maryland Manpower Planning Council operates the Cooperative Area Manpower Planning System (CAMPS) as a way of linking federal and local plans to aid the poor get jobs. The Community Action Agency seeks to improve procedures by which neighborhoods carry out their own self-improvement plans. The Governor's Youth Advisory Council (made up of 115 young persons) exists to communicate the concerns of the young. The Commission on the Concerns of Spanish-Speaking People plans, initiates, and evaluates State programs that accrue to the benefit of this group. The Committee for the Regulation and Study of Migratory Labor in Maryland is a statutory established group that seeks to make certain that out-of-State laborers shall be imported, maintained, and employed under satisfactory conditions of housing, sanitation, health, and welfare.

Organized Labor's Views

The Maryland State and District of Columbia AFL-CIO, representing more than 250,000 workers, has a significant stake and interest in developing programs for labor reforms. The United Automobile Workers of America, the Teamsters Joint Council, the United Mine Workers of America and other nationally organized and independent labor groups, not a part of AFL-CIO, have another 50,000 workers. In general these organizations seek to increase the amount of unemployment insurance benefits and to extend the number of weeks of coverage. They favor extending workmen's compensation coverage to all farm workers, increasing the minimum wage law in terms of higher hourly rates, replacing volunteer firefighting units in urban counties, providing more liberal time allowances for policemen appearing as court witnesses, extending collective bargaining privileges to more public servants, and liberalizing pension plans for civil service workers. The platform of organized labor could bring continuing debate in the Legislature as to philosophy, funds, and the rights of management and the worker.

Chapter 13

EDUCATION: THE MARYLAND SCHOOLS AND LIBRARIES

The sheer immensity of the task is the first observation of one who studies the Maryland schools. In the 1973-74 school year the total enrollment of the Maryland public elementary and secondary schools, kindergarten through twelfth grades, was 911,000 students. Another 130,000 were enrolled in the non-public schools, kindergarten through twelfth grades (100,000 of that number were in Roman Catholic schools). In public and private elementary schools the total would be 1,041,000 pupils.

In 1972 there were 74,000 full-time undergraduates studying in Maryland public colleges and universities (not counting the United States Naval Academy), and 6,400 full-time graduate students in public higher education. There were, in addition, 48,000 part-time undergraduate students and 8,500 part-time graduate students in public colleges and universities. Moreover, in 1972 there were 14,500 undergraduates studying as full-time students in private colleges and universities, and 3,700 more studying there as full-time graduate students. Then there were 8,000 students as part-time undergraduates in private higher educational institutions, and 5,500 more there as part-time graduate students. Thus the total higher-educational enrollment in Maryland, part and full-time, public and private, is about 168,000 students. Therefore, the Maryland school enrollment of 1,041,000 pupils, plus the higher-education enrollment of 168,000, adds up to 1,239,000.

To that number may be added 52,000 students studying in public adult, part-time, basic education classes, with another 46,500 studying in vocational adult-education classes. There are 3,000 inmates studying in Maryland correctional and juvenile-care institutions. Some 3,000 handicapped students receive home and hospital care at any one time, and 2,000 more are in special schools outside the Maryland public schools. At least 20,000 are studying part or full-time in Maryland private proprietary (commercial) institutions below, at or above secondary level. If one adds the 100,000 or more workers studying in non-public industrial labor union, church, and club educational programs that offer formal and informal classes, it is evident that over one-third of the four million Marylanders are attending schools.

True, the State's financial responsibilities are primarily for the one million students studying full-time in Maryland public and higher educational institutions, plus support for the 56,500 part-time students in public colleges and support for 126,000 in public adult, basic, voca-

(Top) Seventh District Elementary School, Parkton, Md. (Board of Education of Baltimore County) (Bottom) Naval Academy Parade before Tecumseh. Annapolis is proud of the national training academy for midshipmen. (Photo by Bob Willis)

College Enrollment as a Percent of Population Age 18-21, 1970

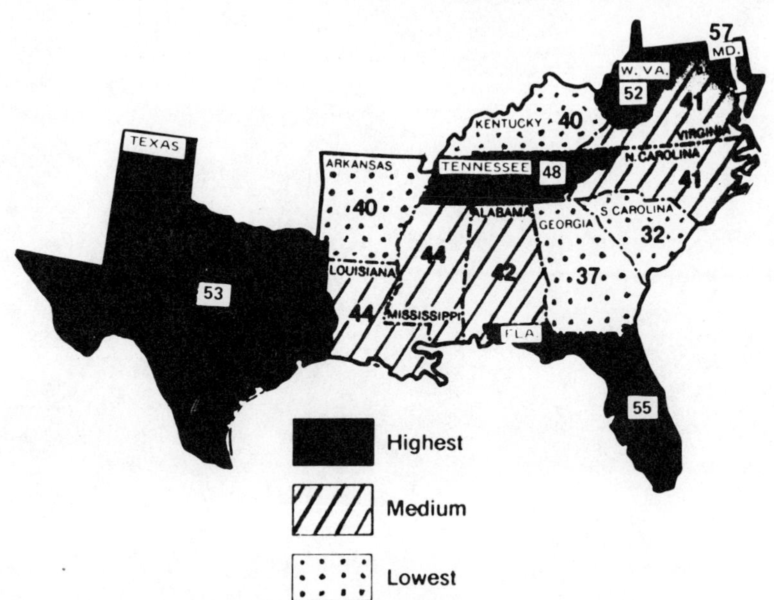

The relation between population and enrollment, expressed in attendance rates showing enrollment as a percent of population, is illustrated by the shaded map. These attendance rates now range from 57 percent in Maryland to 32 percent in South Carolina, compared with 61 percent in the United States.

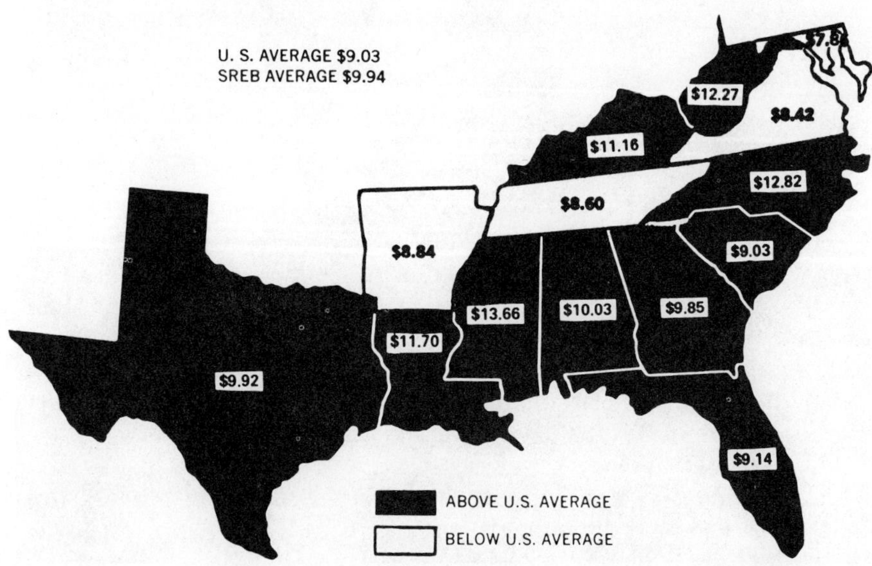

STATE OPERATIONAL FUNDS FOR HIGHER EDUCATION, PER $1,000 PERSONAL INCOME
1971

Source: NASULGC and Survey of Current Business

tional, and rehabilitation classes. Thus 30 percent of all Marylanders are, in public schools or colleges, receiving governmental support.

To put it another way, the average cost per student for Maryland public elementary and secondary education in 1972-73 was $782. The average cost per student for public community college education for the same year was about $1,600, and for public four-year colleges and the State university closer to $2,000.

The State and local units with federal aid together spend over one billion dollars annually in operating costs for public elementary and secondary school education. The State alone spends about $155 million annually for public higher education, to which should be added millions more in county and federal contributions. Added to these costs would be student tuitions for collegiate and university education.

In addition to the operating costs, there are capital costs. The State authorized in 1972-73 alone a bond issue for $300 million to be spent for new public elementary and secondary facilities in the 23 counties and Baltimore City under the Full State Funding for School Construction Law. Some $50 million in State appropriations for public higher educational construction should be added to the 1972-73 capital costs.

There are nearly 1,400 different public elementary and secondary schools in Maryland and, in addition, there are 26 different public higher-educational institutions to support in current operating and capital costs.

Then, too, there are the salaries of 45,000 teachers in public elementary and secondary schools. Add to that about 1,600 full-time faculty employed in the public community colleges and about 3,000 more in the public State colleges and universities. Any way you put it—in terms of students affected, teachers involved, buildings constructed, or current operating costs—the numbers are high.

Education Is an Investment

In fiscal 1972-73 the total State Budget was more than $2.4 billion—the appropriations for public education were about $739 million, or nearly 30 percent of the total. These costs do not include county and Baltimore City local appropriations for public education. In the local units, educational costs represent the largest single expenditure within the tax dollar. But as has been made clear, public education also represents the governmental service that reaches most people.

Government has long recognized that education must be considered as an investment rather than an expenditure. An educated citizenry pours back into the commonwealth that which has been learned. It assures the local community and State that there will be health workers to keep citizens well; will be clergymen to keep us spiritually motivated; skilled craftsmen to build our homes and factories; professionals in fields like engineering and business to operate our economy effectively; policemen and firemen to protect us from crime and fire; musicians, artists and writers to have us enjoy the aesthetic; public officials to perpetuate our government, and skilled and sensitive military to protect us from foreign invasion. Moreover, in a democracy there must be common denominators that go beyond the mere preparation for making a living and include an understanding of the American heritage and traditions. There must also be a feeling for man's role in an interdependent world with respect for all men and for the civilization of which we are a part.

So education is a way of perpetuating and enriching society. But it is also a way of giving promise and fulfillment to individuals. Those who are well educated are more likely to find better jobs and earn higher incomes. But they are also more likely to pour these earnings into more purchases, thus creating a more fluid economy. They are also more likely to support musical concerts and theaters, thus bringing about higher cultural levels. They are more likely to pay more taxes since, for example, college education brings an average of $45,000 additional in life earnings. The extra income alone assures that State and local governments will get back in added tax payments what these units spent to educate the individual.

Most important of all is the inner security that comes to a well educated person. This cannot be measured in dollars, but a person who has self-fulfillment is a better adjusted individual. This is why Maryland puts so much stock in educational rehabilitation of the inmate in correctional institutions and of the welfare client who is not prepared to hold a job in our technological society. Education is still the catalytic agent that promotes social and economic mobility. It is still the main hope of keeping the urban centers viable, of raising the many out of poverty and of harnessing the efforts of thousands of Maryland's citizens who seek to reach their highest potential.

The Maryland Constitution and Public Education

The Constitution of 1851 embodied for the first time the concept "That the Legislature ought to encourage the diffusion of knowledge and virtue" (Article 41, Declaration of Rights). It was not until the Constitution of 1864 that the specifics of educational responsibilities were spelled out. Here Article VIII describes in detail the nature of the State Department of Education and the State Board of Education, explaining that, "The General Assembly. . .shall provide a uniform system of Free Public Schools by which a school shall be kept open and supported free of expense for tuition in each school district, for at least six months in each year. . .The General Assembly shall further provide. . .by the imposition of an annual tax of not less than five cents on each one hundred dollars of taxable property." Here were the beginnings of a State free public school system supported by taxes and Constitutionally established.

The Constitution of 1867, the present governing document, shortened the 1864 statement, but kept as Article VIII the basic concept of a State free public school system, maintained by public taxes. It also kept Article 41 in the Declaration of Rights, which it inherited from the 1851 document.

Public schools were serving local communities earlier than 1864. Baltimore City, by State approval, established such schools in 1829. This earlier action explains why to this day the City is not integrally a part of the State system, though it receives State funds.

The Maryland State Board of Education

The Maryland State Board of Education, a seven-member body, is appointed by the Governor of Maryland to staggered five-year terms. No member may serve more than two consecutive terms. The Board elects its own President and selects the State Superintendent of Schools for a four-year term, to which he may be reappointed.

Powers of the Board of Education are very broad and include legislative, judicial, and policy-making responsibilities. Its bylaws, rules, and regulations have the full force of the law. It has jurisdiction over questions arising out of administrative problems in the county schools, although Baltimore City schools are generally excluded from its jurisdiction. Its so-called "visitatorial" authority has been acknowledged by the courts to be "of the most comprehensive character." The law of Maryland, said a court decision, "invests the State Board with the last word on any matter concerning educational policy or the administration of the system of public education."

The powers of the Board to supersede county actions are not limited to appeals. A 1962 Attorney General's opinion reads, "In view of the fact that the Court of Appeals of Maryland has declared that the power of the State Board of Education is a visitatorial power of the most comprehensive character, it is clear that whenever the controversy or dispute is one involving proper administration of the public school system of the State, the State Board of Education has the power, authority, and jurisdiction *to supervise and control the management of that public school system* and to correct all abuses of authority and to nullify all irregular procedures."

Nor are the powers of the Board limited to intervention in cases of dispute. It also performs a distinct leadership function in the establishment of education policy through such means as decisions on appeals, bylaws, which have the effect of law, broad guidelines for curriculum, graduation requirements, and teacher-certification requirements.

Its posture of moderation is based on two principles: first, a recognition of the value of Maryland's tradition of local control of schools, and second, a reticence on the part of the State Board to substitute its judgment for that of a local board.

State Superintendent

The State Superintendent serves as Secretary to the Board. His powers are also very broad, with general responsibility to enforce the laws, bylaws, and policies of the Board, and to administer the Department of Education. He is empowered to withhold State funds to a subdivision in cases of violation of the law, and, with the approval of the Governor, may remove for cause any member of any of the 18 gubernatorially appointed local boards. He is solely empowered to promote and improve education in the State through conferences, publications, and other means.

The State Department of Education

The State Department of Education includes a staff of about 900, half of which is attached to the Division of Vocational Rehabilitation. Other divisions of the department are:

Division of Compensatory, Urban, and Supplementary programs
Division of Instruction
Division of Instructional Television
Division of Library Development and Services
Division of Vocational-Technical Education
Division of Administration and Finance
Division of Certification and Accreditation
Division of Research, Evaluation, and Information Systems

The instructional divisions in the department are included in the Bureau of Educational Programs. It includes the Divisions of Instructional Television, Vocational-Technical Education, Instruction (Compensatory, Urban, and Supplementary Programs) and Library Development and Services. Also a part of the Bureau of Educational Programs is the Office of Field Services.

The second bureau, the Bureau of Administrative Services, includes the Divisions of Research, Evaluation, and Information Systems, Certification and Accreditation, Administration and Finance and Vocational Rehabilitation.

Public School Construction

In 1971 the Maryland General Assembly enacted a landmark law for elementary and secondary schools which provided that the State would pay "the costs in excess of federal funds of all (authorized) public school construction projects and public school capital improvements." A companion act authorized a State capital improvement loan of $150 million. Subsequent board authorizations have been as follows: 1972, $300 million; 1973, $220 million.

The effect of this legislation has been to substantially improve school ousing in the State. Beside improved learning environments for chil- ren, the new law goes a long way toward providing equal educational pportunity for all children.

The school construction program is administered by the Maryland nteragency Committee for School Construction. The committee is omposed of the State Superintendent of Schools, who serves as chair- nan; the State Secretary of General Services, and the State Secretary of lanning.

Principal Issues in Public Education in Maryland

The State Board of Education has established eight priority areas in ducation:

1. *Human Relations.* The State Department of Education has estab- shed a human relations unit in the Division of Compensatory, Urban, nd Supplementary Programs. Activities since the inception of the pro- ram have included the development of a Statewide roster of blacks and omen who are eligible for promotion and who wish to be considered or promotional opportunities. The roster was developed in early 1973, time for local superintendents to make selections from it. A report n a follow-up to determine the use to which the roster was put is now eing prepared. The human-relations unit maintains contact with local :hool systems and offers its assistance in racially tense areas.

In 1954, after the Supreme Court Decision on school integration, aryland made good progress when compared to states south of its orders. By 1973 most county schools and staffs were integrated; how- ver, Baltimore City, which was the first political unit in Maryland to ntegrate, by 1973, found itself virtually resegregated—with more than 0 percent black students. It appeared that only a merger of the City nd county schools or exchange programs could create a favorable ra- al balance in the elementary and secondary grades. This appeared nlikely.

2. *Reading Programs.* There is general recognition that only as read- g levels are raised can learning fully take place. Many students are ree, four, and more grades behind in reading levels. A three-faceted ate program seeks to improve this condition. The first facet involves e upgrading or competency in reading instruction. The Board has tablished a new bylaw requiring that most teachers present three edits in reading instruction for their certification. The Department s developed model reading workshops that may be used to gain those edits.

The second facet involves the training of reading volunteers. A umber of workshops have been conducted for trainers of volunteers. any thousands are already at work in classrooms across the State. The ird, and most important facet, is student improvement. In this area the schools of Maryland have instituted a wide range of programs fron tutorial and corrective activities to alternate methods of instruction There has been an increase in the variety of materials, system-wid diagnostic identification, reading clinics, and the "reading break," novel approach in which, at a given signal, everything else in schoo stops and everybody in the school reads material of his or her choic for a half hour.

3. *Early Childhood Education.* Since the enactment of the feder Elementary and Secondary Education Act in the 1960's, a strong lead ership feature in that program has been the concentration of feder Title I funds (initiated 1965) to assist children from poor families doin poorly in school, and supplying them with remedial instruction mate rials, special teachers, and teachers' aides in early grades. The State ha cooperated intensely in the development of a model early childhoo center in Baltimore City. So effective was this unusual center in its fir year of operation that it raised the I.Q.'s of its pupils by an average c 18 points. The Department and the Board were sufficiently impresse with the program that they requested, in the 1973-74 State Budget, a appropriation for the establishment of similar model centers in othe parts of the State. An appropriation of $699,000 was made, and thre such centers are now in operation.

4. *Career Education.* In 1972 the U.S. Office of Education calle attention to the importance of schooling for job preparation. This co cept was to go beyond vocational education: it would begin in th earliest grades with readings and neighborhood visits to places of wor encouraging in the young a respect for those who produce goods an services. The promotional and explanatory ideas of the program we begun in 1973 with a Statewide career education conference, sponsore by the State Department of Education, which was attended by publ school administrators from all 24 subdivisions.

Career education in Maryland is now operating under a five-ye plan that includes long-range goals and strategies. The plan reaches ve young children as well as pre-adolescents, adolescents, young adult and older adults. Among the latter groups, job preparation and r tooling for new jobs are especially important.

5. *Teacher Preparation.* The State Department of Education is inte sively investigating the possibilities in competency-based teacher certi cation. At the same time, it is keeping the public fully abreast of developments. The Department seeks answers to such questions a Which competencies make for good teaching? How is good teachi measured? Who does the measuring? One small indicator here was t result of an intimate (200 teachers) State survey conducted in 1973 which teachers were asked what they considered to be the importa characteristics of a good teacher. The first requirement, as far as tho teachers were concerned, is effective "classroom management." Such

esponse is based on the primary need for discipline before any good eaching can take place. If the same questions were asked of 200 stulents the response might be "knows his subject," "can put it across," and "is interested in students."

6. *Accountability*. The Department is required, under a law enacted n the 1972 General Assembly, to present a report to the Governor and he General Assembly in January, 1975, to show students' progress in at least three subjects: reading, writing, and arithmetic. More and more egislators and taxpayers believe that education cannot continue to take he major share of the Budget unless teachers prove that learning is aking place.

The State Board of Education has approved a design for accountaility and a 27-member Advisory Commission on Accountability has pproved procedures for testing students in the three basic areas, with esults to be included in the January, 1975 Report. But many issues emain unresolved, and accountability as an issue will be with us for years to come.

Accountability in education grows out of the idea that if people n business can measure production and profits, why not the schools? ncreases in reading levels are observable as are skills in arithmetic and pelling. But attitudes are not easily measurable and much teaching in ocial sciences, for example, falls into this category. At any rate, the mphasis on accountability has brought about an educational movenent that seeks to measure success of teaching by fulfillment of objecives and by behavioral changes. Thus a teacher of a unit on consumer ducation would check as to whether his students read labels more arefully, purchase more wisely, and make prudent use of credit.

7. *High School Standards.* The State Board of Education determines vhat courses and how many credits are required before a high school iploma can be awarded. In the main these standards were determined y collegiate associations in the early part of the century to assure reparation for college work. Each full-year course was given one redit, and at different times 15 to 18 credits, known as Carnegie units, vere required.

In 1971 the State Superintendent of Schools appointed a blue-ribon committee to examine the standards for high school graduation nd recommend changes. Their report, together with staff comments, vas presented to the Board in mid-1973.

The proposals in the new standards increase the number of credits equired for graduation from 18 to 20, but broaden considerably the neans by which a local school system might grant credit. For example, he new proposals would make it possible for day high school students o gain as many as six credits by examination only. The standards vould also broaden the work-study program by making possible the ollection of as many as ten credits through work experience. The proposed standards would also make it possible for local school systems to institute one-fourth credit programs. This idea would permit high school credits for a wide variety of "mini-courses," and thus enrich the curriculum.

8. *Data System for the Handicapped.* This System is a unique venture that involves six Maryland State agencies in the collection and correlation of data for handicapped individuals. Its purpose is improved services through better diagnosis of learning deficiencies, and more effective instruction.

Local Boards of Education

The Maryland School Laws require that each county and Baltimore City have its own local school board and professional staff. Because of the emphasis on local educational planning (though increasingly there has been more and more emphasis on State funding) it is at the county (and Baltimore City) level that the exciting work in teaching and administration takes place. Apart from the broad standards set by the State Board of Education and the necessity for State accreditation of secondary schools, a good deal of autonomy is left to the local districts.

Local School Boards. Except for Charles, Montgomery, Prince Georges and Washington Counties, where school board members are elected, the rest are filled by the Governor's appointment. In a number of counties such as Baltimore County, civic groups hold nominating conventions and then submit the names of leading contenders to the Governor, who selects the Board members from nominating lists. In Baltimore City the Mayor appoints school board members.

County Programs. The important aspect of the county system is that each of the 24 political units is large enough to have a workable K-12 school structure. In mid-Atlantic states like Pennsylvania, in New England states like Vermont, or in most midwestern states like Nebraska there are many more school districts, with some of them servicing but elementary, junior high, or senior high schools, and most of them with much smaller enrollments than that of the average Maryland county. Maryland has not had to go through the trauma of consolidating school districts to make them workable. The boundary lines for school districts and county political units are coterminous.

So Maryland county schools can be experimental and each can have educational programs adjusted to its unique needs and environment. Allegany County operates an outdoor school for all sixth-graders at which time students spend one week at campsites learning about nature and man's relationship to his environment. Baltimore County designs all its schools for dual use as educational and recreational centers. Baltimore City has decentralized its school system, creating area superintendents and seeking community participation in regional operations. Calvert County has built a new vocational-technical school center containing shops, laboratories, and classrooms where trades, such as carpentry, boatbuilding, electronics, auto mechanics, cosmetology, and data processing are taught. Caroline County offers vocational education in its comprehensive high schools. Cecil County offers low-fee public subsidized adult education in general and vocational education. Dorchester has embarked on a new multimillion-dollar high school building program. In the 1970's the county has been emphasizing human relations in its desire to further improve racial relations after massive changes in shifting school populations to meet integration requirements. The Queen Annes School Board, in concert with those of Kent, Talbot, and Caroline Counties, established an upper Eastern Shore public regional community college operated by the four boards and known as Chesapeake College, located at Wye Mills. The four counties share in those current operating and capital expenditures not financed by the State.

The Problem of Financing

Valuable as is the concept of county schools, it brings problems. In 1971-72 the average cost per elementary and secondary school student in Maryland schools was $782, but the most affluent county spent $1,009 and the least affluent $563. There is no doubt that despite strong support by the State—indeed, a larger percentage than for any other county—Garrett County cannot begin to reach the average expenditures for schools, let alone the heavier costs. In the light of state court decisions in California and New Jersey, such disparities seem unconstitutional, especially for states like Maryland where its Constitution has made the State responsible for education. Baltimore City has already taken court action, hoping to get full State funding for current school operating expenditures, much as is now true for capital costs. State authorities are sympathetic, but point to the fact that it is fiscally impossible for Maryland to pick up all these costs without taking away from the local units some of the funds it now shares with them, such as those from income taxes. Besides, the State indicates that in a recent Texas case the Supreme Court ruled that such disparities were outside the concern of the federal government. But then the Maryland Court of Appeals might rule otherwise. Some propose that State Lottery monies be used to even out school disparities.

Federal financing has been of significant import to local school systems, particularly funds under the Elementary and Secondary Act, the National Defense Education Act, and the Vocational Education Act. The problem with such funds is that when the federal government pulls out (as it did in the early 1970's, in part, when it replaced some portions of these programs with revenue-sharing allocations to states and local units), then Maryland and its sub-units are in trouble, especially since they would not have budgeted to pick up the needed funds often withdrawn without notice, or at the last minute not appropriated as expected.

The Maryland Non-Public Schools

The 130,000 students enrolled in non-public elementary and secondary schools present some special problems. America has long supported the concept of a choice in schooling—private or public. As school costs have risen, non-public institutions have had to raise tuitions to a point where they could price themselves out of the market for modest income families.

In serious financial trouble, the non-public schools have sought federal funds. However, a series of State and federal court decisions have ruled that such contributions are unconstitutional, particularly in violation of Article I of the U.S. Constitution in respect to separation of church and state. Maryland voters, as late as 1972, turned down a referendum permitting State assistance to each non-public school student. The 1974 Legislature again passed a non-public school aid program—$9.7 million—for textbooks, classroom equipment and transportation, again subject to referendum. The theory behind the proposal was that it would keep the non-public (particularly the Roman Catholic parochial) schools from closing some of their buildings and thus loading more students on public schools, with larger accompanying costs. The 1974 bill will be subject to referendum.

Roman Catholic schools have recently employed more lay teachers because of shortages in teaching brothers and nuns. This practice has brought up costs and in some cases has required consolidation of schools, opposed by many parents who seek schools in the neighborhood.

Despite their financial difficulties, non-public schools have entered upon a period of creative planning and innovative teaching. In general, they have not faced the trauma of most school systems in bringing about racial integration. On the other hand, they have not had the advantages that come to both white and black pupils who learn in an integrated setting, though the private schools—Catholic, Lutheran, Quaker, Episcopal, Jewish, and non-sectarian—have been seeking larger numbers of black students where the religious affiliations apply.

Maryland Higher Education

Maryland's colleges and universities fall into four categories:

The University of Maryland. In all there are 31,000 full-time undergraduates and 6,000 full-time graduate students at the University of Maryland and its five campuses at College Park, Baltimore City, Baltimore County, Eastern Shore (Princess Anne), and University College (all part-time students at off-campus classes at centers throughout the State). There are also 13,500 part-time undergraduates and 4,700 part-time graduates. In all, more than 55,000 study at the university, and that does not include those enrolled in its overseas operations.

About 35,000 of these students are enrolled at the main campus at College Park which has highly diversified undergraduate and graduate programs, including doctoral studies in most fields except those offered at the Baltimore City campus. The Baltimore campus contains the so-called professional schools: medicine, dentistry, pharmacy, law, nursing, community planning, and social work. Other doctoral programs are at College Park. The Eastern Shore and Baltimore County units are primarily undergraduate institutions, though the latter has many graduate programs.

The University of Maryland is governed by a Board of Regents whose members are appointed by the Governor and serve for staggered five-year terms. The Board does not have Constitutional power as many state universities do, but it does have the power granted by the Legislature to use its budgetary allotment independently with discretion. This discretionary power caused much debate in the General Assembly in 1973. Most educators believe that such power is essential to a university that seeks to carry out significant research and to be innovative. The Legislature feels that it ought to be able to subject its expenditures to scrutiny.

The University of Maryland Medical School works directly with University Hospital in Baltimore, which is a teaching institution and thus can arrange for and effectively use internship care. Some exciting research and discoveries have taken place in the schools of engineering at College Park and in the schools of medicine, pharmacy, and dentistry in Baltimore. The university has an excellent reputation throughout the country for its high scholarship standards and its effective teaching.

The Public State Colleges. There are eight of these, counting the University of Baltimore, which officially becomes a public institution in 1975. During the 1920's most of these colleges were two- or three-year teachers' training schools. In the 1940's they offered baccalaureate degrees in education and in the 1960's they became general colleges. In the 1970's they introduced graduate work at the master's level. The State colleges are situated at Bowie, Frostburg, Towson, Baltimore City (Coppin, Morgan, and the University of Baltimore), Salisbury, and St. Marys (which is semi-independent and has its own Board).

The Board of Trustees of the State colleges consists of eight members appointed by the Governor, for nine-year terms, and the State Superintendent of Schools. The Board and its staff seek to coordinate the work of all the State colleges, to set policies concerning admissions, curriculum, salaries, graduation requirements, and current operating and capital programs. The Board seeks to avoid unnecessary duplication of offerings among the State colleges.

Each of the institutions is encouraged to major in different programs. Thus, for example, Towson offers health programs, University of Baltimore law and transportation, Morgan urban studies, and Coppin special education. All offer education majors since they were started (all but Morgan, University of Baltimore, and St. Marys) as teacher training colleges. They all also offer general education studies.

About 21,500 full-time undergraduates study at the eight State colleges, as do 8,000 part-time undergraduates, counting the University of Baltimore. Towson has the largest enrollment, 10,200, and Morgan the second largest, 4,500. The State colleges in 1974 also had 4,200 full and part-time graduate students, with 1,400 more counting the University of Baltimore, not yet in the system.

The State colleges are all of good quality, as attested by their full accreditation by the Middle States Association of Secondary Schools and Colleges and their reputation among college educators. The predominantly white schools, such as Towson, Frostburg, Salisbury, St. Marys, and the University of Baltimore, aim to increase their black enrollment, and the predominantly black colleges (Morgan, Coppin, and Bowie) seek more whites. Each segment aims to break away from racially fixed enrollments that go back to the segregated period, previous to the 1954 Supreme Court decision. A State Affirmative Action Plan proposed to the federal government in 1973 has as its goal better racial balance in each of the eight institutions.

The Public Community Colleges. These institutions represent the fastest growing segment of Maryland higher education. The existence of 16 different community colleges places one in virtually each county (with the exceptions of Carroll, Calvert, and St. Marys) on the Western Shore. The sixteen Maryland community colleges include those located in Allegany, Anne Arundel, Cecil, Charles, Frederick, Garrett, Hagerstown (Washington County), Harford, Howard, Montgomery, and Prince Georges counties. Three in Baltimore County are Catonsville, Dundalk, and Essex. A central Eastern Shore college is Chesapeake, located at Wye Mills, in Queen Annes, and serving that county as well as Kent, Talbot, and Caroline. Baltimore City has a large community college.

The first Maryland community colleges were opened in 1935, but the movement did not gain momentum until after World War II. A series of State commission reports and State-aid support passed by the Legislature led to rapid growth of these schools. From a full-time enrollment of 2,361 in 1960, the Maryland community colleges burgeoned to 23,301 in 1972. The part-time enrollment jumped from 3,109 in 1960 to 28,963 in 1972. The colleges approached a total enrollment of about 60,000 in the mid-1970's. This meant that the 16 two-year colleges had about twice as many undergraduate students—full- and part-time—as the public State colleges and slightly more than the University of Maryland.

The phenomenal growth of the two-year colleges is due to the fact that they offer education close to home. Their career programs in health fields, public service, technical education, business, and general occupations offer opportunities for well-paying jobs immediately after graduation. Their good standing with the State colleges and the University of Maryland, as well as their full accreditation by the Middle States Association of Secondary Schools and Colleges, afford easy transfer, with credit, to the third year of higher educational institutions.

The 16 community colleges are governed by local boards of trustees with members appointed by the Governor, except for Baltimore City where the Mayor makes the appointments. The local boards determine general policies, including curriculum, salaries, and plant development. They also appoint the presidents of the colleges. In a few cases the smaller community colleges are governed by the same boards that control the elementary and secondary schools. This was once true of all the community colleges, but in 1968 the Legislature revised Article 77A of the Annotated Code to permit and encourage separate boards. Chesapeake College is governed by representatives from the four cooperating counties. Since the community colleges in Maryland are controlled locally, not by the State, the boards of trustees hold the final answers in many cases.

Coordinating the efforts of all 16 community colleges is the State Board for Community Colleges. Its members are appointed by the Governor for six-year terms. The Board establishes general policies, prepares and maintains guidelines for recommending State financial aid for current operations and capital costs, must approve the building of new community colleges, and establishes guidelines and long-range plans for a State system of community colleges.

Maryland Private Colleges. Three private two-year colleges and 20 (not counting the University of Baltimore) private four-year colleges and universities are recognized in this category by the Maryland Council on Higher Education. In 1972 these colleges had a full-time enrollment of about 14,000 undergraduate and about 3,500 graduate students. In addition they had a part-time enrollment of about 13,000 students.

The private colleges divide themselves into a number of categories: (1) Those like the Baltimore College of Commerce and the Capitol Institute of Technology, which are proprietary, profit-making schools of longtime reputation, specializing in special fields; (2) those like Mount St. Mary's Seminary, Baltimore Hebrew College, Ner Israel Rabbinical College, Washington Theological Coalition, and Washington Bible College that are primarily schools for religious studies; (3) those that had their origins as church-related colleges, but in varying degrees have become general schools serving students of various faiths—Loyola, Mount St. Mary's, College of Notre Dame, Villa Julie, Western Maryland, and Hood Colleges; (4) the nondemoninational schools that may, like Goucher, once have been church-related, or, like Johns Hopkins, never church-related. Some others in this category are Bay College, St. John's College, and Washington College; and (5) the specialized endowed nonprofit colleges like the Maryland Institute College of Art and the Peabody Conservatory of Music.

Washington College in Chestertown, Md. is the nation's 11th oldest institution of higher education. A private liberal arts college, it enrolls about 900 men and women, granting A.B., B.S. and M.A. degrees. (Photo by William A. Coleman, Chestertown)

All private colleges are accredited by the State Department of Education and most have been accredited by regional agencies. Johns Hopkins University, with an enrollment of about 10,000, has an international reputation, particularly in public health and medical education where its students, from all over the world, learn and carry out their studies in cooperation with the Johns Hopkins Hospital. The private colleges in Maryland are of high standing and nationally recognized as being leaders in their fields.

Financial problems have plagued most of the private colleges in recent years. Mount St. Agnes and St. Joseph's Colleges were forced to close their doors, and the University of Baltimore received permission from the Legislature to become a State college in 1975. A number of court cases were decided against full aid for the private Maryland colleges. The Maryland Council for Higher Education has studied their plight and recognizes that if more private colleges close, an even greater burden will fall upon the State to support them.

In 1974 the State contributed $200 for each graduate of an Associate in Arts degree program and $500 for each graduate of a baccalaureate and a graduate degree program. The money goes to the colleges from which the students graduated. In addition, most State scholarships can be applied to private, as well as public institutions. The private colleges would like the State aid increased to include support based on attendance rather than graduates. They succeeded in getting the 1974 Legislature to pass a bill giving just such assistance—$234 aid for each student enrolled. Religious colleges are not eligible for State aid, but the question of church-related schools is in court.

There is no doubt that the private colleges make a very important contribution toward preparing young and older citizens for occupational fulfillment and for fuller participation in American society. Their history and traditions go back many years—St. John's to the colonial period—and they once served most of Maryland's college student bodies. As school costs and tuitions went up in private colleges, students turned to the public institutions. The State needs to find a way to keep these colleges viable and effective in a matrix that acknowledges the importance of both public and private education.

Maryland Council for Higher Education. Seeking to coordinate all higher education in Maryland is the Board and staff of the Council for Higher Education. The Council came into existence in 1963 to bring order into the higher educational spectrum. Increasingly it has been given more power to set guidelines for avoiding duplication of offerings by the various public institutions and to establish the province of each level of the spectrum—the community colleges, the State colleges, and the University of Maryland. Representatives from these three public levels, as well as from the private colleges, are on the Board whose members are appointed by the Governor. Most Board members are lay persons.

The coordination of Maryland higher education is not an easy task since, until recent years, each institution grew without regard to the total needs of the State. The task of the Council is to create coordination without bringing about authoritarian control.

Financial Support. Except for funds from tuition and federal monies, the University of Maryland and the State colleges are fully supported through the State Budget. The public community colleges are supported for operating costs by this formula: 50 percent State aid, 28 percent local aid, and 22 percent tuition. Local communities may and often do raise their own contributions to keep tuition low. Capital costs for community colleges are supported by this formula: 50 percent State and 50 percent local (county) contribution—after deducting federal contributions under the Higher Education Facilities Act. Regional colleges, like Chesapeake, receive an additional 25 percent in State aid for capital costs, and beginning colleges with small enrollments get additional State assistance for current operating costs.

Studies show that Maryland contributes for higher education but $7.85 per $1,000 in personal income. The nation has an average of $9.03 per $1,000, so that while in total contributions Maryland's expenditures for higher education appear to be very good, the State ranks far below the average in terms of its wealth. Indeed, for the southern educational region, Maryland ranks last.

State scholarship funding is one of the controversial areas. For example, Maryland was almost alone in 1974 in having scholarships, amounting to $2.5 million, that are distributed by State Senators. A 1974 bill defeated in the Legislature, would have moved the funds to a general scholarship fund distributed according to need by college financial aid officers.

The Governor's Commission on the Structure and Governance of Education in Maryland

In 1973 the Governor appointed a Commission to look at all of education—elementary, secondary, and higher—with the view toward creating better coordination, recommendations for revisions in structure and governance, and improvements in financing the costs. The Commission is expected to complete its work by 1975. Its findings may lead to a secretariat, or cabinet-level structure, binding together all levels of education and possibly including ancillary activities such as the Maryland libraries.

It is obvious that the State cannot continue to function without greater articulation and coordination. The plethora of boards and the separation of county and State contributions often create problems. As the State contributes more to the support of private colleges, they, too, will need to be brought into the overall planning. The great problem will be to keep the curriculum decision-making at the local level (which has been the strength of Maryland's educational system) and at the same time to coordinate financial and other requirements. Some other states have turned to a commissioner (secretariat) form of State control, and this may be the answer.

State Division of Library Development and Services

The Legislature has recognized on numerous occasions the importance of State support for library services. Article 77 of the Annotated Code clearly states that "Public Library resources and services are essential components of the educational system. They stimulate awareness and understanding of critical social issues, and assist individuals in reaching their highest potential for self-development." With this philosophy as a backdrop the Division was placed in the State Department of Education with a Director at its head and charged with coordinating cooperative efforts of local libraries and administering State and federal funds for public county (and Baltimore City) libraries. The Division is also charged with setting standards for librarians.

Maryland Advisory Council on Libraries. The Council consists of 11 members including representation from the Council on Higher Education, Baltimore's Enoch Pratt Free Library Board, the Maryland Library Association, the School of Library at the University of Maryland, and seven appointees of the Governor. The Council advises the Division staff and the State Department of Education on the needs of libraries in Maryland.

State Library Resource Center. The Central Branch of the Enoch Pratt Free Library, in Baltimore, has been declared the State Library Resource Center in order to supply libraries throughout Maryland with specialized research and reference materials. State funds support these activities.

Regional Resource Centers. Library systems are encouraged to cooperate in terms of three or more county systems—especially those outside metropolitan areas—in the organization of Regional Resource Centers. These Centers would arrange for inter-library loans, cooperative consultant services, and joint in-service training programs.

Boards of Trustees. Though the State makes significant contributions toward support of county libraries, the desire is to keep service under local control, meeting grass-roots desires. Yet the State has set standards for the work of local library boards of trustees.

Funding. In addition to local appropriations, county (and Baltimore City) public libraries are supported by State funds under a formula developed by the Legislature. State aid for programs carried out by local libraries amounted to $2 million in fiscal 1973. The aid is administered under an equalization formula that in general rewards the poorer counties to a greater degree than the wealthier political units. All participating counties must contribute local funds amounting to $1.50 per capita before being eligible for State aid. Entering into the final State aid distributions are such factors as assessed evaluation of property in the county and matching funds contributed by the political unit. For example, in fiscal '73, Baltimore City received $733,000 in State aid;

(Top) The Merrymobile has a special summer schedule to take books to parts of Baltimore County somewhat removed from the branches and not on the bookmobile routes. The truck is painted brilliant yellow, with orange, red and blue lettering. (Bottom) When the candle is blown out the Lullaby Story Hour at the Baltimore County Public Library is over and everyone is ready for bed.

Baltimore County received $320,000; and Montgomery received but $206,000 in State funds; while Prince Georges received $454,000. Many counties contributed more local funds than the minimum amounts required by the $1.50-per-capita formula. Baltimore City contributed more than $7.3 million in local funds for programs at its Enoch Pratt Free Library.

State funds for capital costs (construction) are distributed under a somewhat similar formula, with the poorer local units receiving greater amounts of State aid than the amounts they contribute and the wealthier units in an opposite position.

County Libraries

Outside the direct province of the State Division of Library Development and Services exist the local libraries whose histories in some cases predate that of the State system. It is at these institutions that the direct contact with borrowers of books takes place.

The library service of Baltimore City is one of the nation's finest. It consists of a central library, two bookmobiles and about 30 branches located in various sections of the city. The system is known as the Enoch Pratt Free Library, named after the Baltimore City philanthropist who contributed funds to establish six branches and an additional $1 million for their maintenance. Another philanthropist, Andrew Carnegie, gave the city $500,000 for additional branches. The Enoch Pratt bequest provides the library system with an annual income, which is supplemented by appropriations from the City. The library service is supervised by a non-political board of trustees. In 1932 Baltimore built a beautiful new Central Library Building at a cost of about $3,000,000. Here many thousands of books are housed under the most modern conditions.

The Prince Georges County Memorial Library has a collection of more than one million books, records, and films. Now in its 28th year of community service, the system continues to expand. Its overall circulation figure during one recent 12-month period was 3.5 million books, records, and films at the 17 branch libraries. New libraries are on the drawing boards for Fairmount Heights, Clinton, Beltsville, Accokeek, Palmer Park, Hillcrest Heights, and Glenarden.

Once merely a storehouse of written materials, the branch library in Prince Georges County has emerged in recent years as a center of community activity in the area it serves.

All types of civic and community meetings take place regularly in the libraries, and art exhibits, lectures, and special showings of everything from handicrafts to antiques are scheduled as frequently as possible. The weekly film programs, all family oriented, are well attended, as are children's story hours and a variety of other cultural and educational offerings in Prince Georges County.

Montgomery County has about 20 branch libraries within its borders, and bookmobiles serve anyone who lives or works in the County. A nontransferable identification card can be used at any county library. Library advisory and reference service is available at all libraries. Framed prints may be borrowed from the Rockville and Chevy Chase Libraries; Braille and large-type and talking books may be borrowed from the room for the visually handicapped at Davis Library. Reservations for books, periodicals, and recordings may be made at the branches or administrative offices, located at Davis Memorial Library; reservations for films and projection equipment may be made at the administrative offices.

The Washington County Free Library consists of the Central Library at Hagerstown serving by contract six independent branch libraries at Blue Ridge Summit, Boonsboro, Hancock, Sharpsburg, Smithsburg, and Williamsport; two bookmobiles; and three book deposit stations at Brook Lane, Funkstown, and Keedysville. The library contains approximately 200,000 volumes with an annual acquisition of about 18,000.

Books and other publications may be borrowed, without charge from any public library in Maryland and returned to any other public library in the State, under the terms of the Maryland State Library Network. A borrower must have a borrower's card from his own county library system which may be used in any other system in the State. There are no restrictions on the use of any public library's reference rooms.

Chapter 14

HUMAN RELATIONS AND COMMISSION ON THE AGING

Though Maryland established by General Assembly law an Interracial Commission as early as 1927, the viewpoint was mainly that of benevolence toward the "Welfare of the colored people in the State . . . " In 1943 the Commission's name was changed to "Commission for Colored Problems," with the connotation seeming to be that the black citizens brought about the difficulties.

The years following World War II brought accelerated concern for all Americans since representatives of various racial, ethnic, and religious groups had given their lives for their country. Thus, 1945 found the nation looking at its human relations problems more sympathetically.

The 1954 U.S. Supreme Court decision in regard to school segregation upset the old belief that separate schools for black and white students were permissible if the costs and treatment were equal. The Court's decision, based on the 14th Amendment, made it clear that education could not be equal if separate. From that day on the walls separating black citizens from whites in all categories—jobs, housing, voting, use of public accommodations, and other restrictions, were beginning to crumble.

The federal Civil Rights Acts of 1960 and 1964 extended the protection to include banning of discrimination in employment because of race, color, religion, sex, or national origin. In 1967 Congress extended the protection further by passing the Age Discrimination of Employment Act which states that age (40 to 65 years) should not be a barrier to getting jobs or being promoted.

The Maryland Commission on Human Relations

While the federal government was pursuing fair employment practice laws and other human relations protections in the 1950's and 1960's, the states themselves began to pass more protective measures. In 1951 the Maryland Commission's name was again changed, this time to Commission on Interracial Problems and Relations. The benevolent phrase for the "welfare of the colored people" was deleted in 1960. In 1963 the first Maryland public accommodations law was passed. Though it was not a Statewide law, the power of enforcement was placed in the hands of the Commission. In 1965 enforcement of the State's new Fair Employment Practice Law was a requirement of the Commission. In 1968 the Commission's name was changed yet again to "Commission on Human Relations," indicating that it now had responsibilities for more than racial injustices: discrimination in sex, age, color, religion, and national origin had joined race. Then, too, discrimination cases had been broadened to include employment and housing (including financing). By 1971 the Commission had strong investigatory and enforcement powers in those two areas. In addition, the Commission had the right to study and investigate community relations under its broad power "to promote in every way possible the betterment of human relations." It does not have enforcement power in this area.

The Commission and the Staff. The Commission on Human Relations consists of 12 members appointed by the Governor for six-year terms. By law, members must represent different parts of the State. The Commission has the authority to make such surveys and studies concerning human relations conditions and problems as it may determine, and to promote in every way possible the betterment of human relations. Whenever any problem of racial discrimination arises, the Commission may immediately hold an investigatory hearing in the very place where the problem exists.

The executive director is the chief officer and has the responsibility of carrying out the policies set by the Commission. Staff members have responsibilities of carrying out compliance investigations and conciliations, community relations activities directed toward solving problems, mediating complaints, decreasing tension, and providing information. They prepare public hearings, make reports and studies, and suggest legislation.

Relations with Federal Government. Since a complainant may file his or her charges on job discrimination with both the U.S. Equal Employment Opportunity Commission and the Maryland Human Relations Commission, the two groups often work in tandem. There is usually coordination in the processing of such cases.

The federal government has funded a number of the Maryland Commission's activities. For example, since 1969 federal grants have supported an Affirmative Enforcement Project designed to focus on discrimination in employment. The project includes not only hiring practices, but injustices that may come about due to testing, seniority rules, and termination procedures. The Commission has the power of affirmative enforcement.

Fair Housing Law Enforcement. In 1971 the Commission was given authority by the General Assembly to enforce the law on Discrimination in Housing. The law provides that discrimination because of race, color, religion, or national origin by any person having the right to sell, rent, lease, control, construct, or manage any dwelling, or such discriminatory acts by any agent or employee of such person, shall be unlawful.

Furthermore, violations in Maryland against the added federal laws on discrimination in housing, as stated in the Civil Rights Act of 1968 (Title VIII), are enforced by the State Commission on Human Relations. This enables the Commission to seek restraining orders and preliminary injunctions in those complaints where it believes such civil action is advisable to prevent irreparable harm to the complaining parties.

In recent years the Commission has handled more than 200 cases annually dealing with violations of fair housing practices.

Employment Practices. The area of employment practices represents the largest case load. In any one year nearly 1,000 cases are handled. As stated earlier in this section, much of the work in this area is done in consort with the federal Equal Employment Opportunity Commission.

Most Women Work Because of Economic Need

(WOMEN IN THE LABOR FORCE, BY MARITAL STATUS, MARCH 1971)

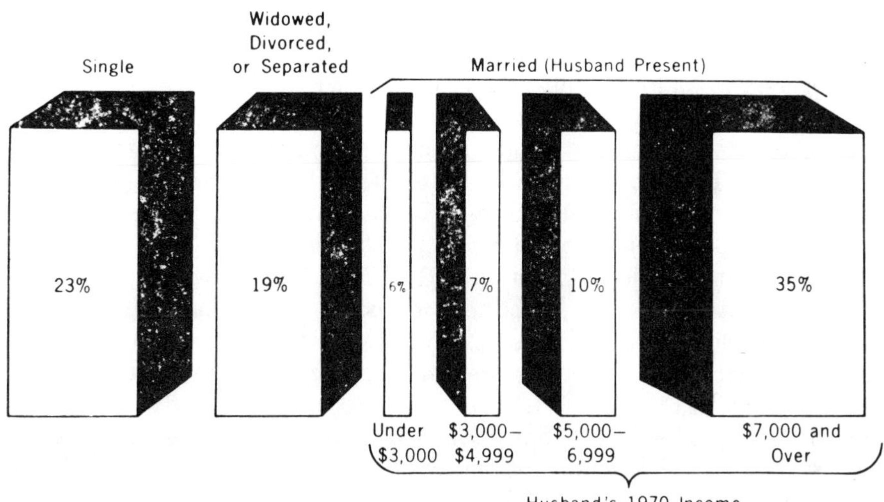

Source: Prepared by the Women's Bureau, Employment Standards Administration, from data published by the Bureau of Labor Statistics, U.S. Department of Labor.

An interesting sidelight on the nature of job-discrimination complaints lies in the fact that in fiscal 1972 about one-third of them—322—had "sex" as a basis. The largest number—605—still were concerned with "race." There were fewer than 25 in the categories of religion, age, and national origin.

Community Relations Division. While the Commission has no enforcement power in the community relations area, it does have study and investigatory powers. In a typical recent year the Commission has investigated racial practices in a Maryland college, the treatment by a proprietary business school of welfare students compared to paying pupils, complaints of racial discrimination in a county high school and by a county school system, and complaints of brutality by members of a county police department. Most of these complaints were settled by discussions with the respondents and by plans mutually worked out.

More recently the Commission has cooperated with other human relations agencies such as the National Urban League, the National Association for the Advancement of Colored People, and the National Conference of Christians and Jews in setting up forums and workshops to improve community feelings and police relations. These steps are preventive in nature.

Local Human Relations Commissions. Most counties (and Baltimore City) have human relations laws and commissions of their own. Where these local laws are in the same field as Statewide laws, the requirements can be more severe, but not less so than those of the State.

Because of the nature of Baltimore City's population—about 50 percent black and 50 percent white—its interracial problems are likely to be more acute and more sensitive. In 1972, for example, 183 new cases were certified and 248 carried over from previous years by Baltimore's Commission. An interesting court case won by the Baltimore City Community Relations Commission was that requiring a Baltimore newspaper to stop separate listings of job opportunities for "males" and "females." The Commission contended that such procedure in the newspaper's classified advertising was discriminatory against women. The newspaper changed its long-held practice in 1973.

The Baltimore City Community Relations Commission has been effective in working with factories, industrial plants, and hospitals to change employment practices that find few black workers at the management level. CRC operates a "rumor clinic" 24 hours a day, seven days a week. For example, in 1972, at the time of a riot at the Baltimore City Jail, the clinic kept families of inmates and others who called up to date, and probably kept matters from boiling over. About 12,000 calls reached the clinic in 1972.

County human relations commissions seek to settle problems at the preventive level. Complaints are more likely to be settled by conciliation between complainant and respondent than by court action.

Progress and the Future. Maryland has come a long way in race relations in the last 20 years. Where once there were separate schools and exclusion of blacks from police work, fire protection, health, and other governmental pursuits, the numbers employed in these fields now are closer to their proportion of the general population. Moreover, there are at least some important beginnings in the matter of blacks reaching leadership levels. In private industry, progress has been slower, but federal, State, and county equal and fair employment laws are causing some headway.

In housing, too, no longer are black citizens relegated to central city areas. Yet, far too few housing opportunities are available for blacks of modest income in suburban areas. In community relations there is more consciousness of the need for improved black-white contacts, but progress is slow, except in education where racial integration at the elementary and secondary levels has been successful. At collegiate levels, progress is beginning to take place.

The riots of 1968, particularly those in Baltimore, Cambridge and Washington, brought inestimable damage and an awakening to all Marylanders. It became evident that there was much that yet needed to happen in race relations. As the State approaches the last quarter of the 20th century, there is enough good will throughout Maryland to build firmer bridges. But polarization of both races was heightened by the riots. A good deal of mistrust is present on both sides, and old sores still fester.

The structures are present in Maryland for better race relations. As a border state its practices were never as severe as in the South nor were the races as detached as in the North. Maryland could be a beacon to the country.

Commission on Negro History and Culture

By General Assembly action the Commission, of nine members appointed by the Governor, was created (first in 1969, revamped in 1971) to bring about a better understanding and knowledge of Negro history and culture. It is to make recommendations to the Legislature and the Governor. The Commission is to unearth, preserve, and collect pertinent historical data and examine the possibilities for the establishment of a Museum of Negro History and Culture.

It is increasingly evident that laws, such as those in human relations, and court decisions, such as the U.S. Supreme Court action on school desegregation, are basic to the furtherance of civil liberties. But along with the strong arm of government for immediate change must be the role of education to change attitudes and destroy stereotypes. This is where commissions such as this one on Negro history can create changes by bringing into the pages of schoolbooks the role of black citizens in Maryland's development.

Black Marylanders

Maryland black citizens have long played an important role in State and national history. Unfortunately, most history books have ignored the contributions of black Americans. It is for this reason that the author of this book deals very briefly with six famous black Marylanders. This short treatment is given for the purpose of interesting readers in exploring further in this field and in filling a gap left by historians. Many more black Marylanders made their imprint on our State, but these six are illustrative of how much we all—black and white people—owe to these illustrious people.

Those who choose to learn more about this fascinating subject should contact the Baltimore offices of the Commission on Negro History and Culture, the Maryland Historical Society, the National Urban League, and the National Association for the Advancement of Colored People.

Benjamin Banneker was born a free Negro on November 9, 1731, near the present Ellicott City, Maryland. He attended country school where he learned to read and write and later became interested in mathematics, astronomy, and surveying. He made friends with his Quaker neighbors, who helped him with his studies. As a young man he made the first striking clock ever made in America of all parts produced in this country.

When the Revolutionary War was over and the new Republic needed to plan the capital city of Washington, Banneker, with his knowledge of surveying, was asked to help plan the District of Columbia under the guidance of Pierre Charles L'Enfant, the French engineer. Work started in 1791 and the federal government moved to Washington in 1800. The Library of Congress contains some of the official writings of Banneker.

Many schools in Maryland are named after Banneker, and there is a memorial in his honor in Baltimore County. His gravesite is unmarked.

To a famous black Marylander has come one of the highest honors to be reached by any American—a seat on the United States Supreme Court. *Thurgood Marshall* was born in 1908 in Baltimore, where he attended public school and graduated from Douglass High School which by the mid-1920's had become one of the secondary schools highly respected for its scholarship standards. The future Associate Justice Marshall graduated from Lincoln University in 1929 and applied to the University of Maryland Law School in Baltimore, where he was refused admission because of race. He then entered Howard University Law School in Washington, where he came under the influence of Charles Huston, a brilliant scholar who sought to make Howard a great institution for Negro lawyers so that one of these days the unfair Supreme Court decision of *Plessy v. Ferguson* in 1894 would be reversed and the whole concept of "separate but equal" school accommodations would fall.

Huston's followers were called "social engineers." Mr. Marshall graduated from Howard in 1933 and two years later won the famous Donald Murray case which forced the University of Maryland Law School to accept black students. Mr. Marshall became the legal counsel for the National Association for the Advancement of Colored People in 1935 and won 32 of 35 cases before the highest court, leading to his supreme victory on May 17, 1954, when the Supreme Court agreed with him and a host of other black and white psychologists, sociologists, anthropologists, and psychiatrists that separate could not be equal. The so-called "integration decision" meant that Maryland schools, like others in border and southern states, could no longer be segregated. Integration of schools later led to other social, recreational, and political reforms for black citizens.

Thurgood Marshall was appointed a judge of the U.S. Court of Appeals by President Kennedy in 1961, became Solicitor General in 1965, and was elevated to the Supreme Court by President Lyndon B. Johnson on October 2, 1967.

Judge Thurgood Marshall of the U.S. Supreme Court.

Harriet Tubman was born a slave in Dorchester County, Maryland, about 1823. After numerous rebellions against her bondage, she escaped to the north and became a "conductor" on the Underground Railway, a planned route over which slaves were guided by white and black abolitionists to free spots in the north and as far as Canada. Miss Tubman helped hundreds to freedom, many finding refuge in Canada, which did not permit slavery after 1833. Because of her heroic exploits, she was known as the "Moses" of her people and many rewards were placed for the return of the 300 slaves she helped set free.

During the Civil War Harriet Tubman became a nurse for the Union armies and cared for the sick and wounded at many camps. On some occasions she even led black troops on raids against Confederate strongholds. She lived to be nearly 90 at her post-Civil War home in Auburn, New York, where her work is memorialized. A monument in the Auburn town square recounts the deeds of Harriet Tubman during the period from about 1850-1913, the date of her death.

Josiah Henson was born a slave in Charles County, Maryland, in 1789. After suffering cruel treatment on a farm near Rockville, Maryland, he escaped and was instrumental in the escape of more than 100 other slaves. Henson established a community for fugitive slaves in Canada, and he himself became a Methodist minister and mill owner. His life on the Rockville farm and his exploits gained the attention of Harriet Beecher Stowe, who was attracted to his selflessness and deep religious convictions and drew from him the theme of Uncle Tom for her classic *Uncle Tom's Cabin.* Though Henson, unlike Mrs. Stowe's character, was not bound to slavery in the deep South, and, also unlike Uncle Tom, he did learn to read and write and, indeed, left a fascinating autobiography.

Frederick Douglass seated at desk at Cedar Hill. (From *Pictorial History of the Negro,* Hughes, L. and Meltzer, M., Crown Publishers, Inc., New York, N.Y., 1956)

Frederick Douglass was born in 1817 in Talbot County, Maryland, of a white father and a black mother; yet he was classified as a slave and raised by his black grandmother. His name for the first years of his life was Frederick Bailey, and his earliest years as a child were spent in Baltimore. After a number of bitter experiences as a slave worker on both Maryland plantations and in Baltimore's shipyards, Mr. Bailey escaped to New York, where he became an abolitionist and active in the Anti-Slavery Society.

In 1841 after changing his last name to Douglass—and by this time he had become a tall, handsome young man—he teamed up with the white abolitionist leader, William Lloyd Garrison, to become an orator for freedom. His preachments included the thought that "no man can be truly free whose liberty is dependent upon the thought, feeling, and action of others." Through his Rochester, New York newspaper, *The North Star Douglass*, he cried out against slavery as he did throughout the North and on various trips to England.

When the Civil War broke out, Douglass counseled President Lincoln and helped him recruit troops—in all, more than 200,000 black troops served in the Union forces—including his own sons. When the war was over, Douglass became a leader in the Republican Party and held many posts, including United States Marshal and Minister to Haiti. His autobiography, *Life and Times*, is full of homespun wit and philosophy such as his belief that what the black man fundamentally wants is a "chance to stand on his own legs, socially, economically, politically and educationally." He died in 1895 and the house where he last lived, namely, the Frederick Douglass Home at 14th and W Streets, S.E., in Washington, D.C., is a public shrine to his memory.

Matthew Alexander Henson, a black explorer, was born in Charles County, Maryland in 1866. He was with Admiral Robert E. Peary when he reached the North Pole on April 7, 1909. After Peary determined

Matthew A. Henson who accompanied Admiral Robert E. Peary, renowned explorer, on numerous expeditions. On April 7, 1908 Peary, Henson and four Eskimos approached the precise point of the North Pole. Admiral Peary asked Mr. Henson to place the American Flag on the spot. (Courtesy Dr. Herbert M. Frisby, Chairman of the Henson Society)

the exact place of the Pole with his sextant, he then asked Henson to place the American Flag on the spot—which would make Henson actually the first man to reach the Pole.

This was not Henson's first exploration with Peary. In 1887 Henson accompanied the admiral on his mission to survey canal sites in Nicaragua. In 1891 the two were together in the unsuccessful attempt to reach the North Pole through Greenland, by use of dog sleds. Henson became very friendly with the Eskimos, who were enchanted by an American of such dark color. Again in 1901, 1902, and 1905 Peary met with continued failure to reach the Pole—each time with Henson beside him.

More than 15 years after the death of Henson in 1955, the State of Maryland officially recognized this great man by placing a bronze plaque in the State House in Annapolis in his honor.

Commission on the Aging

In 1973 the Commission on Aging was removed from Employment and Social Services and became an independent agency. Moreover, in 1973 the Governor pledged that a large portion of the State Lottery profits (25 percent) would be set aside for aid to the aging. There was some talk that in 1974 the Commission might become a cabinet-level secretariat.

These actions were symbolic of the fact that while the older citizen deserved special attention, his treatment was not to be that of the welfare client. In the first place, most senior citizens could manage their financial problems, albeit they were far from affluent. Secondly, they did not want to be thought of as unemployed or unemployable. Many past 65 were vigorous and were neither willing nor required to be put on the shelf.

True, a large number of the aging were in need of health care, and it was in order for the Department of Health and Mental Hygiene to give special attention to their requirements as related to nursing homes (see chapter No. 11). But health care is intimately related to economic security, housing, and social needs. For such reasons, the concept of a separate cabinet-level secretariat dealing with aging is likely to attract increasing attention.

The Commission on the Aging consists of 17 members appointed by the Governor. They include the Secretaries of Health and Mental Hygiene, Employment and Social Services, and State Planning, as well as the State Superintendent of Schools, members of the State Senate and House of Delegates, authorities on aging, and representatives of labor and medical societies. The Commission is responsible for developing the welfare of older persons, particularly as it relates to the interpretations of the U.S. Older Americans Act of 1965.

Maryland's 300,000 citizens aged 65 and over represent 7.4 percent of the total State population. This is a significant rise over 5.9 percent in 1930.

Florida has the highest ratio of older citizens to total population, 14.5 percent, a record attained because many senior citizens go there in retirement. Iowa with 12.4 percent and Nebraska with 12.4 percent are second and third because longevity records are high in those states.

In 1870 the Census showed that 2.9 percent of all Americans were 65 years of age and older. In 1970 the figures for the country were 9.9 percent which shows that Maryland, with a rapidly growing population, tends to bring young people into the State while many older ones leave after retirement. But about one-third of a million older citizens remain in Maryland.

Economics and Financial Needs. A 1971 study by the Maryland Commission on Aging shows that while 10 percent of all families had incomes below the "poverty level," 16 percent of the families with heads 65 or older were at this level. The disparity was greatest between the unrelated individual black male, under 65, whose income placed 36.1 percent at the "poverty level"; while for the same group at 65 years or over, the percentage was 70; moreover, retirement, pensions, and social security failed to meet the economic and financial needs of the older citizens.

Health Care. Health care for the elderly is treated in the chapter on Health and Mental Hygiene; yet some treatment is in order in this discussion. An estimated 55,000 persons in Maryland's population have some degree of restricted mobility; one out of six older persons. The three leading causes of death among older Maryland citizens are diseases of heart, cancer, and cerebrovascular illnesses. Mental illness is prevalent to a high degree and one-third of all such patients institutionalized are in this age group, though the older citizens make up but 7.4 percent of the total population. The Commission studies show that public and private health-care facilities and governmental financial-aid programs such as Medicare and Medicaid do not meet the health requirements since the facilities are not geared to needs and payments are restricted. Too often the facilities are terminal institutional. Some pharmacies do give special rates to older persons.

Housing, Food, Jobs, Social and Cultural Needs. Housing is a special problem for the elderly. Some religious and racial groups have built apartments, with federal subsidies, for older citizens of modest income. Public housing authorities have built low rental apartments for poor, older family heads of households and individuals. But many older family heads prefer to stay in their homes for which they have saved many years. Fortunately, Maryland and its local units give tax credits to the needy elderly. For example, in Baltimore City, if an older citizen has an annual income of less than $5,000, then 50 percent of his assessable valuation is exempt from taxes, up to an allowance of

$4,000. Moreover, Baltimore City, under an urban homestead program, sells vacant homes, acquired by the City because of delinquent taxes, for one dollar to any person who will renovate the premises. The problem with the plan is that the elderly cannot, personally, renovate these rundown homes and usually do not have the funds to pay.

Food requirements are difficult for the elderly who are not institutionalized. Maryland has many "Meals on Wheels" programs handled by volunteers and hospital groups. The charge is low and nonprofit. In early 1974 the Maryland Commission on Aging received a $1.4 million federal grant to provide 3,400 hot meals a day to elderly in the State. Priority would be placed on low-income elderly. One of the important needs of the elderly is to get a part-time job. The country is losing the skills and abilities of people who can contribute a good deal.

Recreational and educational leaders are giving greater attention to the needs of the elderly. Public recreational programs in the counties and Baltimore City have senior citizen activities. A number of colleges exempt the elderly from tuition and encourage them to take classes with persons of all ages. More and more there is recognition that the over-65 citizen has just as many interests as the younger person, and that most are physically and mentally able to participate in a wide range of pursuits. Private, especially religious, groups arrange programs in cooperation with church and synagogue.

Transportation is an acute problem for the elderly. Some municipal transit lines, like the one in Baltimore City, provide lower fares. Volunteer groups often arrange car pools.

The Future. Just as racial injustices received attention in the late 1950's and 1960's and prejudices against women in the late 1960's and early 1970's, so the late 1970's are likely to see more consideration for the elderly. There are some who would even eliminate all mandated retirement laws. Maryland is not likely to go that far, though such bills will be introduced into the Legislature; however, many injustices and stereotypes about the over-65 group are likely to crumble in the 1970's.

Chapter 15

THE DEPARTMENT OF PUBLIC SAFETY AND CORRECTIONAL SERVICES

The Department of Public Safety and Correctional Services in a sense is the soul of the 12 cabinet-level secretariats. No subject has troubled America more than crime in the streets, unless it be how inhumanely we seem to be treating those who committed the crimes and who are in prisons.

Every aspect of the problem is troublesome and frustrating. For example, of the 25 largest cities in the United States, Baltimore during the first six months of 1973 ranked sixth in homicides and fourth in robbery. For years people in Maryland have urged: "Put policemen on foot patrol in the Baltimore streets and crime will go down." Baltimore did just that in 1973 and the homicide rate for the second half of the year went down markedly, but no single cause for the decline could be identified. However, Baltimore homicides increased again in 1974.

A year's controlled study in 1972-73 in Kansas City, Missouri, showed that the basic crime-fighting tactic of all American police departments—regular patrol of the streets by uniformed men in marked cars—does not appear to prevent crime. The Police Foundation, which sponsored the Kansas City study, now believes that policemen can contribute more valuably by talking to people and business leaders, surveying their situations, and advising them how to prevent crime.

America has had no better fortune in dealing with its prisoners. In the two-year period from 1971 to 1973 there were significant riots at the Baltimore City Jail, the State Penitentiary in Baltimore, the House of Correction in Jessup, the Prince Georges County Jail and at the Patuxent Institution, causing millions of dollars of damage. Fortunately, Maryland has been free of the major prison riots that plagued other states, such as the Attica (New York) Correctional Facility uprising in 1971 that took the lives of 39 prisoners and guards and forced penal authorities all over the country to review their policies.

Many penologists and law-enforcement officers now believe that our correctional institutions are overloaded, antiquated, and underfunded. Few correctional industrial programs provide skill-development opportunities or training experience relevant to modern technological requirements—county and local jails are in even worse condition. Here are people not yet convicted, awaiting trial and sometimes in jail, before sentence, longer than the term for which the crime calls. It is a rare jail that has any correctional program. The negative impact of imprisonment often fosters recidivism (additional crimes committed by those released). Parole and probation are often not used wisely; indeed, they tend to be underused.

Fortunately, Maryland authorities are aware of the shortcomings of the present practices in fighting crime and in correctional institutions. As this chapter will show, there are important programs dealing with such reforms as pre-trial intervention and work assignments, more liberal probation practices, halfway houses, work-release programs, weekend and family leaves for inmates, prerelease centers, and community-based correctional projects. This does not mean that there is still not a role for the Penitentiary in dealing with the hard-core criminal. The new outlook in Maryland is to look at alternatives to incarceration for the great bulk of offenders.

In 1970 the Department of Public Safety and Correctional Services under a Secretary was given the unified responsibility to give executive directions and to coordinate activities and programs of the appropriate agencies. This meant that formerly independent agencies, reporting separately to the Governor, such as the State Police, the Fire Prevention Commission and the Fire Marshal, the Police Training Commission, the Corrections agencies, the Parole Board and other boards in this field, would now be under one Secretary. If nothing else, the unified office would (1) identify and concentrate responsibility, (2) reduce proliferation, and (3) reduce functional fragmentation.

Structurally, the Department has two major categories each under a Deputy Secretary. The Deputy Secretary for Public Safety has the following operations under his jurisdiction: civil defense and emergency planning, criminal injuries compensation, fire prevention, State fire marshal, police training commission, traffic safety and Maryland State Police. The Deputy Secretary for Correctional Institutions has charge of these agencies: Division of Correction, Board of Parole, Division of Parole and Probation, Patuxent Institution, and Sundry Claims Board.

The Public Safety Activities

Civil Defense and Emergency Planning Agency. The Agency prepares for and, in the event of enemy attack or major natural disasters, coordinates emergency function of State organs and political subdivisions to minimize and repair injury and damage resulting from such catastrophes.

In the major natural disaster requirement the Agency operates at three levels:

(a) *Emergency Response*. Where a county's regular departments, such as the fire services, cannot operate because of distortions due, for example, to road and bridge destructions, the Agency seeks to coordinate the services available in nearby counties and to secure additional assistance from the federal government.

(b) *Hardships of the Dispossessed*. Disaster emergency centers known as "one stop centers" are established throughout the affected area. For example, at the time of the severe damage done in Maryland by Storm Agnes in 1972, "one stop centers" were established at Ellicott City, Port Deposit, Frederick, Baltimore County, and in the Baltimore City Federal Office Building. In addition, mobile units visited less critically affected areas. In these centers Red Cross aid was provided and food stamps were given to those in emergency need who otherwise were not eligible, and housing was arranged.

(c) *Restoration of Damage.* The Agency is the State's representative in appraising the damage done to State public buildings and structures and to private lives and property. Such appraisal, after Agnes, determined that Maryland would apply through the Governor for federal assistance under the Nation's Declaration of Natural Disaster Law. Maryland was acknowledged as eligible and officials from the federal, State, and local governments evaluated damage to various county and State roads (not federally assisted roads), bridges, and public structures which ultimately were rebuilt with $90 million in federal funds.

A little appreciated accompaniment of the 1972 hurricane damage in Maryland was the economic loss. For example, the pollution of the Chesapeake Bay caused by the storm placed a number of watermen out of work. The Agency assisted by declaring these workers eligible for Maryland unemployment insurance, outside the usual conditions, and in securing for them federal funds to reimburse the costs of storm-damaged equipment.

In carrying out these activities the State Agency operates with the Federal Disaster Assistance Agency, an arm of the Department of Housing and Urban Development. The Director of the Maryland Civil Defense and Emergency Planning Agency is appointed by the Secretary of Public Safety and Correctional Services. He operates with an Advisory Council and a Priorities Board.

Criminal Injuries Compensation Board. In 1968 the Legislature recognized that the State should pay compensation to indigent, innocent, injured persons or to the survivors of those killed through criminal acts committed upon them without any fault on their part. During fiscal 1973 the Board paid out $900,000 to 395 living persons who made claims and to the survivors of 78 victims. Receiving claims were the following victims: 176 assault, 146 shooting, 51 stabbing, nine rape, two mugging, and seven miscellaneous, in addition to some 80 murder victims. The lump sum awards averaged $2,135, which in the main covered medical bills, disabilities, and other hardships caused by being victimized.

Some awards are made on a monthly basis. All claimants must be innocent victims and must show financial hardship. One of the larger claims recently granted was to a woman whose husband was robbed and killed on a Baltimore City street. Her monthly allotment and expenditures were permitted to a total of $27,000. Many claims growing out of family quarrels or revenge combats have not been allowed. An automobile injury or death claim is allowed only if the car is an instrument of crime, rather than a cause of a motor vehicle violation.

Maryland's law, unlike Hawaii's, does not take care of property damage; it merely adjudicates personal injury. In Nebraska only the Good Samaritan who tries to stop a crime is eligible for compensation. In Maryland the Good Samaritan is covered along with the innocent victim.

The Maryland law is a model for proposed federal legislation which would provide compensation for personal injury in federal areas, such as national parks. Most important, the so-called McClellan bill also proposes to pay through the federal Law Enforcement Assistance Administration 75 percent of the cost of any state programs such as Maryland's.

The Maryland program is administered by a three-member Board appointed by the Governor for five-year terms. The Board appoints an Executive Director.

State Fire Prevention Commission and Fire Marshal. The Commission consists of seven members appointed by the Secretary of Public Safety and Correctional Services. The Commission represents paid and volunteer departments in various parts of the State. It promulgates regulations for safeguarding against life and property hazards of fire and explosion. It appoints the Fire Marshal and is also an appeals board dealing with enforcement of the Fire Code.

The State Fire Marshal enforces all State laws dealing with fire prevention, explosives, combustibles, installation and maintenance of fire equipment, and the means and adequacy of exits in case of fire for structures other than public buildings.

The Police Training Commission. As Maryland developed into an urban State in the 1950's and '60's, need arose for more municipal police departments for the smaller cities and even greater need for sophisticated county police departments, particularly in places like Montgomery, Prince Georges, Anne Arundel, and Baltimore Counties. Baltimore City's Police Department goes back to the 1850's, but it was virtually alone in Maryland until 35 years ago. The rest of the State was virtually rural before 1940, except for a few municipalities like Hagerstown, Cumberland, and Frederick that had local police departments.

As the Baltimore and Washington metropolitan areas developed, first the urban centers in the Maryland counties surrounding these two cities developed police departments. Later the counties themselves organized full-fledged police departments using modern crime prevention and control procedures.

As these departments grew, there was the need for State supervision and assistance. Moreover, those counties that are still largely rural do not have police departments but carry out their criminal investigatory and control work through the Sheriff's agencies which in turn are assisted by the State Police. The agents working through the Sheriff's office also needed to become familiar with modern policing methods.

For these reasons the Police Training Commission was established in 1966 to upgrade and standardize police work in Maryland. All State, county, and municipal law enforcement agencies must meet these standards. No law enforcement officer can be appointed unless he meets these standards.

The Commission, using the manpower and facilities of police training departments such as exist in Baltimore City and in the more heavily populated counties, operates two kinds of in-service programs. First, a minimum in-service police training program serves communities and more rural counties having small police departments. These programs fulfill the State standards of at least 245 hours of recruit training for every law enforcement officer. Counties lacking police departments, operating under agencies of the Sheriff, are also invited to send recruits.

In addition, the Commission operates specialized training programs that may run from a few days to two weeks and deal with subjects such as police traffic services, bomb control, photography, and video tapes. Here, too, the personnel may come from Baltimore City or large county police departments or from federal agencies like the FBI.

Funds for the in-service programs may come from federal agencies, such as the Law Enforcement Assistance Administration or from the Department of Transportation.

The Commission consists of 12 members, nine of them representing police departments and police agencies in Maryland. They are appointed by the Secretary of the Department of Public Safety and Correctional Services, with approval by the Governor, for three-year terms.

The Correctional Training Commission. This body was organized in 1971 to improve the skills of correctional officers. The problems of prison riots, difficulties in obtaining qualified personnel, and general problems in upgrading correctional officers caused the Legislature to create the Commission in much the same way as one was created earlier for police personnel. Here, too, the Commission operates, at Jessup, in-service programs of a general nature and of specialized requirements such as riot control.

The Maryland State Police. In 1921, when the State Police first came into being as automobiles became an important part of the Maryland scene, the duties were labeled as "highway patrol." By 1935 it became evident that Maryland needed a full-fledged State Police. It was then clear that criminal investigations and control were to be a key part of its work. At that time there were few police departments for municipalities or counties.

In 1973 there were 1,360 State troopers operating under a Superintendent with the rank of Colonel. The State Police have wide responsibilities to preserve the public peace, to detect and prevent crime, to enforce State and local laws, to apprehend and arrest criminals, and to maintain the safe and orderly flow of traffic on streets and highways.

The force has Statewide jurisdiction except in incorporated communities. Herein its jurisdiction is limited to (1) power of pursuit, (2) when in search of an offender committing a crime outside the incorporated community, (3) when requested to act by the chief executive officer or by the chief police officer of the community, (4) when ordered by the Governor and (5) when enforcing the motor vehicle laws.

Baltimore City policewoman checking fingerprints.

The State Police are especially active in those counties which do not have officially designated county police departments. In such counties the Sheriff designated offices carry out the civil responsibilities and may or may not be very active in criminal matters. Accordingly, they seek aid from the State Police. State Police barracks, located throughout the State, are charged with licensing handgun permits required, under the State law of all who handle guns. A Review Board hears appeals when there are complaints.

The State Police also license garages which are certified to make inspections and corrections as required by State law for used cars that are being sold to new owners. They also operate a helicopter service on call every day and every hour to transport seriously injured persons from highway collisions and other accident scenes to anti-shock treatment rooms in nearby hospitals.

The Maryland Automated Accident Reporting System (MAARS) is a part of a nationally integrated traffic records system operated by the State Police. The system accumulates data dealing with nature of vehicle, driver, accident, highway, and violation. This is coordinated into accident analysis, enforcement assistance, highway improvement, and driver-vehicle administration. The accident data should affect findings dealing with improvement of vehicles, driver education, court procedure, highway construction, and health requirements for driving.

Those wishing to become State Troopers must pass rigid physical examinations and have knowledge of traffic and State laws. They must be at least five feet nine inches in height if men and five feet six inches if women. The latter serve as full troopers and specialists. All attend a six-month basic training program at headquarters in Pikesville. At this time he or she learns about the laws of the State, the use and care of equipment (including revolver, motorcycle or car, radio and teletypewriter), first aid, patrol techniques, and policing. Troopers are on probation for two years.

Under the 1968 Resident Trooper Law a county can contract with the State Police to hire some of their members as additional law enforcement officers, with the State picking up 25 percent of the cost. Carroll County hired ten State Troopers in 1974 and thus increased its police force by one-fourth. Other small counties are looking at the plan.

Local and County Police and Fire-Fighting Services

Local police and fire-fighting services are administered through county and municipal governments. While these activities are not under the Maryland State Department of Public Safety and Correctional Services, no description of policing or fire-fighting would be complete without covering these local services.

Typical is Prince Georges County, which in 1973 had a modern police department including 665 men and women officers. Its efficient law enforcement organization includes its own fully accredited police academy, an extensive police-community relations program, and sophisticated communications and investigative equipment. With main headquarters in Forestville, there are substations in Upper Marlboro, Hyatts-

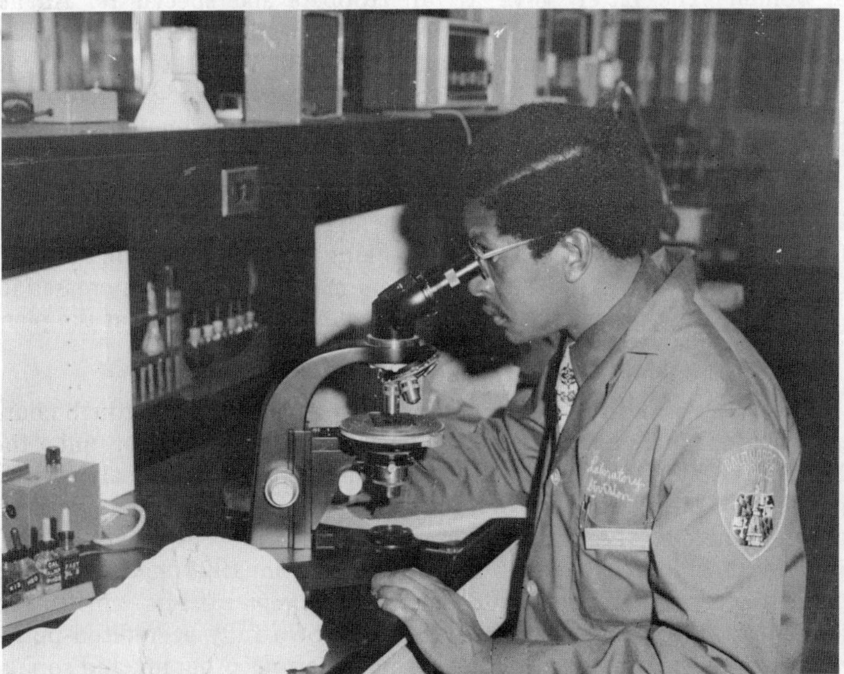

(Top) Baltimore City Police Department's helicopter. (Bottom) Baltimore City's Police Laboratory tracking down criminals through chemical analysis of evidence.

ville, Bowie, Seat Pleasant, and Oxon Hill. The department patrols all of the county except the few municipalities that have their own police departments, and State and federal park areas.

Anne Arundel's Police Department includes tactical operations, youth investigation, and a detention center. Montgomery's Police Department, with various substations—Bethesda, Rockville, Silver Spring, and Wheaton—makes special efforts to protect homeowners and issues "Burglar Proof" cautions to all citizens. Baltimore County has built new and modern police substations, including a Police Training Academy and pistol range in the Loch Raven Reservoir area.

The Baltimore City Police Department underwent a major revamping in both philosophy and structure in the 1960's as a result of a self evaluation, with momentum from national agencies. In 1967 the President's Commission on Law Enforcement and Administration of Justice issued its classic report: *The Challenge of Crime in a Free Society.* In the same decade, and in the early 1970's, court decisions protecting defendants, such as those dealing with right to counsel (even in case of misdemeanors), double jeopardy, right to confrontation, and admissibility of confession, made police work much more complex. An outstanding example of such decisions is the *Miranda v. Arizona* Case in 1966 when the U.S. Supreme Court ruled that the interrogating officer must advise a suspect of his right to the presence of counsel—free if he cannot afford one—and right to be silent. New technologies in fingerprinting and communications required more skillful approaches. New approaches to handling riots and modern uses of tactical police forces brought the need for revised operations. The use of police helicopters is a further proof of changed requirements. Recent sociological findings in race and ethnic relations brought the need for new understandings in human and community relations.

The Baltimore City Police Department was reorganized in the mid-1960's to incorporate these new ideas and to produce a professional policeman, well-paid and highly regarded. At the same time this individual, now likely to have two years of college education with a major in law enforcement, was expected to perform with more sensitivity and effectiveness. Usually his two years or more of college were taken as a law enforcement major and paid for by federal funds. The major debate in Baltimore City is whether its Police Department ought to remain under the Governor rather than the Mayor. For over 100 years Baltimore has been unique among large cities in the respect that it is under State, not city, authority.

Though fire-fighting departments in the counties were still largely manned by volunteers by 1973 changes were marked. For example, Prince Georges services were carried out by 300 paid personnel and 1,000 volunteers who manned the 45 stations of the 37 fire companies. Enforcement of fire laws; inspections of homes, schools, and businesses for fulfillment of county and State fire laws, and actual fire-fighting mark the work of the Department.

Montgomery and Baltimore Counties also have both full-time paid and volunteer departments, with urban areas having professional firemen, and the rural and less crowded, volunteers.

Baltimore City's Fire Department, with full paid personnel, has access to all modern fire-fighting equipment needed in large cities. In addition it has a marine division serving the harbor. A fire-fighting academy trains candidates before they are employed.

The Water Tower—a 1973 American LaFrance built on a 49-foot chassis; equipped with a two-sectional boom with a reach of 90 feet. The tower is capable of delivering 2,000 G.P.M. through two 1,000 G.P.M. pipes and three individual discharge gates located in the basket attached to the boom. Responds on all fire-alarm boxes in the downtown area and all second alarms of fire and special calls when requested.

Volunteer fire-fighting is still the major approach in the counties. Funds come to the volunteer departments from county allocations or from special taxes paid by those in a fire district. Volunteer departments often hold special fund raising events to help pay for equipment. Increasingly, volunteers are attending classes in fire-fighting, such as those at the University of Maryland.

Paid firemen all over the State are improving their skills by attending community college classes in fire-fighting, and some even go on to get their baccalaureate degree at the University of Maryland.

Division of Correctional Services

Division of Correction. By statutory law the Division, headed by a deputy secretary, has control over State adult correctional facilities. Included in its jurisdiction are the following institutions which together house about 5,700 inmates (in 1973) and about 2,000 correctional personnel (not all there at one time) to care for them. Their actual inmate capacity is 4,605, thus overcrowding is evident.

Reception, Diagnostic and Classification Center (Males). The Center came into existence as a result of the Legislature's Act of 1967 providing that convicted persons sentenced to a minimum of 90 days confinement in the State's adult correctional system are to be committed by the Courts to the Department of Correctional Services, which would conduct diagnostic and classification studies on such persons prior to initial assignment to one of the institutions best suited to his needs.

The individual's stay at the Center is from two and one-half to seven weeks. The staff making decision consists of social workers, correctional specialists, psychologists, chaplains, and educators using an interdisciplinary team approach. Age, length of sentence, type of offense, prior criminal record, psychological reports, work history, physical condition, and other factors determine a complete evaluation of each person prior to transfer.

All offenders under 18 years of age are committed to juvenile institutions, under the Department of Health and Mental Hygiene, unless they commit major crimes. Others are committed to adult correctional institutions.

A Center staff of approximately 75 persons is responsible for processing about 5,000 inmates each year, with an average population of 430 at any one time. Temporarily the Center is housed at the State Penitentiary, in its west wing, and thereby the inmates are under the same roof as hard-core criminals. A new Center is to be opened at Jessup in 1976.

On the other hand, it is to the credit of Maryland that while judges in most state courts sentence inmates for a particular institution, in this State the adult male offender is sentenced (since 1966) to the R, D and C Center from where he is placed in the institution that will help him most.

Women are received initially, diagnosed, and classified at the Correctional Institution for Women.

The Maryland Penitentiary. This is a maximum security institution in Baltimore City for the confinement of individuals serving long sentences and considered serious security risks. At any one time more than 800 prisoners are housed there. Assignment to the "Pen" is not final in every case, since individual behavior, attitude, and initiative may result in transfer to another institution within the Division.

The Pen had its own hospital until 1973, but the poor condition of that medical facility was one of the reasons for its closing that year. Very sick prisoners now are sent to local hospitals.

The Pen has scheduled classes for prisoners who seek formal and informal secondary and community college education. It has library and athletic programs and vocational activities. Community interest groups fighting drug and alcoholic addiction and seeking prisoner interest in religion, music and self-help visit the Pen and work with the inmates.

A riot at the Pen in 1972, quelled by Baltimore City police, caused damage amounting to a million dollars, numerous injuries, and a walkout by 100 guards who claimed their lives were in jeopardy. Following the riot a number of safeguards, such as limiting prisoners' personal possessions, were invoked. In addition, an increase in custodial personnel brought the number of guards to 300. Increases in medical and paramedical personnel were also permitted. The problem is that the Pen, like other correctional institutions, is too large and overcrowded. Furthermore, the plant is more than 170 years old and embodies outmoded concepts of punishment in keeping with its age. The way out is to break the maximum security institution into smaller facilities and to carry out some of the forward-looking reforms suggested by authorities. Plans call for a new maximum security institution somewhere in the Baltimore-Washington corridor in 1975. This is not to say that reforms will eliminate the special need for maximum security for hard-core criminals.

It is significant that in the 1972 riot at the Pen three State Use shops were destroyed. With all the supposed advantages of this work program, the rebellion was against low pay (maximum of $1.10 a day) and lack of training experience that leads to jobs after release.

The House of Correction at Jessup. This is a medium security institution housing adult male offenders serving sentences of three months or longer and located on an 837-acre site. The number of average daily inmates is about 1,500. The industrial compound includes a paint shop servicing many State institutional requirements. Other shops engage in baking, butchering, and the manufacture of license plates, highway signs, clothing, mattresses, and furniture.

Formal classes in elementary and secondary education are offered. Recreational and religious activities are present and there is a strong program for the cure of drug addiction. Vocational education is stressed, since many inmates have never had a job.

That problems abound at Jessup is evident by the sporadic riots that take place there—such as the major one in 1972.

The Maryland Correctional Institution near Hagerstown. This is a medium security institution for men. At any one time the number of inmates is about 700.

Total sales in State Use Industries amount to about $700,000 a year with furniture a major product. Unfortunately, a comparatively small proportion of the inmates are involved in State Use work, which manufactures materials and equipment for State governmental offices.

Recreational, religious, and library programs are offered. Medical and psychiatric services supplement self-help and group activities seeking to aid drug and alcoholic addicts.

The Correctional Institution for Women at Jessup. This institution receives adult female offenders convicted of a wide range of crime from misdemeanors to felonies. The average inmate enrollment is about 150. Educational courses at all grade levels and vocational training are offered in fields such as sewing, typing, and key-punch operating. Recreational, religious, homemaking, and civic programs (aid to the blind) are offered to inmates. Medical, psychiatric, and counseling services are available, as are self-help opportunities for drug addicts.

Because the main Reception, Diagnostic and Classification Center is for men only and is at the Penitentiary, this Jessup facility carries out the work for women.

The $10,000-a-year cost for each inmate is a high price to pay for incarceration. True some of these funds were recovered from work-release inmates, but not enough inmates were on the program, nor were those on it serving continuously.

Maryland Correctional Training Center near Hagerstown. This is a medium security institution of 39 acres with an average inmate enrollment of about 1,075. It is for men, primarily between the ages of 18 and 25. Although custody is a factor which is not ignored, the major emphasis is on training. While there an inmate may be assigned to an academic program receiving necessary education from first grade through community college courses offered with the cooperation of the Hagerstown Junior College. Vocational training includes 500-hour instructional programs such as plumbing, machine shop, masonry, carpentry, electronics, print shop, barbering, and auto mechanics.

Medical and religious services are available. A host of vocationally oriented groups such as the State's Vocational Rehabilitation Bureau, the Metropolitan Baltimore Council of AFL-CIO, and the Model Cities project aid in the vocational programs and help ex-offenders to secure jobs.

Correctional Camps and Pre-Release Centers. The Correctional Camp Center at Jessup is the administrative headquarters for four other camp units at Sykesville, Church Hill, Hughesville, and Quantico, and two units at Baltimore City (called Pre-Release Centers). The word "camp" is a holdover from the days when inmates served in work camps situated in various sections of Maryland. Today the Camps are really more like pre-release centers, serving as a midpoint between prison life and community places where the inmate can learn to readjust to community living, to make decisions.

At the Camps a large percentage of the inmates participate in work release. More than one-third are transported each day to and from their jobs and their pay is at the same rate as other workers.

Since working in the Camps is the final step before a man actively rejoins society, it is in these surroundings that he must again learn how to live within a community. Thus, here the emphasis is on training, not confinement. About 1,000 inmates are at the Camps at any one time.

As one inmate at the Pre-Release Camp Center in Baltimore put it, "Stepping from here to the street and stepping from the Maryland House of Correction to the street are entirely different. Here you're given a job. This place puts you back with the community."

The Threshold House for Women is the only pre-release halfway house in Maryland for females. It started its operations as a cooperative venture between private nonprofit groups and the Correction Division with federal funds.

The Baltimore Pre-Release Center for men illustrates an important trend in corrections—community centers in which inmates classified as not hazardous to the public safety live and work in their own communities under strict supervision. Usually qualification for the Baltimore Center requires that an applicant be within three to five months of either release by parole or expiration of sentence, or within but a few months of a parole hearing.

At the Baltimore Center the inmates participate in vocational rehabilitation (in cooperation with activities of the State Division of Vocational Rehabilitation) pre-release, work release, school release, and community service projects. In the latter capacity some inmates working with the Baltimore City Junior Association of Commerce supervise youth recreational programs, tutor children, and conduct cultural awareness programs. Each inmate takes care of his room. Those on work release pay $17.50 weekly for room and board and some additional money may be deducted to assist their families. Weekend leaves permit inmates to spend time with families. Two weeks before parole a resident may join his family.

If a resident of the Baltimore Center is late for work or school he is disciplined. Those having trouble adjusting lose privileges or are remanded back to other correctional institutions.

The Baltimore Center, in its first two years after opening in 1971 reported that about 600 persons had gone through the institution's car and not a single inmate was an escapee.

The County and Baltimore City Jails (not under the Division of Corrections). The County and City Jails are under local rather than State jurisdiction. What happens at these institutions, however, affect the entire progress of correctional work in Maryland. Most inmates (about 75 percent) of the jails are there awaiting trial, some are there for minor offenses (serving sentences for a maximum of 90 days), o awaiting transfer to State or federal correctional institutions. There is common agreement that the jails are undermanned and not physically able to deal with the problems of many frustrated persons who have not yet been tried. The Governor's Community Corrections Task Force found that in 1973 twelve county jails did not meet State standards and should be closed. In the Baltimore City Jail at any one time there may be 1,500 inmates, though capacity is but 950. County jails house about 100 for large counties and a handful for small counties. That conditions can become heated is shown by the riots at the Baltimore City and Prince Georges Jails in 1971-72.

The judges of the Baltimore City Domestic Court have recognized he problems and have taken a number of important steps. Accused persons with good records have been released for trial without bail. Trials have been stepped up so that fewer numbers remain for long periods in jail before hearing and sentence. Unfortunately, some inmates awaiting trial, appeals, sentence and committment may be at the City Jail for a year or more, and these are the frustrating cases. The most exciting experiment now going on is that which sets forth a trial-delay period of three months, especially for young first offenders. The offender in this category is offered an opportunity for a job, vocational raining, or academic study. If he succeeds, the charges against him are dismissed before he even comes to trial. Thus hundreds of so-called offenders are saved the personal problems that would come from languishing in jail and, at the same time, the State is saved the financial burden.

The jails, too, have been looking at their own procedures, seeking to mprove recreational, educational, and other programs. In 1973 the Baltimore City Jail initiated a special program for Confined Addicts Seeking Help (CASH). Yet there is very little rehabilitative work for the ffender who is in a county jail for 30, 60, or 90 days. Local governments have not developed the sophisticated plans of the State's Division of Correction in rehabilitative programs. Many believe that the State should take over all institutional care for anyone who is sentenced respective of the length—the State does now if the sentence is over 90 days. This would leave the county jails with only pretrial inmates.

Patuxent Institution (not under the Division of Corrections but nder the Deputy Secretary for Correctional Services). The Institution pened in 1955 to treat prisoners with severe emotional and mental problems—so-called "defective delinquents." Offenders who fall in this category are given an indeterminate sentence and confined at Patuxent nstitution. All other Maryland offenders are sentenced under the crime aws to serve under minimum and maximum terms.

The rationale of the indeterminate sentence is that Patuxent authorities will know best when a defective delinquent is ready to re-enter society. Actually it is possible for an offender who is labeled as a defective delinquent to remain in prison, at Patuxent, two or three times as long as one who committed the same crime, but was given a fixed sentence. This is why there has been much opposition to the indeterminate sentence and in 1973 there was a wave of court decisions at the State and federal level challenging the right of the Institution to hold inmates indefinitely, claiming there was no due process. Then, too, many inmates have refused to be diagnosed and thus delayed their own progress. The U.S. Supreme Court in 1972 stated that six months was a long enough period for diagnosis and a determinate sentence. The State Legislature is divided on both the philosophy of the indeterminate sentence and its workings.

Actually, Patuxent boasts a recidivism rate of but one-half the national average. The 38 psychiatrists, psychologists, and social workers at Patuxent say that though the annual cost per inmate is $10,000 a year compared to but $5,000 average for other adult correctional institutions, their rate of recidivism is much lower. Presently an inmate can be released by the prison's Board of Review or by appealing to the courts.

The courts have not taken any definitive action as to the legality of the indeterminate sentence and the existence of Patuxent institution. The Legislature could take these steps. So might the Governor's Commission rewriting the Crime Code.

Reforms in Correctional Work. The work-release program started in Maryland by legislative action in 1963 has proven successful. It is important as part of the training and treatment carried on by the correctional institutions and it exemplifies effective utilization of community agencies and resources in preparing inmates for constructive participation after confinement. It is especially valuable as a preparole and prerelease measure. The yearly earnings of inmates on work release runs to over a million dollars average, with the daily number participating being more than 300. Of course, it is most important to the inmate who has the psychological lift of earning money, feeling respectable, and being on the road back. Yet serious incidents such as the cruel murder by a work-release prisoner in 1973 while he was supposedly at work outside the correctional institution led to a public demand for strict supervision. In 1971 the Legislature passed the weekend or family leave bill which permits inmates not on work release to also have the privilege of spending 48 hours at home once a month. An inmate is eligible if he has been in minimum security for at least 30 days and if he is within ten months of parole or two months of completing his sentence. The plan not only permits family life, but encourages inmates to prepare for opportunities for jobs at time of release. Those who are also on work release are accustomed to leaving their institutions and returning daily. They make a better adjustment to weekend release than do those who must return from family leave to the more rigid discipline of the correctional institution.

In fiscal 1973 special leaves (other than weekend) were granted about 12,000 times (multiple opportunities), and only five persons escaped. Family or weekend leaves were given about 4,700 times and only 32 escaped. Most of the runaways were caught.

The main aim in correctional procedures is to establish community correctional facilities. The fiscal 1974 Budget included funds for five such facilities: two in Baltimore City and one in Prince Georges County, and the two Camps at Church Hill and Hughesville were converted to community facilities.

In the early 1970's the Governor's Community Corrections Task Force Interim Report noted that the most effective means of correcting the offender and reducing crime is through the process of reintegrating the offender into his community. It is recognized by most authorities that crime and delinquency are symptoms of failures and disorganization of the community as well as of the individual offender. The Task Force had four key recommendations:

(1) Divert the offender from incarceration by utilizing pretrial diversion strategies,

(2) Direct the offender through adequate diagnostic and evaluation classification into differential treatment,

(3) Provide effective reintegration into community life, and

(4) Minimize fund expenditures per offender by looking to alternatives to incarceration.

The Task Force recommends that there be a system of corrections at the community level with centers of but 100-inmate capacity. That, except for maximum security inmates, rooms have doors not bars, that inmates eat at small tables, and that a campus facility be present for most inmates.

Parole and Probation. The Board of Parole and the Division of Parole and Probation are both under the Deputy Secretary for Correctional Services. The Parole Board is composed of a chairman and six associate members, all appointed for eight-year terms by the Secretary of Public Safety and Correctional Services. The Board has exclusive power to hear cases for parole release and revocation and to authorize the parole of persons sentenced under the laws of Maryland to any penal or correctional institution. Parole is granted to inmates who have served a portion of a given sentence and who are released under certain conditions, including special supervision. The Board conducts hearings at the various penal and correctional institutions for inmates who have at least served one-fourth their sentence. In special cases, where parole and probation officers so recommend, the waiting time may be less than one-fourth the term. It also evaluates activities of parolees and makes recommendations to the Governor with respect to cases, pardons, and commutations.

The Division of Parole and Probation is a staff operation headed by a

Director appointed by the Secretary of the Department. Staff parole officers advise the Board concerning the conduct of parolees and recommend commitment whenever there are parole violations. Staff probation and parole officers advise officers of the County Circuit Courts, the Baltimore City Criminal Courts, and the District Courts throughout the State with pre-sentence reports that may lead to probation or sentence.

Probation is often defined as a suspended sentence given to those offenders found guilty who warrant not being incarcerated, but yet need to receive supervision during the period of suspension. Probation is the prerogative of the court and may not necessarily be related to a conviction or a suspended sentence. It can be an independent decision. Probation officers supervise those under suspended sentence.

Parole and probation officers carry out employment programs, alcohol and narcotic rehabilitation activities, family and personal counseling services, and other activities which seek to readjust the offender and yet protect society. They work through branch offices in all parts of the State. With federal funding they make use of paraprofessionals to bring about community awareness, employment of parolees and probationers, and involvement of volunteers in correctional work. A 24-hour "hot line" is available for offender counseling, as are psychiatric and psychological services.

At any one time in Maryland there would be about 17,000 criminal probation cases and about 6,000 criminal parole cases. In addition there would be an active file of 7,000 nonsupport cases plus 50,000 more nonsupport cases turned over to the Division by the Supreme Bench of Baltimore City in the 1970's under changed law. Each year four to five million dollars are collected in nonsupport cases.

There is a need to extend the services of parole and probation so that more offenders of worth are permitted access to suspended sentence, probation status, and early release. Only in this way can correctional costs be lowered and hope restored, especially to the young and first offender. Such extension will come only as there are more trained parole and probation officers, as laws are more lenient in permitting wider use of these possibilities, as parolees and probationers get jobs and are accepted back into society, and as the correctional system proves that the process does not injure society by creating repeaters or recidivists.

Inmate Grievance Commission. This Commission was created in 1972. It grew out of grievances by inmates and court rulings such as that of a federal district court in Baltimore which ruled that 82 prisoners had been illegally transferred in mass discipline actions because they participated in sit-down demonstrations at the House of Correction and the Sykesville Laundry Camp in 1970. The federal judge in 1971 ruled there was a need for minimum standards of constitutional due process that regulates prison disciplinary hearings. Such due process requires that the offender receive a written statement of his offense within 48 hours after the violation. It requires further that the inmates have an opportunity to appear before the three-man adjustment team—made up of officers at the institution and from the Division—and tell their story. The warden may reduce the penalty noted by the team, but not increase it. He must inform the inmate concerned of the processes involved.

The Inmate Grievance Commission arbitrates disputes between inmates and the institution to which they are confined. The inmate may appeal a disciplinary action taken against him or he may appeal a classification action, stating that he should have been classified as medium security rather than maximum security—thus open to more privileges. The Commission does not have jurisdiction over who and when one goes on parole—that is up to the Parole Board.

Changing the Maryland Criminal Code Itself. Crucial to any reform in correctional practices is the Criminal Code. From arrest to release, criminal justice in Maryland is put together in the Code, which is an accumulation of piecemeal legislative additions to an ancient base. Article 27 of Maryland's Annotated Code deals with crimes and punishment, starting with "abduction" and running for 538 pages to "wire tapping." Each crime such as arson, murder, rape, and robbery, including misdemeanors, is listed and the penalty is stated for each. Many of the laws were passed when the public was aroused about a particular offense, and thus minor offenses sometimes call for more severe punishments than more serious crimes. In general, the thought each time a punishment was noted or revised was that of the specific crime.

In 1965 a commission of distinguished legal authorities, including jurists and lawyers, was appointed to revise the Criminal Code. In 1974, after about nine years of work, their report seemed ready for the Legislature. One of the stated objectives is to replace the present system of sentencing with its stress on "punishment of the crime" with one that emphasizes "punishing the criminal." In this way there will be a more flexible system that tailors sentences to society's and the offender's needs. Thus judges will have more leeway and diagnostic centers of penal institutions and parole authorities will have more flexibility. In addition, the State's correctional system will have more alternatives such as work and weekend release and community approaches. An interesting bill was passed by the 1974 Legislature which requires that persons never formally charged by the State will automatically have the proceedings expunged from public record. This means that persons arrested, but not indicted, will not have the action on record to hound them for the rest of their lives.

A good deal of attention has recently been given to "victimless crimes." One example of what is stirring comes out of a 1972 Baltimore

City police raid on a dice game and the accompanying fatal shooting of one of the participants. Had the playing of dice not been in the Criminal Code and thus an offense, the raid would not have taken place. There is a good deal of hypocrisy, say some legal authorities, in permitting betting at racetracks and in State lotteries, but not gambling in homes. Besides, large-scale home gambling is more likely to be ignored than street-corner dice games. Some say "victimless crimes" should not be punishable.

Not all legal authorities believe that victimless crimes should be wiped from the Code. They say that possession and sale of pornographic literature may not bring any victims into play, but might have a general effect on moral conduct and bring large-scale crime into the actions through controlled sales by gangs. They say the same about marijuana. At the heart of the victimless crime debate is the philosophical question: Does the State have the privilege of proscribing behavior conducted by consenting adults, merely because such behavior offends the majority's moral standards? The failure of the 18th Amendment to the United States Constitution proved that it is difficult to enforce morality. Yet present runaway addiction to drugs shows that morality uncontrolled can be dangerous.

What is the answer? Between 1960 and 1970 in the United States, the crime rate went up 144 percent and the number of offenses per 100,000 population climbed 176 percent—while total population increase was but 13 percent. While new approaches are sought in dealing with offenders, crime in the streets requires that nonoffenders also be considered. Justice requires that there be due process for the offender—it further requires that for the nonoffender there be security of life, limb, and property against crime.

The Congress is in the process of revising and codifying for the first time the 200 years of accretions of federal criminal law. Moreover, the U.S. Supreme Court has recently issued a revision and codification of rules of evidence in federal jurisprudence. The nation and many states, including Maryland, may yet find the answer to both rehabilitating the offender and protecting society.

Militia and Military Department

The Militia is a Constitutionally required structure. Article IX of the Constitution of Maryland states, "The General Assembly shall make, from time to time, such provisions for organizing, equipping and disciplining the Militia, as the exigency may require."

The Adjutant General is appointed by the Governor to head the Military Department, which is an independent agency, not in the Department of Public Safety and Correctional Institutions.

The Ranking Line Officer, often the same person as the Adjutant General, is the custodian of all State and federal property used by the organized militia. He also maintains all State-owned armories located in Maryland and makes all regulations for their use. He is responsible for the administration, training, and supply of approximately 8,000 National Guardsmen and about 1,000 full-time employees.

The Maryland Constitution gives the Governor the power to "call out the Militia to repel invasions, suppress insurrections, and enforce the execution of the Laws." The Governor may not personally take command without the consent of the Legislature. In 1968 the Governor called out the Militia to quell a racial uprising in Baltimore and at about the same time to stop racial strife in Cambridge. On a number of occasions the Governor in the late 1960's and early 1970's called out the Militia to quell campus riots at the University of Maryland, especially as they affected traffic on U.S. Highway 1.

In time of war or other national emergency, when the National Guard is absent from the State and has been nationalized, the Governor as commander-in-chief of the Militia has the power to organize the Maryland State Guard. Such forces are separate and distinct from the National Guard and are composed of commissioned officers and able-bodied male citizens who volunteer and are accepted for service. Members of the State Guard are uniformed as prescribed by the Governor, who may reduce or disband the forces when thought unnecessary. Enlistments in the Maryland National Guard are for a minimum of one year for persons with previous military experience. One who has not had such experience must enlist for six years.

Chapter 16

THE DEPARTMENT OF NATURAL RESOURCES

Formed July 1, 1969 as a cabinet level secretariat, the Department of Natural Resources combined six major departments and eighteen ancillary boards and commissions dealing with the natural resources of the State. They all previously reported directly to the Governor, creating a helter-skelter management structure that had the very real potential of working at cross purposes.

In essence, previous to 1969, most of the natural resources activities were carried out in Maryland by five independent departments—Game and Inland Fish, Chesapeake Bay Affairs, Forests and Parks, Water Resources, and Geological Survey. Each department head and his staff was accountable to a commission in that field for setting forth general policies and decisions. A rather loosely knit organization known as the Board of Natural Resources served as a coordinating unit between the five agencies and with other State departments then involved in environmental affairs, such as the Department of Health. Because of its limited authority, the Board experienced but partial success in resolving these conflicts.

It was evident that such a loose structure could not succeed in the broad scheme, which was to plan the conservation and development of Maryland's waters, shorelines, woods, game, and seafood resources which the State had in such abundance. Moreover, a more unified structure was necessary if Maryland's agencies were to fulfill the responsibility of protecting the natural resources and enforcing the regulations designed to conserve and protect the environment.

With one department headed by a secretariat, the natural resources are now being managed with a unified approach. In addition, it has advantages such as the ability to develop new programs without the formation of a new bureaucracy and the ability to present a united front before executive and legislative bodies of the State and the federal establishment.

The new Department also achieves the ever illusive economies governments say they seek to attain. For example, all service units in the Department serve the major agencies. Services such as legal, bookkeeping, public information, and extension now spread over the entire Department without each agency having its own units.

The transition from autonomous boards and commissions concerned with natural resources into one unit was considered to be a formidable problem. The early 1970's proved that while it was a difficult task it was attainable, and it took place without personnel disruptions and with much good will on the part of those who had served the 24 autonomous agencies before 1969.

In fiscal 1972 the Department managed 185 different programs and rendered direct service on 11 million occasions. About 1,000 persons are on the Department's payroll and its budget for fiscal 1973 was more than $27 million. Of that total, about $13 million came from the State's General Fund; about $12.4 million from special funds, such as hunting and fishing fees, boat registrations and other dedicated funds; another $1.5 million came from federal grants to natural resources programs.

The Board of Review

At the same time that the Department of Natural Resources was created in 1969, a Board of Review was established. The seven-member Board is appointed by the Governor for three-year terms. Four represent the general public and the other three are knowledgeable and experienced in at least one field, such as wildlife, covered by the Department.

The Board hears and determines action to appeals from decisions of the Secretary of Natural Resources or from any heads of Administrations or of other services in the Department. It also makes recommendations regarding the operation and administration of the Department.

Commissions, Boards, Advisory Committees, Trusts

Though the Department itself must operate in a unitary fashion with the view toward looking at the total goal of conserving and developing natural resources, there is still the need for looking at particular problems through the eyes of experts in those specialized fields. Moreover, in dealing with a particular service such as water resources it is significant to get the opinions of those who are going to be affected by the decisions. This is why the Department makes use of so many commissions, boards, committees, and trusts. Through them the Department gets close to thousands of Marylanders who are genuinely interested in the environment. Then, too, the Department understands how its policies affect the ways Marylanders make their living and the ways they enjoy recreational activities.

The Commissions. Each Service and Administration representing a different major activity of the Department has a commission appointed by the Governor. Its task is usually advisory. There are commissions on wildlife, fish, forests and parks, geological survey, mining laws, and water resources. Other commissions seek to draft interstate compacts and agreements. For example, the Susquehanna River Basin Commission involves representatives from New York State, Pennsylvania, and Maryland, as well as the Congress, since the latter must ratify any interstate agreement. Other interstate commissions deal with these subjects: the Potomac River, the Atlantic States Marine Fisheries, the Susquehanna, the Oil Compact, and the Potomac River Fisheries. The Deep Creek Lake Commission involves Garrett County and the commercial and property owners on use and development of the Lake. All commissions dealing with natural resources operate under the Department and issue reports available to the public.

The Committees. Some of these are interstate in nature. The Potomac River Basin Committee, for example, involves four states and the District of Columbia. The Patuxent River Committee advises the State on the avoidance of pollution and the development of park areas along the River. The Susquehanna State Park Committee is charged with advising the Park and Forest Services on the acquisition of land along that River. There is a committee on archaeology and one on watermen's problems, particularly commercial catches of seafood. There is also one on land reclamation.

The Boards. These are largely examining and investigating bodies such as the Mine Examining Board, which issues "certificates of competency" to first-class mine foreman and fire bosses. The Board of Well Drillers examines and certifies well drillers and regulates the business. The Board of Examiners of Landscape Architects certifies people in that field. The Scenic Rivers Review Board inventories rivers and streams of Maryland and related adjacent land areas which offer outstanding scenic, fishing, wildlife, and other recreational values. The Water Sciences Advisory Board makes available the knowledge of water science authorities from Maryland universities, private industry, and fields of government to those who work in this area for the Department.

The Maryland Environmental Trust. This lay group seeks to encourage the people to conserve, improve, stimulate, and perpetuate the aesthetic and cultural qualities of Maryland's environment. They are in a sense the watch-dogs in the effort to "Keep Maryland Beautiful."

In general these boards, commissions, committees, and the Trust serve useful purposes, particularly the interstate and licensing groups. The procedure for the rest can be questionable. Their creation harks back to the time when there were a number of autonomous natural resources agencies, each with its own advisory commission. It was a way to make a lot of people get into the act. In a sense, this is still good, but it could also impede the streamlining and unifying of the natural resources approach. At any rate, a study should be made toward eliminating the less useful ones.

Fisheries Administration

The Fisheries Administration of the Department of Natural Resources is concerned with the State's shellfish and finfish, both sport and commercial. The objective is abundant and healthy fisheries. Maryland's commercial fishery, all tidal, is a $25,000,000-a-year business at dockside. It provides a living for more than 9,000 watermen and more than 4,000 shore-based jobs in packing houses.

Biggest shellfish crop in the Chesapeake Bay and its tributaries is the oyster—providing an annual $15,000,000 value. Maryland ranks first among the states in oyster production. Crabs and softshell clams follow. In the salt-water finfish field, the biggest commercial crop is the popular striped bass or rockfish.

The biggest problems facing the Administration have been water pollution and natural phenomena such as the 1972 tropical storm Agnes. The storm had threatened to wipe out the 1974 oyster crop, which was then spawning, and it caused a die-off of soft-shell clams which kept that industry shut down for a year. Actually, the ban on soft-shell clams was extended for a time into 1973 when the Secretary of the Department of Health and Mental Hygiene indicated that polluted mud beds had contaminated them. The Maryland Watermen's Association refuted the 1973 ban, and after some time the clams were cleared. The debate underscored the hazards of pollution to the State's fisheries.

Pollution of the Chesapeake Bay and its tributaries has caused the closing of thousands of acres of what were once prime oyster and clam beds. Thermal and chemical pollution, soil erosion, pesticides, and sewage from the Patapsco, Back, Magothy, Potomac, and other tributaries flow into the Bay daily and make it uninhabitable for all but the lowest forms of animal life. According to federal and State Water Pollution Control Authorities, about 400 million gallons per day of sewage effluent is discharged into the surface waters tributary to the Bay.

The problem of pollution is particularly important during the spring spawning season. The special danger is to fish eggs and larvae in spawning areas. Rock, herring, hickory and white shad, white and yellow perch, and crappies spawn in Maryland's 30 major rivers and territories.

Fish kills have become increasingly dangerous in the United States. The national fish kill in 1971 was 73.7 million. Maryland was in the middle of the statistics, with the greatest loss about 1.25 million herring killed below Conowingo Dam, according to State authorities, for lack of water from the dam. Another 177,500 fish were killed on Bear Creek; some blamed discharges from the nearby Bethlehem Steel Company plant. A kill of 113,000 fish in fresh-water Piney Run near Taneytown was blamed on effluent from a sewage treatment plant; and 3,000 more were killed in smaller incidents. That Bethlehem Steel paid the State $16,000 (without admitting guilt) showed that fish kills were punishable.

Fortunately, there is recognition that replanting must keep ahead of pollution losses. In the commercial fisheries field, the Administration's most widespread activity is oyster propagation. Through a shell planting and seeding program, the Administration has built up the industry to the point where nearly three million bushels are harvested each year.

In late 1973, the Fisheries Administration announced that it would construct an oyster hatchery on the Eastern Shore that may eventually produce 500 million oysters a year to be planted in the public shellfish beds of Chesapeake Bay. The hatchery would be built in the Tangier Sound area with financial aid from the federal government. Unfortunately, the hatchery will come too late to protect the oyster industry from what could be disastrous seasons in the next few years when the oysters that died as a result of pollution, brought by Storm Agnes in 1972, would have been of harvestable age. Since the early 1960's the State has depended upon "natural seeding" in restricted oyster beds, from which the young would be transported to public areas. Once the production hatchery is fully operative, the natural seeding will be replaced by special disease-resistant strains developed under controlled conditions in the public and private hatcheries.

Langenfelder shell dredge and barge of shells for the State seed oyster areas.

In 1973, the Fisheries Administration stocked 54 Maryland streams and ponds in 12 counties with more than 400,000 trout, including adult fish and fingerlings. Such restocking does much to repopulate the State's fisheries and bring greater opportunities to commercial and sport fishermen.

Several Eastern Shore and Southern Maryland counties and towns, as well as some towns in Anne Arundel, Baltimore, and Harford Counties, celebrate the water resources of Maryland on colorful occasions. For example, the Crisfield Hard Crab Derby is held yearly on the Labor Day weekend along with the nearby Deal Island boat races. The Amateur Anglers Contest and the Surf Fishing Contest are held in Ocean City about the same time. Powerboat regattas are held in Leonardtown in late October and sailboat regattas in early October. Chesapeake Appreciation Day is held afloat and ashore at Sandy Point State Park in late October, just before opening of the oyster dredging season. The big

(Top) Governor Marvin Mandel (r.) presents Woodlawn Trophy to trainer, John Jacobs, while Mrs. Jacobs and jockey, Edward Belmonte, smile their appreciation after Personality's victory in $150,000 added Preakness at Pimlico Race Track in Baltimore, Maryland, May 16, 1970. The Preakness is the "middle jewel" (race) of the Triple Crown horseraces (Kentucky Derby—Preakness—Belmont Stakes). (Bottom) The nation's only workboat sailing race, the skipjack race, draws record crowds annually to Sandy Point on the Chesapeake Bay.

HOOK AND LINE FISHING SEASONS

Open year-round throughout the State, except as noted.

NON-TIDAL

Species	Minimum Size	Creel Limit Daily and Possession
Bass (Largemouth)	9"	5-10 Possession
(Smallmouth)	9"	5-10 Possession
Pickerel (Pike)	14"	5
Northern Pike	20"	2
Muskellunge	30"	2
Striped Bass (Rockfish)	12"	None No Maximum Weight
Walleyes	14"	5
Trout (All Species)	No Limit	7 in Aggregate
All Other Fish	No Limit	No Limit

TIDAL

Species	Minimum Size	Creel Limit Daily and Possession
Bass (Largemouth)	9"	5-10
(Smallmouth)	9"	5-10
Bluefish	8"	None
Catfish	8"	None
Hardhead (Croaker)	10"	None
Perch (White Perch) (Yellow Perch)	None if caught by hook and line	None
*Pickerel (Pike)	14"	10 in aggregate
Striped Bass (Rockfish)	12"	15 lb. maximum No maximum if caught with hook and line except 15 lb. max. from March 1 to May 27 inclusive; limit 1 per day per person. (Not to be sold.)
Weakfish (Sea Trout)	9"	None
†American Shad	None	None
Sturgeon	25 lbs.	None

* May through March 14.

† January through July 5.

Measurement of Fish—Tip of Nose to End of Tail!

feature is the skipjack race, involving the last of the sailing workboats. Tilghman Day, an annual exhibit of oyster tongs and dredges, as well as fishing nets and clam rigs, is held in early November. The National Bass Round-Up is held in Pocomoke City, with monthly prizes through summer and fall. The Winter Codfishing Contest is held at Ocean City from November through early February. Indeed, hardly a week in the year is not taken up by celebrations of fisheries and water sports in Maryland.

Licenses are not required for hook and line fishing in tidal waters. For non-tidal waters, residents of Maryland pay $4.50; non-residents pay $10.50 (seven-day tourist $4.50).

(L. to r.) Trout fishing in Maryland waters; looking up at the Ski Lift at Wisp Ski Area, Deep Creek Lake, Garrett County. This is a prime fall and winter tourist attraction for skiing enthusiasts.

Wildlife Administration

Management of the State's wildlife population, which includes deer, waterfowl, quail, grouse, turkey, and small game, is the task of DNR's Wildlife Administration.

The agency accomplishes it through habitat control rather than stocking. This has been one of its most controversial stands, as hunters see it, it has proven effective and less expensive than stocking. About 35 State-owned wildlife management areas, a total of about 100,000 acres, provide areas for public hunting and other recreational activities. State forests and other State lands are cooperatively used also for pub-

(Top) Marine Inspector working with Wildlife Officer in Carroll County, pheasant hunting. (Bottom) Jousting Tournament, Maryland's Official Sport.

lic hunting, though some conservationists believe multiple use of these lands is dangerous to nature lovers. In addition, large areas of private property have been acquired for public use under the Maryland Cooperative Wildlife Management Program.

Maryland's 1973 Hunting Seasons. Though the dates change somewhat each year, the description below is fairly indicative of what happens annually.

SQUIRRELS: October 5 through January 31 Statewide. Bag limit of six a day, 12 in possession. No bag or possession limits on red or piney squirrels. Season closed on Delmarva (Bryant fox), which are on endangered species list.

WILD TURKEYS: November 1 through 15, fall season only in Garrett, Allegany, and Washington counties. One hen or tom a season. Spring season, 1974, April 29 through May, one bearded tom turkey a season. Hunting open in Garrett, Allegany, Washington, Frederick, Montgomery, Harford and Dorchester counties.

RUFFED GROUSE: October 5 through January 31. Two a day, four in possession.

DEER: Bow and arrow, limit of one antlered or anterless deer a season. September 15 through November 23 and December 3 through January 1. Persons bagging a deer during the bow and arrow season may bag another during the buck season or vice versa. Buck season, November 24 through December 1, one antlered deer bag limit. Special permits will be issued to allow a designated number of hunters to bag antlerless deer in all but the westernmost counties during the buck season.

RABBITS: Western Zone, November 1 through January 15. Eastern Zone, November 15 through January 15. Four per day, eight in possession.

QUAIL: Western Zone, November 1 through January 31. Eastern Zone, November 15 through February 15. Six a day, 12 in possession.

PHEASANTS: Cock birds only. Western Zone, November 1 through January 15. Eastern Zone, November 15 through January 15. Two a day, four in possession. No pheasant hunting in Charles and St. Marys counties.

RACCOONS: September 10 through March 30. No bag or possession limits. Hunting only from sunset to sunrise. Same regulations applicable to opossums.

NOTES: No Sunday hunting of game species in Maryland.

Western Zone includes only Garrett and Allegany counties. The remainder of the State comprises the Eastern Zone.

Maryland hunters are estimated to number between 60,000 and 80,000. Hunting licenses are available throughout the State. Numerous restrictions deal with the hours and days of the week, kinds of animals that may be killed, permissible firearms, ammunition, and the type of bows and arrows, the firing position of the hunter, tagging and checking out deer kill, bag limits, use of traps, use of dogs, chasing of waterfowl by boat, use of ferrets or weasels to hunt or take game birds or game animals, use of live decoys in hunting waterfowl, and the killing of endangered species and song or insectivorous birds. Deer hunters are required to wear some clothing made of day-glow orange. All of these restrictions are carefully outlined in the *Annual Guide to Hunting and Trapping in Maryland*, available from the Wildlife Administration of the Board of Natural Resources in Annapolis.

Some Marylanders say that the turning point in waterfowl conservation came in 1966 when a small group of federal game enforcement officers made more than 1,000 hunter arrests mainly at the practice of baiting or spreading grain to attract large numbers of ducks and geese within gun range. Since that year the waterfowl caseload has dropped to under 300 arrests a year and baiting is down 90 percent. Five federal agents and about fifty State wardens cover more than 60,000 hunters and 3,800 miles of shoreline in Maryland. The agents use planes and helicopters when necessary, though 24-hour stakeouts may keep a suspected violator under surveillance for as long as three weeks.

Others say that these severe measures are uncalled for and do a lot of harm to those who seek to enjoy hunting, especially shooting migratory game ducks. In 1973, the *Preston News and Farmer* ran an editorial satirizing the practices and pointing to how the wardens have gone to absurd lengths in their zeal to enforce the law.

Maryland, through the Wildlife Administration, has developed an "endangered species" list of animals which cannot be hunted, transported, or possessed in Maryland. The list includes bear, coyote, cougar, the Delmarva fox squirrel, and a number of reptiles.

One of the major problems facing the Administration has been declining duck populations in Maryland. For example, the once abundant canvasback and redhead ducks are so scarce that it is no longer permissible to shoot them. Also, the lead poisoning of waterfowl is a problem. An estimated 20,000 ducks and geese die each year from the ingestion of lead shot while feeding off the bottoms of State waterways.

With all the problems in wildlife there is still abundance for hunters in Maryland. For example, the 1972 deer harvest totaled about 12,000 animals from all 23 counties. About 400 wild turkeys were harvested in the six counties permitted. The fur harvest, consisted principally of muskrats, with a total of 15,000 pelts. There were about 5,300 otter pelts and smaller numbers of pelts in fox, mink, nutria, oppossum, raccoon and weasel.

An interesting trend in Maryland is shooting with cameras instead of weapons. Some fascinating shots have been taken by photography enthusiasts—and their catch lasts longer. The Wildlife Administration provides information on times and places for rewarding wildlife photography.

Park Service

The Park Service is responsible for the management and promotion of State parks, environmental areas, scenic preserves, and similar lands.

Maryland has 33 operative State parks (comprising 56,000 acres and in the near future to rise to 125,000) which offer a wide variety of recreational opportunities. These include camping, picnicking, swimming, boating, hiking, and other pursuits such as parking cars and camping trailers. The parks are located in each section of the State—mountain, Piedmont, and coastal plain. As a result, a broad range of scenery and recreation is available to the visitors.

As one might expect, parks have a few problems of a major nature. The sheer bulk of the number of people who use the parks might be classified as a problem. Yearly, an average of approximately ten million visits are registered in the parks. Making certain that the parks are kept in good condition and that everyone enjoys his visit is a herculean task.

The system is growing to meet the demand, and the range of available activities is being increased. One of the programs in that category is the interpretive project in which naturalists conduct tours for park visitors. Twenty-one of the State parks have interpretive programs. There were 900 such tours in 1972 serving 158,000 persons, compared to but eight such tours in 1963 held in two parks and serving but 400 persons.

Most campsites are on a first-come, first-served basis. Group camping is possible in nearly all of the 33 State parks. At least one winterized facility is open in each of the State's camping regions. For summer or winter reservations one should write to the superintendent of the park where he wishes to camp. Individual descriptive folders on any of the following parks give all details and may be obtained free of charge by writing to Park Service, Maryland Department of Natural Resources, Annapolis.

It is well to plan to visit different parks at varying times so that all parts of the State are covered. It is also well for one to consider personal tastes before arranging a trip. For example, if one likes mountains and boating, Deep Creek Lake in Garrett County is exciting. For surf fishing and ocean bathing, Assateague State Park, near Ocean City, is in order. History buffs find St. Clements (also called Blakistone) Island, Fort Frederick, Washington Monument, or Wye Oak fascinating. If there is little time for one who lives near Baltimore and likes hiking, any of the Patapsco State Park sites is in order. The 33 parks are listed below in the four regions of the State:

Eastern Shore. Assateague, Elk Neck, Janes Island, Martinak, Milburn Landing, Shad Landing, Wye Oak.

Central Maryland. Deer Creek, Gunpowder, Patapsco, Sandy Point, Susquehanna.

Southern Maryland. Calvert Cliffs, Cedarville, Point Lookout, St. Clements Island, Seneca, Smallwood.

Western Maryland. Big Run, Casselman, Cunningham Falls, Dan's Mountain, Deep Creek, Fort Frederick, Fort Tonoloway, Gambrill, Gathland, Greenbriar, Herrington Manor, New Germany, Swallow Falls, Washington Monument, Wills Mountain.

Forest Service

The Forest Service is responsible for the overall direction, supervision, and coordination of the activities in State Forests including fire control, forest management in private lands, roadside tree protection, and forest improvement.

(Top) Chesapeake Bay Maritime Museum, St. Michaels, Md. (Bottom) Scenic panorama, Gambrill State Park, Frederick County, Western Maryland.

Within the DNR organization, the Forest Service works closely with other agencies whose activities are concerned with woodland management, such as the Park Service and the Wildlife Administration. The Forest Service is consulted on all proposed public works where trees are involved.

Recreational Activities. Three environmental (low density) recreational activities are receiving special attention. They are:

Establishing the Big Savage Trail. A 16-mile trail atop Big Savage Mountain in Savage River State Forest will eventually be part of the Potomac Heritage National Trail and provide a variety of scenic, geologic, and other attractions together with mountaintop flora and fauna.

Further the Water Canoe-Kayak Races on Savage River below the Savage River Dam (Savage River State Forest). For the last several years Olympic Trials have been held here. The Forest Service cleaned up a small area for rough camping and graded an area for parking, and the Tri-Towns Chamber of Commerce promotes the activity.

Open the snowmobile trails in Savage River, Swallow Falls, and Potomac State Forests.

Tree Care. In all over 1,700 permits were issued in 1972 to persons and utility companies desiring to do tree care work. Forty-three candidates were examined for qualifications to do the work. Licensed tree experts are required to know their job and carry liability insurance as a protection to property owners. More than 1,750 property owners were advised on the care and planting of shade trees. The Forest Service published a mimeographed bulletin entitled "*Keep Maryland Green; Plant a Tree.*"

Tree Distribution in 1972. Approximately 6,500,000 trees were distributed by the Buckingham Forest Tree Nursery for reforestation purposes throughout the State. The major species produced are loblolly pine, white pine, red pine, Scotch pine, and the spruces. Approximately 3,000 roadside trees were distributed to municipalities and public agencies to be planted on public right-of-ways or land owned by the State.

The Nursery. In cooperation with the Natural Resources Institute, University of Maryland, the Forest Service is developing a clonal white pine seed orchard to be planted at the Nursery. Seedlings are in the beds and grafted and some planting was done in 1973, with completion of the clonal orchard possible by 1974. These plantings are to provide seeds to grow superior and faster-maturing trees. Output of trees in the Nursery is generally on the increase, particularly white pine and Scotch pine.

Log Storage Yard. The primary control method was to cut and salvage dead and dying timber to save as much of the resource as possible. However, market conditions drastically declined and salvage operations were hindered. The Forest Service recommended to the Secretary that a log storage yard be established on the Pocomoke State Forest. Tree-length logs were placed under a water spraying system in an attempt to control decay and stain degradation until markets improved. The storage area has a capacity of approximately one million board feet of tree-length logs and will be maintained for two years.

Forest Fires. Fiscal 1972 did not present as severe a forest fire season as some in the past: 586 fires burned 1,667 acres. These figures are higher than for the 1971 season, during which 513 fires burned 1,041 acres. Actually, both seasons were approximately the same in severity, but the Service is now using the uniform forest fire statistic reporting system adopted by the 20 states in the northeastern region. Thus the figures were up in 1972 because they were more accurate.

Fiscal 1972 saw increased use of the spotter plane for detection work, especially in the marshes of Dorchester County. The Service also put into operation two forest fire simulators, which are receiving good use in the training program.

In fiscal 1973, an agreement between the State and the federal government through the Office of Emergency Preparedness was signed. This will provide federal funds to Maryland if the State is faced with a disastrous fire situation.

Problems. Perhaps the most serious of problems facing the Forest Service is the continual pressure brought by development and population increases endangering the State's woodlands. Also, traditional forestry techniques, such as clear cutting and use of herbicides, have come under criticism from the public in recent years.

Natural Resources Police Force

The program is responsible for overall direction, supervision and coordination of the activities of the Inland and Marine police divisions. Specific facilities include the Natural Resources Police Academy at Matapeake, a maintenance and supply center, and an aviation unit to provide airborne surveillance and rescue services.

The Inland Division of the Natural Resources Police Force is charged with the responsibility of enforcing all laws and regulations relative to the protection and preservation of wildlife and to the welfare and safety of the citizenry.

In 1972 the Police Force apprehended 1,473 persons for violations of the fish, game, boating, and litter regulations. It issued warnings to 420 of those persons apprehended, and 1,280 were prosecuted.

Activities. During the year Wildlife Officers performed the following nonenforcement duties:

Rendered assistance to Wildlife Law Enforcement Officials in contiguous states in the apprehension of game and fish violators; Assisted State and local police in the apprehension of felons; Searched for persons reported lost or missing; Searched for and recovered drowning victims; Relayed emergency information to hunters and fishermen;

Rendered assistance to boaters; Recovered drifting unmanned boats; Patrolled boat races; Assisted motorists who were stranded or involved in accidents, and Assisted in rescue and salvage operations during floods caused by Storm Agnes.

Recent reorganization within the Department of Natural Resources has, through reassignment of duties, reduced the number of non-law enforcement activities performed by the officers. The officers did, however, assist with various wildlife and fisheries management projects, and conducted surveys. In addition, Wildlife Officers investigated numerous predator and nuisance animal complaints, issued control permits, and provided various services to land owners.

Permits. The Inland Law Enforcement Division has the responsibility for issuing 11 different types of permits. Investigation of applicants for permits is conducted by the officers and, when necessitated by the type of permit requested, an inspection of the facilities designated in the permit must be conducted by the Wildlife Officers. In 1972 there were issued 1,404 permits of the various types.

Recruit Training and Other Educational Programs in 1972. Expansion of assigned duties necessitated extension of the basic recruit training program for Natural Resources Police Officer candidates to 16 weeks.

Captains and Sergeants of the Inland Law Enforcement Division used sixteen man-days conducting courses of instruction on the fish and wildlife laws and regulations for other enforcement agencies throughout the State. Two new Inland Division Officers successfully completed the basic sixteen-week Police Recruit Training and were graduated from the Maryland Natural Resources Police Academy.

The division continued participation in Project Transition with the U.S. Department of Defense to give military personnel returning to civilian life an opportunity to receive on-the-job training.

Safety in 1972. A record 12,757 people received firearms and hunter safety instruction during the year. Six thousand eight hundred sixty-seven persons successfully completed the full training course and were awarded Certificates of Competency, and the Maryland Safe Hunter shoulder patch. An additional 5,890 persons attended firearms safety lecture-demonstrations.

The incidence of hunting accidents increased slightly during fiscal 1972 in comparison with the previous fiscal year. Fifty-one hunting accidents were reported for the year, six of them fatal. Sixteen of the accidents were self-inflicted.

Boating Accidents. In Maryland waters in 1972 there were 195 boating accidents resulting in 34 deaths and 38 injuries. Recreational boating has accounted for most of the increase in accidental drownings. Studies show that over-confidence and carelessness, improper loading and overloading, and disregard of weather conditions are the leading causes of boating accidents. Hunters and fishermen using boats without full knowledge account for an undue share of the statistics. A fisherman often gets excited, stands up to cast or bring in his fish, and falls overboard.

The Maryland Marine Police state that all these accidents would not have happened had there been knowledge of and conformance with boating safety rules.

The United States Coast Guard Auxiliary, comprised of pleasure boatmen, makes courtesy inspections by invitation and educates small-boat operators in the basics of seamanship. The U.S. Power Squadron also conducts such courses. A recent Coast Guard regulation requires all motorboats under 26 feet in length to display a manufacturer's plate showing safe load capacity.

Marine Police in 1972. The 125 man force of the Maryland Marine Police Division includes headquarters, communications, maintenance and supply, the Marine Police Academy, and field force sections.

Equipment. Units manned by this division include 44 patrol boats, 45 runabouts, 21 vehicles, and one twin-engine amphibian aircraft. All patrol boats and vehicles and most runabouts are equipped with two-way radios.

Inspections. There were 134,587 inspections of boats in 1972 for conservation and boating violations and 37,266 inspections were made at seafood processing houses and of trucks carrying seafood cargo. There were in 1972 as many as 1,448 arrests and 1,678 warnings for violations of boating laws. In 1972 there were also 1,378 arrests, 391 warnings, and 1,669 confiscations for violations of the conservation laws.

Recoveries. The police recovered or assisted in recovery of 35 drowning victims. The force recovered 60 stolen or lost boats and 26 stolen outboard motors. It rendered 1,018 other water-oriented assists to the boating public, including delivery of emergency messages, regatta patrols, tow disabled vessels into port, removal of persons from water, first-aid administration, ice breaking, search for missing boats, fire-fighting on boats, engine repairs, refloating of grounded boats and supplying fuel.

Other Activities. Steel-hull patrol boats keep the harbors free of ice, helping watermen to operate. The scuba diving section, consisting of six skilled officers trained at the U.S. Navy Deep Sea Diving School, in 1972 made 22 dives to make underwater repairs to disabled boats, help refloat sunken boats, and recover lost items.

To insure pleasure boating safety, weather and sea conditions are reported twice daily from all parts of the Chesapeake Bay during the season when boating is at its heaviest. Reports from the field to headquarters are made twice weekly for publication to the sport fishermen, keeping them informed on the best fishing waters.

Daily patrols of seafood areas closed due to pollution and monthly reports of same are made to insure safe and healthy seafood to the public. Inspections of cargo spaces are made on boats and trucks transporting seafood to bring compliance with sanitary regulations set forth by State Department of Health.

Oyster taxes are collected and permits to export oysters are issued by the Marine Police.

Water Resources Administration

This Administration is concerned with matters relating to the protection, enhancement, and management of the State's water resources.

Program activities are divided into three basic categories—Enforcement, Permits and Certification, and Technical Services.

Enforcement. This program is responsible for the inspection, investigation and enforcement activities of the WRA, and encompasses two primary projects: watershed control, which applies prevention-oriented enforcement procedures to those activities directly related to geologic and hydrologic processes occuring in watershed areas. The water quality control activity is responsible for enforcement of the State provisions relating to industries and other point-source discharges.

Permits and Certification. The general permits section is responsible for issuing wetlands permits for the regulation of dredging and filling in tidal wetlands, certification to federal agencies of impact of proposed projects, and issuing of permits involving surface water use, including appropriations, dams and reservoir construction, and construction in waterways and floodplains, and issuing permits involving ground water use, including appropriations and construction of water wells. The water quality permits activity is responsible for issuing waste discharge permits for 1,500 industrial discharges and several thousand discharges from active mines and agricultural sources, and licensing of all persons engaged in storage, transfer, treatment or disposition of oil.

Technical Services. This unit provides technical support to the enforcement, permits, and certification sections. Activities of the Water Resources Administration during 1972 included: 1,000 inspections for sediment control plans, 200 complaints received and responded to; 100 enforcement actions taken; 40 sites evaluated with drill rig. Approximately 1,200 point sources of discharge (industrial, mining, agricultural) were placed under surveillance by staff engineers and technicians.

Wetlands. An important activity of the Water Resources Administration is the regulation of activities in the State's 305,000 acres of tidal wetlands. WRA investigates applications for permits to do work in wetlands and makes recommendations to the Board of Public Works as to what type of permit, if any, should be issued for wetlands activities.

Problems. Probably the largest problem facing the administration is water pollution control. Its 15 programs designed to control pollution include abandoned mine reclamation, certification of municipal and industrial wastewater works, sediment control, oil spill prevention, and issuance of discharge permits.

Water Quality Standards. The Maryland laws on water quality are very specific and enforcement is getting tighter.

Maryland waters must be free from: Substances attributable to sewage, industrial waste, or other waste that will settle to form sludge deposits that are unsightly, putrescent, or odorous to such degree as to create a nuisance, or that interfere directly or indirectly with water uses; floating debris, oil, grease, scum, and other floating materials attributable to sewage, industrial waste or other waste in amounts sufficient to be unsightly to such a degree as to create a nuisance, or that interfere directly or indirectly with water uses; and high-temperature, toxic, corrosive or other deleterious substances attributable to sewage, industrial waste, or other waste in concentrations or combinations which interfere directly or indirectly with water uses, or which are harmful to human, animal, plant, or aquatic life.

Maryland's waterways are divided into four classifications.

Class 1. Water contact recreation and aquatic life
Class 2. Shellfish harvesting
Class 3. Natural trout waters
Class 4. Recreational trout waters

Trout is used as a measure because it is a good indicator of polluting substances.

For each of these classifications there has been established different minimum approvals in terms of five standards affecting water quality: bacteriological matter, dissolved oxygen, ph, temperature and turbidity.

Sampling points all over the State test in terms of the five standards (as a minimum) as applied to the four different classifications. Both long-range monitoring and localized intensive surveys are planned around and take place within 18 major sub-basins, e.g., Patuxent and Patapsco Rivers.

Maryland Environmental Service

This arm of the Department of Natural Resources was established primarily in response to the need for assisting local governments and industry, which could not possibly do this alone, to eliminate pollution resulting from the disposal of liquid and solid wastes.

The Service operates and maintains 17 State-owned institutional waste-water treatment plants and has contracted to operate other public and privately owned liquid-waste management facilities. MES provides supervisory services for five or more additional sewage treatment plants.

Waste-water treatment plant personnel are enrolled in both in-house and formal educational programs in preparation for official State board certification as required by law.

The scope of MES was expanded by the General Assembly during the 1972 session to include water supply in the general powers and duties and in both the planning and implementation functions of the Service. MES now operates five State-owned water treatment plants.

The Service has assisted Baltimore City in its investigation of a pyrolysis method of managing 1,000 tons of garbage and trash daily. The new pyrolysis system of solid-waste handling reduces air pollution through a clean, high-temperature baking process, recycles waste into steam energy which can be sold to reduce operating costs, and eliminates the need to burn significant amounts of fossil fuels, thus conserving valuable resources. The City is now proceeding with the contracts for the pyrolysis plant.

The MES is cooperating with water-resource planning agencies in Virginia and the District of Columbia in a joint effort to produce an action program that will solve the water supply, waste-water treatment, and water quality problems of the Washington Metropolitan area.

Approximately 700 tons per day of excess sludge, generated by expansion of Blue Plains Waste-water Treatment Plant, will be managed by the Environmental Service under contract with eight governmental jurisdictions in the District of Columbia area. Organic materials will be processed and returned to the soil where they originated.

The Service is participating in a scientific study to improve the agricultural capabilities of land by conditioning with sludge. Recycling of this high organic content material into the land also makes reclamation of unusable land possible.

A $142,000 grant from the U.S. Environmental Protection Agency has enabled MES to undertake development of a preliminary design for a system of collection, transportation, and processing of more than 13 million gallons of waste oils. These waste oils are presently being discarded in Maryland. The processing system will be designed so that the end product can be used as oils and lubricants in State-owned vehicles and for heating fuels for State-owned institutions and facilities.

The Service is actively involved in water and waste-water treatment facility design and construction in five specific areas at this time:

Patuxent River. A regional facility to serve portions of Anne Arundel and Prince Georges Counties. Negotiations with local jurisdictions are in progress.

Swan Point. In cooperation with U.S. Steel Corporation, MES has agreed to construct and operate water and waste-water treatment facilities in Charles County, to serve a housing development at Swan Point.

Dickerson. MES has initiated an investigation into the use of treated municipal waste water from a planned Montgomery County treatment facility, to make up consumptive water losses from a proposed closed-cooling-system power generating plant at PEPCO at Dickerson, Maryland.

Freedom District. The service will construct and operate a 1,000,000-gallon-per-day waste-water treatment plant in Carroll County. The facility will service private homes in the district as well as Springfield and Henryton State Hospitals.

Hagerstown. Following study, the MES has recommended a regional waste-water treatment facility to serve Hagerstown and Washington County suburban areas.

To carry out these waste-disposal projects and to create reclamation facilities such as sewage treatment plants, incinerators, sanitary landfills, and reclamation centers, the Service has the authority to sell bonds. It may also enter into contracts with local governmental units or private industries. Before this Service was created those local governments—counties or municipalities—which had neither the funds nor the "know-how," merely ignored the problem. Pollution at their end of a stream or river ultimately affected the health and economy of other Maryland communities farther down the waterway. The Service created regional and Statewide approaches with funds from local, State, and federal governments.

Power Plant Siting

The newest program of the Department of Natural Resources, initiated in 1971, is its Power Plant Siting Activity. A 1971 legislative act, which contains a number of far-reaching features, directs electric utility companies and the Maryland Public Service Commission to engage in long-range planning and to develop forecasts for electric-power demand and supply. Planning calls for study and recommendations of power-plant sites for the next ten years. The energy shortage of 1973 and 1974 showed how foresighted were Legislators who passed the Act.

The program is divided into four sections: monitoring, siting evaluation and selection, research, and land acquisition.

The program is charged with the responsibility of monitoring existing and future power plants with regard to their effect on the environment. This includes surveillance of discharges from power plants into the water as well as into the air and onto the land.

Perhaps its most active program is site evaluation and selection. Under the law, power companies must present a ten-year plan to the Public Service Commission. This plan must give proposed sites and sizes of power plants the various utilities intend to build over the ten-year period. Then the DNR agency is given the overall ten-year plan and is charged with assessing the environmental impact of each proposed power plant. This includes judging the effect on water, air and land, fisheries, wildlife, and plants.

The research phase of the program includes all possible effects electrical generating stations will have on the environment and the population. Principally, the work is done by a consortium of scientists representing many professional disciplines.

The Environmental Trust Fund was created in 1972 to further research in this area. The Act calls for a 1973 surcharge of .147 mill per kilowatt hour (with a ceiling of 0.3 mill) on all Maryland electrical consumption bills. Homeowners in the State have paid little attention to this electric environmental surcharge, for it adds to but ten to 20 cents on the average monthly bill. Yet, for the first quarter of fiscal 1973 alone, it netted the Fund more than $770,000.

Site research is usually carried out with the assistance of environmental engineers, physicists, and geographers at Maryland universities. The objective is better understanding of the basic physical, chemical, and biological impacts of electric power plants on the environment. The Chesapeake Bay Cooling Water Studies Group studies the aquatic impact problems while the Human Health and Welfare Studies Group investigates the air quality, radioactivity and socioeconomic impact.

By 1973, nine sites for possible construction of new generating facilities were identified. Three of these—at Brandon Shores, Perryman, and Dickerson—had advanced to detailed investigation.

The Power Plant Siting Act requires the Department of Natural Resources to acquire lands that might be used for power plant sites and to hold them on standby for future use. Temporary use of these State-owned sites for recreation or other activities is permitted. The land acquisition phase appears to be the most difficult part of the program because, while everyone wants electricity, no one wants a power plant in his backyard. The first serious debate in this regard was triggered in 1974 when the Maryland Public Service Commission granted the Baltimore Gas and Electric Company permission to continue construction of the $347 million Calvert Cliffs nuclear generating plant.

Maryland Geological Survey

The Maryland Geological Survey is both a research and a regulatory agency of the Department of Natural Resources. It is the only DNR agency not headquartered in Annapolis. Its main offices are at the Johns Hopkins University in Baltimore. It is concerned with hydrogeology, environmental geology, coastal and estuarine geology, archeology, and mining.

It is its regulation of mining which might be considered the Survey's most controversial task. Although Maryland is producing but 1.4 million tons of coal per year, more than three-fourths of this comes from strip mining in Allegany and Garrett Counties, it is a relatively small operation. Stripping has aroused the interest and, sometimes, the ire of conservation groups throughout the State. Stripping is a technique which, if not carefully supervised, can permanently scar the surface of the land. The studies of the Survey should show what must be done to prevent pollutants such as sulphuric acids and other contaminents from entering streams after leaving abandoned mines.

The strip mining process is supervised by the Land Reclamation Committee, whose work is coordinated by the Maryland Geological

Survey. Strip miners must apply to the Committee for a permit to mine any vein of coal. The applicant must assure the committee that he will backfill and revegetate the land after the stripping operation is concluded. A bond must be posted.

In 1974 there were moves in the Legislature to govern strip mining of sand and gravel, two important resources in Maryland.

Other work of the Survey includes publication of topographical maps, bulletins on many phases of geology, and popular booklets on many phases of its work.

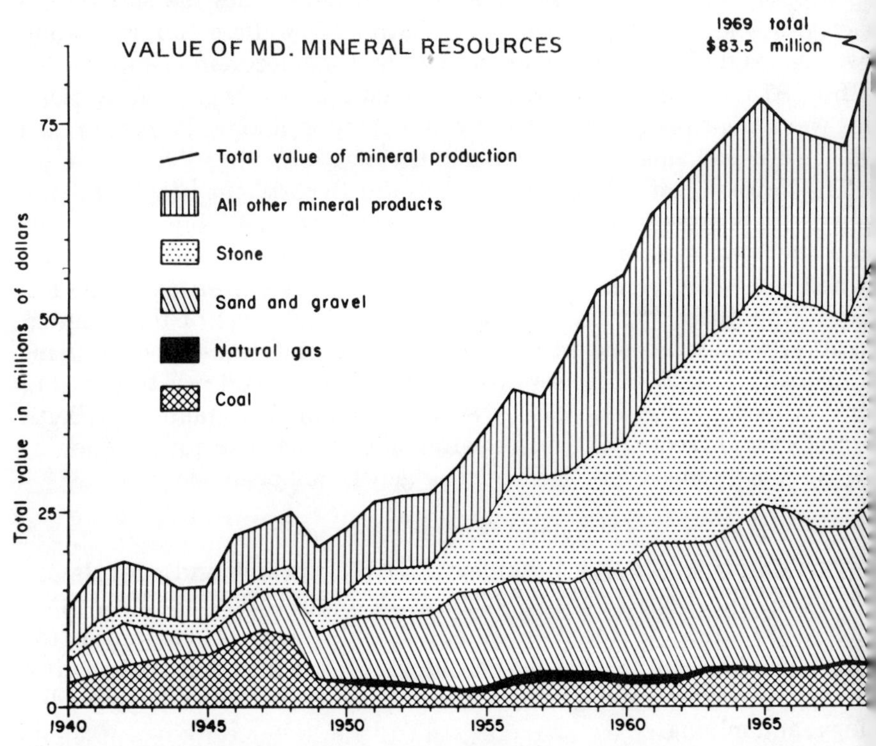

Unsolved Problems

Land Use. The most controversial subject in the Legislature in 197: and 1974 sessions was land-use bills. Those who favored strict State wide legislation indicated that the continuing expansion of Marylan suburban areas, chiefly around Baltimore and Washington, meant de struction of prime agricultural land, inroads on open space, and th lessening of future recreational opportunities. Since the problem was regional one, municipal and county political units could not deal with i effectively in terms of local zoning laws. Besides, say proponents o land use, the local jurisdictions had too many vested interests in som of the proposed expansion plans.

Those opposed to Statewide planning indicate that such would do damage to county planning and zoning. For example, the Maryland Association of Counties believes that the State should have some determinations in land use since what happens in one part of Maryland is bound to affect nearby communities. However, the Association wants county control over most planning decisions, and it especially wants local recommendations and public hearings.

One of the proposals would require the mapping of land-use areas, with five-, ten-, and 25-year goals. A commission would draft a State land-use plan, restricting further development where there has been over-expansion, as for example in the Baltimore-Washington corridor; on the other hand, encouraging further development where there has been less than proper-expansion, as is true for Western Maryland. The Commission, to be known as the Maryland Land-Use Agency, would need approval from the Legislature for any projected plans.

Permits would be required from the State Commission for development of more than five acres or of more than one acre when within 250 feet of a State waterway, historical site, or scenic location. Applicants would have to show that their proposed projects would not cause air or water pollution, place an undue burden on area water supplies, and cause erosion, and, that the projects conform with State and local plans and goals.

Some compromise plans would set forth "critical areas" of environmental concern and would require all developers to meet the criteria for these areas, letting local zoning units handle the local controversies, but giving the State the right to intervene. The Land-Use Agency would safeguard those areas from local decisions that conflict with broader State land-use policies.

The 1974 Legislature adopted a compromise plan which would not create a separate land-use board but would permit the State Department of Planning to intervene in an advisory capacity in local zoning decisions when the effect might be widespread.

Wetlands. Maryland's wetlands, which follow the shoreline along the Atlantic Ocean, Sinepuxent Bay, Chincoteague Bay, and other bays facing the ocean, provide natural barriers between subsurface drinking water and the salt waters of the sea. They cushion interior lands against the force of eroding waves, and provide spawning areas for fish and breeding grounds for birds.

According to some marine biologists, the wetlands are a source of food for the commercially valuable seafood taken from East Coast waters. Once filled or destroyed, they will never again produce their natural harvest.

Wetlands come into being by periodic buffeting of the land by tidal waters. As the tide rises and falls, the water is slowed by the buffer of marsh grasses and drops its nutrients into the wetlands to nourish animal and marine life. Yet some shortsighted governmental officials, in the name of development, have permitted these precious lands to come within the hands of the real estate developer. When Maryland's landmark Wetlands Act was passed in 1970, the State had more than 300,000 acres of salt and freshwater marshes, bogs, swamps, ponds, and seasonally flooded meadows. The problem lies in the fact that under the Act each case is handled individually.

Many of the violations have been in the Ocean City area and south of the resort where speculative land investors sell filled-in wetlands at skyrocketing prices. Both private realtors and local governments have made large profits by building along the marshes. But the Maryland Wetlands Act, to prevent loss or despoliation of land, requires private as well as public property owners to secure State permits.

The private owner of marshlands believes that this is his property and he should not be required to get a permit to dredge his own wetlands. The conservationists say that he is affecting the livelihood of others—for example, those who make a living fishing, crabbing, or clamming—when he injures his own wetlands.

State officials, particularly the Water Resources Administration of the Department of Natural Resources, have issued a number of cease-and-desist orders to builders, but have been willing to compromise where a minimum amount of dredging is involved. In 1972 the U.S. Army Corps of Engineers, for the first time, entered the debate to force private real estate owners to seek permits for dredging and filling their own wetlands. The Corps quoted an old federal law requiring permits for "activities affecting navigable waters."

Recreational Activities

Maryland is rich in hunting, bicycling, fishing, hiking, water, equestrian, and competitive sports, skiing, camping, and other outdoor recreational opportunities. Indoor opportunities are equally abundant. Practically every county (and Baltimore City) has a public recreation program. For example, at low cost, the Montgomery County Public Recreation Department offers literally hundreds of recreational activities in different parts of the county. There are arts and crafts courses, exercise and physical fitness classes, music groups, and special interest activities—for all age categories. Practically every school building in the county is used from morning until late evening.

The Department of State Planning, in cooperation with the Department of Natural Resources, has developed a Comprehensive Plan for Statewide Outdoor Recreation and Open Space Use. Every last resource—virtually every land and water public possession—has been catalogued in terms of present and possible future consumer usage. A suggested priority list is established for completion of projects. It is a major step forward in recognizing that Maryland resources for recreation should be coordinated to save money and increase opportunities.

Chapter 17

STATE DEPARTMENT OF AGRICULTURE

Since the University of Maryland evolved from the older Maryland State College of Agriculture going back to 1856, the State's agricultural affairs were under the University until 1973. Indeed, the Board of Regents of the University of Maryland was also the State Board of Agriculture. In the latter capacity it administered the State laws related to livestock-disease control; plant-pest control; inspecting, grading, and promoting agricultural commodities; soil conservation and drainage; inspection laws relating to seed, feed, fertilizer, pesticides, and liming materials; weighing, sampling, and testing of milk; and a meat and poultry inspection service. Actually three members of the Board of Regents and its adjunct, the Board of Agriculture, were selected from

(Top and bottom, l. to r.) Maryland Department of Agriculture officials grade both vegetables and fruit crops for marketing; tomatoes represent an important crop for Eastern Shore farmers. A new type of tomato has been recently developed, which can be harvested mechanically; greenhouse and nursery products produce about $14 million in annual income for Maryland; raising beef cattle has become a multimillion-dollar business in Maryland. Shown here is a herd of Black Angus, highly prized for their excellent steaks and roasts.

nominees submitted by the Maryland Agricultural Commission, which consisted of farming experts.

Because the University of Maryland is the State's Land-grant college, the Maryland Agricultural Experiment Station has its main location at the College Park campus. The Station was established following passage of the federal Hatch Act in 1887 making available to the states grants-in-aid for the conduct of agricultural research. Here are located laboratories for research in animal and plant sciences, as well as experimental herds, flocks, field and tree plots, and investigations of soils, and insect and disease control. Off-campus stations include an experimental tobacco farm at Upper Marlboro, a dairy-agronomy research station at Ellicott City, a poultry-vegetable research farm at Salisbury, and an experimental livestock farm at Waterloo. Results from these research findings are turned over to Maryland farmers to improve agricultural practices.

The Cooperative Extension Service in Agriculture and Home Economics was established by federal and State laws in 1914 and is funded by both governments, with some county contributions. Each county and Baltimore City has extension agents who conduct educational programs in agricultural production and marketing, home economics, public affairs and community development and youth affairs. The State's 4-H Club activities operate through this Service. The main office is located on the College Park Campus of the University of Maryland.

Until 1973 the prime agricultural agency in the State was the Maryland Agricultural Commission, which served as an advisory body to the State Board of Agriculture, really the University's Board of Regents. The 19-member Board, appointed by the Governor, embraced representation from the University's agricultural college and from its Board of Regents, as well as those in different agricultural pursuits such as livestock, horticulture, field crops, and tobacco. Then, too, there were representatives from the Maryland State Grange and the Maryland Farm Bureau.

Separate agricultural boards and commissions—such as the Apple Commission, the State Fair Board, the State Superintendent of Weights and Measures, the Soil Conservation Committee, the Maryland Tobacco Authority, the Wholesome Meat Advisory Council, the Wholesome Poultry Advisory Council, and the State Veterinarians—acted independently of broader agricultural requirements.

A Cabinet Level Department is Created

In 1973 with unification and coordination of services in the same field in the air in Maryland, a cabinet-level secretariat was created for the Department of Agriculture. The Maryland Agricultural Commission and the Board of Review were brought under the new secretariat, as were all the separate agricultural boards and commissions and their activities named above. This meant that the secretariat had replaced the University of Maryland's State Board of Agriculture. Actually the University had long wanted to shed the responsibility of doubling as the main State agricultural body. The regents had enough to do running an institution with an enrollment of 55,000 students and five campuses.

The Maryland Agricultural Commission. This body was to continue as an advisory agency, but to serve the Secretary of the Department, not the University of Maryland. Its membership was cut to 17, but it still represented the different agricultural pursuits, such as livestock, field crops, and tobacco.

Board of Review. A seven-member Board of Review was established with appointments by the Governor. It was empowered to hear and determine appeals from any decision of the Secretary of the Department of Agriculture or from any one working under the Secretary. The Board also hears appeals on failures to act.

The State Board of Veterinary Medical Examiners. The Board was established under the Department of Agriculture for the purpose of establishing standards and licensing veterinary physicians.

The Director of Marketing and Manpowers. He has the task of promoting market development and coordinating the operations dealing with agricultural labor, tobacco, apples, and the State fairs.

Inspector of Tobacco and the Tobacco Authority. The Inspector, with his staff, is responsible for operating tobacco warehouses and promoting the tobacco industry. The Inspector establishes grades for leaf tobacco and opens hogsheads to check for uniformity.

The Authority consists of eight members appointed by the Governor, representing sellers, purchasers, and producers of tobacco. They operate under the Department and regulate the tobacco industry in Maryland.

The Apple Commission. This Commission regulates standards of size and quality of the fruit.

The State Fair Board. Coordinates the schedules and operations of the State and county fairs.

The Director of Animal Industries. He is responsible for animal disease control and meat and poultry inspection. All carcasses are inspected to make certain that there is no adulteration or false labelling. Wholesome Meat and Poultry Advisory Councils implement inspection laws for livestock and poultry.

The Director of Plant Industries, Environmental Affairs and Rural Development. He and his staff are responsible for soil conservation and drainage; pollution, pesticide, and mosquito control; apiary inspection; enforcement of planning, zoning and open space; seed and sod laws; plant pathological studies, and nursery inspection.

Maryland's laws are very definitive in these areas. For example, the State's Pesticide and Labelling Law is very detailed in respect to the sale and use of pesticides which are highly toxic to man. The law on nursery

(Top) Cattle raising both for dairy products and for beef is very prevalent in Maryland. This picture shows a typical parade of prize winning bulls in a county fair. (Bottom) Blacksmith, Carroll County Farm Museum.

inspection requires that nursery stock be destroyed if it contains injurious insects or plant diseases. Apiaries may be quarantined upon discovery of foul brood or other infectious or contagious diseases harmful to honeybees.

The Director of Inspection and Regulation. Under him are three major operations. The State Chemist registers fertilizers, lime, and pesticides for fulfillment standards. He conducts laboratory tests for meat and poultry adulteration; diagnostic examinations for plants and animals; and examines water and air pollutants. The Chief of Field Inspection sees that Maryland's laws dealing with feed, seed, and fertilizers are obeyed; examples would be the test for adulteration of commercial feed and the check on meeting required standards for fertilizers and soil conditioners. He also enforces the State's Egg Law and its requirements for setting size, such as jumbo and extra large, as well as quality measures, such as AA and A. The Chief of Weights and Measures tests scales, meters, and timing devices, as well as laboratory calibrations. He also inspects dairies.

The Secretary of the Department of Agriculture has great police powers under the 1973 law which established it as a cabinet-level office. For example, he may establish a quarantine of livestock and poultry and may prohibit import, from any state, of any animal believed infected or exposed. He has the power to force full county support by the sheriff or enforcement officers.

As the chapter on the geography of Maryland shows, the State's farms are diverse as are its agricultural products. The presence of a Secretary of Agriculture should do much to solve many of the problems of Maryland's farms. For example, in 1974, as gasoline and other energy fuels were in short supply, the farmer sought to make it clear how his mechanized operations were no longer as dependent on manual labor, but rather needed fuel. The farmer had a strong spokesman now in the Secretary and his lot could be improved.

Chapter 18

THE MARYLAND DEPARTMENT OF TRANSPORTATION AND THE PUBLIC SERVICE COMMISSION

It was evident by 1970 that the fundamental approach to transportation in Maryland, indeed in the nation, would have to be changed from separate treatments of basic modes such as waterways, air, rail, and highways. Before 1971 Maryland had separate departments dealing with State roads, motor vehicles, mass transit, port usage and aviation. Transportation revenues in Maryland and throughout the country were traditionally earmarked for use by the generating agency. Motor fuel taxes and vehicle registration fees were used to build and maintain highways. Fare-box receipts purchased and maintained buses. Registration and license fees for pilots and aircraft supported the agency which regulated aviation.

The Creation of the Maryland Department of Transportation

It was clear that multi-faceted approaches could not solve the overall problems of transportation. Goods and people were being moved in the last third of the 20th century in volume far beyond any earlier known rates. The growth of the Maryland suburbs to a point where their populations outnumbered the cities they surrounded, Baltimore and Washington, meant that people now lived quite a distance from where they worked. On superhighways and expressways thousands of motorists sped to and from suburbs daily. Moreover, buses, planes, and, to a decreasing degree, trains, moved people all over the United States. Ships and modern jet planes permitted mobility of people all over the world. Trucks, trains, planes, and ships carried goods to and from all parts of the globe. Just as people no longer lived close to where they worked, so they no longer depended on consumer goods that were nearby. The world's markets were at Maryland's doorsteps.

But the narrow approach to transportation in Maryland could not continue to let each mode work it out for itself alone. For example, many farm owners and city dwellers did not want to be relocated to make room for ever-increasing multiple highways. Indeed, antifreeway groups in urban communities claimed that the suburbanite was chewing up city land in his hurry to get in and out of the metropolis as rapidly as he could without concern to destruction of valuable properties that brought lower total industrial and commercial assessments and often displaced the poor. Residents of housing projects near airports protested the loud noises and extra hazards of low-flying jets. Ecological experts sought to ban large parking areas in Maryland suburbs and cities, claiming that engine emissions brought a general lowering of air quality. Moreover, conservationists were disturbed by oil spills and other pollution damage to the Port of Baltimore and to Maryland waterways, especially the Chesapeake Bay. Bus riders wanted faster service, and many Baltimoreans and Washingtonians sought to keep all but necessary commercial traffic out of the downtown streets.

(L. to r.) The interchange in Druid Hill Park, near downtown Baltimore connecting the Park, the Jones Falls Expressway and the 28th-29th St. bridges. (Photo by M.E. Warren); loading container cargo from the Port of Baltimore.

It became evident in 1970 that each mode of transportation was interdependent with the others. If motor cars were choking traffic in the downtown streets of Baltimore City, there would need to be more bus transportation or other mass transit, such as subways. The gradual elimination of railway services and the accompanying destruction of roadbeds meant a greater dependence on motor vehicles and planes for moving goods and people.

The Federal Government's Influence

In the 1960's the federal government encouraged movement away from the single modal approach to transportation. The Housing Act of 1961 made federal planning money available to states for transportation planning as well as part of comprehensive urban planning. By 1972 completion of the first round of the continuing, comprehensive, coordinated planning was a prerequisite for a metropolitan area wishing to qualify for further Urban Mass Transportation funding.

At present, the major effort of the federal government lies in the demands of the U.S. Department of Transportation that each state prepare a biennial estimate of transportation facilities throughout the state. This national transportation study will create in cooperating states, including Maryland, a transportation data bank and associated analytical planning methods which justify all transportation efforts.

On August 13, 1973, the President signed into law the $22.9 billion Federal Highway Act, which for the first time permits gasoline taxes to be used for expansion and improvement of urban rapid transit systems. The Highway Trust Fund, once limited only to road usage by the federal government, now permits distribution to cities and states so that they may use the money as is necessary to create balanced transportation systems.

The Department

All these causes—in addition to far-sighted legislators and Maryland executive officers, from the Governor down, including an eight-member task force working since 1969—brought about in 1971 the establishment of a Statewide, cabinet-level Department of Transportation. Headed by a Secretary, the Department was to incorporate the five previously independent, transportation-oriented agencies as constituent Administrations. It was now to have the responsibility for the management and development of highways, ports, mass transit, aviation and motor vehicle operating programs, and physical facilities. The Department includes the following Administrations: State Aviation, Maryland Port, Mass Transit, Motor Vehicle, and State Highway. In 1973 there was a movement to bring in railroad assistance and ultimately include this mode.

Maryland's Transportation Trust Fund

To give financial meaning to the unitary approach to transportation, the earlier used modal approaches to financing, such as the specially earmarked State gas taxes for roads improvement only, were abandoned. In their places, in 1971, was established a Transportation Trust Fund, which combines into one single discretionary account all of the taxes, federal-aid funds, automobile and driver fees, and other revenues which had traditionally been dedicated to specific transportation purposes or modes.

All transportation expenditures are made from the Trust Fund on a priority basis to meet needs in accordance with the coordinated plans laid out by the Department. This permits a simultaneous attack upon the full range of transportation problems, and it keeps one agency from hoarding its dedicated funds while others suffer from under-financing.

Then, too, it permits flexibility so that if, for example, construction slows down in one mode of transportation, such as highways, the money can be shifted by the Department to usage by other modes. Moreover, bonds can be floated for the entire Department's use, thus eliminating market competition between the different modes.

Unique and significant is the fact that the Trust Fund holds on to unexpended monies, at the end of fiscal years, instead of turning them over to the State's general fund. In this way there can be better continuity of planning instead of year-by-year adjustment. Of course, the budget for the Department, like all other departmental budgets, must be approved by the Governor and the General Assembly, and each purchase must be approved by the Board of Public Works.

The funding of the Department's current operations comes from two sources—special and federal funds. The federal funds come from acts that aid particular transportation programs. In fiscal 1974, federal monies turned over to Maryland included $182 million for highway construction, $32 million for improving mass transit (including bus purchases), and $2.8 million for airport improvement. The special funds collected by the Trust Fund include motor vehicle titling and gasoline tax receipts, three-fourths of one percent of the corporate income tax, registration fees for pilots and aircraft, bus fare-box receipts, wharfage fees, and other miscellaneous revenues—all of which added up to $361.5 millions in special funds received by the Department in fiscal 1974. No money is received from the State's general fund, and this is one of the justifications for not turning surpluses back to the general fund at the end of a year.

To give added support to the Trust Fund, especially to the new requirements of supporting mass transit subway systems in the Baltimore and Washington areas, the State in 1972 raised its gasoline tax from seven to nine cents per gallon. This should raise about $40 million in new revenues in 1974 and by 1980 as much as $58 million annually. Moreover, the State increased the consolidated transportation bond ceiling from $500 million to $950 million. The capital improvements are supported by the sale of these bonds.

Boards and Commissions

The Board of Review hears appeals from certain decisions of the Secretary or of any administration or agency in the Department. The Transportation Commission is comprised of 17 members and serves as the public's formal advisory body to the Secretary on matters of program and policy. The Maryland Transportation Authority is responsible for the financing and operation of all toll bridges—those spanning the Chesapeake Bay (William Preston Lane, Jr. Memorial Bridge), the Susquehanna River, and the Potomac River (Governor Harry W. Nice Memorial Bridge). It does the same for the Baltimore Harbor Tunnel Thruway and the John F. Kennedy Memorial Highway. The Governor's six appointees and the Secretary of Transportation serve as the Authority.

Community Involvement

The Federal Highway Administration requires each state to develop a new highway planning process—action plan—that assures full consideration of the economic, social, and environmental effects of federal-aid highway projects. A major requirement of this process is public involvement in the consideration of transportation facilities.

Though in past years there have been public hearings before highways and airports have been built, or before bus routes have been established, in the main they have come after planning has been completed. As a result, polarized feelings arise between the local populace and governmental officials. If the plans were big, so were the misunderstandings. The Maryland Department of Transportation seeks to change this and establish community awareness, involvement, and interaction in the planning. For example, if the Department forecasts a need and the public is strongly against the plans, they will be revised or abandoned.

Two examples of cummunity involvement illustrate the desires of the Department. First, the transportation needs in the northwest corridor in western Prince Georges County include possible alternatives. The same holds true for a selection of a route for a new road parallel to the Reisterstown Road corridor from the Baltimore City line through Baltimore County. Actually, this northwest transportation corridor is part of one of the proposed legs of the future Baltimore subway. In both cases the Department plans to review citizen opinion and to include this into the decision making before the open forum of design and location hearings. In both cases a single mode of transportation may be in order, but it is more likely that multi-modal possibilities—bus, subway, and possibly rail—should be considered. Perhaps after community involvement there will materialize a modal mix.

The State Highway Administration

Maryland's roads may be classified into two categories: The State Primary System and The State Secondary System. The entire State highways system totals about 5,200 miles.

The State Primary System. This has two sub-categories: the federal Interstate and other primary roads. The total Primary System as structured in 1972 included about 1,146 miles of highways.

The Federal Interstate Highways. The theory of the federal Interstate highways system funded in 1956 and advanced by President Eisenhower was that when these highways were completed, one could travel across or up and down the country, without passing a traffic light or a cross road. It was thus that the federal government pledged to pay 90 percent of the costs of constructing the Interstate highways, leaving 10 percent to the states.

In Maryland, I-95 is the leading north-south Interstate highway. Its northern leg is the John F. Kennedy Memorial Highway, a toll road from Baltimore to the Delaware line. The southern leg of I-95 was opened in 1972 and tied together the Baltimore and Washington Beltways before reaching into Virginia. I-70 is the east-west Interstate highway and it has two eastern arms, one (I-70 N) reaching west from the Baltimore Beltway and the other (I-70 S) going west from the Washington Beltway—both converging in Frederick and then stretching farther west across the State as part of the National Freeway. Some of the western parts were still not complete by 1974, but scheduled to be finished in a few years.

Construction of Northeast Expressway (1962), S.W. of Md. Route 22, Harford County.

Two Interstate highways reaching into Maryland from Pennsylvania are I-83, which comes down from central Pennsylvania through Harrisburg and York on the way to Baltimore, and I-81, entering Maryland by way of Chambersburg, Pennsylvania, somewhat farther west than I-83 and then passing through the Hagerstown valley and on into the West Virginia Panhandle before continuing south through Virginia.

The numbering system on Interstate roads is such that even numbered ones like I-70 are east-west highways and odd numbered ones like I-95 are north-south routes.

The Baltimore Beltway, I-695, and the Washington Beltway, I-495, are circumferential roads tying together the three Interstate highways, I-70, I-83, and I-95.

All of Maryland's Interstate roads, which total 328 miles, are part of the State primary road system.

Other State Primary System Roads. The theory of the State primary road system is that all regions of Maryland should be tied together with all the counties. In this way major urban and employment centers would be linked. Some of the non-Interstate roads, like U.S. Route 40, which ties in with I-70 N going west, have long histories as leading highways across the nation. Route 40 was long known as the Cumberland or National Road, authorized by Congress in 1806, and it helped tie together the East and the Middle West. Route 50 from Washington to Ocean City for many years has carried Maryland vacationers to the Atlantic beaches. U.S. Route 1 has long been an Eastern Seaboard highway from Maine to Florida. In Maryland it was the first State road and marked a break from the past when all roads were county roads. Construction of the first thirty-odd miles of Route 1 was started in 1906 and finished in 1915 at what is now the unbelievable cost of $20,000 per mile—bridges and all.

Funding the Primary System. In 1972 the Department of Transportation took over the sole responsibility for funding the construction and maintenance of the primary road system, releasing counties of any responsibility in this area. Of course, the Department's funds for these roads come from the Trust Fund (explained earlier), which gets its money from federal appropriations and special funds such as the gasoline tax and other revenues collected by different transportation agencies, as well as by sale of bonds.

The State Secondary Highways. The State secondary highways system consists of all State highways and bridges not designated as part of the State primary system and including approximately 4,078 miles of highways, ranging from narrow country roads to multilane thoroughfares. The main purpose of these routes is to provide a local travel function or service to adjacent land users.

A total of $308 million has been allocated by the State for improvement of these secondary roads in the five-year program period of 1973-77. This represents the greatest State attention to State secondary road needs in recent years. Every county stands to receive significant amounts, from Prince Georges, which is scheduled to get about $74 million, to Calvert and Worcester Counties which are to get somewhat more than $1 million each.

The Critical Needs Study. Selection of projects for inclusion in the State highway construction and reconstruction program and the allocations of available funds has been based on the Twenty-Year Needs Study. Under the consolidated transportation program, allocation of funds—$308 million—for secondary roads in the period 1973-77—permits at least 30 percent of the 20-year needs to be met in each county during the first five years.

The Chesapeake Bay Parallel Bridge. Of all the bridges in Maryland, this double span has the most unusual history. As early as 1907 there was talk of such a structure, but two world wars and an economic

(Top) Tred Avon Ferry, Talbot County. (Bottom) William Preston Lane, Jr. Memorial Bridge over the Chesapeake Bay, June, 1973.

depression kept plans from materializing until the original Bay Bridge was opened in 1952, providing a two-lane, two-way crossing of the Bay. Its official name is the William Preston Lane, Jr., Memorial Bridge, after a former Governor.

It was soon apparent that a parallel structure was necessary so that each would carry traffic in different directions. After much debate in 1967, the Legislature passed an act authorizing a second bridge to run parallel to the old one, but with three lanes rather than two. In June, 1973, the second structure was opened. The length of the new structure, 3.987 miles, is slightly less than the 4.03 miles between abutments of the first Bay bridge.

In 1972 as many as 6.5 million vehicles crossed the original two-lane bridge. It is estimated that the annual increase of one-third of a million cars is likely to double now that there are parallel bridges with a total of five lanes.

Certainly the Eastern Shore is likely to move away from its rural and rustic modes to more urban and suburban environments. Indeed the added presence of a large convention hall in Ocean City and the growth of condominium apartments led to predictions that the resort could become overly crowded.

The Baltimore Harbor Tunnel. For years previous to the opening of the Harbor Tunnel, travelers moving north and south through Baltimore saw traffic in that City as a nightmare. Discussions concerning a tunnel took place in the 1940's with the view toward having travelers skirt the city. In March, 1955 the contract was let and on November 29, 1957, the Canton-Fairfield crossing was completed. Sixteen miles of approaches lead to the tunnel, which is 6,300 feet long and has four traffic lanes. It is one of the largest metropolitan expressways in the country.

The tunnel approaches tie in with Routes 1, I-95, 301, and 2 going south and I-95 and 40 going north, as well as 40 and 70 N going west. In almost all cases the time saved in avoiding city traffic is about 15 minutes. It is a toll highway that ultimately will pay for its total costs, approaches and all—$130 million.

Maintenance of the State Highway System. The State Highway Administration is responsible for constructing and maintaining more than 5,200 miles of road in its system. The operations involve thousands of workers. In the purchase of land for roads "right of way" experts examine each piece of property and their appraisals are subject to review by outside appraisers. The Bureau of Materials and Research tests materials used. The maintenance operations include snow and ice removal, surface and subsurface patching, shoulder improvements, bridge painting and repairs, preparing and posting traffic signs and installation of automatic signals. Landscaping and soil conservation are other necessities. Picnic areas are provided. Bike lanes are established on some roads. Five toll facilities are operated by the Administration.

The County (and Baltimore City) Roads—not in the State Highways System. The County road system consists of about three times as many miles—about 16,000—as the State system. The counties themselves contribute money for building and maintaining these highways, but much of the funds come from the State in terms of shared gasoline excise taxes and shared automobile licensing fees.

The State has a nine-cent-per gallon gasoline tax. Seven cents of the nine is shared, with the State keeping 65 percent, all the 23 counties together getting 17½ percent, and Baltimore City receiving 17½ percent. The two cents per gallon that are not shared bring funds that go entirely to the State, and like all other transportation revenues are placed in the Trust Fund.

The shared automobile licensing fees are distributed as follows: 17½ percent to the 23 counties; 17½ percent to Baltimore City, and the remaining 65 percent to the Department of Transportation's Trust Fund.

Some of these roads, as Joppa Road in Baltimore County, have long histories as farm-to-market routes, originating with the old wagon trails. Others are newly created highways to serve rapidly developing suburban areas or rich farm lands.

Seventeen counties have their own highways departments and six pay the State Highway Administration to maintain their roads. Baltimore City's Department of Public Works, with the allocated State funds and its own monies, maintains and builds a 2,000-mile system of streets. Some of the City's streets are part of the State Highways System and are built and serviced by the State.

The Division of Transportation Safety

In August, 1972, the Division became operational. It is estimated that the Statewide economic-societal cost of traffic accidents in Maryland during 1972 came to more than $650 million. Traffic accidents continue to exact substantial, needless tolls in lives, suffering, and money. Nationwide, the 57,000 traffic deaths in 1972 alone exceeded total U.S. deaths in Vietnam during the ten war years.

In Maryland, traffic accidents and casualties keep going upward as in 1972 to more than 130,000 accidents, 813 deaths, and 63,621 persons injured annually. The Statewide fatality rate did drop some in 1972 to 3.4 deaths per 100 million vehicle-miles of travel, somewhat below the 4.5 national rate. The $654 million of traffic costs to Marylanders in 1972 represents $305 per licensed driver. If accidents could be lowered by as little as one percent—1,300 fewer accidents—there would be a saving of one-half million dollars.

The Highway Safety Coordinating Committee is the central coordinating agency in the planning and execution of highway safety programs. The Governor is chairman of the Committee and the director of the Division of Transportation Safety is the chief executive. The Governor has the responsibility for dealing with the federal government and its requirements and funding under Federal Highway Safety Acts of 1966 and 1970.

The Division works with other arms of the Department of Transportation, such as Motor Vehicles and Highways and with other departments, such as the State Police, to improve Maryland's safety records. Thus, for example, tests for alcoholic content of drivers are continually being improved, since one out of every two serious accidents is caused by a drunken driver. Revocation of licenses and schooling for violators are additional functions. In all, the three E's still hold—enforcement of laws (including safety of automobiles), education leading to better drivers, and engineering leading to better roads.

Motor Vehicle Administration

In 1973 there were about 3,000,000 registered motor vehicles in Maryland. Headquarters of the Motor Vehicle Administration is in Glen Burnie, with nine regional offices located in different parts of the State. At these offices the following divisional services are carried out:

1. Vehicle safety and reciprocity with other states in use of highways in Maryland and other states.

2. Vehicle titling and registration, including the collection of taxes, totaling $125 million annually, from these two sources.

3. Coordination of field services established at nine regional offices.

4. Data processing keeps computer records on all drivers, including suspensions, revocations, arrests, and point-system status.

5. Driver examination and licensing—available in regional and county offices—including testing of applicant's visual acuity, knowledge of motor vehicle laws, and ability to safely operate a motor vehicle; five different kinds of licenses differentiate types of vehicle to be operated.

6. Driver review and rehabilitation seeks to assist in the rehabilitation of unsafe drivers; license review officers in conjunction with professional consultants advise on cases with physical-disability or mental-disturbance elements.

7. Driver improvement and records—concerned with suspension, revocation and restriction of driving privileges of those not responsive to rehabilitation or who have committed very serious violations.

8. Financial responsibility—processes require accident reports on personal injury or property damage in excess of $100.

9. Investigation—agents effect the return of operators' and chauffeurs' licenses and tags from those drivers who have had their privileges revoked or suspended; also regulate automobile dealers, wreckers and scrap processors.

Driving Licenses. All those driving motor vehicles in Maryland must have licenses. Eligible persons are issued permits lettered "A" to "E" to denote the type vehicle they seek to drive—passenger car, light truck, bus, heavy truck, or tractor-trailer. A learner's license costing $8, permits the learner to drive a car for as long as 60 days before taking an examination, providing a qualified driver is seated beside him. One must be at least 18 years of age before he is permitted to drive unless he has passed an approved driver-education course, which makes him eligible at 16.

Officers and employees of the United States are exempt from license requirements while driving a federally owned or leased vehicle on official business. Also exempt are those operating farm equipment on their land or temporarily on State highways. Any nonresident of the State may drive with out-of-state licenses providing his qualifications conform with Maryland law or there is reciprocity.

Mentally disabled persons, habitual drunkards, or drug addicts are refused licenses. Those with refused, suspended, or revoked licenses are not permitted to drive, nor are those who cannot understand signs. Persons with physical disabilities have restricted licenses.

Operators' licenses are renewed in Maryland every two years, without examination, at a cost of $2.

Mandatory Revocations. Licenses are revoked for a number of conditions, such as manslaughter resulting from motor vehicle operation, driving impairment due to narcotic drugs or alcohol, failure to stop and render aid in event of accident causing death or bodily injury, fleeing or eluding a police officer, and the accumulation of 12 traffic violation points.

Express Consent for Chemical Test. Since July 1, 1969, any person making application for a Maryland driver's license must sign the Express Consent Pledge to take a chemical test to determine the alcoholic content of his blood, breath, or urine. The declaration of consent makes it clear that the driver may refuse to take the chemical test, but if found guilty of operating a car while intoxicated, would be automatically subject to revocation of license for 60 days or more for a first offense and for not less than one year for a second or subsequent offense. In addition to these administrative penalties, there are severe criminal penalties for driving while intoxicated, which may be fines of $1,000 and two years imprisonment. There are also lesser but serious penalties for driving while impaired by smaller blood-alcohol content.

The Point System. In 1960 Maryland adopted a Point System whereby persons convicted of moving violations were assessed points according to the seriousness of the offenses. This legislation requires suspension review of a violator's license upon accumulation of eight points and mandatory revocation upon accumulation of 12 points. Points assessed are retained for a two-year period; violations, however, remain permanently on the record. Punishment is required at prescribed point levels, but suspension or revocation of license may take place whenever a driver is deemed unsafe. Therefore, two convictions occurring in a relatively short time could result in punishment even though the point assessment is short of suspension or revocation levels.

Driver Rehabilitation Clinic. Problem drivers who have accumulated penalty points are assigned to attend the Driver Rehabilitation Clinic. These include those who have accumulated eight points, have had licenses revoked, or are referred to the Clinic by the Medical Advisory Board or the License Reviewers of the Administration, or by the courts. The four-week course includes topics such as accident causes, motor vehicle laws, and defensive driving. Examinations are given at the end. In fiscal 1973 more than 27,000 drivers took the course.

Titles, Taxes and Tags. All cars driven with permanence in Maryland must have titles and tags in this State. Titles for vehicles not subject to inspection, normally new cars, cost $2. Titles subject to inspection (all used passenger cars that are sold require inspection by a State-approved facility) cost $4. All sales or transfers of cars are subject to a State excise tax—four percent of the selling price. Annual passenger car tag fees are $20 for vehicles up to 3,700 pounds and $30 for heavier cars.

Vehicle Safety. The Division of Vehicle Safety tests and approves equipment in conformance with standards established by the federal Vehicle Equipment Safety Commission. For example, the 600 school buses in Maryland are inspected three times annually, and temporarily suspended usage of 151 of these buses at different times in the year has occurred. Tire safety standards and trailer hitch requirements are checked.

The Compulsory Motor Vehicle Insurance Law. Initiated January 1, 1973, the owner of every motor vehicle registered in Maryland was required to maintain automobile liability insurance in the amount of $15/30,000 for bodily injury, $5,000 for property damage, and $2,500 economic loss coverage. In 1974 the bodily injury requirement was changed to $20/40,000 and $2,500 medical coverage was added. Under this law all Maryland licensed insurance companies are required to notify the Administration of every automobile liability insurance policy that is cancelled or terminated. The Motor Vehicle Administration in turn notifies the affected vehicle owner that his or her registration is retrieved.

In order to sell insurance coverage to those persons who find it difficult to get policies from traditional companies, the State established the State-owned Maryland Automobile Insurance Fund. MAIF must insure for at least minimum coverage any motorist rejected by at least two private insurers. Thus there is no reason for anyone not to fulfill the mandated insurance requirements. Of course, there are some serious problem drivers whose licenses have been revoked and who are not even eligible for insurance with MAIF. Driving is a privilege and the 816 deaths on Maryland highways in 1973 attest to the seriousness of determining who may drive. For the first six months of 1973 alone, insurance companies cancelled or terminated insurance for 160,000 motorists; not all of these—yet many—were due to unsafe driving.

State Aviation Administration

On July 26, 1972, the State purchased from Baltimore City the then 24-year-old Friendship International Airport for $36 million. It then became a part of the unitary State Department of Transportation.

The Airport's name was changed to Baltimore-Washington International in 1973 with the view that air travelers would recognize the wide geographical area that it served. The Airport is situated near Glen Burnie, in the center of the golden triangle of Washington, Baltimore, and Annapolis, and is the area's only regional commercial air facility.

Terminal Expansion Program, Baltimore-Washington International Airport, State Aviation Administration of the Maryland Department of Transportation. Construction period: 1973-1976.

When the State took over the Airport it promised improvements enlarging and modernizing all facilities and services. The expansion program to be completed by 1976 represents an investment of $39 million. The program will be funded through airline user charges, space rentals, and grants under the Federal Airport and Airway Development Program. The terminal building will be expanded from its present 350,000 square feet to 514,000, with expanded ticket offices, boarding facilities, baggage areas, and customs facilities for passengers arriving from overseas. New air cargo facilities are to be built. Runways will be resurfaced and centerline lighting is to be installed. The expansion plans are so exciting that BWI was named "Airport of the Year" in 1973 by *Airport World.*

In the search to reduce aircraft engine noise over neighboring communities, the State Aviation Administration and the Federal Aviation Administration are using a revised instrument landing approach procedure. The new procedure requires all aircraft approaching from the east and southeast to remain as high as possible for as long as feasible, consistent with established safe operating regulations.

All these improvements are designed to serve some 5.6 million passengers annually who will be boarding airplanes at Baltimore-Washington International Airport by 1982. In 1972 the Airport accommodated 1.5 million passengers.

The Maryland Department of Transportation feels that Baltimore City would not have had the fiscal capabilities to carry out such improvements at BWI. Furthermore, it feels that the unified Maryland Transportation Fund can bring about progress in short order, particularly with federal assistance. At the same time the State can make the Airport an integral part of the larger regional air facilities which include Washington National Airport and Dulles International in northern Virginia. The latter two are federal government facilities and receive more funds from federal budgets, thus making it more difficult for BWI to compete.

In 1973 there were 12 municipally owned airports serving Maryland: Cambridge, Crisfield, Cumberland, Easton, Frederick, Garrett County, Hagerstown, Montgomery County, Ocean City, Pier 4 Heliport (Baltimore), Salisbury-Wicomico County, and St. Marys County. In addition, 28 privately owned public-usage airports dotted the State. These 40 commercial airports range from very limited facilities at Gill Airport, Chestertown to very full accommodations for a city the size of Salisbury. More attention is to be paid by the State Aviation Administration to these airports which lack the glamor of BWI.

The question of airports for Maryland's smaller communities is becoming increasingly important. The Administration will need to turn to this issue, since some cities that once had acceptable facilities show a need for State support.

Effectiveness of the Aviation Administration's drive to strengthen air service in Maryland was demonstrated early in 1974 when the agency argued successfuly against an attempt by Pan American Airways to suspend its European and South American flights from BWI. The Administration won the case before the U.S. Civil Aeronautics Board, contending that Pan Am's proposed action would seriously damage international commerce of the Maryland area and that the airline's plea of insufficient fuel had not been validated.

Maryland Port Administration

The Port of Baltimore is a crucial component in the economy of the State. It produces $1.6 billion in Maryland's economy annually, thus generating $38 million in taxes each year. It provides jobs for 63,000 who are directly employed in the Port's activities and for an additional 100,000 persons whose jobs are indirectly related to the Port. It is evident that the Port of Baltimore is the industrial heart of the State.

Baltimore's port began in 1706, twenty-three years before the City was founded. Movement of wheat to the West Indies brought Baltimore fame in the 18th century. But it was the freedom from British blockades during the Revolutionary War and the War of 1812 that brought fortune to the city on the Patapsco. Baltimore shipwrights outfitted the first frigate of the Continental Navy and its two cruisers. During the War of 1812 Baltimore-built privateers preyed on enemy shipping. When the two wars were over the local builders and shippers turned their attention toward South American and China trade. In the 1830's they built the famous Baltimore Clippers—the fastest ships then afloat. The close of the Civil War brought to Baltimore such rapid development as a port that in 1874 *Scribner's Magazine* called the City "the Liverpool of America."

The opening of the Panama Canal in 1914 gave Baltimore's port great advantages over the more northerly ports, enabling it to move more westbound tonnage through the Canal than any other Atlantic port. World Wars I and II raised the Port to new heights of importance, not only for foreign traffic, but because of its key activities in tying together industrial development such as steelmaking in the then newly established Maryland Steel Company (later acquired by Bethlehem Steel) and shipbuilding at the Bethlehem-Fairfield shipyards and at Maryland Shipbuilding and Drydock Company. Moreover, the railroads brought grain and coal from the states to the west of Maryland, and the Port gained prominence for its grain elevators that permitted transshipment to European markets.

In 1956 the Maryland General Assembly recognized that the Baltimore Port was the State's most important single factor in economic growth, and thus it passed legislation establishing the Maryland Port Authority. This was to be a single agency coordinating the efforts of city, State, and private groups on behalf of all Maryland ports.

In 1971, when the State Department of Transportation came into being, the Authority became a part of the Department and its name was changed to the Maryland Port Administration.

The Port of Baltimore

Oceangoing vessels make their way through the deep channel of Chesapeake Bay and on up the Patapsco to Sparrows Point, Dundalk, Canton, Locust Point, Fairfield, Port Covington, and the Inner Harbor. The Port has approximately 45 miles of waterfront area and 1,589 acres of sheltered waters. There are 88 general cargo berths, 65 special cargo berths, and 25 public bulk cargo berths. The nine major international cargo terminals provide multiple services, such as warehousing, heavy lift, ground storage, and simultaneous loading and discharge. The large size of the harbor permits loading and discharging of 175 vessels at any one time, with easily accessible berthing.

The Port of Baltimore is one of the world's greatest centers of international commerce. In 1973 it handled 36.0 million long tons of export-import cargo or about 13 percent of all the foreign tonnage loaded and unloaded at major North American ports. Grain exports alone reached an all-time high in 1973 of over 100 million bushels of food and feed. Petroleum imports handled at the Port's 12 oil piers totaled 10.7 million tons; iron ore 12.2 million. Coal is the greatest export. The main channels, now 42 feet, are hopefully to be increased to 50 feet.

An exciting development that has completely revolutionized the transfer of cargo is containerization. Container ships carry truck-sized steel or aluminum shipping boxes (eight feet wide and 20 to 40 feet long). Once packed and sealed, these boxes can be mounted directly on a truck chassis or dropped onto a railroad flatcar by Baltimore's ten-story cranes, for hauling to and from a seaport terminal. The Port Administration has provided a special site—the Dundalk Marine Terminal—where massive amounts of container cargo can be transferred and where expansion is possible. New cranes were purchased to handle the containers. The wisdom of this special attention to container cargo is shown by the fact that in 1968 there were 77,455 tons of container freight handled, whereas in 1973 the tonnage was 1.8 million. Moreover, the total number of container ships from various parts of the world increased for those same years from 104 to more than 700. Piggy-back trailers arrive on three trunk line railroads serving between Baltimore and the north, south and midwest—the Baltimore & Ohio and Chesapeake & Ohio (Chessie System), Penn Central, and Western Maryland. The three railroads have facilities at the Dundalk Marine Terminal to handle piggy-backs and containers on their flatcars.

Each year the Port handles $2 to $3 billion worth of cargo, including from 2.0 to 2.5 million tons of containerized cargo and 225,000 foreign-made automobiles. Seventy overseas steamship lines make regular calls at the Port and more than 440 vessels each month sail to and from the Port to 109 different countries. About 4,500 ships call annually at Baltimore, an average of about 12 new vessels a day. Then, too, while the number of vessels arriving each day has diminished some in Baltimore, as in other ports, the size of the freighters has increased markedly.

Servicing the foreign and domestic lines are 34 well established steamship agents and operators. They arrange for the vessel's berthing, pilots, tugs, longshore labor, and repairs. Working with brokers, they process bills of lading, manifests, and consular invoices. Then, too, there are about 50 firms specializing in freight forwarding or customhouse brokerage. Eight shipbuilding, repair, and dismantling yards offer overhaul and drydocking.

Foreign consuls from 22 countries work with these agents, as do international banking firms, marine insurance agents, expert packing and crating firms, inspectors, weighers, and surveyors. A highly skilled labor force of about 4,800 dock workers meet stevedore and other needs. In 1973 they logged about 5.2 million hours of work.

Cruise Service—A Growth Industry. From a meager beginning in 1962, when there was but one sailing with a total of 296 passengers, Baltimore's cruise business now includes about 20 yearly sailings, averaging about 520 passengers per cruise. The City is ideally located to draw from a regional population of 32 million, including Maryland and nearby states.

The World Trade Center. After years of discussion, on October 4, 1973, ground was broken at Pier 2 in the Baltimore Inner Harbor for the $21 million World Trade Center. The 30-story pentagonal structure is to be operated by the Maryland Port Administration and will house the MPA offices and offer rentable space to private port-oriented businesses. The Center is but part of a broader plan costing $250 million to be expended by the Maryland Transportation Trust Fund in the 1970's and 1980's for development of needed terminals, cargo areas, berths, a cruise building, and other waterfront facilities.

The Future of the Port. While the number of visiting ships is not likely to go beyond 5,000 annually, the vessels of the future are likely to be bigger and faster, thus bringing more cargo. There is no doubt that world trade is likely to be accelerated. Deepening of the Port's main channels from 42 feet to 50 feet is imperative for the handling of ore, coal, and grain. These cargoes move in very large ships and need deep water.

Then there is the big problem of dredge materials—how to get rid of them? Flotsam, oil spills, and debris are troublesome. Raw sewage emptied into the harbor waters presents another problem.

Basic to all plans is the hope that the future will bring a larger, more active United States Merchant Marine. At present only a small percentage of American ships carry foreign cargo and participate in world trade. Development of a nuclear-powered Merchant fleet could change the picture.

Maryland's Other Ports

In addition to Baltimore's deepwater facilities, two other Maryland ports serve oceangoing ships, with a third planned for the near future. The Piney Point facility on the lower Potomac River is owned by the Steuart Petroleum Company and caters to bulk shipments of fuel and petroleum products. The Eastern Shore port of Cambridge is on the Choptank River, a tributary of the Bay. The Cambridge Marine Terminal is a single 500-foot marginal pier, served by a 25-foot channel. The cargo handled there is largely frozen fish to supply local packing plants.

A third port facility is planned for Cove Point, in Calvert County. It will specialize in handling imported liquefied natural gas and is to be built by a private company supplying natural gas to a market covering seven mid-Atlantic states and the District of Columbia.

Mass Transit Administration

No transportation study can neglect the importance of mass transit solutions. For too long commuter railroad lines have been reducing service or disappearing entirely. Mass transit was left to ever increasing passenger cars, which cluttered roads and covered the countryside with more and more expressways. When the Department of Transportation came into being in 1971 and established the Mass Transit Administration under it, there was evidence that a unified public bus system was needed for the Baltimore metropolitan area, which had a population of over two million.

The Baltimore Metropolitan Transit System. The Metropolitan Transit System was established within the MTA to create a unified public mass transit bus service for Baltimore City, Baltimore County, and Anne Arundel County, and to purchase any private transit lines within those local units. It has authority to extend the services into Carroll, Howard, and Harford Counties in the future.

By the close of fiscal 1973 the MTA's bus fleet in the Baltimore metropolitan area included 869 service-ready buses operating on 40 different routes. Some of the new features included:

Park 'n Ride services providing free parking at suburban locations and nonstop transit to and from downtown Baltimore.

Streamlined transit to Colt football games at the Baltimore Memorial Stadium.

Lower fares on in-town Baltimore shuttle buses.

The purchase of 100 new buses, hopefully with federal assistance which was changed in 1973 to permit urban mass transit improvements to be financed out of the U.S. Highway Trust Fund, heretofore earmarked for roads.

Installation of two-way radios on all buses, thus assuring greater safety for passengers and greater efficiency.

Reduced fares for senior citizens and for elementary and secondary school students.

Express buses from heavily populated suburban areas to downtown Baltimore.

The Statewide Public Transit System. The Mass Transit Administration is also interested in small urban areas throughout Maryland. Its officials have met with local officers in Salisbury, Hagerstown, and Cumberland to help draft plans for federal and State aid for public bus transportation in smaller cities. Comprehensive transportation studies have been prepared to analyze needs in the Annapolis and the Bel Air-Edgewood-Aberdeen-Havre de Grace corridors. Similar studies are to be made for Easton, Frederick, Ocean City, Cambridge, Greenbelt, and Columbia.

Baltimore's Regional Rapid Transit System. For many years there has been much talk of a rapid underground transit system serving the metropolitan Baltimore area. Traffic conditions have gone from bad to worse, with streams of cars, bumper to bumper, jamming the main arteries of Baltimore daily. Rapid transit is a necessary complement to the automobile and the bus system.

To the worker who must commute to the city, rapid transit will mean getting to work and home in less time than it takes the suburban motorist to fight a twice-a-day battle with traffic. Moreover, rapid transit will reduce air pollution, rescue land in downtown Baltimore from conversion into parking lots, attract new businesses, and prime the economic pump.

A number of key steps toward rapid transit in Maryland were taken between 1971 and 1973. The official establishment of the Maryland Department of Transportation in 1971 ensured a unitary approach to transportation problems, including a strong consideration of rapid transit plans. The passage by the Legislature in 1972 of a two-cent increase in the State gasoline excise tax to help pay for Maryland's share of Phase I of the Baltimore Regional Rapid Transit System was another good omen.

On October 31, 1972, the Urban Mass Transportation Administration of the U.S. Department of Transportation approved a capital grant request to finance initial construction of Phase I of the Baltimore Regional Rapid Transit System. The federal government made available a first installment of $22.5 million on a total grant of $270 million for construction of all of Phase I. The 8.5 miles of Section A of Phase I between the Inner Harbor and Reisterstown Road Plaza in Baltimore County was to be one portion of the north-west corridor.

The federal grant of $22.5 million implied that the U.S. government would financially assist all of Phase I, which consists of a northwest corridor from Owings Mills to Charles Center and a southern leg from Charles Center to Marley, with a spur to the Baltimore-Washington International Airport. The fiscal 1974 estimate of the cost of Phase I was $956 million, with inflationary rises creating even greater costs unless the schedule of 1980 was met. Unfortunately, in June, 1974 the federal government seemed to renege on its full promise.

In 1973 the State appropriated funds for design drawings for Section A, which would include five miles of subway tunnels, three miles of aerial tracks, and ten stations. Construction was scheduled to begin in the fall of 1974.

High speeds will be maintained with cruising at 75 miles per hour, thus permitting passengers to travel from Owings Mills to Charles Center in less than 22 minutes. The subway vehicles will be approximately

75 feet long and will seat about 70 in each car. It is estimated that 153,000 riders will use Phase I when it opens in 1980. Fares would be based on distances traveled and are planned to cover total operating costs. Four other corridors planned beyond Phase I would represent north, northeast, southeast, and west lines, reaching out to all nearby suburbs of Baltimore and connecting them with one another. Completion of these lines was set at "before the year 2000."

The investment in rapid transit for the Baltimore metropolitan area represents a strong belief in future growth of the region. It is a daring venture that shows faith in Baltimore City, and support by the State indicates that Maryland as a whole stands to profit.

Washington Metropolitan Area Rapid Transit System. To distribute transportation funds equitably throughout the State and to assure passage by the Legislature of funding for Baltimore rapid transit, the MTA was authorized to support the Washington Metropolitan Area Rapid Transit System. In 1972 the State assumed the remaining $161 million capital commitment of Montgomery and Prince Georges Counties for their portion of the Metro's costs, which involve the 23 Metro stations within Maryland. The Metro has planned to complete a $3.1 billion subway much earlier than Baltimore's, and it, too, held promise for easing problems in the heavy commuter traffic between the Maryland and Virginia suburbs and Washington. Like the Baltimore rapid transit plan, it met with many frustrations due to rising costs and multiple funding involving the District of Columbia, Maryland and Virginia.

The Railroads

It is strange that one of the older forms of transportation—the railroads—should have been left out of the Maryland unitary system of transportation as established in 1971. The railroads had their American beginnings in Baltimore in 1823, yet in the last 25 years important commuter roadways like the old Maryland and Pennsylvania "Ma and Pa" line were abandoned and the roadbeds were allowed to be sold. Perhaps too late has Maryland found that these commuter trains and the rights of ways could have been rejuvenated and made worthy substitutes for other forms of transportation which have choked our roads. Trains are environmentally preferable in many situations to truck carriers. They result in less noise and congestion, and they require less land for rights of way.

In 1972 the Secretary of the Maryland Department of Transportation won support for a commuter rail improvement program. The Legislature later appropriated $1.5 million to purchase new cars for commuter services conducted by the Chessie System and the Penn Central. Other conditions needed to be cleared, such as the Department's request for the Washington Terminal to reduce terminal fees, and its desire to have the Interstate Commerce Commission permit the railroads to increase fare structures.

Another factor that led the railroads to gain new attentions in Maryland was the 1973 accident in which a freighter collided with a railroad bridge spanning the Chesapeake and Delaware Canal and disrupted rail service to rural Eastern Shore areas. The Penn Central wished to abandon the route entirely after the accident, saying it was unprofitable. Fortunately, the route was reopened. Federal assistance is being sought for subsidized support, on a federal-State matching agreement for retention of disputed trackage in northeastern United States.

As 1974 unfolded, as the nation's energy crisis became more severe,

Bridge crossing the Chesapeake and Delaware Canal at Chesapeake City, Md.

and as Marylanders became more ecology conscious, it was evident that the railroads ultimately would have to be considered important in any unified transportation plan. Fortunately, the federal government has kept many rail lines alive through subsidies such as Amtrak. The states are beginning to recognize that they, too, must assist. For example, in 1973 Maryland and West Virginia agreed to share with Amtrak, a federal agency, the subsidy of maintaining passenger service between Cumberland and Washington, with intermediate West Virginia and Maryland points. The annual deficit to be subsidized was $400,000.

Public Service Commission

The PSC is not a part of the Department of Transportation; it is an independent State agency. The Commission is composed of three members appointed by the Governor for six-year terms.

The PSC has jurisdiction over common carriers, including railroads, sleeping car companies, bus lines, express companies, water transportation carriers, aircraft carriers, toll bridges, and other carriers engaged in public transportation of passengers or freight within the State (except for those passenger carriers under the jurisdiction of the Washington Metropolitan Area Transit Commission). The PSC also has jurisdiction over all taxicabs in Baltimore City and County, and Hagerstown and Cumberland. It further has jurisdiction over all gas, electric, telephone, telegraph, water, sewage disposal, heating, and refrigeration companies operating in Maryland. In a broad sense it has jurisdiction over all public utilities and common carriers in the State.

The Commission has the power to set minimum and maximum rates and to suspend schedules pending the determination of the reasonableness of rates for such utilities as gas, electricity, telephone service, or transportation services. The Commission holds hearings and it may penalize the utilities or require deductions in rates, as it did with the Baltimore Gas and Electric Company in the 1960's.

It hears matters related to rate adjustment, applications to exercise franchises, approval of issuance of securities, promulgation of new rules, quality of utility and common carrier service, and railroad safety.

The General Counsel. The General Counsel of the PSC is appointed by the Governor for a six-year term. He is the legal adviser to the Commission. He also represents the Commission in appeals from court decisions. The General Counsel does not participate in any proceeding before the Commission. He sometimes appears before federal regulatory bodies such as the Federal Power Commission, the Interstate Commerce Commission, and the Federal Communications Commission to express opinions on topics affecting Maryland. He may appear before a federal agency as a representative of the National Association of Regulatory Commissions, a body tying in the interests of all 50 states. He is a part-time officeholder at a low salary frozen by statutory law. As a result, the office is often vacant. It should be a full-time job with salary open and set in the annual budget.

The People's Counsel. Maryland differs from many states in having a People's Counsel operating in public service activities. The People's Counsel, appointed by the Governor, represents the public and is a sort of ombudsman, taking the public's pleas and arguing its causes. He appears before the PSC when a hearing is in original jurisdiction, and in the courts on behalf of the public. His main pleas deal with the reasonableness of rates, services, and practices. In recent years he has argued against sharp hikes in telephone, gas, and electric rates in the Metropolitan Baltimore area. He has also opposed extension of high-voltage electrical transmission lines in Montgomery and Frederick Counties. The Commission has no control over him, and he often takes opposite views from that group arguing the people's side.

Problems. The PSC must follow the law, which says that every utility is entitled to a fair return for its investment. On the other hand, the consumer must be protected. To walk this tight rope is not easy. Public utility operation is a complex activity involving elements such as engineering, labor, economics, accounting, and law. It is not always easy for the consumer to recognize these complexities.

Chapter 19

THE DEPARTMENT OF LICENSING AND REGULATION

Until 1970 more than 30 State agencies and boards responsible for licensing and regulating businesses, professions, and trades acted largely independent of one another, with each reporting directly to the Governor. In 1970 the Department of Licensing and Regulations was created as a cabinet-level secretariat. The Secretary of the Department is appointed by the Governor.

In many ways this department can be thought of as "the protector of the public." If the Marylander works in industry—and most of the State's labor force does—the Division of Labor and Industry protects his wages and safety. If he has savings in a bank or building and loan association, the Bank Commissioner and the director of the Building, Savings and Loan Associations protect his funds. If he borrows small cash, then the new Consumer Credit Office protects him from excessive interest rates. The Home Improvement Commission protects the consumers from overcharging on home repairs, and the Real Estate Commission checks on the integrity of a person who sells him a house. Even his recreational pursuits are protected to assure honesty in athletic affairs and horse racing and avoidance of outright pornography in moving pictures.

Then, too, there are a number of boards that assure standards on jobs by licensing skilled workers who serve the public, such as barbers, cosmetologists, plumbers, and engineers.

In a sense the Department is a consumer's protection agency. The old concept of "the consumer beware" has been changed to "the consumer be protected." Services for and to persons have become complex, and the consumer has no recourse except through the law and protective agencies.

The State is likely to see a greater demand for more legislation dealing with licensing and regulation. For example, in 1974 a bill was introduced into the Legislature to regulate automobile repair and to require warranties for six months or 6,000 miles for major repairs. Other bills seek to regulate the repair of home appliances. Then, too, there are some who believe that automobile mechanics should be licensed as should other repairmen. While the 1974 Legislature did not pass bills going that far in regulation, it did pass legislation requiring that no automobile repair bill can exceed the estimate given the customer by more than 10 percent in jobs costing $50 or more.

This chapter deals with an analysis of the agencies now providing these protections.

Division of Labor and Industry

The field of labor has undergone some radical changes in recent years. To begin with, the 1960's and early 1970's saw a virtual turnabout in laws related to women in industry. The women's liberation movement brought about the removal of many restrictive (some would call them "protective") laws that came into being in the 19th and early 20th centuries. The modern thought is that the State does not need laws protecting women from hours as long as those worked by men, or from so-called extra-hazardous jobs. Practically all of those laws have been scrapped.

The rapid rise of collective bargaining has brought the need for additional mediation and conciliation services by the State. New State and federal laws dealing with equal opportunity in employment require more supervision. Increased industrial accidents and new interests in this field by the federal government require more inspections.

Indeed, some labor specialists, especially organized labor leaders, believe that there should be a cabinet-level Department of Labor in Maryland with its own secretariat. Their point is that the activities are scattered; many are in the Department of Employment and Social Services, some in the independent agency known as the Workmen's Compensation Commission, others in the Division of Labor and Industry under the Department of Licensing and Regulation. They say that if the federal government has a Department of Labor, why not the State? At present the people of Maryland, at least the Governor and the Legislature, are not yet ready for this view.

The Division is one of the oldest governmental labor and industry agencies in the country; it actually predates the U.S. Department of Labor by one year, having been established in 1884. During the first thirty-two years the agency was known as the Bureau of Industrial Statistics and Information. In 1916 it became the State Bureau of Labor and Statistics and added to its tasks the investigation of unemployment and the mediation of labor disputes.

In 1970 the agency became a Division under the Department of Licensing and Regulation. The Division has three main tasks: to promote harmony between industry and labor; to promote the welfare of wage earners; and to collect, systematize and report statistical details relating to matters within the jurisdiction of the Division.

By law the Division is responsible for and administers activities in the following areas: consent collective bargaining; representation elections; apprenticeship and training; occupational safety education; boiler inspection; child labor; wage and hour; collection of unpaid wages; equal pay for equal work; prevailing wages on public contracts; hours of work in factories; licensing and regulation of fee-charging employment agencies; licensing of workshops; licensing of homeworkers, and industrial registration.

The Division is comprised of six operating services: Labor Standards, Safety Engineering and Education, Safety Inspection, Apprenticeship and Training, Mediation and Conciliation, and Research and Information. A number of these services have boards which set policies.

The Labor Standards Service. This Service is responsible for administering the protective labor laws and for issuing the licenses and certificates required by these statutes. Investigative personnel are assigned to monitoring these laws: wages and hours, wage payment and collection, equal pay for equal work, child labor, hours for work in factories, industrial registration, contracts for public works, and fee-charging employment agencies.

An example of the investigatory work makes clear the breadth of the operations. The new Wage and Hour Law passed by the Legislature in 1965 states that, with certain exceptions, all employees be paid a minimum wage and time and one-half for all work beyond 40 hours in any work week. Investigations in 1972 showed 277 firms in violation, with 1,772 employees underpaid and $166,355 recovered.

The Child Labor Laws of Maryland set forth the conditions under which minors may be employed, types and hours of employment, and ages of employables. The investigators working for the Bureau of Contracts for Public Works seek to establish, under the prevailing wage laws, hourly wage rates for various crafts within the industry and then to apply them to contractors for public buildings. For 1972 alone, the wage rates were applied to payrolls of $371 million.

Safety Engineering and Education Service. The primary functions of this Service are to develop and present safety courses, conduct accident prevention surveys, and analyze employers' reports of injuries.

Mediation and Conciliation Service. This Service has major responsibility for labor management relations. The Service conducts consent elections; these votes determine whether employees want to have a bargaining group represent them. The Service seeks to aid both employees and employers from growing so far apart that work stoppage takes place. The Service in 1972 assisted in obtaining a settlement in labor negotiations at Johns Hopkins Hospital, and the terms set a bargaining pattern for all hospitals in the Baltimore area.

Safety Inspection Service. The Service has adopted 67 nationally recognized safety and sanitary codes for minimum standards. New machinery, chemical processes, production methods, and new safety devices are analyzed. In 1972 alone the 38 inspectors of the Service conducted 27,241 safety inspections. Passenger elevators, cranes, derricks, and construction hoists get special attention. The boiler safety unit of the Service enforces the State law on this subject, since boilers can be highly hazardous. Special certificates are given where inspections are passed.

Other Services. The Apprenticeship and Training Service operates with the Maryland Apprenticeship and Training Council (six members appointed by the Governor representing management and labor) in the supervision of registered apprentices. In 1972 these two groups cooperated with the U.S. Department of Labor in reviewing the activities of 3,600 apprentices registered in 71 trades, especially the construction, metal, printing, and automotive trades.

The Research and Information Service seeks to analyze quality and quantity of inspection activities and the work load in the department, as well as to respond to questions by the public.

Injury Frequency Rates in Various Manufacturing Industries, 1950-70

(The number of disabling work injuries for each million employee hours of work)

Standard industrial classification	1950	1955	1960	1965	1970
19 Ordnance and accessories	6.2	6.1	2.4	2.8	9.8
20 Food and kindred products	18.9	18.6	21.1	23.4	28.8
21 Tobacco	6.8	6.6	8.7	9.5	11.9
22 Textile mill products	11.0	9.7	9.2	9.6	10.4
23 Apparel and other textile products	6.6	6.9	6.7	6.8	7.7
24 Lumber and wood products	49.8	40.5	38.0	36.0	34.1
25 Furniture and fixtures	21.0	18.1	18.8	19.9	22.0
26 Paper and allied products	16.1	12.9	12.3	12.6	13.9
27 Printing and publishing	8.2	9.1	9.5	10.0	11.7
28 Chemical and allied products	11.1	8.0	7.4	7.5	8.5
29 Petroleum and coal products	9.3	6.5	6.8	8.6	11.3
30 Rubber and plastic products	10.0	6.9	4.4	5.2	18.6
31 Leather and leather products	10.8	11.8	11.4	13.4	15.2
32 Stone, clay, and glass products	20.5	19.0	18.3	18.7	23.8
33 Primary metal industries	14.8	12.2	10.5	12.9	16.9
34 Fabricated metal products	19.0	15.4	15.4	18.1	22.4
35 Machinery, except electrical	13.8	11.1	10.8	11.9	14.0
36 Electrical equipment	7.4	5.6	5.2	5.9	8.1
37 Transportation equipment	8.3	5.7	6.1	6.6	7.9
38 Instruments and related products	7.7	5.8	5.8	6.2	7.9
39 Miscellaneous manufacturing	13.3	12.5	12.7	13.3	15.8

Sources. U.S. Department of Labor: Press release 71-663, 20 Dec 71; press release 1484, 23 Feb 56; Bureau of Labor Statistic *Handbook of Labor Statistics 1970*, p 364-74; Bulletin 1098, *Work Injuries in the United States During 1950*, p 12-15.

Occupational Safety and Health Planning ties in with the federal government's Williams-Steiger Act of 1970 on this subject. The Act, with nearly full federal funding, requires the State to take initiatives in this field. The intent of the Maryland Safety and Health Planning Act passed in 1973 was similar to that of the federal government—namely, to assure each worker a safe and healthful place of employment and to reduce the ever rising incidence of work-related accidents and injury. Occupational Safety and Health Service requires the employer to submit a first report on a job-related injury or illness after three days absence to the Division of Labor and Industry as well as to the Workmen's Compensation Commission.

With all the good work taking place in State inspection of factories and industrial plants there are some authorities who believe that more inspections are necessary if industrial accidents and occupational diseases are to be diminished. The belief is that most manufacturing plants should be inspected at least once a year and construction sites once every three months. Moreover, permanent inspectors might be assigned at each large plant.

State Insurance Division

In the Department of Licensing and Regulation the State Insurance Division authorizes and licenses insurance companies, agents, and brokers to do business in the State. The Insurance Commissioner approves all policies for life, accident, health, fire, casualty, title, and other insurance offered for sale in the State by authorized companies. The Department approves or disapproves the rates for most kinds of insurance other than life, accident, and health.

It is the function of the insurance examiners to examine the affairs of insurance companies authorized to transact the business of insurance in the State. The examiners verify and evaluate assets and check on whether investments are in compliance with State requirements. The examiners determine whether the companies are solvent, the treatment of the policy holders is fair, and the companies are in compliance with State insurance laws.

Rate requests are not always upheld. For example, in 1973 the St. Paul Companies, which write more than 75 percent of medical malpractice insurance in Maryland, asked for an 80 percent premium hike in Baltimore because amounts paid out were so large. The company was turned down by the Insurance Commissioner and it refused to appeal saying it would rather leave the State. Fortunately, in 1974 a compromise was effected but that, too, seemed tenuous.

The Life-Health Actuarial Section. It is concerned with the actuarial aspects of the regulations of life and health insurance. It makes an annual valuation of the reserve liabilities of life insurance companies. Rates are checked to see that they are sufficient, secure, and practicable, and in the case of health insurance to see that the benefits provided are reasonable in relation to premiums paid.

Approximately 2.6 million persons in Maryland are covered by life insurance, the face amount being $26 billion.

Rating and Forms Reviews of Property and Casualty Insurance. Reviews cover rates, manuals, policies, rate schedules, and rating scales.

Education and Licensing Section. It is responsible for approving study programs, examining agents for insurance qualifications, issuing agents' and brokers' licenses. Separate examinations for agents and brokers are given annually in Baltimore, Cumberland, and Salisbury.

Complaints and Investigations. Policy holders complain about virtually everything, though most concerns are about cancellation or nonrenewal of policies, delayed or unsatisfactory service, denial of claims. During 1970 there were more than 10,000 complaints and about 2,500 were found justified.

Hearings and Enforcement Section. Hearings decide when insurance laws are violated and more than 300 hearings were held in 1973. Decisions have been in favor of complainants in 60 percent of the cases. Those not settled satisfactorily are turned over to the enforcement branch, which can order policy termination, agent license termination, disciplinary action, denial of application for license, and adjusted rate determination.

Insurance Reparations Reform Bill. The Insurance Reparations Reform Bill became effective January 1, 1973. Foremost, it abolished the Unsatisfied Claim and Judgment Fund and required that all drivers be insured and that all those not able to get automobile insurance with a private company because of accident history seek and be accepted by the newly created public Maryland Automobile Insurance Fund. MAIF had to accept these high-risk drivers (at a somewhat higher premium rate than that of the private insurance companies) if they had been turned down by two private companies unless the cancellations were causes for refusal to pay. If so, MAIF could turn them down, too.

Even with MAIF, which required all drivers to be insured, it is recognized that accidents could be caused by unauthorized drivers and normally, in such cases, there would be no recourse for claims from an insurance company. Here MAIF would pick up the responsibility previously held by the Unsatisfied Claim and Judgment Fund and would pay the valid claims.

The Reform Bill also tightens up on cancellations of policies and sets limitations by which insurers could cancel agreements with agents or brokers. It forbids increases in a premium unless it is part of a general increase approved by the Commissioner or unless it is due to reclassification. It forbids the setting of motor vehicle insurance rates partially or entirely on geographic area itself as opposed to underlying risk considerations. Though it still permits territorial rate distinctions, e.g., those who live in Baltimore City pay higher rates than those in nearby counties. It permits any party to appeal to a court of law decisions of the Commissioner of Insurance.

It seemed for a time in 1973 as though the Maryland Legislature, like New York's, New Jersey's and Connecticut's, would pass a "no-fault" automobile insurance law. Under the no-fault law, regardless of who caused the accident, drivers are reimbursed through their own insurance companies for medical expenses and wage losses. In New Jersey an accident victim receives unlimited medical coverage and $100 a week, up to $5,200, to compensate for lost wages. Suits for injuries are forbidden for soft-tissue damage such as sprains and permitted for severe injuries. New Jersey lowered liability premiums by 15 percent after one year of no-fault. Lawyers who specialize in torts were largely against no-fault in Maryland, so it failed in 1973, but the Reparations Reform Bill was an important victory.

Bank Commissioner of Maryland

The Bank Commissioner is appointed by the Secretary of Licensing and Regulation. The Commissioner's office has supervision over all banking institutions in the State other than national banks. There are currently 75 different State-chartered banking institutions in Maryland, many with a number of branch offices. In addition, there are about 40 national banks, which are required to be members of the Federal Reserve system.

The Commissioner and his staff charter and certificate new banking institutions and approve the opening of new branches and amendments to charters. Each institution is examined at least twice in 18 months and at other times when the Commissioner deems it expedient or when the board of directors of the bank so request. The Commissioner has the authority to take possession of a bank when the capital stock is impaired and not made good as prescribed by law. He retains possession until it is ready to resume business or is placed in final liquidation.

The Commissioner also approves and supervises all credit unions which, like banks, must have his permission to operate.

The Commissioner's office, under the Maryland Currency Exchange Law, supervises and regulates the selling or issuing of checks, drafts, and money orders where fees or service charges are required. The Commissioner also has jurisdiction over the operation of the Maryland Higher Education Loan Corporation from which college students may borrow money with low interest payments and government support. It further supervises the activities of the Development Credit Corporation and licenses those agencies working under DCC's terms which are not banks, nor building and loan associations, nor credit unions, yet lend money.

Maryland's usury laws protect the person who wishes to borrow money. Maximum interests are identified. The Banking Commissioner requires all Maryland banks to be insured by the Federal Deposit Insurance Corporation, which protects deposits to $20,000 (some Congressional leaders want it hiked to $50,000) before his office will approve them. Maryland bankers find some of the federal activities helpful: for example, they can lend money to businessmen more readily when the loan is covered under the Small Business Administration Act, since the federal government guarantees 90 percent of the loan.

There is a significant trend in Maryland, since 1960, toward mergers of banks. In some places the small independent banks of urban neighborhoods and country towns are disappearing and branches of Statewide institutions like the Suburban Trust Bank and Equitable Trust

Bank are replacing them. Banking as a profession in Maryland offers opportunities not usually known by the general public.

Commissioner of Consumer Credit

The Commissioner of Consumer Credit is appointed by the Secretary of Licensing and Regulation. Actually, the Commissioner's office spends most of its time on matters of consumer credit, retail sales accounts, and sales financing, such as master charges and all consumer loans not handled by banks. Previous to July 1, 1974 this office was known as the Commissioner of Small Loans.

The office is responsible for the licensing of consumer loan companies and conducts investigations of them. It may revoke or suspend a license, following a hearing before the Commissioner if the Small Loan Act has been violated.

The penalty on overcharge is three times the amount of the overcharge, repaid to the customer. The law is very clear on small loans, placing in that category a maximum loan of $500 for a maximum period of 30 months and 15 days, with the equivalent of an annual interest rate or 33.36 percent, reverting to but six percent after six months beyond the maximum period. Most borrowers making such loans also take out life, accident, and health insurance to cover the loans; the cost of that would be about $35 for the 30-month period.

The Commissioner also has jurisdiction over industrial finance companies. The Industrial Finance Law provides that no person or corporation may charge interest or other charges in the aggregate above that permitted by law on loans of $3,500 or less unless licensed by the Commissioner.

The more difficult problems are in the area of sales finance companies, which are licensed by the Commissioner. As third party contracts have come increasingly into the sales picture, consumer problems have mounted. For example, the automobile company that sells one a car usually turns the financing over to a third party, a sales finance company; thus three parties are involved in the sales contract. Problems arise if a customer wishes to pay in less time than the loan period. The law is clear on the refund action, but computers are not always accurate. Defaults on loans and repossession of automobiles always present problems.

Sales finance companies are supervised and investigated annually. Complaints against them are also open to hearing by the Commissioner, and revocations of licenses may result. The Maryland Retail Installment Act is clear on permissible business practices.

To consumers the best advice is use small loans only after you have investigated other possibilities, such as refinancing or just delaying the purchase. Companies in this field are usually reliable, but the cost is high.

Real Estate Commission of Maryland and Hearing Board

The Commission is composed of seven members appointed by the Governor with the advice of the Secretary of Licensing and Regulation under whom the Commission operates. Members represent different parts of the State and all but two must be in the real estate business.

The executive director and his staff license and approve applicants as real estate salesmen and brokers. A salesman must complete a basic course in real estate. After three years as a salesman, or after passing the Maryland Bar examinations, a candidate may apply for a broker's license. He must complete three semester credit hours in basic real estate principles at a degree granting college and then pass the State broker's examination.

The Real Estate Hearing Board consists of three members of the Real Estate Commission. The Board reviews complaints against real estate salesmen or brokers. The Board has the power to reprimand, suspend, revoke, or fine those found in wrongdoing.

The Division of Building Savings and Loan Associations

The Director of the Division is appointed by the Secretary of Licensing and Regulation under whom he serves. The Division supervises and regulates the organization and operations of State-chartered building and loan associations. It examines the affairs of each association at least once a year to determine compliance with the law. The Maryland law is clear as to the nature of investments, withdrawal of accounts, management, securities, allocation of profits, reserves, dividends, consolidation, merger, and dissolution.

The Board of Building Savings and Loan Association Commissioners consists of nine persons appointed by the Governor. It acts as a policy-making group, recommending methods and standards to be used in making examinations of associations for evaluation of assets, and suggests changes in the regulations.

In all there are 176 State-chartered building and loan associations in Maryland. All must carry insurance. Some associations are covered by the federal government's Federal Savings and Loan Insurance Corporation; most use the Maryland Savings Share Insurance Corporation, which insures deposits to $30,000.

Outside the jurisdiction of the State are the 58 federally chartered building and loan associations. They are chartered and supervised by the Federal Home Loan Bank Board and under its regional office's control. They all carry insurance under the Federal Savings Loan Insurance Corporation, where insurance is currently $20,000; some members of Congress seek to make it $50,000.

In 1959 and 1960 there was a scandal among some of Maryland's building and loan associations. It was this scandal and the closing of some 17 institutions, with heartbreaking losses to depositors, that caused the Division to come into being in 1961. In the early 1970's the 17 companies were still in receivership largely because the company that insured them, the Security Financial Insurance Corporation, was itself defunct. Fortunately, some of the 17 were showing recovery and were able to apply for reinstatement and recharter.

Another scandal in building and loan operations is not likely to come to Maryland because of four factors: (1) the existence of the Division since 1961, (2) the passage of stringent laws, (3) the requirement about insurance and the joint supervisory efforts of the insurers and the Division, and (4) the rigorous efforts of the Division to investigate practices, and the surveillance of the Board.

Maryland Home Improvement Commission

Five members of the Commission are appointed by the Secretary of Licensing and Regulations. The Commission licenses and regulates contractors and salesmen in the home improvement industry. Any contractor who does home residential improvement work with a job or single contract of $200 or more must be licensed. Exempt are contractors doing commercial or industrial improvement. Failure to be licensed can bring a fine of up to $5,000. In all 8,000 contractors have been licensed under the act governing home improvements.

In 1973 there were 1,800 complaints to the Commission. Most of them involved service, though many dealt with failure to do the work properly and resultant difficulties such as roof leaks. The most serious complaints involved abandonment of the job though money was paid for services. Most complaints, after investigations and hearings, are amicably adjusted. The Commission has the power to revoke or suspend a license. In cases of abandonment of job, it can issue a warrant. Though jobs under $200 do not come under its jurisdiction, the Commission will seek redress if blame is clear, or especially if it is abandonment.

Other Agencies that Regulate

All the agencies herein noted operate with boards appointed by the Governor and with the advice of the Secretary of the Department of Licensing and Regulation.

The State Athletic Commission has supervision of all boxing and wrestling matches in Maryland. It licenses sponsors, referees, managers, and participants.

The Racing Commission licenses those who hold meets where there is a stake. It may regulate the size of the purse. The Maryland-Bred Race Fund seeks to sponsor State-bred horses. The Board of Inspection of Horse Riding Stables licenses all riding stables where horses are let for hire, and auction and sales barns.

The State Board of Motion Picture Censors examines all film, except newsreels, to be exhibited or used in the State and disapproves those which might be thought of as obscene, debasing or corrupting of morals, or inciting to crime. Maryland is almost alone in censorship of films, and increasingly liberal interpretations by federal courts have cut down on what can be disapproved. Some legislators seek to abolish the Board; others say it is needed now more than ever.

Agencies that License

These agencies all have boards appointed by the Governor and approved by the Secretary of the Department of Licensing and Regulation. The boards are made up of practitioners in the field.

The Board of Barber Examiners examines and licenses all barbers and barber schools. The Board of Cosmetologists licenses all cosmetologists and beauty culture teaching schools. It supervises beauty shops and schools for compliance in health and sanitation.

The Board of Electrical Examiners and Supervisors examines and licenses master electricians and adopts regulations for installing and operating electrical apparatus in Baltimore City. No major electrical repair or installation is legal except those under the supervision of a master electrician.

The Board of Examining Engineers examines and licenses operators of steam engines, boilers, and engines.

The Board of Registration for Professional Engineers and Land Surveyors certificates those who practice in these fields. Certification is voluntary.

The Board of Commissioners of Practical Plumbing examines and licenses journeymen and master plumbers. All certificates must be renewed annually.

The Architectural Registration Board registers architects in the State. Qualifications are submitted and judged before licensing.

The Board of Examiners of Maryland Pilots licenses those who pilot ocean-going vessels.

The Board of Examining Motion Picture Machine Operators examines, licenses, and supervises operators of these machines in Baltimore City only.

The Board of Public Accountancy examines and certificates those who pass the CPA (Certified Public Accountant) tests. It also passes on applications from other states in reciprocal recognition.

There is general agreement in the State that lay persons should be added to the practitioners on each of these boards so that there is no inbreeding.

Chapter 20

WORKMEN'S COMPENSATION COMMISSION

Maryland was one of the first states to provide for the protection of workers against industrial accidents. As early as 1914, the State set up agencies for the enforcement of its Workmen's Compensation Law. Since that date the law has been amended many times and in many ways. Today it covers more occupations, is more justly administered, and insures compensation for a larger number of industrial accidents and occupational diseases than ever before in the history of the State. Responsibility is now in the hands of the Workmen's Compensation Commission, an independent agency not in any cabinet-level secretariat and thus reporting to the Governor.

1. *Workmen's Compensation Commission.* Reconstructed in 1957 this body consists of seven Commissioners and a chairman appointed by the Governor for overlapping 12-year terms. Its general function is to administer the Workmen's Compensation Law. The Commissioners are full-time executive officers. The determination of occupations covered is by statutory law—Maryland Code: Article 101, Section 21. With their staff (appointed through the merit system) the Commissioners receive and investigate reports of accidents; hear and adjudicate claims for compensation; investigate companies which fail to carry insurance under the terms of the Act. The Commissioners have the power to issue subpoenas, compel attendance of witnesses, administer oaths, and take depositions. Taxpayers of the State are not called upon to provide for the expenses of the Workmen's Compensation Commission; they are borne by the insurance companies and self-insurers which underwrite compensation insurance for employers.

2. *How Employees Are Insured.* Employers are permitted to meet their compensation responsibilities toward employees in any one of the following ways:

a. By taking out policies of worker insurance with any stock corporation or mutual association authorized to transact workmen's compensation insurance in this State.

b. By furnishing satisfactory proof of their own financial ability to pay such compensation claims as may be made against them. In such instances the Workmen's Compensation Commission may require a deposit of security and have the privilege of periodic checks on the ability to pay insurance.

c. By taking out insurance with the State Accident Fund. This project is administered by five salaried Commissioners of the Fund appointed by the Secretary of Personnel (subject to the Governor's approval) for overlapping five-year terms. Employers who hold this type of insurance pay premiums at regular intervals, as directed by the Commissioners. Premium rates are based upon the size of the payroll and classification of risk. When the financial condition of the Fund so warrants, the Commissioners are empowered to declare a dividend.

3. *Compensation Payments.* The basic purpose of the compensation system is to provide financial help for an employee who is injured at his job and thus unable to work either temporarily or permanently.

An employee suffering any injury should file a claim within 60 days of the event. Failure to file within two years may constitute a complete bar to the claim. Within ten days after the employer is notified of the injury, he must send a report in writing to the Workmen's Compensation Commission or its local representative. If he fails to do so, he may be fined. Following submission of these reports, the employee must file his claim for compensation, together with a physician's statement. Members of the Commission investigate claims at their discretion, and may set a hearing in any case at the request of either the claimant or the employer. After the claim has been filed, however, the claimant may make an agreement directly with his employer or the insuring company subject to the approval of the Commission. In this case, a hearing is not necessary, but a medical report must be filed before the final agreement will be accepted by the Commission.

Awards in compensation cases depend upon laws which are changed by the Legislature from time to time. (The awards noted below are for 1974.) The award made to a claimant also depends upon his normal earning power and the nature of the injury he has sustained. In all cases medical fees are paid in addition to the awards. In cases of serious injuries, rehabilitation arrangements are also made.

Some compensation claims relate to cases of *temporary partial disability;* for example, an injury to a finger permits the employee to continue to work, but with lowered earning power. In such cases, the worker receives 50 percent of the difference between his regular salary and his present earning capacity, up to a maximum of $40 per week, for as long as the healing period or until maximum improvement has been reached and he enters the permanent partial wage category. Total compensation cannot exceed $4,000. In addition, the injured worker is entitled to medical treatment of the injury at no cost to himself. Even if the injured employee's earnings are uninterrupted, as sometimes happens, he may have a right to free medical services.

In cases of *temporary total disability*, in which an employee is completely unable to work for a healing period, the injured person is entitled to two-thirds of his average salary, not to exceed 66-2/3 percent of the average weekly wage in Maryland as determined by the Department of Employment Security (changed to 100 percent of Maryland average wage in July, 1975). With a minimum of $25 per week (unless his wages were less) no time limit exists as to the period for healing or total amount of payment.

While the temporarily injured worker is receiving compensation payments, he must present himself for periodic medical examinations, as the Workmen's Compensation Commission directs. If he fails to do so, he may lose all right to further compensation payments.

With regard to cases of *permanent partial disability*—such as the loss of a finger, hand, or leg—which does not necessarily prevent further employment, the maximum period for which payments may be made varies according to injury. For example, in cases of loss of a thumb, payments may continue for 100 weeks; in cases of loss of a leg, 300 weeks. A worker receives the amount, provided by law, at the rate of 2/3 of his wage, not to exceed $35 per week, unless his permanent partial disability is extended (because of the nature of his injury) so that it must equal 250 or more weeks, in which case the number of covered weeks are then increased by 1/3 and the maximum per week is increased to $65 per week.

An employee suffering *permanent total disability* (for example, loss of both hands, arms, legs, or eyes) is entitled to 66-2/3 percent of his average salary, not to exceed two-thirds average Maryland wage (changed to 100 percent of average Maryland wage in July, 1975) with a minimum of $25 per week. The compensation payment continues during the entire disability period.

If death results from an injury, the surviving total dependents may receive as much as $45,000. This amount is paid under the same weekly arrangements as if the worker were alive and receiving 66-2/3 percent of his average weekly wages (based on two-thirds average State weekly wage until July, 1975 when it becomes 100 percent of State average) for as long as the surviving total dependent person lives or is in the dependency category, even beyond the $45,000 limit. Partially dependent persons shall receive an amount at a maximum of $17,500.

Compensation for Occupational Diseases

In 1939 the Workmen's Compensation Law was amended to include compensation for so-called occupational diseases. The law listed 34 specific diseases (*e.g.*, lead poisoning and pulmonary dust diseases such as asbestosis, silicosis, and dermatitis) and indicated the occupations with which these maladies are commonly connected. It proved extremely difficult, however, to administer the law realistically on this basis. Accordingly, in 1951, the schedule of diseases was replaced by an amendment stating that all persons who contract diseases as a direct result of their employment are entitled to compensation.

The Medical Board of Occupational Diseases has the responsibility of reviewing all contested cases. This body consists of three paid physicians, appointed by the Governor from a list of nominees submitted by the deans of the medical schools of Johns Hopkins University and the University of Maryland and by the Medical and Chirurgical Faculty of Maryland. Members of the Board serve six-year terms. They are empowered to investigate working conditions, to order and carry out autopsies, and to conduct hearings on medical questions relating to occupational diseases.

In recent years the concept of occupational diseases has been clarified and this definition accepted by courts: "the event of an employee's becoming actually incapacitated, either partly or totally because of an occupational disease, from performing his work in the last occupation in which exposed to the hazards of such disease." Under this definition, occupational deafness or losses of hearing due to industrial noise is compensatory if the losses are within the range of established standards.

Interpretations of the Compensation Laws and Appeals

The laws in compensation cases are continually changing and subject to court review. In general, recent statutory laws and court decisions tend to liberalize settlements of claims. For example, in an important court case in 1971 the word "accident" was expanded to include "any mischance resulting in physical injury to the bodily tissues produced by some unusual and extraordinary condition or happening in the employment." Thus, it would include pulmonary and cerebral hemorrhages, hernia, infection, heart dilation, and rupture of an aneurism arising from some unusual or extraordinary condition in the employment, even where the injury was due in part to pre-existing disease or physical abnormality of the claimant.

Any employer, employee, or beneficiary may appeal a decision of the Commission in the Circuit Courts of the counties or the common-law courts of Baltimore City. Where compensation is awarded on appeal, the claimant gets the award and six percent interest. Before he asks for an appeal for a court hearing, the claimant may move for a rehearing by the Commission itself.

Number and Kinds of Cases

About 20,000 cases of accidental injury were heard in fiscal 1973 by the Commission. In addition 24,000 cases were handled without being heard by the Commission. The Medical Board also heard 159 more cases of accidental injury. Then, too, there were about 150 cases in the field of occupational diseases. Eighty-one of the injuries were fatal and three were permanent and total; while more than 2,000 were permanent partial injuries, and more than 17,000 were temporary (healing period) injuries. Almost every type of job classification was included in both the serious and less serious compensatory claims, though carpenters and construction workers, machine operators, truckers, health service workers (including nurses and doctors), steelworkers, and warehousemen ranked highest on the list.

Chapter 21
ECONOMIC AND COMMUNITY DEVELOPMENT

Prior to establishment of the Department of Economic and Community Development in 1970 as a cabinet-level secretariat, there were 13 independent agencies seeking to advance Maryland's economic, aesthetic, and cultural welfare. The need for a coordinated and unified approach was obvious: there was duplication of efforts to encourage new industrial enterprises in the State and, even more seriously, some wrong approaches were being used.

In a sense it was more difficult for this Department to identify its task than for any of the other eleven cabinet-level secretariats. After all, Health and Mental Hygiene, Transportation, Agriculture, Natural Resources, Personnel, and the other departments had more clearly delineated responsibilities. What are the ingredients that bring about economic and community development?

There are as many views as there are responses. For example, it has long been recognized that industrial firms will settle in an area where labor conditions are favorable, energy power is abundant, and tax laws are liberal. But recent studies show that skilled and professional workers in short supply are much more likely to come to a community if there are nearby places of worship, good schools for their children, healthful living conditions, stable and safe neighborhoods, good housing, abundant recreational and cultural pursuits, and a stimulating environment.

Thus, the objective of the Department might really be thought of as the creation of opportunities for fuller and more meaningful communities to come into being in Maryland so that individual citizens can be enriched. Such an assignment can thus be interpreted philosophically in different ways. What is the good life? Do we build superhighways to entice industrial and community development which in turn present ecological problems? On the other hand, unless our economy grows, where will the funds come from to give us the effective schools and cultural opportunities, let alone the improved housing and health care increasingly required?

It is this very dilemma which has brought forth this statement: *The mission of the Department is to improve the well-being of the citizens of Maryland by:*

* Optimizing employment and income opportunities throughout the State.

* Reducing unemployment and underemployment.

* Fostering expansion and improvement of housing opportunities.

(Top) *Harbor Queen* scenic tours of Severn River, Annapolis. (Bottom) Cruise Ship, Baltimore Port. (Photo by Jerry Wachter)

* Assisting communities by working with local officials in maximizing opportunities to provide for suitable living environments for all their citizens.

* Enhancing the development, availability, and utilization of the State's cultural and historical resources.

* Cooperating with and assisting organizations and groups, both public and private, in reaching the goals stated above.

It is evident that the Department believes that there can be both growth and the preservation of ecology and the State's heritage. To build new industry does not mean despoliation of natural resources or historical treasures. It does mean, however, that there are planned and well understood developments, mutually arrived at by citizens and governmental officials seeking to bring about such balanced growth.

Board of Review

The board has seven members appointed by the Governor, for three-year terms. Four members represent the general public and three are from fields embraced in the Department. It hears and determines appeals from the decisions of the Secretary or from any agency within the Department of Economic and Community Development. This is the typical review process set up for all the secretariats.

Advisory Commissions

As is true for other cabinet-level secretariats, the Department has numerous commissions whose members are appointed by the Governor to advise it on both broad and specific topics. The Economic Development Advisory Commission has broad geographic representation from all parts of Maryland and from private industry as it advises that Division. Another group advising the Division of Economic Development is the Tri-County Council for Western Maryland. The Division cooperates with the Appalachian Regional Commission, which is a federal agency, with Maryland representation aimed at the development of the State's western counties, as well as the land in other states in the Appalachian region.

Other commissions advising the Department include: The Advisory Commission on Atomic Energy, the Ocean City Convention Hall Commission, and the Advisory Commission on Industrialized Building and Mobile Homes.

All these commissions help the Department and the State to draw on the resources of fifty or so outstanding experts in the fields of economic and community development.

Economic Development

The work of the Division of Economic Development is perhaps the most ubiquitous activity of the Department. Not only does it perform at the State level, but the Division works intimately with each county and municipality to help it develop new industries and to promote growth of established firms. The Division, in collaboration with the local units, has published basic economic data on Statewide and county levels.

The Office of Business and Industrial Development (BID). In 1972, in cooperation with the local and regional groups, BID helped to bring 54 new firms to the State. It also played a part in expansion of 37 established plants. Capital investments in the new plants and facilities amounted to $57 million and created about 3,900 new jobs.

BID maintains on a current basis essential economic data which is made available to those companies expressing an interest in locating or expanding in the State. The Maryland Basic Plant Location Data indicate the nature of labor supply, energy availability, market proximities, foreign trade opportunities, transportation, science and research centers, educational services, natural resources, industrial financing, and tax requirements in this State compared to others. The general economic picture is a good one for Maryland.

A recent adjunct of BID is the Business Liaison Office, which gives full-time attention to projects to retain resident business and to encourage them to expand.

Federal funds have been extremely important in the work of BID. For example, the Appalachian Regional Commission, on which the director of BID serves as Maryland's representative, allocated more than $75 million to the State in the period 1965-1973. In addition, the ARC contributed nearly $15 million toward $30 million in contracts to further construction of the National Freeway from Cumberland west through western Allegany County, then through Garrett County to the West Virginia line toward Morgantown. At different times the Federal Economic Development Administration contributed about $4 million for public works and technical assistance projects.

The Maryland Industrial Development Financing Authority. The Authority consists of five members appointed by the Secretary of the Department, the State Treasurer, and the Secretary himself.

The Authority provides State insurance for industrial mortgages and guaranteed loans to stimulate new industries. During 1972 MIDFA approved 15 loan applications valued at more than $10.7 million, and there were no defaults. The loans are distributed throughout the State and have provided financial stimulation to businesses and communities all over the State. The 1972 loans have a potential for 2,000 new jobs.

An Industrial Land Bank assists counties in solving problems of industrial sites.

Tourist Development. The Division of Tourism promotes a Maryland industry which has an annual yield of $300 to $500 million and is growing at a rate of about 11 percent a year. In 1972, State sales tax receipts from hotels and motels alone netted about $4.3 million. Each visitor spends on the average of $32 a day during his stay in Maryland.

The tourism director works with regional groups such as the Central States Travel Council and national groups such as Discover America. The office has formed new groups such as the Potomac Valley Hosts and the Monocacy Valley Hosts in Hagerstown and Frederick, and aided local groups in the formation of programs such as the Very Important Visitor to Annapolis.

Efforts to promote the Ocean City Convention Hall as a year-round site for meetings have been partially successful.

Ocean City Convention Hall.

Seafood Marketing Authority. The seafood industry induces some 25,000 jobs in Maryland. The Authority seeks to develop better methods of harvesting and marketing seafood so that there will be greater profits and more consumption. The promotional efforts are directed at both bulk purchasers and individual consumers.

The Authority has printed cookbooks, participated in food demonstrations, and promoted 12 seafood festivals which were attended by 200,000 persons. It cooperates with the Chesapeake Bay Seafood Industries Association, an organization of those Maryland firms engaged in the industry.

Community Development

The community development goal of the Department is an elusive objective. In a sense, the work of all twelve of the cabinet-level Departments and the independent State agencies are concerned with community development.

Historical and Cultural Affairs. Working with this section of the Department is the Maryland Bicentennial Commission, which has a publication program dealing with Maryland's role in the Revolution. It works closely with federal, regional, and other similar State groups to present an integrated picture in 1976. The Commission has received a $45,000 federal grant.

The St. Marys Commission has acquired historic town land holdings and conducted archeological investigations of early sites in its task to preserve and develop Maryland's first capital and original settlement. The Commission has received numerous research grants from the National Endowment for the Humanities and from private corporations such as the Rockefeller Foundation.

The Maryland Historical Trust is authorized to acquire, preserve, and maintain historic, aesthetic, and cultural buildings and property. A good deal of restoration has taken place in Annapolis, rich in colonial history. In some cases the Trust has been willed historic properties with endowments suitable for maintenance. It also works with county governments that seek to preserve historic landmarks.

The Trust cooperates with the Committee for the National Register in Maryland and prepares a Statewide survey and plan for historic preservation in conformance with the National Historic Preservation Act of 1966. It further cooperates with the Maryland Historical Society, in Baltimore, which has the best collection of Maryland memorabilia. The Trust also cooperates with county historical societies.

The Maryland Arts Council lends advice and consultant aid to performing groups, and in some cases grants funds in direct support of cultural events and programs. For example, in the early 1970's it contributed money to four major cultural institutions: The Baltimore Symphony Orchestra, Center Stage in Baltimore, the Maryland Ballet, and the Baltimore Museum of Art. All four used the funds to make programs available to school and youth groups. The Council also granted funds for traveling art shows, and high school literary competitions in the schools.

The Baltimore Symphony is partly supported by municipal funds. It is recognized as one of the leading city orchestras in America. Its tours are national and sometimes international. The Baltimore Museum of Art enjoys an international reputation.

Housing. The Department's Division of Research recognizes that private housing requirements represent a need that has not been given enough attention in the State. It is planning a complete analysis of the need for new and upgraded housing in local areas.

Housing and Community Development in Counties and Municipalities: Not a Part of the DECD

A number of counties (and Baltimore City) have housing agencies that handle problems falling into three areas:

Public housing built, owned, and operated by the local governmental unit and rented to low-income families and low-income elderly individuals.

Moderate-income housing built, owned, and operated by private developers (nonprofit or limited dividend) and rented or sold to families of an income above that for public housing, roughly $6,000 to $11,000 a year, depending on family size.

Urban renewal is the means used to buy and prepare the site which may be used for public or moderate-income housing.

Following are two case studies of how public housing and urban renewal work in a large community like Baltimore and in a smaller one like Cambridge. In both cases it is evident that Maryland communities with federal assistance can rejuvenate business, give better housing to the poor, increase the assessable base of property and tax funds, and thus give new hope to urban centers.

Baltimore City's Department of Housing and Community Development. This city agency ordinarily is heavily supported by federal funds under the U.S. Department of Housing and Urban Development. For example, in fiscal 1970, of $33.5 million in sources of funds, $8.2 million came from the federal government.

The public housing segment of HCD is operated by the Housing Authority of Baltimore for more than 11,000 low-income families. Rentals vary according to income and size of family, but the National Housing Act forbids families in public housing from paying more than 25 percent of their income for rent. Special attention in public housing is given to the elderly. HCD plans to build 1,000 units for the elderly yearly until all needs are met.

Urban renewal in all parts of Baltimore is crucial, for it means changing the nature of run-down neighborhoods by renovating, tearing down, and reconstructing. Once deterioration takes place, the entire neighborhood goes down, people move out, and assessable values depreciate.

On the other hand, when renewal takes place, people and city gain. For example, in 1970 the Baber-Daniels Gardens was built in the North Avenue section with apartments for 268 moderate-income families. The developer, a nonprofit organization formed by the Prince Hall Masons and the African Methodist Episcopal Church, produced an attractive development replacing old structures which were torn down. Before renewal the land was assessed at $1.1 million; after renewal at $1.9

million. Thus, there were more homes for people and more tax funds for the city.

Unfortunately, in 1973 the federal government said it would no longer approve the insurance of construction loans and insurance of mortgages which it has provided to developers of moderate-income housing. Nor will it approve open-space land programs or water and sewer grants (which are related to urban renewal).

Many citizen groups, such as the Citizens Planning and Housing Association for Metropolitan Baltimore, are seeking to end the federal moratorium. When this occurs, the Baltimore Department of Housing and Community Development can continue its plans to literally change the face of the city. County housing groups can do the same.

Public Housing and Urban Renewal in Cambridge (Dorchester County). In 1973 Cambridge had about 300 public housing units, some restricted for use by the elderly. In addition there are some 150 dwelling units of "rent supplement" apartments for low- to moderate-income families. Then, too, there are some 65 three-bedroom townhouses built by a private developer but with mortgage interest payments, to qualifying moderate-income families, partially subsidized by the federal government.

Each action of the Cambridge urban renewal agency must be approved by the mayor and city commissioners. However, the federal government's guidelines are used and federal agencies provide technical and financial assistance as the city makes the requests and as they meet federal requirements.

Cambridge's urban renewal project is immediately adjacent to the central business district. Thirty-nine parcels of land were acquired in 1970, with accompanying relocation of families, individuals, and businesses. Objectives of the project are as follows: To remove blighting influences adjacent to downtown; to provide better access to parking; to widen and extend a main street; to provide a pedestrian access point and mall from the parking lot to downtown stores; to provide land for commercial development immediately adjacent to the central business district; and to provide an atmosphere of improvement in which the central district will upgrade existing facilities.

There is no doubt that such an urban renewal project can give new hope to Cambridge.

Community Economic Inventories

Each county (and Baltimore City) through its county development corporation, with the aid of the Maryland Department of Economic and Community Development, has produced a *Community Economic Inventory*. Purpose of the publication is to encourage new industries to settle in the county. Each Inventory includes data under the following categories: geography, economy, climate, population, labor and wages, business advantages, existing industry and industrial sites, transportation facilities, market area, communication facilities, utilities, government and taxes, planning and zoning, educational and other county resources, and recreational and natural resources. The inventories give the prospective Maryland industrialist an opportunity to judge his possible new venture.

Some illustrations from the 1972 edition of the *Inventory* or similar publications indicate the incentives held out by the various county development corporations:

1. Allegany County gives attention to the Western Maryland Regional Development Office, which coordinates economic development activities in the area. WMRDO has relationships with the federal Appalachian Regional Development Act, funding many economic pursuits, including the new National Freeway through Allegany County. The county has a labor force of more than 27,000.

2. Anne Arundel County states that its updated general development plan calls for allocation of more than 7,000 acres of industrial and commercially zoned land in prime areas throughout the county, with eight industrial parks. It also praises its "hold-the-line" tax posture.

3. Baltimore County cites the fact that its 1980 Guideplan (master plan) will aim toward making more than 30,000 acres of commercial and industrial land area available for new pursuits. This includes land that was vacant in 1970 but zoned for redevelopment. The County points to the rapid business development in the Cockeysville area within the Hunt Valley commercial and industrial community and similar growth at the Pulaski Industrial Park, North Point Boulevard, Canton Center, Woodlawn, Halethorpe, and Owings Mills.

4. Calvert County points to its labor force of more than 5,000 and the success of firms already engaged there in seafood and meat processing, boatbuilding, and lumber and millwork.

5. Caroline County cites the testimonial of Maryland Plastics, which states that it started business in Federalsburg in 1938, occupying a building of 5,000 square feet and employing twelve persons. In 1972 it occupied 60,000 square feet and employed 200 persons.

The Preston Trucking Company, which also employs 200, tells why it has kept its headquarters in rural Caroline though it now services the nation. Other firms employing a labor force of more than 7,000 persons are mainly in the processing of seafood and in truck farming pursuits.

6. Carroll County calls attention to its labor force of more than 27,000 and its 1973 retail sales of $132.5 million. It points to its total farm land (1969) of more than 188,000 acres, with about 1,400 farms averaging 135 acres.

7. Cecil County boasts about its Conowingo Dam and its hydroelectric power plants. It has a potential labor force of 32,000 persons

and is the home of the explosive and propellant industry. It is known for boatbuilding and boat maintenance shops. Industrial parks are being developed.

8. Charles County announces that the St. Charles Industrial Park has about 208 acres available along the main U.S. 301 highway and that sites will be provided with access roads and all utilities.

9. Dorchester County, with a labor force of 14,000, boasts of the port of Cambridge, the Eastern Shore's only deepwater seaport and handling over 55,000 tons of cargo annually. Freezer-storage facilities are owned by private enterprises and permit frozen fish products from other regions of the world to be imported with ease. Hopefully, the future will bring red meats from Argentina and movements of Delmarva Peninsula chickens to Europe, as well as Delmarva-produced vegetables to Europe and South America.

10. Frederick County points to the fact that it is the largest supplier of fluid milk for Washington and annually ships more than $20 million worth to that city and Baltimore. Purebred dairy cattle raised in Frederick County are shipped all over the world to start herds.

11. Garrett County offers a ten-year tax exemption on real property, machinery and tools, and raw materials provided assessment value exceeds $10,000 and 20 or more persons are employed. In 1967 Bausch & Lomb opened a new ophthalmic plant (eyeglass lenses) near Oakland which eventually will employ about 1,000 workers.

12. Harford County boasts of its two large U.S. Army research and development installations—Aberdeen Proving Ground, with its multi-million-dollar Nuclear Pulse Reactor, and Edgewood Arsenal, with its electron-volt Tandem Van de Graaff Accelerator facility. The County has 60 manufacturers, more than 1,200 businesses, 11 industrial parks, and 5,000 acres of industrial-zoned land.

13. Howard County claims it is one of the fastest growing units in Maryland and calls attention to its key location between Baltimore and Washington. It believes that Columbia ultimately will have a population of more than 100,000, and as a planned city will contain important industrial developments.

14. Kent County has phased out its tax on manufacturers' inventories, machinery, and equipment in order to attract new industry. Arrangements are available through the Small Business Administration to supply capital for financing new and expanding plants. It calls attention to the 13-foot channel in the Chester River permitting coastal oil tankers and grain barges to serve Chestertown. The Rock Hall harbor serves fish and oyster boats.

15. Montgomery County boasts that the average household income was $24,500 in 1973. It is said to lead the nation in doctors, lawyers, and scientists. Its health, science and government agencies make it one of the country's great research centers.

16. Prince Georges County has a labor force of about 300,000, more than 40,000 of whom are professional, technical, and kindred workers. It has 13,600 acres zoned for commercial and industrial use. There are 10 key industrial areas ranging from a 200-acre industrial complex for heavy industry at Ammendale Road to the 78 acre Aerospace Science Research Center. Practically every type of manufacturing, industry, and commerce, including federal government operations, are in this county with the largest population in Maryland.

17. Queen Annes County has a labor force of 6,390 and praises its Bay Bridge Industrial Center, with an airpark, and the Ritchey Industrial Center, at the eastern terminus of the Bay Bridge. Eight other sites are zoned for industrial use, including some in Centreville which has municipal water and public sewerage.

18. St. Marys County notes that it has an ample labor force, with about 10 percent commuting out of the County to work. It has a comparatively low county tax rate of $2.30 per hundred. It has public sewerage at Leonardtown and Lexington Park with planned facilities at Piney Point. The first two communities have public water supply outlets. The County has 400 miles of shoreline.

19. Somerset County has a labor force of 7,200. Most employers are in the seafood, frozen and canned vegetables, and marine industries, though Rubberset Company has a large paintbrush operation in the County. The County exempts manufacturing inventories from property taxes and will exempt industry from all taxes for a period of up to a year at a time (maximum of three years) provided ten or more persons are employed.

20. Talbot County has a labor force of 10,600. Its main industries are seafood, poultry (the largest), printing (next largest), and clothing manufacture. The County and City of Easton jointly own the Airport Industrial Park and will assist selected firms in financial arrangements.

21. Washington County has a labor force of 43,000 persons. It exempts manufacturing inventories from taxation and helps finance new and expanding industries. It has 17 industrial sites mainly centered around Hagerstown, with one each near Hancock and Boonsboro. Every form of transportation is available in abundance.

22. Wicomico County grants temporary tax abatements for manufacturing inventories, machinery, and equipment, and assists in financing through industrial revenue bonds. The Salisbury Area Chamber of Commerce aids new and developing business firms. Salisbury has a significant number of frozen and canned food, clothing, construction, and poultry businesses. It takes pride in its modern Peninsula General Hospital.

23. Worcester County has one of the fastest growing hotel and motel businesses on the East Coast. It boasts of its new Ocean City Convention Hall and its large tourist trade. In the effort to accommodate

growing numbers of tourists, millions of dollars have gone into construction of condominiums in recent years. Nearby, Assateague Island National Seashore is a "primitive paradise."

24. Baltimore City's economic assets have been described in various sections of this book. It is often referred to as the City with most drive, as illustrated by its rejuvenated Charles Center and Inner Harbor development, and the East Coast city most likely to prove that urban centers can thrive.

(L. to r.) Ocean City Boardwalk, Maryland's Atlantic Ocean Beach; Downtown Baltimore. (Photo by Bob Willis)

Corporations

One of the independent agencies not included in any cabinet-level department is the Department of Assessments and Taxation. The director of DAT approves and records charters and amendments to charters of domestic corporations. The director also has charge of the qualifications and registrations of foreign (out-of-state) corporations.

Domestic corporations (with some exceptions as those having no capital stock, building associations, and credit unions) pay a tax for the franchise to be a corporation. The annual rates are $10 for a capital of $10,000 or less to $480 on a capital of $10 million and $30 for each $2 million in excess. The tax funds are divided between the State and the county of residence.

Foreign corporations pay a recording fee of $4 to $40 for registration and certificates.

Chapter 22

DEPARTMENT OF PERSONNEL

The State Merit System, which governs virtually all State government positions, came into existence in 1920 when the General Assembly passed the merit law. Before that time, under a system of patronage, jobs went to loyal supporters of the party in power. The latter practice is often referred to as the "spoils system" in that it grew out of the belief that to the victors belong the spoils.

Maryland became the eleventh state to enact a merit system. Thirty-seven years elapsed between the time New York State passed its civil service law in 1883 and Maryland's passage in 1920. Actually, the concept of civil service should be credited to the federal government, for numerous political scandals among appointed federal employees in the 1870's led to the formation of the National Civil Service Reform League in 1881. (In a sense, the cry for a new system of government job procurement was somewhat like the 1973 call for a new way of financing election campaigns.) At the national level, there were people like Senators Charles Sumner and Carl Schurz, Congressman Thomas Jenckes, and reformers like E.L. Godkin and George W. Curtis who wanted a federal civil service plan modeled on Great Britain's. Fortunately, with Presidential support, the Pendleton Act was passed in 1883 and it set in motion the substitution of examinations and other civil service techniques for appointments to federal positions. States soon followed.

For the 50-year period between the introduction of the Maryland law and 1970, there were two important extensions that needed to take place. First, the law needed to be adopted by Maryland county and municipal governments. Since these governments were operating close to home and since Maryland was a rural state in 1920, each appointment had a personal relationship. The elected officer making the appointment usually knew the one selected for the job from boyhood days. So the local units came along more slowly than the State in adopting civil service.

The exception to the local units was Baltimore City, which established a City Service Commission in 1918. As the larger counties became urbanized in the 1950's and '60's, they, too, moved away from patronage appointments. This was especially true in the 1960's, when home-rule counties wrote strong merit system regulations into their new charters. As municipalities gained more home rule they, too, adopted merit systems.

The second required extension was that moving the system from civil service to merit and personnel plans. The civil service system was largely concerned with original appointments.

The new requirements came into being in the 1930's when the federal government and President Franklin D. Roosevelt's Social Security plans made it clear that protection for workers involved more than how the original job was procured. The labor unions and employee groups, too, fought for rights for workers. Pensions, merit promotions, protection against the high cost of illness, collective bargaining rights, proper vacations, grievance privileges, fair employment practices, and decent wages were all important factors in employer-employee relationships. By 1970 the State had made many revisions to the 1920 civil service law and had created effective personnel practices for the 34,500 classified Maryland State employees and 6,500 unclassified. Thus it was certainly justified to establish a cabinet-level Maryland Department of Personnel in 1970.

State Employment Practices for Classified Employees

Equality in Employment. It is the policy of the State of Maryland that race, religion, sex, and national origin shall not be considered in: recruitment and employment of new State employees; promotion, demotion, transfer, layoff, and termination; selection of State employees for training and development; establishment of rates of pay, salary adjustment, and merit salary increments. State employees who believe they have been discriminated against because of race, religion, national origin, sex, or age may file complaints with the Secretary of Personnel or with the Maryland Commission on Human Relations. Any complaint against any State agency will be investigated thoroughly and appropriate action will be taken. Employees will not be disciplined in any way for filing complaints of discrimination.

Job Classification. Each job in State government is given a job title based on assigned responsibilities and duties performed. All jobs are carefully studied and those with similar duties and responsibilities are given the same job classification and rate of pay within the same salary range. Qualifications and requirements are established for each job classification and these standards are the same everywhere in the State. It is the responsibility of each State agency and the State Personnel Department to make certain that each employee's job classification is correct. At times this requires that jobs be restudied, redefined, or adjusted to fit changing conditions or requirements.

Salary. "Equal pay for equal work" is the rule. Most job classifications are assigned a salary grade having minimum, maximum, and intermediate pay steps. An employee whose work is satisfactory receives automatic increases each year (in January or July) as he moves from base pay to the final step of his salary grade. A limited number of trainee and specialized professional classifications are paid at a set amount referred to as a *flat rate*.

Job Performance and Rating. Upon assignment to one's position, an employee receives on-the-job instruction from his supervisor. He is given time to learn his duties and the established standards which must be met. During his probationary period, his work will be observed continuously and compared with these standards. The objective of the probationary period is to help him develop satisfactory job skills. At the end of his probationary period and at yearly intervals thereafter, his supervisors will rate his work performance in the areas of work quality, quantity, habits, and attitudes.

Promotions. Promotions are based mainly on competitive examinations. Employees are encouraged, therefore, to prepare for and participate in examinations in order to obtain a place on an eligibility list. Applications for examinations must be filed before the closing date set for the receipt of applications. Permanent employees should not wait until the examination is announced to file applications. Employees are urged to file applications for positions in which they are interested as soon as they are within six months of meeting the minimum experience and educational requirements.

The eligible list established as result of the examination ranks successful candidates in the order of test score. In awarding promotions, then, the department head must choose from among the top five employees on the eligible list. Permanent employees whose names appear on eligible lists stay on the lists for two years. Employees selected for promotion are required to serve a probationary period in the new position.

Annual Leave (Vacation). Annual leave is the term used in State service for paid vacation. The number of leave days one receives each year depends on the years of employment in State service. New employees are credited with five days of annual leave after working six months. Then one begins to earn a little less than one day (.83 days) for each additional month of service for a total of ten days of leave for the first full year. State employees with one or more years of service are entitled to from ten to 25 days of annual leave in accordance with years of service.

Sick Leave. Each employee is allowed 30 days of paid sick leave each year. Sick leave is not due an employee, but is available if an employee is ill. It accumulates at the rate of two and one-half days per month and is available when earned. Sick leave may be accumulated up to 100 days, the maximum number of sick days which may be carried into a new calendar year.

Health Insurance. Three types of health insurance coverage are available for State employees and their families. The State and the employee share the cost, giving the employee much greater protection per dollar than he could purchase alone. Benefits covered include hospitalization, medical and surgical treatment, nursing services, drugs and medicines, ambulance services, and prosthetic appliances.

Workmen's Compensation. Employees who are injured or disabled on the job are protected by Workmen's Compensation.

Retirement. The Maryland State Employees' Retirement System guarantees retirement income for members or their surviving dependents. It also provides disability or death benefits, should either occur prior to retirement. Enrollment in the Retirement System is mandatory upon entering State service. The appropriate percentage of salary is deducted from each paycheck and deposited in an annuity savings account with the Retirement System. The percentage deducted is called the contribution rate and is determined by the Retirement System from a standard table based on age at the time of enrollment in the Retirement System, and sex.

Retirement is compulsory at age 70. An employee may retire at age 60. After 25 years of service, an employee may retire at any age and receive actuarially reduced benefits. For teachers, after five years of work, the State makes retirement contributions.

Grievance Procedure. The State recognizes that legitimate problems, differences of opinion, complaints, and grievances will exist in the daily relationship between the State as an employer and its employees. It is the responsibility of all supervisors, administrators, program directors, appointing authorities, and employees to establish and maintain a work climate within which an employee problem or complaint may be promptly identified, presented, discussed, and given fair, timely consideration.

Every employee, permanent, temporary or probationary, has the right to present his grievance through established steps and procedures free from interference, coercion, restraint, discrimination, or reprisal. In accordance with these principles, there is a procedure for the resolution of employee grievances for all employees.

Employee Organizations. Every State employee is guaranteed the right to join, if he wishes, any employee organization, with assurance that he will not be discriminated against for being a member of such a group.

Retirement Systems for State Workers

The Assistant Secretary of Personnel is the executive officer for the retirement systems operated by the State. Retirement salaries (pensions) are determined by years of service and contributions into the system. The latter is a percentage of the total salary.

The Employees' Retirement System covers classified workers. It is governed by a seven-member board of trustees chaired by the State Comptroller. Some of the members are elected by employees. It provides a plan of retirement for, and administers pensions to, retired State employees.

The Teachers' Retirement System covers all teachers in the Maryland public elementary and secondary schools as well as faculty members of the University of Maryland and the public State and community colleges. It is governed by a five-member board of trustees including the State Treasurer, the State Comptroller, the State Superintendent of Schools, and two elected members.

In 1973, a major concession was won by teachers in this system; the State agreed to vest (match with State contributions) pension contributions by teachers after they had taught but five years. It also raised State retirement contributions to a point of one-fifty-fifth of average salary for last three years (for each year of service) instead of one-sixtieth.

The State Police Retirement System is administered by a six-member board of trustees chaired by the Superintendent of State Police. The board administers the retirement system and rules on disability and other retirement requests. Only uniformed members of the State Police are in the system.

Some Unresolved Questions

The most controversial question is that related to collective bargaining. As 1974 opened, it seemed almost certain that the General Assembly would pass laws permitting faculty members in Maryland public colleges and universities the privilege of collective bargaining. The Maryland public elementary and secondary schools were already operating under State collective bargaining laws. States to the north and west of Maryland had already established such legislation for higher educational faculties. At least three college teacher organizations—the American Federation of Teachers, the American Association of University Professors, and the higher education division of the National Education Association—were vying with one another to be elected the bargaining unit in the various institutions.

In general, Maryland's pension system ranks high among State plans in terms of liberality. Yet there are some questions that need attention. First is the one of reciprocity with other state systems. College teachers, who are very mobile, believe they should have the right to elect to join one of the national organizations, which would permit them to move about the country and yet keep their pension vested contributions. This right would require the State to contribute matching funds for some teachers to the national organization instead of to its own teachers' pension system. For this reason some members of the Legislature believe the Maryland system would be weakened. Besides, the State would be contributing funds to a national organization over which it has no control. Actually, a teacher could join the national organization and contribute both his part and what the State would normally match.

Another unresolved question is that of the State worker's contributions to the pension system. Some officeholders—for example, State judges—are exempt from personal contributions. Legislators are under less liberal provisions.

The question of salary raises for State workers is always an aggravating point. Maryland's proximity to Washington, and its more liberal wage scales require the State to continually adjust salary schedules to be competitive. Inflation also plays havoc with scales, especially for unskilled or semi-skilled employees. In the early 1970's many conflicts over salaries took place between State hospitals and workers at middle- and lower-level jobs. It was for these reasons that the fiscal 1975 budget called for a 6.7 percent increase for State workers.

After raising all these questions, it is fair to say that Maryland has gone far in its personnel relations since the first civil service laws of 1920.

Chapter 23

DEPARTMENT OF STATE PLANNING

The Department of State Planning is the computer of the 12 secretariats. Underlying its existence is the belief that any action taken by any State department in terms of development of physical resources, improvement for human progress, long-range planning, and other extensions of activities requires coordination. For example, if the Department of Natural Resources seeks to establish a new State park, it is necessary for the Department of Transportation to arrange to build roads leading to the park. If the Department of Health and Mental Hygiene aims to extend the Medicare program, it must work in concert with the Department of Employment and Social Services in order to integrate Medicare with the public assistance services offered by the latter department. The State Department of Education could hardly plan for new local elementary and secondary schools without considering relationships to main highways (developed by Department of Transportation) which might well become hazards to safety. Unfortunately, a good deal of haphazard planning did take place before the Department of State Planning became the agent responsible for proper articulation of State projects. Indeed, hardly a single activity carried out by one of the 12 cabinet Departments, or for that matter any of the independent agencies, can be performed unilaterally and yet be fully effective.

This is why the Department of State Planning, reorganized in 1970 as a cabinet-level secretariat, has a division known as the State Clearing House, another division known as State Planning Research, yet another dealing with Regional and Local Planning, and one dealing with Comprehensive State Planning.

State Planning Commission

The State Planning Commission was created, as were other commissions within the framework of the State government, to provide and guarantee that lay thinking and advice would be available to the State in the formulation of its policies and programs. The Commission has nine members and is advisory to the Secretary of the department. It is charged, under the terms of Article 88C of the Annotated Code of Maryland, with advising the Secretary on the State Development Plan.

Capital Improvements Programs

The many operating departments and institutions of the State are required to submit annually to the Department of State Planning all projects proposed for inclusion in the State's capital program. The department is required to review, evaluate, recommend, and schedule those projects of greatest operational priority and importance to ensure that the State's physical plant facilities keep pace with program needs and an increasing population.

The procedure for formulating the annual Capital Budget begins more than a year prior to the fiscal year for which it is planned. It includes the preparation and distribution of detailed instructions and project submittal forms, on-site inspection of physical plant facilities, departmental hearings, and maintenance of continuous, close relationships with all State agencies and institutions. This process is facilitated through the cooperation of the Department of General Services, the Department of Budget and Fiscal Planning, the Legislature's Department of Fiscal Services, and the Capital Budget Committee of the Legislative Council.

In addition to the annual General Construction Loan Bill, the General Assembly enacts other general obligation bond bills to authorize funds for other special capital projects. All bills which provide for the authorization of general obligation bonds are submitted prior to legislative action for review by the Department of State Planning assisted by the Departments of General Services and Budget and Fiscal Planning, and the Comptroller's Office. The review is made in terms of effect on the State's structural indebtedness, as well as conformity with general policy guidelines. Findings and recommendations are submitted simultaneously to the Governor and to the chairmen of the pertinent committees of the General Assembly.

During the 1972 session of the General Assembly, the following debt authorization bills, in addition to the General Construction Loan Act, were reviewed and evaluated:

Other Bond Authorization Bills 1972 Legislative Session

General Public Junior or Community College Construction Loan of 1972	$ 10,000,000
Home Financing Loan	10,000,000
State Public School Construction and Capital Improvement Loan of 1972	300,000,000
Baltimore City Detention Center for Women Loan of 1972	155,000
Solid Waste Reclamation Loan	10,000,000
Anne Arundel County Water Loan of 1972	3,000,000
Maryland Regional Cancer Center Loan of 1972	2,000,000
Friendship International Airport Loan of 1972	36,000,000
Maryland Industrial Land Act	6,000,000
Nursing Home Loan of 1972	1,000,000
Community Mental Health Center Components and Mental Retardation Facilities Loan of 1972	1,000,000
Senate Bill 626 includes a provision that the State shall bear the amortization cost on $20,000,000 of the $25,000,000 appropriated in the Urban Mass Transit Loan of 1970	20,000,000
Total	$399,155,000

State Clearing House

The State Clearing House refines and improves procedures for coordinating the review of specified federally aided projects.

Increase in Programs Reviewed. The Clearing House performs a major service to State and local agencies related to proposed projects on which planning has not progressed sufficiently to warrant a formal review. An informal "early warning" notification and review system is in existence. This proves to be especially helpful to the State Highway Administration in obtaining comments prior to corridor public hearings and in notifying affected agencies of requests for railroad abandonments submitted to the Interstate Commerce Commission.

Quality of Plans Enhanced. In the area of review of State plans, the Clearing House, in conjunction with the Comprehensive Planning Division, enhances the quality of the plans prepared by all State agencies. A list of the 59 federal grants-in-aid programs, which require a State plan as a condition of federal assistance, is provided to all State agencies. All required State plans are submitted to the Clearing House for review.

Coordinating Legislation. Accordingly, the DSP drafted legislation which would mandate the department to make rules and regulations to systematize early coordination of such programs and projects among affected agencies of the State and local governments.

A major purpose of the Clearing House is to raise the level of federal grant funding in Maryland. This effort is pursued by advising State and local agencies of the available federal grant programs, assisting in the mechanisms and procedures for applying for such grants, and improving the quality of applications. In addition to individual advice and assistance in response to specific requests or as a result of the receipt of sub-standard notification of intent, the Clearing House publishes and distributes thousands of special and periodic reports such as "Federal Grants-in-Aid Awarded in Maryland, July 1, 1970 to June 30,1971."

By providing the link between planning and implementation through its PNRS (federal Project Notification Review System) reviews, the State Clearing House substantially reduced uncoordinated development and associated resource wastage, frequently initiating communication between governmental agencies which should have been working together. Federal grant funds awarded in Maryland increased 48 percent from $381 million in FY 1971 to $563 million in FY 1972.

State-Owned Land Inventory in Process. In conjunction with the Department of Taxation and Assessments, an inventory of State-owned and federal land has been tabulated. A complete listing and mapping of State-owned land for Baltimore City and all counties, except Allegany, Anne Arundel, Garrett and Washington, has been completed.

State Planning Research Program

Activities of the Research Program center around the development of comprehensive information for use in Statewide planning. Activities vary from the development of data bases of useful socioeconomic information to the design and construction of predictive models essential for the identification and evaluation of development issues.

Interstate river basin and regional water and related resource planning programs also enlist the department's participation. Endeavors are directed toward the Susquehanna and Ohio River Basin Commissions, the North Atlantic Regional Water Resources Study, and the Northeastern United States Water Supply Study.

In addition the Research Program provides technical assistance to the executive departments and the Legislature, as well as to other State agencies.

Studies, Analyses, and Reports. Among the urgent priorities faced at all planning levels is improved planning and management of environmental resources. To meet this need, the Research Program has developed a State Planning model capable of forecasting economic-environmental impacts of alternative regional development proposals. Major components have been utilized to forecast output, employment, income, and migration for counties and to indicate the effects of specific development proposals upon government revenues and generation of waste. This effort produced a 1970 interindustry model of the Maryland economy and an accompanying computer-based impact analysis program which has the capability to evaluate development alternatives in terms of critical Statewide economic and environmental variables. As the model is refined to operate on local and regional levels, it provides an invaluable device for identifying and analyzing a wide range of future resource problems and issues.

Census Data. Important data bases for State government are provided by the servicing of census data users. The program published a *Census Data Newsletter*, which enabled users to become informed of all census-related activities undertaken within the State.

River Basin Planning Programs. The Susquehanna River Basin Commission, established in 1971, made substantial progress during the early 1970's in completing organizational arrangements. A policy statement, based upon the provisions of the Susquehanna River Basin Compact, was prepared to inform the public of guidelines that will govern future commission activities. The statement was published in the *Federal Register*, as well as in appropriate publications of member-state jurisdictions. In the aftermath of Storm Agnes in 1972, the commission performed a vital coordinating role among federal, State, and local agencies in identifying and cataloguing areas within the basin vulnerable to flood damage and in the preparation of flood-plain maps essential to redevelopment planning.

The Ohio River Basin Commission, also established early in 1971, is responsible for coordination of numerous federally funded water and related land resources studies. Of particular interest to Maryland is the preparation of a plan of study for preparing the Monongahela sub-basin portion of the comprehensive plan for the Ohio River Basin, which calls for the incorporation of the ongoing Youghiogheny Wild Rivers Study of the U.S. Department of Interior's Bureau of Outdoor Recreation.

North Atlantic Regional Water Resources (NAR) Study. The NAR study is part of a long-term survey of all major river basins in the United States, as required by the President's Water Resources Council. NAR, begun in the mid-sixties, covers all or parts of 13 northeastern states and the District of Columbia with drainage into the Atlantic Ocean.

Maryland's interests focus on the Susquehanna and Potomac River Basins and the Chesapeake Bay and Delmarva Peninsula drainage areas. The State, represented by the Department of State Planning, works in close cooperation with the Department of Natural Resources and presses for proper recognition of important relationships between the estuarine and coastal zone resources and other up-basin components and uses of the various river systems embraced by the NAR study.

The overall objective is to provide broad-scale analyses of water and related land resources problems on a regional and sub-regional basis. Three planning objectives were considered as they relate to human needs and demands—regional development, national income, and environmental quality. The NAR study's planning horizon extends to the year 2020, with intermediate benchmark years set at 1980 and 2000.

Northeastern United States Water Supply (NEWS) Study. The NEWS study is a companion to the NAR study, but specifically addresses local critical water supply problems. Its goal is to create an action program that will provide an ample supply of water for the people of the entire northeastern United States with particular emphasis on metropolitan areas. Recommendations will be transmitted to Congress.

Regional and Local Planning Programs

Encouraging active and relevant comprehensive planning in the municipalities, counties and regions of Maryland is a major responsibility of the department's regional and local function. A division of the department works with local governments to stimulate and increase their planning capabilities, encourages cooperative approaches to regional problems, and coordinates and develops plans at each level of government within a common, coordinated policy framework.

At this time, all 23 counties and Baltimore City have active planning agencies and programs. There are 55 active municipal planning agencies. Five of the seven regions of the State are organized into multi-county areawide planning operations.

Comprehensive Planning Assistance Projects. The department is the applicant for, and the division administers, the "701" federally assisted comprehensive planning assistance projects for local and non-metropolitan planning agencies. In administering the 701 program, the staff meets with each local applicant to review its 3-year work program, which serves as the local 701 application. The division advises the local jurisdiction of planning activities required by the U.S. Department of Housing and Urban Development or State legislation that should be emphasized in the jurisdiction's work program and application. The division advises non-charter counties and municipalities of the need to comply with this law and of ways in which the 701 program can assist the jurisdiction in meeting these State requirements.

The division also meets with each grant recipient throughout the year to review work being undertaken.

Community Technical Advisory Services. The division remains on call to assist communities and planning agencies. The degree of this technical assistance varies considerably, as is evident in these examples: Ocean City—preparation of an open space plan and beach preservation program; Cecilton—preparation of a comprehensive plan; Sharpsburg—design of a neighborhood park; Dorchester County—assistance in the reorganization of the County Planning Commission and program; Tri-County Council for Western Maryland, Inc.—assistance in the initial organization and subsequent operations; Charles County—assistance in the preparation and review of zoning regulations for a large new community; Model Cities Project areas in Baltimore and Prince Georges County—701 funding to the Department of Economic and Community Development; Overall Program Design—assistance to all 15 municipalities and counties included in the fiscal 1972 Comprehensive Planning Assistance Program.

Areawide Planning Organizations. The Department of Housing and Urban Development requires that prior to the federal funding of water, sewer, and open space facilities, grants to the local governmental jurisdictions must be a part of a multi-jurisdictional areawide planning organization. The Areawide Planning Organizations Division explains these requirements to jurisdictions throughout Maryland and works with localities in applying and qualifying for areawide certification.

There are three separate certification requirements to be met by each areawide planning applicant:

Planning Area and Organization. Each areawide planning organization must have the legal status and authority to carry out comprehensive planning and a policy body composed of two or three elected officials. Membership in the organization must be open to towns and areawide citizen interests must be represented. In addition, the organization must adopt a 12-month work program, have a staff capable of carrying out this planning program, and document its program of equal employment opportunity.

Comprehensive Planning Program. The comprehensive planning program, as outlined in the 12-month work program, must include a statement of the organization's goals and objectives and an area-wide land-use element.

Functional Planning and Programming. Each organization must adopt functional plans and short-range programs for open space, water, and sewer services.

Regional Planning Coordination. The staff serves in an advisory and coordinating capacity to the two metropolitan planning agencies and three non-metropolitan planning agencies. In addition, the staff serves as advisory representatives to the Delmarva Advisory Council and the Wilmington Metropolitan Area Planning Coordinating Council.

Comprehensive State Planning

Realization of the department's legislative directives is being accomplished through an increased emphasis on State development planning—an approach to solving problems facing government by providing assistance and alternatives to decision makers. In order to increase the department's capabilities in this area, the division continually refines and updates overall State plans and recommends policies. This includes formulation of a State Development Plan, program reviews, and the analysis and formulation of policy alternatives relative to their impact on the pattern of population distribution with reference to physical, economic, and sociocultural resource utilization in the State.

State Development Planning. The Plan creates a framework and context to aid, guide, and contribute toward the establishment of a clearer State direction. The word "State" is used in its broadest sense and does not merely mean State-level government. What is intended is a means of cooperative, coordinated public and private action at all levels of government.

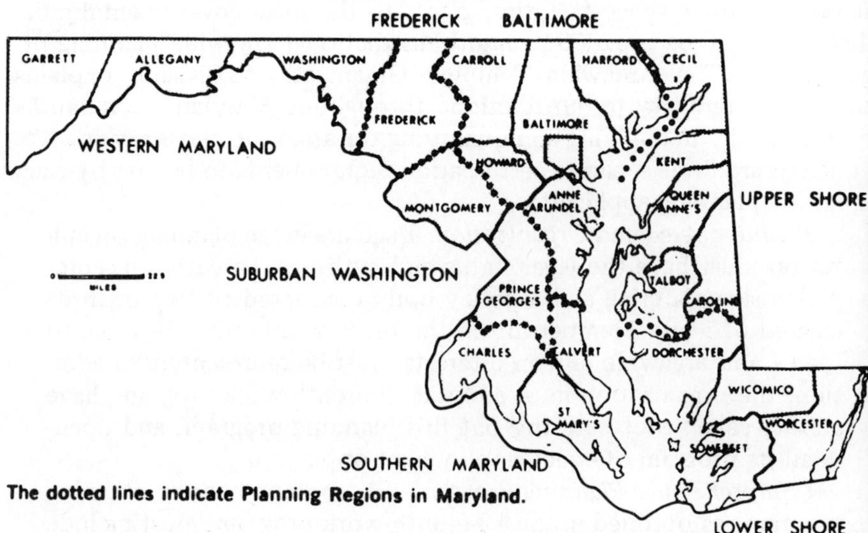

The dotted lines indicate Planning Regions in Maryland.

A Generalized State Land-Use Plan is scheduled for completion in 1974. It will identify new work elements and create a mechanism for incorporating existing sub-elements, *i.e.*, open space plan, historical preservation plan, housing element and other functional plans. Preparation of the plan includes 1) analysis of the consequences of existing State, regional, and local plans and policies which influence land use; 2) identification of those natural features and processes which establish land-use capability, suitability and environmental sensitivity for various uses; 3) consideration and protection of historical, cultural, ecological, recreational and aesthetic resources; 4) analysis of the land-use influence posed by supplying utilities, transportation networks, and other public services and facilities; 5) development of standards for public services and facilities and methods of assuring their implementation; and 6) the projection of population levels, including characteristics, densities and distributions.

A second project is the Human Resources Plan. As envisioned, the plan will depend partially on a survey of social indicators. The first phase is under way both through the census data retrieval work of the Research Division and previous studies done by this division. Social indicators will be utilized to investigate current conditions in Maryland.

A second phase of the Human Resources Plan will involve the definition of goals, in an attempt to describe desirable human capabilities and attainments. Phase 3 will result in the identification of agencies and institutions that are, or should be, involved in the effort to attain each goal. Based on a determination of where Maryland currently stands in relation to the goal statements, Phase 4 will suggest broad directions in which to move in order to attain the long-range goals. Finally, a process for planning and program development will be recommended to assist functional agencies to perform these tasks. The final phase is based on the recognition that it is the functional agencies of State government, as well as local government, that must actually devise and administer the programs which will lead to goal attainment.

Transportation—Land-Use Planning Coordination. Practically every land-use project in the State requires that there be a transportation component tied in with it. For example, the building of a new road in the heavily traveled I-95 corridor in Prince Georges County will have an immediate effect on shopping patterns, housing patterns, and other life requirements.

Economic Growth Center Development Highways. Under a new provision in the 1970 Highway Act, each state is asked to designate areas and highways which would "demonstrate the role that highways can play . . . (in promoting) . . . . the desirable development of . . . natural resources . . . revitalize and diversify the economy of rural areas . . . (and) enhance and disperse industrial growth."

The Department of State Planning was requested by the Department of Transportation to supply its assessment of where such funds could be most profitably used in the State. Each region of the State was considered and recommendations prepared. The decision was that the initial application of these monies would be made to expedite the improvement of U.S. Route 11 north from Hagerstown.

Incorporating Environmental Considerations into the Transportation—Land-Use Planning Process. An increasing awareness of the environment has prompted a more thorough consideration of both noise and air pollution in planning studies. The department is participating in several interagency committees established to deal with these issues. In the Baltimore area, the department participates in an interagency task force guiding the efforts of a consultant study. This study will propose some regional strategies for reducing the amount of air pollution from transportation sources. These strategies, if found to be feasible in helping the State to meet the 1976-77 air quality standards, will be incorporated into the State's overall air-quality control plan. One means to be investigated is the more rational arrangement of land use to reduce the amount of travel needed by people each day.

Areawide, Multi-disciplinary Planning of Transport Facilities. In order to adequately assess the actual impacts of newly developed transportation facilities, the department is participating in two unique efforts. To restudy the I-95 Corridor in western Prince Georges County, a 70-member steering and citizens' advisory committee has been formed. This committee will be responsible for generating alternative solutions to transportation needs of the area.

While Prince Georges County wrestles with the problems of directing booming growth, Western Maryland has an opposite challenge—how to gain the maximum benefits from proposed highway improvements in the area.

Planning Related to Environmental Quality. As man seeks to improve the environmental quality of life, it is necessary for comprehensive planning to take place. For example, one cannot build a new outdoor recreational center without tying in requirements of roads, population studies, and recreational needs.

Water Supply and Waste Management. Since responsibilities for planning, operation, and regulation of water supply and solid liquid waste management are divided between two principal State Departments (Planning and Natural Resources) and local jurisdictions, emphasis has been placed on developing and improving coordination between State agencies and between different levels of government.

The county sewer and water plans are an important element in carrying out and controlling land use and development. To improve the county plans the Department of Planning and the Department of Health and Mental Hygiene have jointly drafted guidelines for county sewer and water projects.

Chesapeake Bay Program. The Chesapeake Bay Interagency Planning Committee (CBIPC) was established in 1969 to improve planning and management procedures between State agencies with Bay-related responsibilities. The Bay's natural resources require comprehensive study to minimize adverse land- and water-related impacts through the promulgation of policies for balanced use.

Neither the Susquehanna River nor the Chesapeake Bay is entirely within the boundaries of Maryland. Therefore, proper management requires interstate coordination. Maryland and her sister states have entered into the Susquehanna River Basin Compact with the federal government. However, no formal attempt has been made to address comprehensive management planning for the Bay. Maryland must continue to work for a formal agreement for the Bay. In the absence of a formal agreement, Maryland continues to coordinate its Bay planning efforts with Virginia and with federal agencies to insure common purpose.

Open Space and Outdoor Recreation. Increasing leisure time, mobility, and income are creating a growing demand for additional park, recreation, and open-space areas to meet the changing needs of a modern population. The Department of State Planning is addressing these needs through preparation of the State Outdoor Recreation and Open-Space Plan which, when completed, will be the open-space element of the State Development Plan.

The first phase of the plan presented in preliminary form the overall direction for the outdoor recreation components. This was essentially a "natural features" approach. Upon the completion of this stage, a further refinement of the approach, along with extensive feedback from other State agencies and local governments, was incorporated into the plan. This then represented the Phase 2 report, which provides among other things, detailed Statewide and regional recommendations for areas to be preserved as open space and areas to be developed for recreation.

Historical Preservation Plan. The Department of State Planning assists the Maryland Historic Trust, through and with the assistance of the Department of Economic & Community Development, in the development of a Statewide Historic Preservation Plan.

An essential part of any historic preservation plan is an inventory of cherished sites, structures, and objects throughout the State. A second and equally important part of the preservation program is the study of historical forces which have influenced the State's political, social, economic, and geographical development.

C & O Canal National Historical Park Commission. In preparation is a master plan for the preservation and development of the national park, priorities for acquisition and development, review of the damage to the canal as a result of Storm Agnes, riparian rights, recreation use of the Potomac River, and the impact on the park of development external to the area.

Assateague Island Study. The study includes all aspects of ownership, utilization and development of the Maryland portion of the island. The committee is composed of six legislators and representatives from the Departments of Health and Mental Hygiene and Natural Resources.

The committee report recommends that Maryland retain its ownership of Assateague Island State Park, that the emphasis be placed on day activities, and that there be a minimum of physical development. The report further recommends that the National Park Service adopt a similar philosophy, and calls for the preparation of joint federal-State management and development plans to insure compatibility of the various activities with the fragile barrier island environment.

Power Plant Siting. The role of the Advisory Committee is to furnish Maryland's Secretary of Natural Resources with expert advice on technical appraisal of the State's power plant siting program. The Human Health and Welfare Studies Group was established to identify and evaluate potential power plant problems as they impinge on human health and welfare.

Housing and Community-Development Planning. The Department of State Planning's involvement in community-development planning has been primarily in the realm of preparing and recommending preliminary Statewide housing goals and policies directed at confronting the housing and housing-related problems of the residents of the State.

Review of all federal housing assistance applications is conducted by the Department of State Planning. This process gives relevant State agencies the opportunity to review and comment on projects while in the early planning stage, thus promoting compatibility between the proposed housing developments and housing-related environmental factors.

Multi-Purpose Centers. Concern has developed in recent years over the accessibility and convenience of State services and the skyrocketing space needs and associated costs to government agencies. As a result of this concern, the Department of State Planning recently received funds from the Legislature to "prepare a program and plan, including a feasibility study, for State multi-purpose centers to provide for convenient and efficient service delivery."

Multi-purpose centers are a recent innovation in government facilities. These centers bring together in one location all services needed by the public. Government responsiveness can be increased by eliminating duplication of activities and improving coordination and communication.

Chapter 24

THE DEPARTMENT OF GENERAL SERVICES

Too few persons recognize that the State government is a large land and building owner in its own right. The State buildings maintained by the Department of General Services include more than a million square feet in Annapolis and about the same amount in Baltimore. This would not count the property falling under the care of the various secretariats other than that for General Services. For example, it would not include State schools, roads and bridges, airports, hospitals, correctional institutions, and police and fire headquarters. It would, however, include the State House, the Government House, the Treasury Building and the new House of Delegates Building—in all, 17 buildings in Annapolis; as well as five buildings, such as the State Office Building, the State Highway Administration Building, and the new Herbert R. O'Conor State Office Building in Baltimore.

The State is a big real estate developer. Each year it spends millions for State buildings and structures for education, health, natural resources and other services. These costs are lumped together yearly into that portion of the State Budget known as Authorizations for Capital Improvements, and are passed on by the legislators with the knowledge that they are financed in large part by the State taxes. For fiscal 1974 alone the Legislature passed a $435 million total Capital Budget including such items as a new $17.8 million University of Maryland School of Medicine Teaching Facility in Baltimore to permit expansion to an enrollment of 1,000 students. Other capital expenditures included State Public School Construction (under full State Funding support for all county and Baltimore City elementary and secondary school buildings) amounting to $245 million, and $70 million for State support of county and local sewage treatment plants and water quality projects.

These items have to be priced. In the case of the elementary and secondary school buildings the whole procedure, from origin to completion is supervised by the Department of General Services. On the other hand as for the new buildings at Coppin, Morgan, and Towson State Colleges, plans would be developed by the Board of Trustees of the State Colleges, but the Department of General Services prices out the projects and passes on its findings to the Department of State Planning, which puts the Capital Budget together. After the Capital Budget is passed by the General Assembly, the Department of General Services reviews and advises the Board of Public Works as to whether the contract bids for land and buildings are financially reasonable. The Secretary of General Services and his staff select and appoint the architects and engineers for these projects. In a sense, General Services is the State's realtor and real estate agent.

At the end of 1972 the Department was involved in the design or design supervision of some 440 projects. Some recent examples are the $32 million Herbert R. O'Conor State Office Building (Baltimore), the $5.5 million House of Delegates Building in Annapolis, and the $13 million Baltimore Community Health and Retardation Center.

Moreover, the sheer maintenance and repair of State governmental structures is a gigantic task. All of this comes under General Services. In 1971 there were 279 employees engaged in operating, maintaining, and protecting 1.5 million square feet of office space to become 2.3 million when the new Courts of Appeals and Natural Resources Buildings in Annapolis and the Baltimore Laboratory Building are fully occupied.

The central purchase and storage of supplies and equipment for all State functions in order to buy at minimum prices is a complicated and mammoth activity carried out by General Services. The State is probably the largest single consumer of goods in Maryland, and the question of amounts of money involved makes up but one facet of the requirement. Bidding without favoritism, judgment of quality, standards for usage, and other issues become paramount in an age when there is collusion and breach of ethics in governmental purchasing. The 1973 charges surrounding Vice President Spiro T. Agnew and leading to his resignation particularly those related to his Maryland gubernatorial administration, raised some questions about the need for more ethical practices in awarding contracts, particularly to engineers.

The question of official State records and archives is crucial to legal decisions. The Department of General Services acts in this area through the Hall of Records at Annapolis. The Archivist of the Hall doubles as Commissioner of Land Patents, a task that protects land holdings.

Thus it is evident that the Department of General Services is the guardian and watchdog of State holdings. Because its activities receive less publicity than, for example, those of the Departments of Health and Mental Hygiene or Transportation, it is often the unsung hero in Maryland government.

Activities of the Department of General Services

The Department of General Services became operational in 1970. The head of the Department is the Secretary of General Services, who, like other Secretaries, is appointed by the Governor with the advice and consent of the Senate. The Secretary is directly responsible to the Governor. The Deputy Secretary is appointed by the Secretary with the approval of the Governor. All staff assistants in the Secretary's office in charge of particular areas of responsibility serve at the pleasure of the Secretary.

The Department is a consolidation of the duties and functions previously performed and exercised by the Department of Public Improvements, the Board of Architectural Review, the Office of the Superintendent of Annapolis Public Buildings and Grounds, the Office of the Superintendent of Baltimore Public Buildings and Grounds, the Hall of Records Commission, the War Memorial Commission, the Washington (County) Cemetery Board of Trustees, the Commission on Artistic Property, and the Purchasing Bureau. The Department has been organized into three functional offices: Office of the Secretary (Administration), Office of Engineering and Construction, and Office of Central Services. The Act which created the Department of General Services abolished the Department of Public Improvements and transferred its functions to it.

Office of the Secretary. The Secretary advises the Governor on all matters assigned to the Department of General Services and is responsible for carrying out the Governor's policies with respect to such matters. The Secretary advises the Board of Public Works and other State agencies on all matters of engineering, surveys, plans, specifications, and contracts for public improvements that may come before the Board or in which a State agency may be interested. The Secretary selects and appoints architects and engineers subject to approval of the Board of Public Works; he reviews and makes recommendations to the Board of Public Works on all contracts for the expenditure of sums appropriated for the acquisition of land, buildings, equipment, new construction, and other capital expenditures, except in connection with State roads, bridges, and highways.

The Secretary is responsible for the budget of his office and for the budgets of the boards, offices, and agencies within the Department's jurisdiction. The Secretary is also responsible for the promulgation of rules and regulations and planning activities for his office and he is authorized to approve, disapprove, modify, or revise the rules, regulations, plans, proposals, or projects of the boards, offices, divisions, commissions, and agencies within the Department.

The Director of Administration is responsible for general overall administrative coordination in the Department. This office distributes plans and specifications to bidders for all State building construction and purchasing. It also receives and tabulates bids and furnishes the results to the Board of Public Works with the Secretary's recommendations. The office contracts with all successful bidders and maintains cost records and accounting data on all bond issue funds. Administrative staff support is provided by this office in the areas of budget, finance, contract awards, personnel, legal counsel, and management service to all line programs in the Department.

Numerous boards set policy for different activities.

Board of Architectural Review. The Board consists of seven members appointed for four-year terms by the Secretary of General Services from lists of nominations submitted by the Baltimore Chapter, the Potomac Valley of Maryland Chapter, and the Chesapeake Bay Chapter of the American Institute of Architects. The Board advises the Secretary about specifications related to proper architectural treatment of proposed buildings. The Board also reviews all architectural designs and drawings and recommends any changes necessary to make the proposed buildings functional and practical for the use intended.

Commission on Artistic Property. The Commission consists of four persons appointed by the Secretary of General Services with the approval of the Governor. Its task is to keep a continuing inventory of valuable paintings and other decorative arts in all State buildings in the Annapolis area. The Commission also provides for the location, proper care, custody, restoration, display, and preservation of these paintings and decorative arts. The Commission is empowered, with the approval of the Secretary or the Governor, to receive and accept gifts and loans of paintings and other decorative arts. With the approval of the Governor, the Commission may accept gifts of money from any source, public or private, and thereafter administer and expend the funds according to the conditions and terms of the gift.

War Memorial Commission. The Commission consists of ten members, five of whom are appointed by the Secretary of General Services, with the approval of the Governor, and five who are appointed by the Mayor of the City of Baltimore. Each member serves a five-year term and must be a Maryland war veteran. It has custody and supervision of the War Memorial Building and the War Memorial Plaza in Baltimore which were erected to honor Marylanders who fought in World War I. The maintenance cost is shared equally by the State and the City of Baltimore. The building is open and available for meetings of veterans' groups and civic and patriotic societies, and for civic gatherings, providing that no collection or donation is taken or any admission charged.

Washington Cemetery Board of Trustees. The three Trustees, appointed by the Secretary of General Services for three-year terms, are responsible for the maintenance of Washington Cemetery, Hagerstown, where the Confederate dead of the battles of Antietam and South Mountain are interred.

Engineering and Construction. The Director of Engineering and Construction is responsible for supervising the functions of the office and coordinating the design and construction of all State public work projects.

The Land Acquisition Division is responsible for the purchase of all land acquired under Program Open Space, as well as all land acquired for State construction projects, except roads and bridges.

The Division of Design and Approval renders advice and assistance to State agencies on all matters involving engineering, surveys, plans, specifications, and contracts for construction and repair of State buildings.

The Division prepares and reviews plans and specifications for all public improvements, assists the Department of State Planning with the development of technical detail in the preparation of the Capital Improvement Program, and collects and maintains a file of plats and surveys of the location of all State-owned property.

The Construction Supervision and Inspection Division maintains representation on all major projects to insure adherence to established standards and specifications. In addition, all fire losses and casualty claims are handled through this Division.

The Division of Plant Management is responsible for directing the functions of Annapolis and Baltimore Public Buildings and Grounds, and the continuing study of maintenance programs for all State facilities.

The Public School Construction Division reviews and approves consulting architects' and engineers' plans and specifications for public school buildings throughout the State.

The Office of Annapolis Public Buildings and Grounds has a Superintendent who is in charge of the operation, maintenance, and protection of the following State-owned buildings: Government House, the State House, William S. James (Senate Office) Building, Courts of Appeals, Hall of Records, Treasury Building, Legislative Services Building, Treasury Building Annex, Stokes Building, Shaw House, the Income Tax Building, Central Services Building, which houses the Power Plant, Tawes State Office Building, Jeffrey Building, House of Delegates Building, the new offices of the District Courts, and State Police Barracks and Garage. He is also responsible for the several buildings which are leased by the State. The Superintendent is appointed by the Secretary and serves under the merit system.

The Office of Baltimore Public Buildings and Grounds has a Superintendent who is charged with the responsibility of operating, maintaining, and protecting the State Office Building, the State Highway Administration Building, the former Department of Motor Vehicles Building, and such other buildings and grounds owned or controlled by the State in the Baltimore area as designated by the Board of Public Works.

Office of Central Services. The Director of the Office of Central Services is responsible for supervising and coordinating the Purchasing Bureau, the Communications Division, the Printing and Publication Division, and the Hall of Records Commission.

When the *Department of Budget and Fiscal Planning* was created by Acts of 1969, the Purchasing Bureau was assigned to that Department, but it was placed under the Secretary of General Services in 1970. The Purchasing Bureau is responsible for the purchase of all materials, supplies, and equipment for the use of every State agency. The Secretary, through the Bureau, formulates standards for all materials, supplies and equipment to be purchased for the using authorities of the State. It maintains a warehouse for storing supplies and purchases them from a $700,000 Revolving Fund. These supplies are bought by State agencies which receive invoices and then replenish or repay the Revolving Fund in the same manner as do other vendors.

The Purchasing Bureau is also responsible for the distribution of donatable foods from the production and Consumer Food Programs of the U.S. Department of Agriculture and for administering the Special Milk Program for summer camps and child-care institutions.

(Top) Model of the State Office Complex, City of Annapolis. (Bottom) Model of Maryland State Office Center, Baltimore.

The Communications Unit is responsible for studying and coordinating Statewide telecommunications, including radio and telephone services, and for adapting modern techniques to eliminate duplication and overlapping.

The Division of Printing and Publications provides central management for all printing, publications, graphic arts, and other activities related to printed materials in the State service. Also provided are centralized duplicating services to agencies located primarily in the Baltimore area.

The Hall of Records Commission supervises and controls the Hall of Records and appoints the Archivist, who manages the building and its contents. State agencies, counties, cities, and towns in Maryland are authorized to offer for deposit at the Hall of Records all files, documents, and records not in current use. The Hall is located in Annapolis.

All records which are in the courthouses of the State and which were created prior to April 28, 1788, the date of ratification of the United States Constitution by Maryland, must be deposited at the Hall of Records. The records of all State agencies, boards, and commissions which are abolished or otherwise cease to function must also be transferred to the custody of the Hall of Records Commission.

State agencies are required by law to establish a continuing program for the management of their records. The Commission provides assistance and guidance in the development of the State Records Management Program, including the establishment of record retention schedules and microfilming activities.

All current deeds, mortgages, and releases recorded in the courthouses of the State are microfilmed and preserved at the Hall of Records for security purposes. Limited facilities are available for the filming of records of State agencies.

By several Acts of the General Assembly, the Hall of Records has been designated as an official depository for the publications of State agencies and for all codes published by local governments, both county and municipal. Since 1967, the Hall of Records has been a depository for measures changing the charters of municipal corporations. The Hall of Records Commission also edits, compiles, publishes, and distributes the *Maryland Manual*, a comprehensive directory of State government.

Under the provisions of Chapter 355 of the Acts of 1967, the Archivist was designated as the Commissioner of Land Patents and assigned the responsibility of issuing land patents and conducting *caveat* hearings. In performing these duties, he acts independently of the duties imposed on him as Archivist. The Hall of Records Commission serves as the official depository for the duplicate copies of subdivision plats formerly sent to the Land Office as insurance against the loss of originals.

Maryland Capital Improvement: A Step-by-Step Case Study

1. Towson State College needs new Library. Faculty, Administration and Board of Trustees for State Colleges appraise need.

2. Board of Trustees evaluates this capital improvement need in terms of other college proposals in the State college system and sets up 5-, 10-, 20-year priorities.

3. Department of General Services (Office of Engineering and Construction) aids with estimate of costs.

4. Through State Board of Trustees request goes to Department of State Planning which appraises project in terms of need, proposed location, and long-term State plans (Hearings held).

CAPITAL IMPROVEMENTS AUTHORIZED BY GENERAL ASSEMBLY, 1961-1972

CAPITAL IMPROVEMENT FUNDS AUTHORIZED BY THE GENERAL ASSEMBLY BY MAJOR FUNCTION, TWELVE YEAR PERIOD, 1961-1972

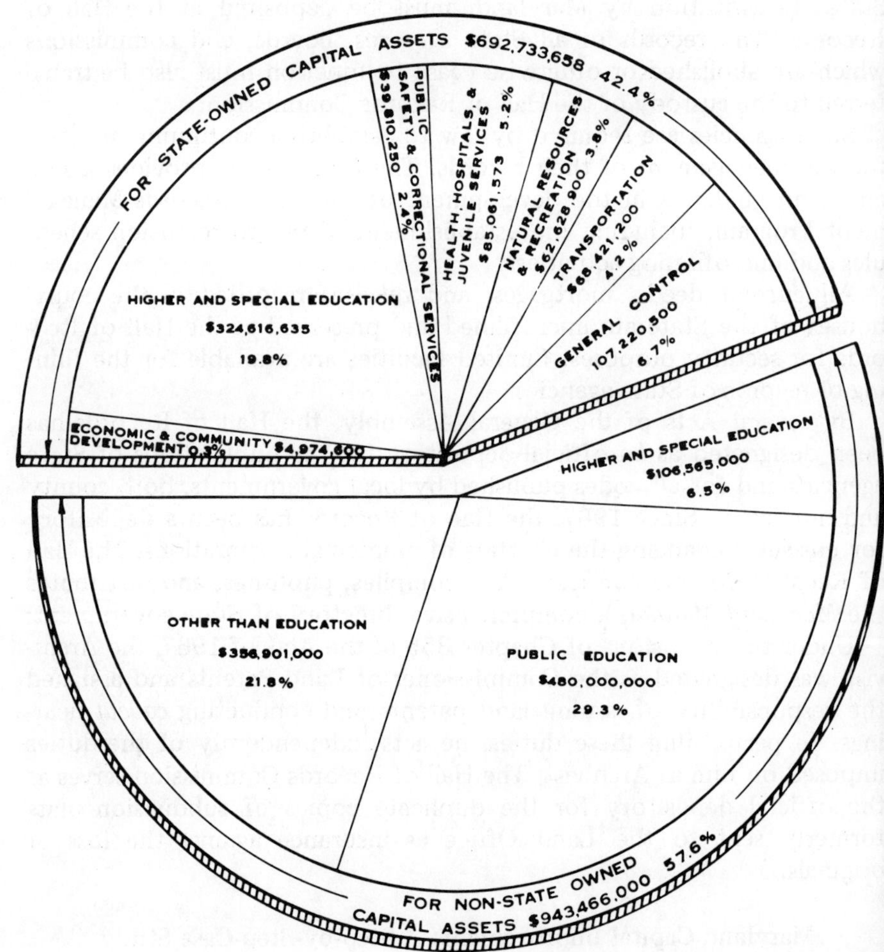

GRAND TOTAL—$1,636,199,658.00

5. Secretary of Budget and Fiscal Planning consulted by DSP about relation of capital program to operating program and general need for the Library.

6. DSP either accepts the request, fitting it into its public works program for submittal to the Secretary of Budget and Fiscal Planning to determine how much, if any, can be paid for by "pay-as-you-go" in current operating budget. If not, it remains as Bonded Capital Budget.

7. DSP (in cooperation with Secretary of Budget and Fiscal Planning and Department of General Services) works the Towson State College request into the total bonded capital program and submits it to Governor at same time B. and F. P. is submitting current operating budget to Governor. The two come in as a package (though voted on by the Legislature separately).

8. The Legislature through its Capital Budget Sub-Committee may recommend that the Governor increase or decrease the capital budget.

9. Action of Legislature is not an appropriation, as in case of operating budget; only an authorization to issue State bonds for specific purpose.

10. Board of Public Works determines the proportion of the total loan to be authorized at a given time, the denomination of the bonds, interest, and other matters.

11. Department of General Services uses its own architects and engineers to design small projects. Major projects contracted to private firms—supervised by DGS.

12. The Library goes up.

Chapter 25

THE DEPARTMENT OF BUDGET AND FISCAL PLANNING

The 20th Century has witnessed a vast increase in the services which our governments supply to the people. This applies on all levels of government—federal, state and local.

There has always been considerable debate regarding the proper limits of governmental activity. Some people believe that the trend toward dependence on government (particularly the federal government) has gone too far. They argue that it would be beneficial to foster more individualism, meaning reliance on individuals and private groups. Where governmental participation is unavoidable, they prefer operations on the local or state level to the federal level. On the other side of the issue are those who maintain that the increasing role of government in our daily lives is, on the whole, a good thing, and that we must expect it to continue in the future.

Without attempting to settle this debate, we can see readily how and why governmental services have widened in number and in scope. Many examples have been provided in earlier chapters of this book. Increased urbanization and suburban growth have made it necessary for governmental units to undertake services which could have been attended to by individuals in sparsely settled communities. Such developments as the automobile and suburban growth have given government new responsibilities in terms of highways and mass transportation which it did not have only a few generations ago. Many present-day governmental activities are connected with the typical American concern for an ever higher standard of living. Out of this desire for a fuller, richer life for all have come constantly expanding school systems, colleges, libraries, museums, public recreational facilities, and various other programs and services. Our recent stress on ecology has brought new requirements for governmental regulation of air and water pollution and furtherance of land-use laws and planning. Increase in life span and the accompanying need to support good health for the elderly has brought government support for hospitals and nursing homes. The goal of eliminating prejudice has created governmental enforcement agencies. The belief that decent housing is right has brought about public and low-cost housing support. A humanitarian view of helping the needy has created government aid for social services.

Even this fragmentary listing provides some conception of the vast range of functions which American democratic government will be undertaking in the last quarter of the Twentieth Century.

Increased Cost of Government

There is one thing that all governmental services have in common—they cost money. This is clearly reflected in the financial picture of present-day governmental cost in Maryland. In 1939, about 35 years ago, Governor Herbert R. O'Conor submitted a biennial budget for a two-year period calling for General Fund Expenditures—money primarily from State taxes—of about $21 million for each of the two years. In fiscal 1959 Governor J. Millard Tawes's General Fund Expenditures for the Budget were $204.8 million. In 1968 the General Fund Expenditures under Governor Spiro T. Agnew were $660.2 million, while the total Budget was $1.1 billion. For fiscal 1974 the General Fund Expenditures under Governor Marvin Mandel were $1.34 billion and the total Budget was $2.467 billion. For fiscal 1975 there was a leveling off to a General Fund Expenditure of $1.41 billion and a total Budget of $2.760 billion.

Local government units in Maryland also spend huge sums. For example, Montgomery County's Operating Budget for fiscal 1974 was $354.3 million. Anne Arundel's Operating Budget in 1973 exceeded $130 million. The Prince Georges Operating Budget for fiscal 1973 was $201 million. Baltimore City's for fiscal 1974 was about $725 million. The smaller political units, of course, would have smaller budgets; for example Charles County's Operating Budget for fiscal 1974 was but $16.3 million, and for the same year Wicomico's was $15.9 million.

It is important to note that inflationary factors have been significant in the rise of governmental costs. But even if these were 1940 dollars being spent in the 1970's, the comparisons would still show that State and local governmental budgets have skyrocketed in the last 35 years largely because citizens have demanded more services.

The State Constitution and Governmental Expenditures

The Constitution of Maryland gives much attention to fiscal matters. Article VI deals in detail with the Treasury Department and establishes by Constitution the methods by which the Comptroller and Treasurer are elected and their duties. The Comptroller holds a four-year term and is elected by the people as a Statewide officer at Gubernatorial elections. The Treasurer is appointed by the two Houses of the Legislature in joint ballot at the regular session when a Governor first goes into office and he, too, holds a four-year term.

The Comptroller. This officer is the general superintendent of the State's fiscal affairs. He prepares plans for the improvement and management of the revenue and for the support of the public credit; prepares estimates of State revenues and expenditures; enforces the prompt collection of all taxes and revenues, and issues warrants for all monies to be paid out of the Treasury in pursuance of appropriations by law. He is a member of the highly important Board of Public Works and the Board of Revenue Estimates.

The Treasurer. This officer receives the monies of the State and deposits them in banks which, with the approval of the Governor, he selects. He disburses the funds received by the State upon warrants drawn by the Comptroller. Also, upon similar warrants, he makes payments on the State debts. He, too, is a member of the Board of Public Works and the Board of Revenue Estimates.

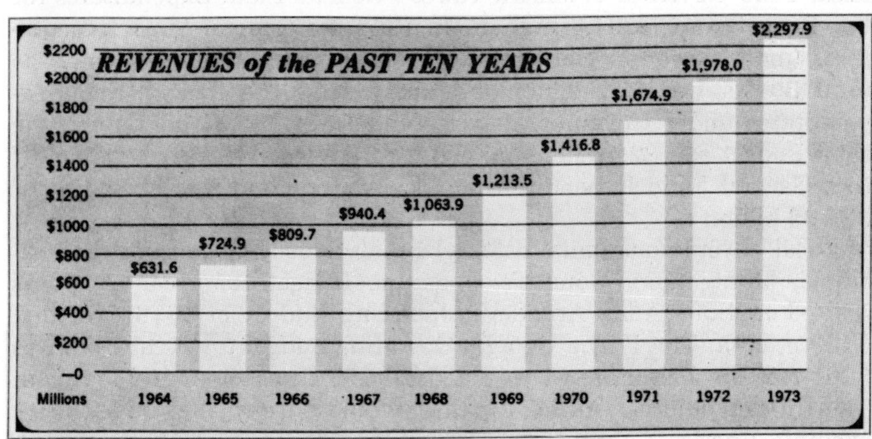

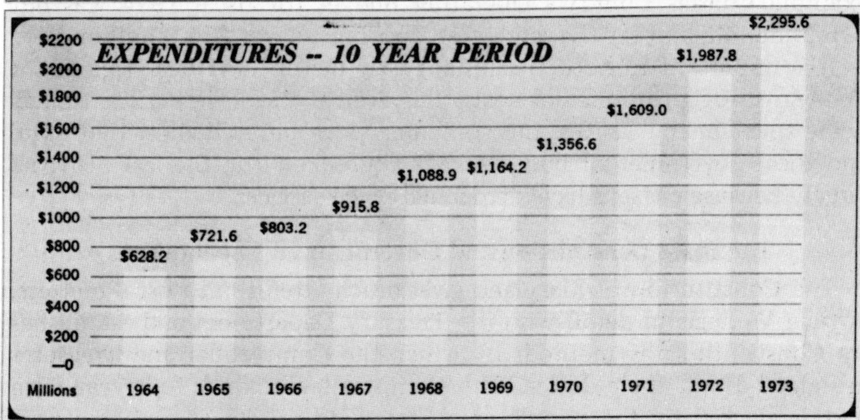

The Budget Bill. A large portion of Article III of the Maryland Constitution describes in detail how the Legislature must deal with the Budget. Section 52 of that Article makes it clear that "The General Assembly shall not appropriate any money out of the Treasury except in accordance with the provisions of this section."

The Constitution requires that the Governor (except when the year is his first of the term or unless the Legislature itself extends the time) submit to the General Assembly on the third Wednesday in January the

Budget for the next ensuing year. Each Budget must contain a complete plan of proposed expenditures and estimated revenues for the said fiscal year. It must also indicate the current assets, liabilities, reserves, and surplus or deficit of the State.

The Constitution permits a Supplementary Appropriations Bill, but only after the Budget Bill has passed both Houses. Each such supplemental appropriation must be embodied in a separate bill and the provisions made as to the revenue required.

The Legislature may reduce the Operating Budget items, but not increase them. The Operating portion of the Budget must be a "balanced budget" and not place the State in deficit. This, of course, is not true of the Capital Budget portion, which requires borrowing money and selling bonds.

If the Budget Bill is not finally acted upon by the Legislature seven days before the expiration of the regular session, the Governor may extend the session and not permit other discussions until the Bill is passed.

State Debts. Section 34 of Article III deals with the State debt and makes it clear that the General Assembly has the power to authorize the Board of Public Works to direct the State Treasurer to borrow in the name of the State, in anticipation of the collection of taxes.

This, of course, gives the Legislature the right to pass the Capital Improvement Bill (General Construction Loan). For example, the Loan Authorization of 1973 was for various departmental building construction, demolition, acquiring real estate and options, and the sale of bonds accruing to $108.5 million, plus $300 million more bond money authorized for school construction and sewage treatment plants in the next few years.

The State debt incurred as a result would be financed in part by the State tax rate on property, which in fiscal 1974 was 21 cents per $100.00.

There would, of course, be money from the General Fund to pay for the debt service that would have to supplement the funds that accrue from the State Property Tax. The addition of full State funding for public schools alone cost $200 million spread out over a number of years so the State Property Tax alone couldn't pay the yearly interest and principal requirements of the bonds.

It is important to note that while *authorization* for loans of $400 million was given in fiscal 1974, the money was *not spent that year.* Bonds were not even sold that year; they are sold as the contracts are let. Therefore the expenditures for capital funds are usually spread out over a 15- or 20-year period with each year bringing debt service costs for interest and principal. It is this debt service that is included in each year's Budget and paid for through revenues from Special Funds (including State Property Tax), Federal Funds, and General Funds. The debt service involved $56.8 million or 2.3 percent of the total Budget of $2.46 billion in fiscal 1974.

The State Sources of Revenue

The State gets its power to tax from the Constitution, but the forms of taxation are established by the Legislature. In practice, the Governor and the General Assembly are continually looking for new sources of revenue, particularly those not preempted by the federal government.

REVENUES

Where the money came from Fiscal Year 1973

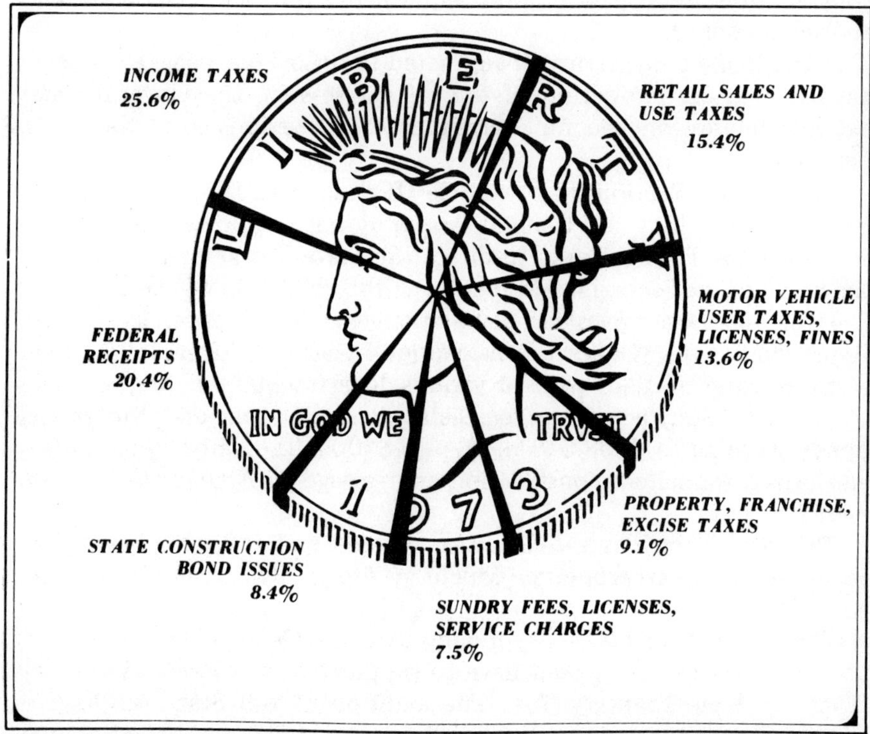

This is one reason why the State sales tax is such a good source, since there is no national sales tax. On the other hand the sales tax does not follow the key principle, "A tax should be based on ability to pay," as well as does a graduated income tax.

The Budget's Revenues. General taxes depend to a degree upon the revenue necessary to go into the General Funds—money which comes largely from State General Taxes and is the non-earmarked portion of the Budget. For example, in fiscal 1974 the General Fund Revenue from non-earmarked taxes and licenses amounted to $1.37 billion. General Fund revenues are monies which are available for any purpose not earmarked for a special purpose.

In addition to the General Fund monies that go into the Budget, there are Federal Fund revenues. For example, for fiscal 1974 the federal government contributed $508 million, largely to support transportation facilities, employment and social services, public education, health services, administrative operations, natural resources, State planning, public safety and correctional services, and economic and community planning. These federal funds represent State-aid programs passed by Congress to encourage the states to offer more public services and to contribute state money. The federal funds are generally earmarked for a particular purpose, such as aid for vocational education.

Then, too, one must add to the Budget monies that come from Special Funds. Special Funds are monies collected for a special or earmarked purpose. These Funds include such things as private grants for colleges and hospitals, fees paid by students and earmarked for student activities, cafeteria, and extracurricular events. For example, the University of Maryland alone collected $52 million in Special Funds in fiscal '74. Special Funds would also include fines, certain licenses, lottery funds, and payments for services. It would also include, for example, gasoline taxes, which go into Special Funds to finance operations of the Department of Transportation.

Of course, all the Debt Service (principal and interest) on the State's costs for airports and port facilities would be paid from the Special Funds collected by the Department of Transportation. This means that in addition to gasoline tax money, some motor vehicle revenue and titling tax money would be earmarked for the Department of Transportation and thus go into their Special Fund.

The State Property Tax is earmarked for payment on capital improvements; thus its revenue would go toward the payment of Debt Service. Other portions of taxes and licenses such as the tobacco tax, income tax, and horse racing tax are earmarked for return to local subdivisions and would go into Special Funds.

The Federal Fund, Special Fund, and Debt Service take a large portion of the total Budget, with more and more funds earmarked for certain purposes, thus leaving smaller portions for the General Fund that can be distributed any way the State desires. This can be bad in that there is not much flexibility in earmarked appropriations.

If one adds the General Fund of $1.3 billion, the Federal Funds of $508 million, and the Special and Debt Service Funds of $613 million, he would arrive at the total Revenue Fund figure of $2.4-plus billion for the Budget of fiscal 1974.

The State Taxes. As stated earlier, General Fund requirements in the main determine what general taxes shall be used and what rates are to be set.

In general it is difficult to initiate a new tax; the public is alert to such innovations. The initiation of the Maryland sales tax in the late 1940's kept Governor William Preston Lane, Jr., from winning a second term, even though his victorious opponent kept and increased that tax. It is easier to raise rates on older taxes.

Following is a summary of State taxes as of fiscal 1974. Since rates often change, readers should check on the figures herein quoted:

Income Taxes. Maryland's income tax on individuals is a graduated tax of 2 percent on the first $1,000 of taxable income, 3 percent on the second $1,000, 4 percent on the third $1,000, and 5 percent on all taxable income in excess of $3,000. There are exemptions of $800 for each dependent.

In addition, each person pays what is known as a "piggy-back" income tax to his county (or Baltimore City). This piggy-back is usually as high as 50 percent of the State tax. It is collected by the State and turned back to the local units.

The Corporation Income Tax is 7 percent of the net income of corporations (domestic or foreign). Those corporations doing a unitary business partly in and partly out of the State apportion their tax.

Income taxes brought the State about $650 million in revenue in fiscal 1974. The sum represented nearly 50 percent of General Fund Revenues.

Sales and Use Taxes. Maryland Retail Sales and Use Taxes are imposed on purchasers at the rate of 4 percent. Sales that are portions of one dollar pay one cent on each 25-cent purchase or fraction thereof. Fuels used in manufacturing or motor vehicle fuels are exempt; they have their own taxes. Use taxes are collected on purchases outside the State.

The monies collected are paid to the General Fund. In fiscal 1974 collections were about $356 million, representing 27.3 percent of the General Fund Revenues.

Inheritance and Estate Taxes. The inheritance tax is levied on transfers of property at death. This tax is set at $1 on every $100 worth of property inherited by direct descendants of the deceased. On legacies to collateral descendants the tax is $7.50 on every $100.

Maryland also has an estate tax, passed by the General Assembly to enable the State to benefit from the Federal Estate Tax. Actually, the Maryland Estate Tax costs the State's citizens nothing additional, since persons concerned would have to pay the same amount whether or not the State had such a law. Because Maryland has this law on its books, however, it is able to collect 80 percent of the tax receipts, which otherwise would go to the federal government. As it is, the federal government retains only 20 percent of the total. Since the State inheritance tax is deductible from the estate tax, only beneficiaries of very large estates are affected by the latter levy. In fiscal 1974 the death tax yield to the General Fund was $14.35 million.

Alcoholic Beverages Excise Tax. The tax on distilled spirits is $1.50 per gallon, 100 proof or less; a proportional advance if more than 100 proof. Wine is taxed at 40 cents per gallon and beer at nine cents per gallon.

A share of the distilled spirits revenue is distributed to the counties (and Baltimore City). The State's share going into the General Fund was $16.75 million in fiscal 1974.

The Tobacco Tax. The cigarette tax is six cents per package of 20. The funds are distributed, after deducting for the expense of operating, with 50 percent to the State General Fund and 50 percent to the counties (and Baltimore City) according to population. The State's share going into General Fund was $17.36 million in fiscal 1974.

Admissions Taxes. These taxes on amusements vary from county to county. The State collects the money for the counties and turns it back to them.

Tax on Horse Racing. Mile tracks pay to the State a license fee of $1,000 per day, 5 percent of the money wagered and one-half of the "breakage fee" (the rounding out of bets). Half-mile tracks pay (to county offices) a license fee of $50 per day and to the State a wager fee of 1 percent on the first $2.5 million wagered and 6 percent above that. Harness tracks pay a license fee of $25 a day, a wager fee of 3½ percent of the first $125,000, and 7 percent after that.

Taxes on horse racing are shared by the State and counties. The total collected in State General Funds for fiscal 1974 was over $12 million.

Corporation and Business Taxes. Corporations pay a graduated bonus tax on the authorization of stock (this tax is paid only when the corporation is first formed), an annual graduated franchise tax on capital stock, and a net income tax. Foreign (out-of-State) corporations are not liable for the bonus or franchise tax, but they do pay an income tax, a qualification fee, and a filing fee. Like individuals, corporations (including public utilities) pay a tax on the property they own.

In 1974 such utility companies as telegraph and cable lines, express and transportation systems, parlor cars, sleeping cars, telephone companies, oil pipelines, and electricity and gas companies paid a gross receipts tax. This ranges from 2 to 2.5 percent, and is applicable to all receipts from business done within the State.

Another business tax of 2 percent on net premiums in previous year is paid by insurance companies on premiums collected within the State.

In fiscal 1974 all these and other business taxes were expected to bring about $65 million into the State General Fund.

State Property Tax. There is a State tax on real and personal properties of individuals and ordinary business and foreign corporations. In fiscal 1974 it was 21 cents per $100. The tax is collected by the local units (counties and Baltimore City) when they collect their own property taxes. The tax is earmarked to be used to pay off a portion of the State capital improvements. As made clear earlier, other capital im-

ESTIMATED REVENUES AND EXPENDITURES FISCAL YEAR 1975

WITH AMOUNTS IN THOUSANDS OF DOLLARS AND PERCENTAGE OF ESTIMATED TOTAL REVENUES AND EXPENDITURES

WHERE THE MONEY WILL COME FROM

Source	Amount	Percent
INCOME TAX	$ 732,605	26.5%
SALES AND USE TAX	$ 389,582	14.1%
FEDERAL FUNDS	$ 608,185	22.0%
GASOLINE TAX, MOTOR VEH. REVENUE	$ 310,411	11.2%
OTHER RECEIPTS	$ 330,943	12.0%
GEN'L BUSINESS TAXES	$ 74,582	2.7%
STATE EDUCATION HOSPITALS ETC.	$ 84,852	3.1%
PROPERTY TAXES	$ 63,656	2.3%
TOBACCO TAX	$ 35,700	1.3%
ALCOHOLIC BEVERAGES TAXES	$ 26,500	1.0%
RACING REVENUE	$ 18,205	0.7%
DEATH TAXES	$ 14,373	0.5%
REVENUE SHARING	$ 41,000	1.5%
SURPLUS	$ 30,089	1.1%

WHERE THE MONEY WILL GO

Expenditure	Amount	Percent
ECONOMIC AND COMMUNITY DEVELOPMENT	$ 6,117	0.2%
NATURAL RESOURCES AND RECREATION	$ 40,945	1.5%
PUBLIC DEBT	$ 68,656	2.5%
PUBLIC SAFETY AND CORRECTIONAL SERVICES	$ 74,502	2.7%
PAYMENTS OF REVENUE TO CIVIL DIVISIONS	$ 81,172	2.9%
GENERAL	$ 299,677	10.8%
EMPLOYMENT AND SOCIAL SERVICES	$ 252,384	9.1%
HEALTH HOSPITALS MENTAL HYGIENE	$ 417,943	15.1%
TRANSPORTATION	$ 741,734	26.7%
PUBLIC EDUCATION	$ 789,553	28.5%

provements, like highways, are paid for by Special and Federal Funds, while yet others are paid for by General Funds.

Motor Vehicle Taxes. The State Gasoline Tax (when used for highways only; boating and farm use exempt) of nine cents per gallon is used to pay for operations of the State Department of Transportation. The first seven cents of the tax is divided thus: 60 percent to the State, 20 percent to Baltimore City, and 20 percent divided among the counties. Two cents of the nine-cent tax is earmarked for mass transportation in Maryland.

There is a motor vehicle titling tax of 4 percent of the purchase price. This thus exempts one from the retail sales tax. The tax brings $16 million into the State General Fund.

Vehicle annual license fees vary according to weight of car. Passenger cars are $20 or $30. Trucks have annual fees that range from $25 to $335, with trailers even more.

Licenses and Fees. Other sources of State revenue include various kinds of licenses, fees, taxes, and fines. Every business that sells merchandise, for example, must have a trader's license. Special licenses must be taken out by chain stores and amusement enterprises. Recordation taxes on purchases of property vary from county to county. All these, together with marriage licenses, may be obtained from the clerk of the Circuit Court in each county and from the clerk of the Court of Common Pleas in Baltimore City.

The State Lottery

In 1972 the people of Maryland amended the State Constitution to permit a lottery, thus following the steps of other states such as New Jersey, Pennsylvania, and New York. The Lottery went into effect in 1973.

The Lottery Act called for the establishment of a State Lottery Agency, including a State Lottery Commission and a Director with a working staff.

The Commission. The Commission consists of five members appointed by the Governor, with the advice and consent of the State Senate. After a period of staggered terms the members would serve for four-year periods. No salaries would be paid to commission members, but reasonable expenses would be provided.

The Director. The Director has the power to supervise and administer the operation of the Lottery in accordance with the provisions of the Lottery Act and with the rules of the Commission. In accordance with the provisions of the act and the rules of the Commission, he can license as agents to sell lottery tickets persons who will best serve the public convenience and promote the sale of tickets or shares. The Director requires a bond from every licensed agent, in such amount as provided in the rules of the Commission. Every licensed agent must prominently display his license, or a copy thereof, as provided in the rules of the Commission. Subject to the approval of the Commission and to any applicable laws relating to public contracts, the Director may enter into contracts for the operation of the Lottery, or any part thereof, and into contracts for the promotion of the Lottery. All contracts shall be awarded to the lowest responsible bidder and shall be let for such period of years, not exceeding three, as the Commission may determine. No contract awarded or entered into by the Director may be assigned by the holder thereof except by specific approval of the Commission.

Members of the Maryland State Lottery Agency set up the lottery's colorful "drawingmobile" as the audience begins to gather at Bethesda's Montgomery Mall. The weekly drawings are held at different sites around the State and members of the audience are asked to come on stage and choose the winning six-digit number at random.

State Lottery Fund. All monies received from the sale of lottery tickets or shares, less the commission of the agent, and any other revenues received under the granting legislative article, shall be accounted for to the State Comptroller and placed into a special account known as the State Lottery Fund.

From the fund, the Comptroller shall first pay for the operation and administration of the Lottery including the expenses of the Agency as allowed in the annual State budget. Fifty percent of the remainder of the monies in the fund shall be distributed as prizes to the holders of winning tickets or shares; and the remaining 50 percent shall be the State's share. The State's share shall be accumulated in the Fund on a calendar year basis and each 12-month share shall be placed into the General Fund of the State. These monies are available as General Fund Revenues in the fiscal year which begins in the calendar year following the year in which collected.

Its Workings. Maryland's lottery, known as "Twin Win," in early 1974 featured a weekly drawing of a six-digit number with weekly prizes ranging from $5 to $50,000. Additionally, a "Millionaire's Party" was held periodically, with participants receiving cash prizes of from $500 to $1 million, payable at the rate of $50,000 a year for 20 years. The Agency plans to make changes in order to increase the funds.

The first drawing took place on May 24, 1973; therefore, not much money came in during fiscal 1973 which ended on June 30, 1973. However, during 1974, the Lottery Agency expected to report a profit of $20 million, which would accrue after paying all the winners and after paying for administrative costs. Beyond 1974, the hopes are even greater, with talk of a daily drawing and daily lottery. If that were to take place, the Agency feels that the State would get even more money. It is important to note that of the $20 million that goes to the State for fiscal 1974, 25 percent may be pledged for aid to the aged and the other 75 percent for General Funds.

Budget Appropriations to Civil Divisions

It is not commonly known that slightly over one-half the total State Budget is turned over to civil divisions—that is, counties and municipalities. For example, for fiscal 1974 the total Budget was $2.4 billion, and $1.29 billion or 52 percent was appropriated to civil divisions.

As indicated earlier in this chapter, portions of certain State taxes—franchise tax on savings banks and building and loan associations, alcoholic beverages, tobacco, unclaimed property, franchise tax on ordinary business corporations, gasoline and motor vehicles—are budgeted in Special Funds and earmarked for civil divisions. These directly contributed tax monies added to certain grants by the State directly to the subdivisions (for example, Police Protection Fund) totaled $129 million for fiscal 1974.

Then there are funds which the State (largely from its General Fund) turns over to civil divisions through their operating departments. For example, the State turned over to the counties (and Baltimore City) over $400 million for local school aid for general use and for earmarked assistance toward local special services such as libraries, food service, transportation, school construction, handicapped children, and community colleges. The State turned over to counties (from the General Fund) about $100 million for local social services. It gave them about $190 million for local health services and more than $40 million (from Special Funds) for county and municipal roads. The State contributed about $90 million toward county (and Baltimore City) public school teachers' retirement and personnel benefits. In all, the State turned over to county departments (including Baltimore City) about $840 million. Most of this money came from the General Fund.

Indeed, the turnover to the civil divisions represented 60 percent of the total General Fund.

Finally, about 65 percent of all the federal funds which reach the State are turned over to operating departments in the counties (and Baltimore City). For example, in fiscal 1974 more than $127 million in Federal Interstate Roads money went to county (and Baltimore City) government treasuries. More than $100 million in federal money went to local social service departments. More than $50 million in federal money was turned over to local school systems for earmarked programs such as education of low-income families, school lunch, and vocational and manpower activities. The total, about $330 million of federal funds, was distributed by the State to the counties. Actually this amount was about 65 percent of all the money the State received from the federal government in fiscal 1974.

There is no doubt that without this State and federal money county and municipal taxes would be even higher.

County and Baltimore City Taxes

The problem of county taxation might be made clear by giving an illustration: Baltimore City in fiscal 1973 had a Budget of $726 million. It received $426 million from the State and federal sources both in direct contribution through State tax sharing and in contributions to its operating departments, such as health, education, police, model cities, social, hospital services, and community action.

That left $300 million to be picked up by the City. Fortunately, the piggy-back on State income tax gave it $33.3 million. Public service enterprises brought in $20.6 million. Various city taxes and licenses, plus miscellaneous revenues such as parking meter funds, brought in $65 million.

That left about $175 to $180 million to be picked up by real and personal property taxes. On Baltimore City's total assessable base of $3.13 billion, to get that $175 million in property taxes would mean a tax rate of $5.86 per hundred of value.

Other local units faced similar problems. For example, for fiscal 1974, in order to take care of a $354.3 million Budget, Montgomery County had to raise $143.2 million, or 40 percent of its budget, from property taxes. Fortunately, the assessed valuation of all real and personal property in the County was $4.1 billion. Assessments in Montgomery County are 55 to 60 percent of market value.

The question of county and Baltimore City property taxes has become increasingly difficult in Maryland. The 1974 Legislature recognized the problem by passing two important bills on this subject. The so-called "circuit-breaker" bill sets aside $59 million in tax credits for homeowners and renters by tying in property taxes with income and setting a ceiling for those with low income. This bill would go into effect in fiscal 1976 if funding is available.

The second passed bill was strongly contended. It permitted Baltimore County, subject to its County Council, to eliminate the county property tax (as applied to residential use) entirely and to raise the needed funds by an additional county income tax to be added to the State and county "piggy-back" income taxes already in existence.

STATE OF MARYLAND—1972-1973 TAX RATES

STATE TAX RATE	$ .21	*HARFORD COUNTY	2.82
ALLEGANY COUNTY	2.80	Town Rate	2.62
ANNE ARUNDEL COUNTY	3.12	*HOWARD COUNTY	2.75
In City of Annapolis	2.82	KENT COUNTY	2.79
BALTIMORE CITY	5.86	*MONTGOMERY COUNTY	2.62
BALTIMORE COUNTY	3.85	*PRINCE GEORGE'S COUNTY	3.57
CALVERT COUNTY	2.77	QUEEN ANNE'S COUNTY	2.48
CAROLINE COUNTY	2.90	SAINT MARY'S COUNTY	2.30
CARROLL COUNTY	2.65	SOMERSET COUNTY	2.30
*CECIL COUNTY	2.82	TALBOT COUNTY	2.25
*CHARLES COUNTY	3.10	WASHINGTON COUNTY	2.50
DORCHESTER COUNTY	2.84	WICOMICO COUNTY	2.15
FREDERICK COUNTY	2.54	WORCESTER COUNTY	1.90
GARRETT COUNTY	2.73		

*These counties contain additional special taxing districts.

Assessments of Property

The big question tied in with property taxes is that of assessments. If the assessable base is determined by 50 percent of the market value, then the property tax rate would have to be higher to bring in the same amount of money as one would get on a base determined by 60 percent of the market value.

Until 1971 each county used a different percentile of market value to determine the assessment of property. A low percentile of market value worked to the advantage of a county that showed a low assessable base and then showed its tax rate as fairly high. On the other hand, the State Property Tax (21 cents per hundred dollars) was based on the same assessment in that county; thus the residents there paid less money to the State on a house where the market value might be the same as in a nearby county where the assessment was higher.

In 1971 it was decided to even out assessments and to have the State Department of Assessments and Taxation administer it for all counties and Baltimore City. In early 1974 the Legislature discussed *annual assessments* so that in inflationary periods all homes would be treated the same way. For example, assessments every three years (previous practice) meant that those assessed in 1971 would be paying on a lower base than those assessed in 1972, or particularly in 1973 when market values skyrocketed. Indeed, there was some talk about a *rollback* for those assessed in 1972 and 1973 to even them out and then not to permit more than a ten percent increase in assessments of property in any one year (except where there have been major improvements), irrespective of rise in market values.

Of course, as assessments are rolled back by the State, which now has the control, it then becomes necessary for the counties and Baltimore City to raise the tax rate for the money they need. (Remember, the lower the assessment the higher the rate, to get the same money.) Thus, the homeowner should look at the total tax payment before he passes judgment on assessment or rate.

Annual assessments will mean more assessors, and they are not easily found since they are highly trained persons.. It will also mean that more persons are likely to go to tax court to seek adjustments. In 1972 there were about 900 cases handled in the Maryland Tax Courts; 267 were adjusted, 261 were affirmed, and the rest are pending.

Municipal and Special District Taxes

In addition to county taxes there are municipal taxes for those who live in incorporated communities. Usually, when one pays municipal taxes for services, such as trash and garbage collection rendered to everybody in the county, such taxpayers are given a credit deduction on the county tax.

For example, the Prince Georges County property tax for fiscal 1974 was $3.37 per hundred valuation. Some of the municipal taxes in Prince Georges for the same period were: Capitol Heights, $1; Takoma Park, $1.55; Bowie, 47 cents, and Laurel, $1.08 to $1.15 (according to section).

Special tax districts as library, fire, water, sanitary and planning areas also require taxes for those using the services.

In general, Maryland has fewer tax districts than most states.

Bond and Debt Services

As was explained earlier, the mere fact that a capital improvement has been authorized by the Legislature does not mean that bonds are sold for the project. The sale of bonds is spaced so the State will not borrow the money until payments are due on the project. The State Treasurer does the preliminary planning, preparation, and advertising for State of Maryland Bond Issues, receives bids, and arranges for settlement, signing, and delivery.

Counties borrow money for capital projects in the same way. Many county projects are paid for in whole or part by the State or federal government. For example, the State pays all construction costs (unless there are unusual additions) for elementary and secondary schools. The county and Baltimore City pay site costs. The State pays 50 percent of the costs for county community college buildings and the federal government adds another portion from the Higher Education Facilities Act funds. The county pays the rest. County government buildings are paid for by the counties.

Counties, like the State, usually borrow money for a 15—20-year period. Usually they set a limit on the amount of capital funds authorized in any one year and on the total debt assumed. In this way, new projects can be launched and new bond issues floated while others mature.

The credit rating given to the State and a Maryland county is determined by the assets, the amount of outstanding loans, and its general financial condition. The highest available rating by experts, such as Moody's Investment Service, helps bring the sale of the bonds on a low interest rate since the risk is not great. In 1973 Montgomery County was given this "AAA" rating by Moody, thereby noting "the well-designed debt structure, strong financial position—aided by prompt tax collections and excellent fiscal management and planning."

Debt service makes up a significant portion of the Annual Budget for the State and counties.

The State Budget Procedure

The Maryland Constitution requires that the Governor submit the Budget early in the session and that the Legislature complete its work on it before adjournment. But other routines are set in motion by the Code and by regulatory or administrative rules.

New budgets go into effect at the beginning of a fiscal year, July 1st. On virtually the same day a new budget goes into effect, the head of a State agency must start to prepare his budget for the next year.

Below is a sample schedule of Budget Procedure (the exact days may vary each year):

BUDGET CALENDAR
FISCAL YEAR 1976
(July 1, 1975 - June 30, 1976)

Dates	*Description of Activity*
July 1974	Program evaluation and management appraisal.

July 3, 1974	Governor's budget letter and budget instructions mailed to all agencies.
July 3 - Aug. 31	The departments evaluate their programs and prepare fiscal 1976 Budget requests and related policy position papers with assistance, on request, from analysts in the Department of Budget and Fiscal Planning.
July 7 - Aug. 4	Conferences with major agencies. The objectives of these meetings is to promote a closer working relationship between the agencies and the Department of Budget and Fiscal Planning, prior to budget formulation; to improve communications between agencies to clarify existing policies; and to enable the Governor to have sufficient time for consideration of: new programs to be requested, priority ranking by agency secretaries of all programs within the agency, estimated number of new positions to be requested, and estimated increase or decrease of anticipated Federal or Special Funds.
Sept. 1	Agencies to submit fiscal 1976 budget requests to the Department of Budget and Fiscal Planning. Exceptions to this date are: University of Maryland - September 21 Department of Transportation - September 21 Aid to Education - November 1
Sept. 15 - Dec. 15	Department of Budget and Fiscal Planning makes recommendations for allowances.
Oct. 2 - Dec. 7	Obtain Governor's approval on those requests which have been finalized. Conferences may be necessary regarding any major policy changes by the Governor.
Oct. 6 - Dec. 14	Begin forwarding completed budgets to the printers.
Oct. 9 - Dec. 11	Proofread copy from printer.
Dec. 15	Final projection of General and Special Fund revenue estimates.
Jan. 1975	Department of Budget and Fiscal Planning distributes fiscal 1976 revisions to manual relating to any changes in program and performance budget preparation format.
Jan. 15, 1975	Submission of Governor's Budget to the General Assembly.
Jan. - Apr., 1975	Agency budget hearings before General Assembly; budget analysts to support Governor's Budget allowance before appropriate legislative committees. Department Secretaries also appear before Legislature's hearings.
Feb. 15 - 28	Agency submission of fiscal 1976 *Supplemental Budget Requests.*
April	Department of Budget and Fiscal Planning team meets individually with department Secretaries and staffs to discuss programs and policy analysis of approved fiscal 1976 Budget.
Apr. 15	Department of Budget and Fiscal Planning furnishes fiscal impact data and recommendations to the Gov-

Apr. 15 (cont.)	ernor on selected legislation which was passed by the General Assembly.
May 16	Letter from Governor to heads of all agencies requesting plans for the fiscal year 1977 Budget.
June 11	Department of Budget and Fiscal Planning develops summary of all significant laws enacted during 1976 with 5-year fiscal impact.
July 1, 1975	Budget for fiscal 1976 goes into effect.

The Board of Revenue Estimates

While the Department of Budget and Fiscal Planning is studying the proposed new fiscal 1976 Budget during July and August of 1974, and the accompanying possible appropriations, another group is continuing its year-round study of possible revenues.

The Board of Revenue Estimates is made up of the State Comptroller, Treasurer, and Secretary of the Department of Budget and Procurement. It prepares an itemized statement of anticipated revenues for the succeeding fiscal year, together with its recommendations. The Board gets its data from the Bureau of Revenue Estimates, which is a full-time agency dealing with this subject.

For example, the Bureau looks at the past year's revenue brought in by the State income tax and extrapolates rises or falls in that item based on employment records and size of labor force. Sales tax returns are studied in terms of population trends, price movements, employment, and other factors. Thus gasoline shortages and fuel rationing would affect returns from gasoline taxes. Attention is given to new federal funding bills passed by Congress, for federal monies make up a large part of the State's revenue.

The science of revenue estimating is nearly an exact one, until an unforeseen circumstance takes place. At any rate, over the years, the Bureau and the Board have set forth estimates of revenues that are very close to what comes into the State Treasury.

Because the State Budget must be a balanced budget, appropriations can be no higher than expected revenues.

The Board of Public Works

The most prestigious group in State government is the Board of Public Works. It is made up of the Governor (chairman), the State Comptroller, and the State Treasurer. The Board supervises the expenditures of all sums appropriated through State loans. It also supervises the expenditures and approves the contracts of all general and other funds appropriated for capital improvements, except for roads, bridges, and highways.

The Board may borrow up to $50,000 upon the credit of the State between sessions of the Legislature. The Board approves the sale, lease, or transfer of any real property belonging to any State agency. The Board may make allocations from the General Emergency Fund.

For example, at a meeting of the Board of Public Works on February 7, 1973, an item of $133 was approved for the purpose of testing the concrete and placing reinforced steel in the renovation of the Boiler Plant at the Women's Correctional Institution. At a similar meeting that year, the Board approved the contract for the $21 million World Trade Center in Baltimore and appropriated funds for the design drawings for Phase I of Baltimore's Rapid Transit, a $956 million project.

The Secretaries of the Departments of Planning, General Services, and Budget and Fiscal Planning are always present at the meetings of the Board of Public Works and they, of course, advise the Board on numerous decisions; thus the range and the enormity of the job is not as overwhelming as it might be. Yet some believe that the Board needs study and change.

A very important change in the awarding of consultant fees and contracts was made by the Legislature in 1974. The "kickbacks" in fees and other illegal procedures that were often characteristic of dealings with contractors at both the State and county levels (leading to the conviction of one former Maryland governor and at least one county executive) forced tighter regulations. Former practices of awarding bids without contracts were changed to require all fees and contracts over $25,000 to be subject to bids so that price, as well as quality of work design, would be considered.

The Department of Budget and Fiscal Planning

In 1916 the State moved, by changing the Constitution, to provide for an executive budget system. This action brought an end to the previously accepted practice of considering and voting upon budget appropriations in independent actions, and introduced a procedure for consolidating budget requests into a total figure and measuring this against estimated revenues. Thus, the sole responsibility for the Budget is the Governor's. In 1969, after operating under various titles, the Department received its present name and its Secretary was made a Cabinet-level position.

It is within this responsibility that the Department of Budget and Fiscal Planning operates as an agent of the Governor. The Budget it prepares is based on the Governor's policy, and when he delivers it to the Legislature each January the Governor includes a message with the details. In essence, the Budget reflects what is important in executive policy. If, for example, the Governor believes strongly in health support for the indigent, the Budget will show it. Priorities are clear in the Budget. Money will go to where the action is desired. A department that gets little money is not held in high regard.

The taxpayer, too, must be held in high regard, especially if the

Governor wants a second term. In essence, there is no single document that reflects the philosophy of the Executive and Legislative Departments of the State more than the Budget.

Thus, the work of the Department of Budget and Fiscal Planning is not just an accountancy and computer task.

The Secretary of the Department. He must carry out the Executive direction of the Department and the planning and execution of its program. He coordinates the needs of the State in relation to its resources and provides the best information available to those responsible for allocating resources, and exercises continuous review of the execution of approved operating budgets, in accordance with legislative spending authorizations.

Division of Administration. Administers the fiscal operations of the Department's headquarters, which include personnel administration, payroll, purchasing, and maintaining the Department's general ledger.

Division of Budget Analysis and Formulation. Works closely with departments and institutions toward improving agency programs and develops yardsticks to measure workloads and program effectiveness. It analyzes proposed legislation with respect to fiscal and budgetary impact, and makes recommendations as to Gubernatorial action on legislative enactments. It continuously studies the maintenance and operational costs of all State buildings and recommends, on the advice of engineering analysts, necessary operational and maintenance expenditures.

Division of Fiscal Planning. Monitors the economic conditions of Maryland and the United States and provides both short- and long-range projections of revenues and expenditures. It analyzes and proposes modification of tax laws and conducts management analyses, performance audits, and program analyses of the various State agencies and programs.

Division of Management Information Systems. Coordinates automatic data processing (ADP) activities between State agencies and data processing centers, controls the acquisition and leasing of data processing and associated services, and provides technical expertise to the data centers and State agencies. It exercises administrative authority over the Baltimore Data Center, which is responsible for providing a centralized facility to serve the data processing needs of the agencies in the State offices in Baltimore. Services rendered by the Center are paid for by the user agencies on a time basis according to a predetermined rate schedule.

REVIEW QUESTIONS

Chapter 1: The People of Maryland

Review Questions

1. Give statistics to show that Maryland's growth in population was strong between 1960 and 1970.
2. Show that Maryland's growth in population between 1960 and 1970 was "uneven." Which counties and sections showed the largest increases? Which the smallest increases or even decreases?
3. Give statistics to show that Baltimore City's population in relation to the rest of the State has been increasingly diminishing in the last thirty years.
4. Show that Maryland's black population is large in some portions of the State, but small in others. How does the black population in Baltimore City compare with the same group in the surrounding counties?
5. Counties vary in median yearly family income. Give statistics to prove this.
6. Average income indicates educational attainment. Show that this is so in Maryland.
7. How are population statistics significant in terms of federal and State financial aid?
8. Show that age counts in population—for example, the number of very young and older citizens—determine factors such as schools, voting, labor force, and other activities.
9. What are the predictions about future population in Maryland?
10. Show that significant number of Marylanders come from many lands, from other states, and are of different faiths.

Key Generalizations and Concepts. Support these by facts.

1. Maryland's richest resource is its people.
2. Population growth has been heaviest in the suburban areas around Baltimore and Washington, D.C.
3. The black population of Maryland is a significant portion of the total, especially in Baltimore City.
4. Population statistics affect developments in education, health care, and other fields.
5. Population growth takes place through natural increase and in-migration.
6. Marylanders are a migrant people.

Questions for Discussion. Take a point of view.

1. Baltimore City's influence in State affairs is likely to decline in the future.
2. The next 20 years will see large population spurts in southern Maryland areas and the counties going west of Carroll.
3. Maryland's rate of growth in the next ten years is likely to be lower than in the past ten years.

Chapter 2: The History of Maryland

Review Questions

1. After whom was Maryland named and when is Founders Day?
2. What is the significance of the Mason-Dixon Line?
3. Who were the Maryland signers of the Declaration of Independence?
4. What key role did Maryland play in the American Revolution?
5. How did Maryland influence policy on the western lands at the time of the Articles of Confederation?
6. Tell the story of *The Star-Spangled Banner.*
7. Show that Maryland was a divided State during the Civil War.
8. How did Maryland play an important role on the battle front and home front during World War II?
9. Describe the key developments in industrial growth since 1950.

Key Generalizations and Concepts. Support these by facts.

1. Maryland's beginnings are associated with the search for religious tolerance.
2. Maryland, though a small State in the early history of the nation, played a highly important role in winning independence.
3. Maryland was important in the formulation of key objectives of America's basic written documents such as the Declaration of Independence, the Articles of Confederation, and the Constitution.
4. Loyalties of Maryland, as a "border state," were divided during the Civil War.
5. Highly important social, political, and industrial reforms took place in the State after 1950.
6. The last 25 years in Maryland have been filled with controversial questions, some yet unsolved.

Questions for Discussion. Take a point of view.

1. Because *The Star-Spangled Banner* is so difficult to sing, it should be replaced as our national anthem.
2. The people of Maryland were right in rejecting the proposed Constitution of 1968.
3. Maryland has not gone far enough since 1950 in solving its social problems. The pace has been too slow.

Chapter 3: The Geography of Maryland

Review Questions

1. Show that both land and water make up important portions of Maryland's area.
2. Point out the diversity in Maryland's topography.
3. Show how there are important differences of climate between one part of the State and another.
4. What are the important mineral resources of the State and where are they found?
5. Show that the Chesapeake Bay is important for commerce and for food.
6. Point out that while the number of farm workers are declining in Maryland, agriculture is an important industry.
7. What three farm products would you rate as of most importance in Maryland? Why?
8. Indicate some of the leading agencies in Maryland that help the farmer.

Key Generalizations and Concepts. Support these by facts.

1. Maryland's topography is so diversified that the State might be referred to as "America in miniature."
2. Maryland's coal mines are diminishing in total output, but energy shortages in oil could rejuvenate their value.
3. The Chesapeake Bay is Maryland's most valuable single natural resource.
4. Maryland's agriculture is diversified.
5. The State's industrial development is diversified and not dependent on any single industry.
6. Important branches of key industrial firms are located in the State.
7. So-called science-oriented industries are beginning to take hold in Maryland.
8. Baltimore City no longer has a monopoly on industry in Maryland. Virtually all over the State there are important industries.
9. The Port of Baltimore is one of Maryland's great assets.

Questions for Discussion. Take a point of view.

1. Maryland has not fully capitalized on its diverse topography by attracting more tourists.
2. Strip mining should be permitted, especially since there are fuel shortages.
3. The Chesapeake Bay needs stronger protection against pollution.
4. Maryland could develop its science-oriented industries to a greater degree.

5. We let the railroads down in Maryland. There should be more State and federal support for them.
6. The State is shaped wrongly and boundaries should be redrawn in new ways after agreements with neighboring states.

Chapter 4: The Constitution of Maryland

Review Questions

1. Show that the State regulates large areas of our daily lives.
2. Each one of Maryland's four Constitutions came into being as a result of important historic events. Show that this is true.
3. How can the Maryland Constitution be amended?
4. Give examples to show that the Maryland Constitution can be changed by U.S. Constitutional revisions, by courts, and by rulings of the Attorney General.
5. Indicate and explain three characteristics of a good Constitution.
6. Name three functions of a good Constitution and give illustrations.
7. What are some of the basic guarantees in the Maryland Declaration of Rights.
8. What departments of government, governmental units, and officeholders are described in those Articles of the Maryland Constitution referred to as the Frame of Government?
9. Show that the federal government has, in recent years, taken over some of the responsibilities of the state governments.
10. What is the belief of the New Federalists?

Basic Generalizations and Concepts. Support these by facts.

1. Government should be the "servant of the people."
2. In Maryland, Constitutions last a long period of time and they are not completely rewritten except at critical points in the State's history.
3. The United States Constitution is the "supreme law of the land."
4. While the courts are not ordinarily conceived of as legislative bodies, their decisions often remake constitutional law.
5. The Attorney General of Maryland is often the interpreter of constitutional law.
6. Constitutions must create both a sense of stability and flexibility, contradictory as this may seem.
7. Constitutional law should deal with broad fundamentals, leaving the details to statutory and regulatory law.
8. A Constitution should include a "bill of rights" protecting fundamentals which government cannot take away from people. In this sense it is a "compact" between the people and government.
9. The structure of government is clearly defined in the Constitution so that there is a balance and interrelationship among the three departments: executive, legislative, and judicial.
10. The Maryland Constitution has provisions that permit amendments.
11. Constitutional laws can be changed only by the direct vote of the people.
12. Since the United States is a federal government, with states sharing powers with the nation, the interrelationships need clarification.

Questions for Discussion. Take a point of view.

1. Maryland should have another Constitutional Convention and completely rewrite the present Constitution written in 1867.
2. The federal government, in recent years, has taken over much power that belongs to the State.
3. The Maryland Declaration of Rights should be expanded to include such modern protective articles as those on civil rights, consumer protection, fair housing requirements, equal employment opportunities, and ecology.
4. The "rights" noted above belong in statutory law—not in the Constitution.

Chapter 5: Elections and the Election Process

Review Questions

1. Give three illustrations to show how the United States Constitution has affected election laws in Maryland.
2. How did the 1962 *Baker v. Carr* case affect Maryland?
3. Show that the United States Congress affects election procedures.
4. Point to three articles in the Maryland Constitution that deal with election procedures.
5. How does the referendum operate in Maryland?
6. How do the local Boards of Election Supervisors operate?
7. What is the work of the State Administrative Board of Election Laws?
8. What are the requirements for filing for office in Maryland?
9. Describe the way primary elections operate in the State.
10. How might one get on the ballot in the general election without winning in a primary election?
11. Name five different kinds of officeholders on the ballot in Maryland's gubernatorial general elections.
12. What are some of the safeguard measures in the Fair Election Practices section of the Maryland Election Code?
13. How does absentee balloting operate in Maryland?
14. What is the role of State Central Committees in the election process?
15. Show how the State courts and the Maryland Attorney General affect election laws.

Basic Generalizations and Concepts. Support these with facts.

1. Americans, including Marylanders, are in a period of great disillusionment with respect to politics.
2. The United States Constitution is an important determinant of voting rights.
3. Laws passed by the United States Congress have influenced voting privileges and procedures.
4. The Maryland Constitution is the basic source of election procedures for Marylanders.
5. The referendum is a way by which the people can protect themselves against the legislature from laws they don't want.
6. The election laws are primarily statutory laws passed by the General Assembly and deal with election procedures.
7. Through the local Boards of Election Supervisors, elections become operative at the grass-roots level.
8. The easiest way to run for office is to participate in the party system. But being unaffiliated with the major parties still gives one a chance to gain office.
9. The Election Code seeks to protect the public from bribery and dishonest election practices, yet much remains to be done.
10. There is some control over the internal operations of political parties in Maryland.

Questions for Discussion. Take a point of view.

1. The United States courts had no right getting into the election process, as for example in the Tennessee case, thus forcing reapportionment of the Maryland legislature.
2. Maryland is unfair to independent voters who refuse to join a political party.
3. Maryland should permit the "recall" of officeholders.
4. Only public money should be used in political campaigns.
5. No firm nor any individual who does business with the State of Maryland should be permitted to contribute to a political campaign.
6. Politics is dishonest and you cannot clean it up.
7. Politicians are of as high integrity as businessmen or industrialists.

Chapter 6: The Governor and Administrative Offices

Review Questions

1. Show how the office of the Governor in Maryland changed in power from time to time.
2. How did Governor Albert C. Ritchie increase the power of the Governor's office?
3. How many years in a Governor's term and how long may he serve?
4. What are the qualifications of the Lieutenant Governor and what are his duties?
5. What are the laws regarding replacement of the Governor in case of death or illness?
6. How do impeachment proceedings take place in the case of the Governor?
7. Name the 12 cabinet-level secretariats.
8. Indicate three agencies that are independent and not represented in the cabinet.
9. Give illustrations to show that the Governor has important executive, legislative, and judicial powers.
10. In the case of each power illustrated, show that there is also a restriction.

Basic Generalizations and Concepts. Support these with facts.

1. The Maryland Colonial Governor was a strong chief executive.
2. The power of the Governor was strongly diminished under the first Maryland Constitution.
3. At different times the General Assembly or the Governor has had the more dominant power. The times and the person determine whether the chief executive or the legislative body will have the greater influence.
4. The Lieutenant Governor in Maryland is a weak office.
5. The laws of succession with respect to the Governor assure continuity in office.
6. The current Constitutional and statutory powers held by the Governor of Maryland make him a very strong officeholder.
7. The Governor is not just the chief executive; he holds legislative and judicial power of great moment. This shows that the so-called concept of separation of powers does not always hold.
8. The recent creation of cabinet-level secretariats gives the Maryland Governor more power than ever.
9. Within the concept of balance of power among the three branches of government, there are restrictions by the legislative or judicial department on virtually every power held by the chief executive.
10. More cabinet-level secretariats are likely to join the 12 established by early 1974. Two agencies which are early likely candidates are education and problems of the aging.

Questions for Discussion. Take a point of view.

1. The Governor's term of office should be unlimited.
2. The Lieutenant Governor should also be President of the State Senate.
3. Some of the Governor's present powers should be relinquished to the State legislature.
4. The newly created system of cabinet-level secretariats needs continual review.
5. The Governor's emergency powers should have an ending date.

Chapter 7: The Legislature and Legislative Processes

Review Questions

1. How does the Maryland General Assembly differ from the Nebraska Legislature?
2. How does the United States Constitution place limitations upon the powers of the Maryland General Assembly?

3. Indicate three restrictions that the Maryland Constitution places upon the State legislature.
4. Show how the Maryland Constitution, through expressed and implied grants of powers, gives the State legislature the right to pass laws in many fields.
5. Indicate five major responsibilities of the State legislature.
6. Give the "pros" and "cons" of a *limited session* such as the Maryland legislature has, over a *continuous session* such as that held by states like New York and Pennsylvania.
7. What are the terms of office and the age and residence qualifications for members of the State Senate? The House of Delegates?
8. How will the Maryland legislature of 1975 differ from earlier ones in numbers and in the way legislators are elected?
9. What is the purpose of reapportionment and redistricting the Maryland General Assembly after every U.S. decennial census?
10. If you live in Maryland, in which legislative district are you located? How many State Senators and Delegates have been allocated in whole or part to your county?
11. How are the presiding officers of the Senate and House of Delegates selected?
12. What is the pay and compensation of members of the legislature?
13. Name the five kinds of committees that operate in the legislature and tell what each does.
14. Indicate the powers of the President of the Senate and the Speaker of the House of Delegates.
15. Describe how a bill becomes a law in the Maryland General Assembly.
16. Name the major standing committees in the Senate and in the House of Delegates.
17. Describe the requirements of members of the legislature under the laws of disclosure and ethics.
18. Give the "pros" and "cons" of legislative agents or lobbyists.
19. What is the role of the Legislative Council?
20. What is the role of the Department of Fiscal Services?

Basic Generalizations and Concepts. Support these with facts.

1. A bicameral body such as the Maryland General Assembly permits greater checks and balances than a unicameral body.
2. The United States Constitution restricts rather strongly the State legislature's area of operations.
3. While the Maryland Constitution offers some restrictions to the legislature's powers, in the main it gives widespread powers to this body.
4. The Maryland Constitution places the State legislature in between the tightly limited session and one that is continuous or virtually unlimited.
5. Maryland does not distinguish between the term of office for members of the lower and upper Houses.
6. Single-member districts as a concept for electing legislators is gaining hold in Maryland.
7. Every ten years the Maryland legislature will have to be reapportioned and redistricted.
8. The executive, legislative, and judicial branches of government all have roles in making certain that the State legislature is based on "one man, one vote."
9. The day of at least one legislator from each county in the State Senate and in the House is over.
10. The suburban counties have wrested the power of representation away from Baltimore City.
11. The party in power, almost always the Democratic Party in Maryland, holds tremendous influence in State politics.
12. Presiding officers wield much hidden power.
13. Salaries of legislators are not determined by the Constitution; thus they are easier to change than, for example, the compensation of the Governor.
14. The select committees virtually determine the laws of the small non-home-rule counties which are made in the main by remote control at Annapolis. Since the

Senator or Delegate from the county involved in a bill discussed by such a committee holds the key vote, he virtually makes the laws for his own county.
15. The joint conference committees are the compromising agents between the two Houses.
16. The party caucuses that select the leaders of the Senate and the House of Delegates really operate through the power of a small group.
17. The three readings required for a bill to pass in each House assure more reasoned study.
18. While the Governor is not a member of the legislature and cannot vote on bills, his beliefs are usually more influential than those of any legislator.
19. The public has its best chance to have its opinions heard while a bill is in committee. Committee hearings represent the best avenue for an individual to express his beliefs.
20. The standing committees represent the "bread and butter" activities of the State legislature. Little gets passed without support of such committees.
21. Until proper safeguards, such as enforcement of tight ethics codes and disclosure laws, are taken, the public will be leery about trusting lawmakers.
22. The legislature does and should have a financial service arm just as the executive department does. Otherwise, the two departments could not check on each other.

Questions for Discussion. Take a point of view.

1. Maryland should have a unicameral legislature.
2. The Maryland General Assembly should be in continuous session.
3. The legislature should have the right to increase the proposed current operating budget as well as to decrease it; suggesting ways of getting the additional required revenue.
4. The Maryland legislature should be patterned after the Congressional plan, viz., members of the Senate holding office for six years and those of the House of Delegates elected every two years.
5. The Maryland legislature should be a much smaller body than it is now with approximately 50 Delegates and 25 Senators.
6. Redistricting and reapportionment of the legislature should be done differently than current practice, possibly by the State courts.
7. Maryland legislators should be paid $25,000 a year and serve full-time on the job, not being permitted to earn other income.
8. Maryland legislators should not be able to vote on any bills that even remotely affect any work they or their families are carrying out or are likely to be carrying out.
9. A proposed bill should be carried over from one year to another (as long as it is in a four-year term) without dying at the close of a session if it has not been passed. In Congress a bill does not start from scratch each year within a Congressional term.
10. The legislators from my county are effective (or not) at Annapolis.

Chapter 8: The Judiciary and the Judicial Processes

Review Questions

1. Give illustrations of the following sources of law: constitutional law, statutory law, court-made or decision law, common law, and equity.
2. The rules of law (with exceptions) might be divided into criminal law and civil law. Give two examples of the more serious criminal laws, viz., the felonies. Give two examples of the less serious criminal laws, viz., the misdemeanors. Give two illustrations of cases that are handled in civil law courts.
3. Why is *habeas corpus* important?
4. Illustrate how *due process* protects the accused from unfair decisions.
5. The United States Constitution governs the conduct of Maryland and other state courts. Illustrate.
6. The Maryland Constitution governs many of the actions of the State courts. Give examples.

7. The legislature, through statutory law, often governs court actions. Explain.
8. Name the courts in the Maryland four-tier system.
9. Explain the current District Court structure as established in 1971. Over what kinds of cases does it have jurisdiction? How do the judges get their jobs and for how long do they serve? What is the work of the court commissioners?
10. Explain how the Circuit Courts are organized. Over what kinds of cases do they have jurisdiction?
11. Because the Circuit Court for Baltimore City has so many cases, there are various sections specializing in different kinds of cases. Name the various sections and their specializations.
12. What special functions are carried out by the masters?
13. How do Circuit Court judges get their jobs and how long do they hold office?
14. What is the jurisdiction of the Court of Special Appeals? How do the judges get their jobs?
15. How can the Maryland Court of Appeals be compared with the U.S. Supreme Court? How do these judges get their jobs?
16. What is the role of the Orphans' Courts? How do these judges get their jobs?
17. How does the Commission on Judicial Disabilities protect the public against improper practices by judges?
18. What are the four major functions of the Attorney General? How does he get his job?
19. What is the work of the State's Attorney?
20. How does the grand jury differ from the petit or trial jury?
21. Explain the indictment and the investigatory functions of the grand jury in Maryland.
22. How are members of the petit jury selected? What is its main role?
23. Describe the workings of the Maryland Public Defender Law.
24. How does the work of the Legal Aid Bureau differ from that of the Public Defender Office?
25. Suggest some court reforms.

Basic Generalizations and Concepts. Support these with facts.

1. "Equal justice under the law" is a concept hopefully pursued, but difficult to attain.
2. Constitutional and statutory laws are continually subject to interpretation by the courts and by the Attorney General.
3. The courts—State and federal—are in a sense legislative bodies in that they create "decision laws." This concept in a sense challenges the typical belief that there is a fine separation of powers between the three branches of government—executive, legislative, and judicial.
4. The law and punishment to be meted out when the law is broken has many sources—both constitutional and statutory.
5. The Maryland Criminal Code is a document that clearly states what punishment (within a range) is to be meted out for particular crimes.
6. Though the distinction is open to some debate, in general, criminal offenses are crimes against society; civil offenses are crimes against individuals. The State is, of course, responsible for seeing that the offender is punished or pays for damages in either a criminal or civil offense.
7. The concept of "due process" is a basic Constitutional protection by both the Maryland and the United States Constitutions.
8. The Maryland courts and the court system are Constitutionally established structures. In the last analysis only the people, by vote, could make changes in the structure.
9. The State Constitution has delegated to the legislature the power to create certain changes in court procedures and processes.
10. The creation in 1973 of a State four-tier court system was a major reform in a previously disjointed court system.
11. The District Courts are the ones that handle by far most of the offenders, including those charged with minor offenses such as illegal parking. How the judge

in these courts deals with offenders determines in large part how the public views the laws of the State.

12. Judges in the Maryland Circuit Courts or trial courts, particularly those in criminal court sections, handle more hard-core criminals.

13. Circuit Court judges must have widespread knowledge of both criminal and civil law.

14. The Maryland Court of Special Appeals is increasingly handling all cases of appeal from the Circuit Courts.

15. The Maryland Court of Appeals should have judges especially learned in Constitutional law.

16. It should be fairly easy to eliminate an incompetent judge.

17. The open election of judges tends to discourage many of the better candidates from seeking the job.

18. Judicial selection commissions help in the screening and tend to make the selection process less political.

19. The grand jury is an old and Constitutionally established protective process for the accused.

20. The petit jury goes back to old English traditions that a person should be judged by his peers.

21. The public defender system helps assure the accused who is indigent that he will get a fair trial.

Questions for Discussion. Take a position.

1. Some of the minor offenses, usually classified as misdemeanors (e.g. receipt of a parking ticket), should not be included within the Criminal Code and should be handled by an administrative board outside the court system.
2. All judgeships should be appointive positions and not subject to the electorate.
3. Newly appointed judges should receive in-service training in court practice and procedures before taking office.
4. The Orphans' Court should be abolished (or not) and its duties merged into a newly created section of either the Domestic or Circuit Court (and kept separate, as is).
5. The grand jury has served its usefulness and should either be abolished or radically changed.
6. Except in trials of murder cases, a unanimous decision of the jury need not be required in criminal cases.
7. Petit juries sitting in civil cases should have but six to nine members.
8. Judges are usually too easy on criminals.
9. The accused does not get fair treatment in present court proceedings.
10. Judges should get their jobs through special training rather than come in through law practice.
11. We need to train and certify attorneys specifically as trial lawyers and not assume that passing the bar examination qualifies them for court work.
12. The courts in our county are well run (or not).

Chapter 9: County Government

Review Questions

1. Why did the county take hold as the most important political sub-unit in the State early in Maryland's history?
2. Indicate five functions which the county in Maryland assumes as an agent of the State.
3. Name three functions the Maryland county assumes as an instrument of local government.
4. Show that county government in Maryland cannot be divided into the conventional patterns of executive, legislative, and judicial branches.
5. How does a Maryland county attain home rule? Which ones have such rule? What powers are held by home-rule counties?
6. Why has code county status not been selected by counties other than Kent?

7. How would the proposed 1968 Maryland Constitution have changed county government?
8. How does the State legislature influence county government?
9. Describe the structure of government in the commissioner counties.
10. Name the leading office-holding positions in home-rule counties and indicate their responsibilities.
11. What are the tasks of the county treasurer, auditor, attorney, purchasing agent, finance director, highway engineer, director of public works, and police commissioner?
12. Why is the county seat important?
13. Give illustrations of intercounty cooperation.
14. Why is reform of county government likely to come slowly in Maryland?
15. Describe the difficulties involved in fiscal interrelationships between the Maryland counties and the State.

Basic Generalizations and Concepts. Support these with facts.

1. The county unit in Maryland is of great importance in our daily living.
2. The county is a political unit established by the Maryland Constitution and governed by a charter which is the organic law.
3. The Maryland General Assembly has a good deal of control over the operations of the counties.
4. A county's operations are intertwined with those of the State.
5. The concept of "home rule" seeks to give the county more autonomy and even independence in some areas of government.
6. In the main, only the larger counties have availed themselves of the opportunity to have home rule.
7. Home rule is not freedom from Statewide general laws passed by the legislature.
8. The concept of "code counties" has not taken hold in Maryland.
9. The traditional commissioner county form of government is still preferred by most Maryland counties.
10. The outstanding characteristic of a home-rule county is that it has a council or legislative body.
11. Maryland's home-rule counties, in the main, are urban counties and, therefore, their governmental structures and officeholders resemble those of big cities.
12. There are interesting examples in the State of intercounty cooperation.
13. In many ways the strong county system in Maryland has protected the State from a plethora of governmental units, multiple in nature and repetitive in services and costs.
14. Relationships between the county and the State of Maryland are often complex, especially in fiscal matters.
15. Baltimore City operates as though it were a 24th county.

Questions for Discussion. Take a position.

1. Much of Maryland's progress is due to its county form of government.
2. Home-rule government should be required of all counties.
3. Maryland should have full State funding of education, social services, hospital care, and roads construction.
4. Counties should be abolished and combined into four or five regional governments which should be established in the State (or counties should be kept as they are).
5. Article XI F dealing with code counties should be eliminated from the Constitution and Kent County encouraged to develop home rule.
6. All county officers should be under the merit system and required to follow State disclosure laws.
7. County governments should combine some of their services such as police, fire protection, and jail into regional arrangements.
8. Baltimore City operates as though it were a county; therefore, the State Constitution should be changed to make it a county.
9. I would make important changes in the county I live in.

Chapter 10: Local and Metropolitan Government

Review Questions

1. What conditions usually cause a community to incorporate and become a municipality?
2. Why did requests for municipal incorporation come to a dead stop in 1953?
3. What reasons might fairly heavily populated communities in Baltimore and Howard Counties give for not seeking incorporation?
4. Show how regional arrangements may replace the need for municipal incorporation.
5. How does incorporation place the municipality in somewhat the same position as a corporation?
6. Show that Maryland municipalities vary in size and population.
7. What is the role of the Maryland Municipal League?
8. Name the 10 largest incorporated municipalities in Maryland. For each indicate its population, some of the industrial assets, and its form of government.
9. Name some of the fairly heavily populated unincorporated communities in Baltimore, Anne Arundel, Howard, Prince Georges, and Montgomery Counties.
10. For each of these forms of municipal government name a Maryland incorporated community and indicate how government is organized there: (a) strong mayor-council, (b) weak mayor-council, (c) town commissioner, (d) city-commissioner and (e) council-manager.
11. How does Baltimore City differ from other municipalities in Maryland?
12. Indicate the unique powers which Baltimore City has under its charter.
13. Describe the duties of Baltimore City's Mayor, Comptroller, Treasurer, Solicitor, Director of Public Works.
14. How is the Baltimore City Council organized? How are bills passed in this body?
15. What is the work of the Baltimore City Board of Estimates?
16. Describe the conditions that bring problems to Baltimore City and Washington.
17. How is Baltimore seeking to rejuvenate the city?
18. Why is metropolitanism important to both those who live in the city and those who live in the surrounding suburbs?
19. Why is annexation outmoded as a way of solving regional problems?
20. Why would merger of adjoining communities in different counties present problems?
21. Show how intergovernmental service contacts have brought about progress in regional planning.
23. How might changes in Constitutional and statutory laws help solve metropolitan and regional problems?

Basic Generalizations and Concepts. Prove these with facts.

1. Municipalities come into being for definite reasons.
2. As counties have become more urban in Maryland their governments have turned attention to urban problems, and thus earlier needs for municipal incorporation are not as present today.
3. The incorporated municipality as a political unit is recognized by the Maryland Constitution, which grants it governing rights.
4. Some Maryland counties have no incorporated municipalities.
5. Regional service arrangements often replace the need for incorporation.
6. The municipality's charter is the granting of power by the legislature that can modify or revoke the privilege.
7. The more than 150 incorporated communities in Maryland differ in size and in problems, but all point to the importance of such political units.
8. Maryland is unique among the states in that its largest city has more than 900,000 persons and its second incorporated municipality has but 41,000 population.
9. Many of Maryland's unincorporated communities, especially in the urban counties, are larger in population than any of the incorporated municipalities except Baltimore City.

10. Every major form of municipal governmental structure is in existence in Maryland: the strong and weak mayor-councils, the town commissioner, the city commissioner, and the council-manager forms.
11. Baltimore City is so markedly different from the rest of the State that its problems bring it closer to other big cities like Cleveland, Pittsburgh, Detroit, and Philadelphia rather than to other Maryland municipalities.
12. Baltimore City is virtually a state within a state. It is given separate treatment often in the Maryland Constitution.
13. Baltimore City's charter gives it widespread powers.
14. Baltimore City's Mayor has much power in governmental affairs.
15. The Baltimore City Board of Estimates is an all-powerful body in fiscal matters.
16. Baltimore, like other large cities in the country, has serious problems.
17. Metropolitanism is an idea whose time has come—the big city and the surrounding suburban areas cannot survive alone.
18. Mergers and annexations are virtually outmoded as ways of creating regionalism in Maryland.
19. Intergovernmental service contacts and progress through regional planning council recommendations seem to bring most progress in Maryland.
20. While Constitutional and statutory laws seem to bring about more regionalism in some parts of the country, they have had little impact in Maryland.

Questions for Discussion. Take a position.

1. Communities should not need the approval of their counties before the legislature grants them permission to incorporate.
2. With home-rule counties that are largely urban oriented, all municipalities should be abolished (or kept and given more powers) in Maryland.
3. Before granted incorporation papers a community should reach a population of at least 10,000.
4. Baltimore City should abandon its mayor-council form of government and take on the council-manager structure.
5. Baltimore City and the five nearby counties in the standard metropolitan area should merge into one political unit which arranges for services such as schools, police and fire protection, incineration, garbage collection, health and social services, and education. There should be a merged government handling these activities.
6. Metropolitan or regional government for the Baltimore area would be harmful.

Chapter 11: Department of Health and Mental Hygiene

Review Questions

1. Illustrate how and why single-purpose health institutions were being changed to comprehensive care facilities.
2. What were the fears about integrating former separate health and mental hygiene activities into one coordinating department?
3. How does the Board of Review protect the public from any wrong decisions by the Secretary of the Department of Health and Mental Hygiene or by his coworkers?
4. How did the federal government help to create the Comprehensive Health Planning Agency? What is its purpose?
5. Show that the advisory council to the Planning Agency is broadly representative of consumers and producers of health.
6. The Planning Agency operates partly through regional counterparts. What is their work?
7. What are some of the accomplishments of the agency?
8. How has the Drug Abuse Administration solved some of the drug and alcohol problems?
9. In what way might the 1970's be a turning point in the treatment of Maryland's mentally ill and emotionally disturbed?

10. Show how federal and State legislation support community based mental health services.
11. What is the significance of the change of name of the five public mental health institutions (previously known as State Hospitals) to Hospital Centers?
12. What are the problems still to be faced in the establishment of community based mental health services?
13. Of what value are the 1973 legislature's "right to treatment" bills for the mentally ill patient?
14. The Mental Retardation Administration seeks to bring reform on a number of fronts. Describe some of its plans.
15. What is likely to happen in the future to the former State retardate institutions: Rosewood, Henryton, and Great Oaks?
16. What is the extent of juvenile delinquency in Maryland and how do such violations in Baltimore City tend to differ from those elsewhere in the State?
17. How has the new view of the actions of the juvenile delinquent as being "symptomatic of underlying emotional, psychological, and social problems" affected Maryland legislation in this field? How has it affected court action?
18. How does the Juvenile Services Administration coordinate its findings and actions with other State and local departments in the search to treat juvenile offenders on the basis of underlying problems?
19. Each of the public institutions offering juvenile services has different specializations. Name the institutions and describe their programs.
20. How has the federal government's Older American Act recognized the problems of the aged?
21. What were the key recommendations of the Governor's Commission on Nursing Homes?
22. Who handles the private home care of the indigent aged? How does the program operate?
23. How does the State Medicaid program operate? How might a more liberal, general federal program of health insurance reduce the cost of Medicaid?
24. How does the Environmental Health Administration, through its bureau on air quality control and its divisions of general sanitation, food control, and radiation control, protect the air, water, and food we take into our bodies?
25. How does the federal government give financial support and legislative stimulation to air and water quality?
26. Describe the activities carried out by the Preventive Medicine Administration, particularly those in communicable diseases.
27. How do the State health laboratories fight disease?
28. Why might the local (county) health services be referred to as the operational bases for the department's work?
29. Name some of the health professional fields whose workers are examined and certified by different licensing boards under the Department of Health and Mental Hygiene.
30. What is H.M.O. and how has the federal government aided this program?

Basic Generalizations and Concepts. Support these with facts.

1. The problem of health care can no longer be treated in piecemeal fashion.
2. Single-purpose hospitals are outmoded and too expensive. They are being made into comprehensive health care institutions.
3. A cabinet-level secretary, such as the head of the Department of Health and Mental Hygiene, has tremendous powers, but his decisions are open to review and appeal by the Board of Review.
4. Long-range planning in health care is a recent but highly important development.
5. Practically every endeavor undertaken by this department has had federal stimulation and funds. The desire to receive the federal monies has helped encourage the State legislature to pass conforming bills.
6. The federal government has supported the concept that the *consumers* of

health care should join the *producers* in determining the nature of health care programs.

7. Regional agencies have moved the decisions to the grass-roots level.

8. Private hospitals can no longer be started without concern as to whether the facilities are in under- or over-supply. State health agencies must give their approval before new hospitals are opened.

9. Drug addiction and chronic alcoholism are receiving much attention in Maryland.

10. The whole field of mental health is moving from earlier institutions, largely terminal care, to community-based services tied in with new treatments.

11. At last insurance companies are recognizing that the mentally ill and the emotionally disturbed should be protected in the same way as those physically ill.

12. The public institutions for the mentally retarded recognize that behavior modification is possible for many retarded who had been previously condemned.

13. The National Association for Retarded Children has developed the new philosophy: "They possess the right to be treated with dignity."

14. The philosophical change most likely to create change in the treatment of the juvenile offender lies in the new conviction that juvenile anti-social or deviant behavior is symptomatic of underlying emotional, psychological, and social problems.

15. The new 1969 Maryland law, that before a youngster may be adjudicated legally as a delinquent, allegations must be proved "beyond reasonable doubt," is likely to create important changes.

16. The former public State institutions dealing with juvenile delinquents are scheduled to change radically.

17. Private nursing homes are only partially answering the needs of the elderly who are ill. The subject is being carefully scrutinized and significant reforms are on the way.

18. Public support for private home care for the indigent aged is likely to get increased attention in the future.

19. In the near future there is likely to be a cabinet-level secretariat on problems of aging.

20. State aid for the medically indigent (Medicaid) is but a stopgap program until a comprehensive federal health insurance bill is passed. There seems to be no end to expenditures for Medicaid in Maryland, and yet needs are unmet.

21. Air and water quality protection are getting increased attention as ecology becomes more important.

22. Industrial growth often runs counter to ecological needs: the dichotomy is our problem of this decade, especially with nuclear power under study.

23. Noise studies and the effects of loud noises will receive new attention in the 1970's.

24. Preventive medicine and laboratory testing will become more widespread especially as H.M.O. makes it important for the physician to keep patients well rather than to treat them when ill.

25. The licensing practices of boards certifying health practitioners are likely to change so that recertification every few years also becomes the practice.

26. America has not delivered health care to the degree that modern technology permits. The answers have not yet come and it is shameful that a nation with so much health know-how is still far from providing its citizens with the kind of health that brings joy in living.

Questions for Discussion: Take a position.

1. The Secretary of the Department of Health and Mental Hygiene has the most difficult task of all the Secretaries.
2. The only way out of the health care problem is a strong federal health insurance law.
3. Medicaid should be replaced.
4. Rosewood should be closed (or should be kept and strengthened).
5. All public mental institutions should disperse their patients among community service centers.

6. There is still need for institutional care for hard-core mental retardates and emotionally and mentally disturbed persons.
7. Over one-half of those assigned to public institutions for the juvenile delinquents could be treated in other ways.
8. The private nursing home as an institution needs to be revised radically if it is to fulfill its requirements.
9. Smoking in all public places should be banned, except for designated areas.
10. We should pay physicians for keeping us well.
11. The predetermined monthly flat fee to physicians for all health care services is a better way to handle medical services than the present way (which is to pay the doctor on the basis of the number of patients he sees).
12. My county (or Baltimore City) health department is operating effectively (or needs to improve).

Chapter 12: Department of Employment and Social Services

Review Questions

1. What were the two main problems that the federal Social Security Act of 1935 aimed to solve?
2. In 1970 employment security and social services were (along with some related agencies) combined into the Department of Employment and Social Services. What are the general objectives of the department?
3. Why do the remedies or the objectives not meet with easy success?
4. How does the Board of Review protect the public from unfair or unwise decisions of the Secretary or his staff?
5. What was the main purpose of the 1972 SERVE program?
6. How does Legal Aid assist those on public welfare?
7. What is the role of the Comprehensive Offender Model Program?
8. Indicate and explain the four important forces that seriously affect the social services activities carried out by the department.
9. What is the value in decentralizing service offices and creating outreach stations rather than handling social service clients in one central city or county office?
10. Describe the protective services and the single parent service available to clients by the Social Service Administration of the department.
11. How does the Social Services Administration share with the State Department of Health and Mental Hygiene the requirements for meeting the need of the indigent seeking nursing home care?
12. Describe the homemaker service.
13. Describe the "foster care," "adoption," and "food stamp" programs.
14. What role is played by the Department of Employment and Social Services in the Medicaid program?
15. How many people in Maryland are on public assistance programs? How do the percentages of welfare clients to the general population differ from county (including Baltimore City) to county?
16. Describe the extent and the operation of the AFDC social service program.
17. How does General Public Assistance to Employable operate?
18. What is the broad aim of SSI? What payments are made to the eligible?
19. How does the new federal SSI operate? How will it save the State millions of dollars?
20. How might SSI ultimately relieve the local units from contributing to the operation of social services?
21. Why should unemployment insurance not be looked upon as a welfare program?
22. Show how the federal and State governments both passed acts to ease the sad results of severe unemployment.
23. Why are advisory councils to the Employment Security Administration helpful in solving unemployment problems?
24. Show that the Maryland employment picture varies from one county to another.
25. Indicate the extent of unemployment payments in 1971 and 1972.

26. Why should credit be given to employers who have good work records and why should they pay lower unemployment insurance rates?
27. What unemployment insurance payments are made to claimants?
28. Indicate five key reasons why a claimant may not qualify for unemployment insurance payments.
29. How does the Employment Service Division use Statewide job banks, urban-federal job banks, rural manpower services, and employer services functions to get jobs for the unemployed?
30. How does the Maryland Office of Economic Opportunity help alleviate unemployment?
31. Show that there is much point to the argument that the State and the nation are not using the resources of women.
32. Name three human services agencies under the aegis of the Department of Employment and Social Services.
33. What are some of the major goals of Maryland's organized labor for the 1970's?

Basic Generalizations and Concepts. Give supporting facts.

1. Job security and a job for any one who wants to work should be the ultimate guarantee of our country.
2. The federal Social Security Act of 1935 marked a turning point in the country's attitude toward job security and poverty.
3. Loss of job and poverty are multiple-caused and simplistic treatments will not work.
4. The federal government has taken the initiative and given strong financial and leadership support in getting people back to work, insuring them against unemployment, and assisting them if they are in poverty.
5. In the main, when it comes to unemployment insurance and public welfare, Maryland has ridden on the coat-tails of the federal government, which passed enabling State laws and granting matching funds.
6. Though federal contributions are high, it is the State, through its local social service departments, that administers the service requirements and in some cases the disbursement of funds to the needy.
7. Increasingly the disbursement of funds is being separated from the services to needy clients.
8. The federal government is taking over disbursements, such as the new SSI, in order to establish a national ceiling so that payments to the needy will not vary greatly from state to state.
9. The federal government is likely to take over the disbursement of funds for other assistance programs.
10. The State of Maryland should be able to handle more "services" for the needy as the federal government takes over the disbursement responsibilities.
11. The theory of the State keeping the "services" responsibility is that this should vary from state to state, with those at the grass-roots level, including the needy themselves, having a role in the decisions.
12. Increasingly there is the view that those on the public rolls who are able to work should do so.
13. Public assistance for the needy suffers from many stereotypes, including the belief that many are "chiseling" funds.
14. Actually the numbers of needy who are dishonest is but a small portion of the relief rolls.
15. The payments paid to those on relief meet but minimal demands in food, clothing, and shelter.
16. Urban centers like Baltimore tend to have larger portions of their population on public assistance rolls.
17. Minority groups, particularly the black population in Maryland, because of environmental influences, have a large proportion of their populations on assistance rolls.
18. Child and family care programs are getting more attention at the national and State levels.
19. The local departments of social service are decentralizing their operations and

it is at these neighborhood levels where there is most promise for solving the problems.

20. The local departments are likely to remain the key scenes of action, but the State is likely to assume all of the funding (except for the federal portions) and to have the chief control.

21. Job banks and other job procurement devices are crucial for the success of employment services and cutting down on poverty.

22. Unemployment insurance is not a welfare program; employers contribute to a fund for this protection of their workers.

23. The Maryland Unemployment Insurance Fund carries the burden of payments to the unemployed. Employers contribute a percentage of their payrolls on the basis of their employment record.

24. Not all unemployed are eligible for insurance—the qualifications are reasonable.

25. The concept of appeal is present for those who think their payments should be larger or longer in period.

26. We have set up many stereotypes about women and as a result the State and nation have not made the best use of their resources.

27. State and federal laws now protect women from prejudice in work and promotional opportunities.

28. We forget our veterans too soon after wars are over.

Questions for Discussion. Take a position.

1. The entire social service program—all phases, disbursement, and services—should be under the federal government.
2. America should pass a "guaranteed annual wage" law.
3. Clients on welfare relief are not being assisted as much as they should.
4. Relief rolls need to be investigated more thoroughly.
5. General Public Assistance to Employable should receive federal funds.
6. Urban job procurement projects are not operating effectively.
7. Those workers on strike with good cause should be entitled (or not entitled) to unemployment insurance.
8. Rates and periods of payment for unemployment insurance need to be extended.
9. Placing the former social services and employment services under one department is a good idea (not a good idea).

Chapter 13: Education: Schools and Libraries

Review Questions

1. How many students are studying in public elementary, secondary, and higher educational institutions?
2. What are the costs for educating these students?
3. How many teachers are involved?
4. Why should education be viewed as an investment rather than an expenditure?
5. How does the Maryland Constitution support public education?
6. What is the role of the State Board of Education? How does it represent the public?
7. How does the full State funding for construction of public elementary and secondary school buildings operate?
8. Name any five of the eight priorities set forth for the Maryland public schools.
9. Give illustrations to show that the local (county) school boards and departments of education have autonomy and are creative.
10. Show that there is a disparity from one county to another in Maryland public school costs.
11. Describe the activities of the University of Maryland.
12. Name the eight State colleges and indicate some of their programs.
13. Why have the Maryland community colleges made such rapid progress?
14. What are the major categories into which the private colleges fall? Show how financial support is their major problem.

15. What is the role of the Maryland Council for Higher Education?
16. How is higher education funded in Maryland?
17. What are the special problems of the Maryland non-public elementary and secondary schools?
18. What are some of the problems dealt with by the Governor's Commission on the Structure and Governance of Education in Maryland?
19. What is the statutory authority for the State Division of Library Development and Services and what are some of its programs?
20. Show that the exciting activities are at the local (county-Baltimore City) libraries.

Basic Generalizations and Concepts. Support with facts.

1. Any way you put it—pupils, buildings, funds, teachers—the Maryland public and private schools are a gigantic undertaking.
2. Public education at the elementary and secondary levels is a Constitutionally established undertaking in Maryland.
3. Education is an investment, not an expenditure.
4. The State and local boards of education exist to establish policy and regulatory laws concerning schooling.
5. Numerous statutory laws have been passed by the legislature dealing with State aid and the conduct of the schools and colleges.
6. Full State funding (other than federal contributions) for construction costs of public elementary and secondary schools has taken a large burden off local governments.
7. Along with traditional problems such as reading, the local schools are currently giving more attention to career education, race and human relations—and especially to teacher accountability.
8. The tripartite system of public higher education assures most high school graduates in Maryland opportunities to go to college.
9. Private schools and colleges are direly in need of public financial aid. How to supply this funding represents a serious problem, especially the Constitutional question of church and state.
10. The unique and historic contributions of public and private schools at all levels—elementary, secondary, and college—are accepted by most Marylanders. How to keep both kinds of schools financially supportive is an unanswered question.
11. In contrast to the interest shown other services of government, such as transportation, health and mental hygiene and natural resources, there has been little inclination to create a cabinet-level secretariat handling all of education.
12. Maryland has come to the aid of public libraries late in its history, but recent State support should mark the beginning of rapid progress.

Questions for Discussion. Take a point of view.

1. The State should give greater financial support to private elementary and secondary schools, including Roman Catholic parochial institutions.
2. The State should increase support to private colleges.
3. All members of public elementary and secondary, as well as college, school boards should be elected.
4. Public community colleges, like the State colleges and the University of Maryland, should (should not) be State controlled and fully financed.
5. There should (should not) be a cabinet-status secretariat coordinating all educational levels.
6. A new system of State scholarships needs to be established.
7. College and graduate school admission procedures need to be changed.
8. New methods of grading in schools and colleges need to be established.
9. Schools and colleges have (have not) been too easy on students.
10. College education should (should not) be fully supported by public funds—no tuition.
11. The federal government should (should not) undertake all costs for public schools and colleges.
12. Public libraries should (should not) be a State undertaking.

Chapter 14: Human Relations and Problems of Aging

Review Questions

1. Show how the federal government has taken the lead in establishing rights for black citizens.
2. Show how Maryland has moved from a benevolent position toward "colored citizens" to a strong enforcement position.
3. What groups are now protected on the basis of the current responsibilities of the Maryland Commission on Human Relations?
4. How does the Commission operate and how does it interrelate with federal agencies in the human relations and rights fields?
5. What are major concerns in the fields of housing, employment, and community relations?
6. Indicate the kinds of cases handled by the Baltimore City Community Relations Commission.
7. What are some of the unsolved problems in human relations?
8. Name five black Marylanders who have played important roles in American history. Describe their contributions.
9. How is the Commission on Aging organized?
10. How many Marylanders are over 65 years of age and what are their main problems?
11. Why are the activities on aging likely to be placed under a separate cabinet-level secretariat?

Basic Generalizations and Concepts. Support with facts.

1. Late in its history America, including Maryland, awakened to the need for giving dignity and security to its black citizens.
2. The May 17, 1954, Supreme Court decision on school integration was the turning point in rights for minorities.
3. The U.S. Congress and Presidents have taken the lead in giving fuller meaning to the American dream that "all people are created equal."
4. It took the tragedy of Dr. Martin Luther King's assassination to awaken us even more fully to human rights.
5. The Maryland Commission on Human Relations is the enforcement arm of the State's statutory laws in this area.
6. Black history and the contributions of blacks to America's advancement are given little attention in history books.
7. Local human relations boards like the Baltimore City Community Relations Commission deal with grass-roots problems.
8. Civil rights have been expanded to deal with sex, ethnic background, creed, religion, and age—as well as race.
9. There are still many unsolved problems and though the schools are desegregated, they are not integrated.
10. Polarization and stereotypes exist among blacks and whites.
11. Maryland as a border State has an opportunity to be a beacon to the north and south in the human relations field.
12. Problems of the aging are getting more attention at last.
13. America, including Maryland, is beginning to realize that important man- and womanpower are lost by shelving the elderly.
14. The greatest problem the elderly face is health and the ability to pay for proper health care.
15. There is a great range in differences in health, mental ability, physical condition, job competency, and intellectual acumen among the 65-plus group. It is wrong to stereotype them into one homogeneous group.

Questions for Discussion. Take a position.

1. We have (have not) made good progress on the racial question in Maryland.
2. School busing should (should not) be used to bring racial integration.
3. The Maryland racial disturbances of 1967-68 set back (advanced) progress in racial affairs.

4. Employment opportunities represent the greatest need in racial progress.
5. Textbooks need to be rewritten to include contributions of minority groups.
6. The federal government has gone too far (not far enough) in requiring conformance with the laws on job employment and advancement of minority workers.
7. The county human relations commissions are ineffective (effective).
8. Quotas based on Maryland's black population of 18 percent should (should not) determine job preparation and college entrance.
9. There should be no compulsory retirement age.
10. Elderly persons should be given the same chance to hold jobs as others—based on ability.

Chapter 15: Department of Public Safety and Correctional Services

Review Questions

1. Show that we do not seem to have the answers to crime control or the treatment of criminals.
2. What are some alternatives to incarceration of prisoners?
3. What are the two major categories in the department and what activities fall under each category?
4. Describe the three-level approach of the Civil Defense and Emergency Planning Agency.
5. How are innocent victims of crimes compensated?
6. What is the role of the State Fire Prevention Commission and the Fire Marshal?
7. How does the Police Training Commission upgrade and standardize police work in Maryland?
8. Show that the Maryland State Police are no longer concerned with highway patrol alone.
9. Give illustrations to show that local police services in Maryland are scientific.
10. Paid and volunteer fire fighters are much more sophisticated than they were but a few years ago.
11. Describe the work carried out at the Reception, Diagnostic and Classification Center (males) located in the State Penitentiary.
12. Why is the State Penitentiary referred to as a maximum security institution?
13. Describe the activities carried out at the medium security institutions for offenders.
14. What provisions are there for women offenders?
15. How do the pre-release camps and minimum security centers bridge the gap between incarceration and freedom?
16. Why do the county (and Baltimore City) jails represent what appears to be the lowest level of progress in correctional institutions?
17. What are the points in debate about Patuxent Institution and the concept of the indeterminate sentence?
18. How do parole and probation operate in Maryland?
19. Describe the "pros" and "cons" of work-release, weekend and family leave, and other reforms tried in Maryland.
20. Why might the substitution of community correctional facilities for large institutional care be a good move? What cautions would you suggest?
21. How might pre-trial diversion and early diagnosis, evaluation, and classification into differential treatment improve correctional practices?
22. What changes might be made in the Maryland Criminal Code?
23. What is the role of the Maryland National Guard? Illustrate its operations at times of emergency.

Basic Generalizations and Concepts. Give supportive facts.

1. Crime is on the serious increase in America, including Maryland, and may well be the major concern of America today.
2. The problem of crime is particularly complex in that there is so much of it and we do not seem to have the answers.

3. Penologists and law enforcement officers believe that our correctional institutions are overloaded, antiquated, and underfunded.
4. The new trend in Maryland is toward looking at alternatives to incarceration—pre-trial intervention, work assignments, more liberal probation practices, halfway houses, work-release programs, weekend and family leaves for inmates, pre-release centers, and community-based correctional projects.
5. Civil defense tied in with emergency defense combines peace and wartime needs.
6. State compensation to innocent victims of crimes is a new and humane development.
7. The pre-service and in-service training of police officers and correctional officers has helped to lift these positions to a higher professional status.
8. The federal and State governments are giving greater financial support to the staffing and training of local police departments and local jails.
9. The task of the State Police trooper has changed radically in recent years.
10. Modern fire-fighting is becoming more dependent upon science and training.
11. The Maryland correctional system is undergoing radical change.
12. The county jails need sharp improvement.
13. Patuxent and the indeterminate sentence bring sharp division of opinion in penal circles.
14. Parole and probation hold promise for reducing the high numbers incarcerated in Maryland.
15. The Maryland Criminal Code needs thoroughgoing revision.
16. The Maryland National Guard is a citizens' defense unit.
17. The problem is to both protect society and rehabilitate the offender.

Questions for Discussion. Take a position.

1. We should stop the incarceration of all offenders but the hard-core criminals and put others in smaller community centers with outside work schedules.
2. The federal government should compensate for all damage done by storms, hurricanes, tornadoes, earthquakes, and other natural phenomena to private property.
3. The Maryland Criminal Injuries Compensation law should take care of property damage as well as personal injury.
4. Pre-trial intervention, parole, and probation should be used to a far greater degree than at present.
5. Capital punishment should (should not) be instituted in Maryland for heinous crimes.
6. Victimless crimes should not be included in the Maryland Criminal Code.
7. The county (and Baltimore City) jails should be operated by the State.
8. The Baltimore City Police Commissioner should be appointed by the Mayor instead of the Governor.
9. We are too soft on offenders. (We are too hard on offenders, not really rehabilitating them.)
10. Maryland needs special facilities for the seriously mentally disturbed, chronic criminal.
11. We should (should not) close Patuxent.
12. We give too much attention to offenders and not enough to the protection of non-offenders.
13. The underlying causes of crime—poverty, lack of education, poor housing—receive too little attention.

Chapter 16: Department of Natural Resources

Review Questions

1. Which five independent agencies were operating in the field of natural resources before 1969?
2. Why was unification a necessary step?

3. Show that in terms of programs, services, persons on payroll, and total budget, the department represents a big operation.
4. How does the Board of Review protect the public from unfair or unwise decisions by the Secretary or his staff?
5. Show how the department makes use of various commissions, committees, and trusts in order to hear from the so-called experts.
6. The independent boards are largely examining and investigating bodies. Give illustrations.
7. Show how extensive and important are Maryland fisheries.
8. Indicate the danger of pollution to the fisheries of Maryland.
9. How is oyster replanting seeking to keep ahead of pollution losses? How will the oyster hatchery on the Eastern Shore have some advantages over natural seeding?
10. How extensive is restocking of fish in Maryland?
11. Give illustrations to show that fishing and water resources are honored in Maryland by festivals.
12. Indicate five different restrictions on hunting in Maryland.
13. What are some practices used by federal game enforcement officers to trap hunters who violate hunting laws?
14. Show that Maryland has both abundance and scarcity in game and fowl.
15. Show that Maryland's State parks offer a variety of opportunities in recreation, scenic beauty, and natural lore.
16. Describe tree care, tree distribution, the nursery, and the log storage activities of the Forest Service Division.
17. Describe the work carried out by the Inland Division of the Natural Resources Police Force and that carried out by the Marine Police.
18. The Water Resources Administration carries out programs primarily divided into three basic categories—(1) enforcement, (2) permits and certification, and (3) technical services. Give illustrations of each.
19. Indicate five kinds of violations not permissible under the water quality standards laws of Maryland.
20. How extensive is the work carried out by the Maryland Environmental Service in maintaining and operating waste-water treatment plants?
21. What contributions are made by MES in incineration and processing of waste oils.
22. Why is the regional (and sometimes Statewide) approach to sewage treatment more effective than county or municipal approaches?
23. What are the main objectives of the power-plant siting activities of the department? How does the Environmental Trust Fund get its money and how are the funds spent?
24. What work is carried out by the Maryland Geological Survey?
25. What are the issues at odds in Statewide land use laws?
26. Why are Maryland's wetlands so important and how are they endangered?
27. Show how public recreation is given attention in Maryland.

Basic Generalizations and Concepts. Give supporting facts.

1. Before 1969 Maryland's approach to natural resources was through a number of independent agencies, boards and commissions, each operating with a single purpose such as forests, water resources, State parks, and game and fish.
2. Since 1969 there has been a unified approach to natural resources.
3. The department seeks the advice of expert practitioners through the use of many commissions and committees.
4. The fisheries represent one of Maryland's richest resources both as a commercial enterprise and as a recreational activity.
5. Water pollution represents a serious threat to Maryland's fisheries.
6. Oyster hatcheries are likely to replace natural seeding as a way to combat the losses due to pollution and natural phenomena such as storms.
7. Restocking is a way to insure the future of the fish catch.
8. The rodeo emphasizes the importance of cattle in the midwest and southwest.

So the various crab, oyster, clam, and boat-race celebrations in Maryland indicate the importance of fisheries in this State.

9. The Wildlife Administration has chosen to manage the State's wildlife population through habitat control rather than through stocking.
10. There are all sorts of hunting restrictions as a result of the control policy. In the cases of "endangered species" they cannot be hunted at all.
11. There is strict policing of hunting laws, at times to the dismay of hunters.
12. Maryland's State parks offer a wide variety of opportunities for camping, nature and history lore, hiking, boating, and other recreational activities.
13. Maryland's Forest Service has extensive programs in reforestation, fire prevention, and log storage.
14. Maryland's Inland Division of the Natural Resources Police Force apprehends violators of hunting and fishing laws.
15. Safety, in hunting and in boating, represents serious problems for the sportsman.
16. The Marine Police carry out numerous activities to lessen fatal and serious accidents on the water.
17. Many Marylanders are adding boats to their assets of a house and two automobiles; thus the water lanes are getting as crowded as the highways.
18. The establishment of a Maryland Water Quality Standards Law has assured more pure water and fewer polluted waterways. Industrial firms now know the State means business.
19. The view that environmental factors of sewage and waste-water treatment are not local (county or municipal) matters, but regional and even Statewide concerns has brought Maryland far in environmental concerns.
20. One result of the view noted in point 19 is that the State operates some and supports other waste-water treatment and waste-management facilities.
21. The new pyrolysis system of solid waste handling has moved the State in giant steps in incineration of waste.
22. With energy shortages likely to hound Maryland and the rest of the country for many years, the work of the power-plant siting activity in Maryland is especially important.
23. Geologic studies may well rejuvenate some of Maryland's former mineral wealth.
24. We face a debate in Maryland over ecology—whether it is more important than coal mining and use of marginal energy-producing resources.
25. The federal government has often led the way and stimulated the State with financial aid and legislation dealing with natural resources.

Questions for Discussion. Take a position.

1. The concept of a unified Department of Natural Resources makes good sense (or is all wrong).
2. Some of the advisory commissions might well be closed out now that the unified approach is stressed.
3. The interstate commissions are doing important work.
4. Fish kills should be punishable by heavy fines.
5. The Wildlife Administration should combine both habitat control and stocking (instead of just control) as a means of assuring an adequate wildlife population.
6. Game wardens are too severe in their policing (or not severe enough).
7. Hunting should not be permitted in State parks.
8. Maryland needs more year-round State parks.
9. Maryland's Forest Service can do more in encouraging tree planting in urban centers like Baltimore and in numerous suburban sections of the State that are as barren of greenery as inner cities.
10. All small-boat operators should be required to pass boating tests, as are motorists.
11. Water quality standards should be strictly supervised and enforced.

12. The Calvert Cliffs nuclear power plant should not (or should) have been permitted to be built.
13. All surface mining of coal, gravel, and sand should be controlled.
14. Maryland should have (or not have) a strict Statewide land-use bill.
15. Strict laws in reference to the development of Assateague Island should be passed—no private development.

Chapter 17: Department of Agriculture

Review Questions

1. Why was the State Board of Agriculture tied in with the University of Maryland for such a long period of time?
2. What activities take place at the Maryland Agricultural Experiment Station both on and off campus of the University of Maryland?
3. Show how federal and State support carries out activities of the Cooperative Extension Service in agriculture and home economics.
4. What is the task of the Maryland Agricultural Commission under the unified cabinet-level Secretary of Agriculture established in 1973?
5. Why is the State Board of Veterinary Medical Examiners a key body?
6. What activities fall under the responsibilities of the director of marketing and manpower?
7. What work is carried out by the director of animal industries?
8. What is the role of the director of plant industries and environmental affairs?
9. What products and activities are inspected and regulated by the State Chemist, the chief of field inspection, and the chief of weights and measures.
10. Show how the Secretary of the Department of Agriculture has tremendous power in dealing with crucial problems.

Basic Generalizations and Concepts. Give supporting facts.

1. It was natural for the University of Maryland to take over control of State agricultural activities for the past 117 years.
2. It was just as right to set up a separate State Department of Agriculture apart from the University in 1973.
3. The Agricultural Experiment Station is the State's research agency and has contributed widely to the advancement of agriculture.
4. The Cooperative Extension Service enables research and scientific agricultural methods to reach the individual farmer.
5. The Maryland Agricultural Commission enables experts to funnel their knowledge into State progress.
6. The commissions and councils set up policies dealing with agricultural products and activities.
7. The State protects various agricultural products for the consumer through inspectional and regulatory practices.
8. The Secretary of the department has strong powers of a regulatory nature.

Questions for Discussion. Take a position.

1. The Maryland Agricultural Experiment Station should be under the Department not the University of Maryland (or should remain where it is).
2. Pesticides containing DDT should be prohibited.
3. Many of the commissions dealing with single products (e.g., Apple Commission) should be abandoned since they may injure the unified approach to agriculture (or should be kept).
4. Maryland should seek to diversify even more widely its agricultural pursuits.
5. Farming still offers a grand opportunity in Maryland though the number of farms is decreasing.
6. There is no future for young Marylanders in farming—it takes too much capital.

Chapter 18: Department of Transportation and Public Service Commission

Review Questions

1. Show that before 1971 the various transportation modes were treated separately.
2. Why was it inefficient for the individual modes—highways, planes and trains—to continue to operate independently of other modes of transportation?
3. What stimuli (acts and funds) toward a State unified transportation plans were offered by the federal government in the 1960's and the 1970's?
4. How does the Maryland Transportation Trust Fund permit a simultaneous attack upon the full range of transportation problems?
5. Both federal and special funds support transportation's current operating expenditures—give illustrations.
6. How will the extra two cents in gasoline tax help transportation needs?
7. What are the roles of the Board of Review? The Transportation Commission? The Maryland Transportation Authority?
8. How does the Department of Transportation plan to involve community opinion in its programs for improvement?
9. What is the theory of the federal interstate highways system? What are the main Maryland roads in that system?
10. What is the theory of the State primary roads system? Name some primary roads not in the federal interstate system.
11. What is the purpose of the State secondary highways system? Describe the five-year funding plan for that system.
12. What is the importance of the Chesapeake Bay Bridge? The Baltimore Harbor Tunnel?
13. What maintenance activities are carried out in the highways system?
14. How are the county (Baltimore City) roads systems funded?
15. Indicate the economic and human loss caused by traffic accidents in Maryland.
16. Indicate five different activities of the Motor Vehicle Administration.
17. What kinds of restrictions exist in eligibility for driving licenses in Maryland? Under what conditions may licenses be revoked?
18. How does the chemical test for driving violations operate? The point system?
19. How are school buses safeguarded?
20. What are the terms of the compulsory motor vehicle insurance law? How does the Maryland Automobile Insurance Fund operate?
21. What are the plans for improving the Baltimore-Washington International Airport?
22. What is the status of the airports in Maryland's small towns?
23. Show that the Port of Baltimore is a crucial component in the economy of the State.
24. Review the history of the port.
25. Show that the port is one of the nation's greatest centers of international commerce.
26. How does containerization work?
27. What plans are offered for the port's future?
28. What important ports other than Baltimore exist in Maryland?
29. Describe some of the features of the Baltimore buses in the Mass Transit Administration. What is MTA planning for small urban areas throughout Maryland?
30. How has the federal government assisted mass rapid transit systems being planned for the Baltimore and Washington metropolitan areas? Describe the importance and the funding of the systems.
31. Why are the railroads important in any integrated transportation plans? What is the State doing in this connection?
32. What is the role of the Public Service Commission? What is the work of the General Counsel? The People's Counsel?

Generalizations and Concepts. Give supportive facts.

1. The modal approach to transportation is passé and the unitary approach has replaced it in Maryland.
2. Each mode in transportation is interdependent with other modes.
3. The federal government took the leadership role in moving away from the single-modal approach to transportation. Federal acts and federal financing were important incentives for Maryland's movement in this direction.
4. The Maryland Transportation Trust Fund facilitates the operation of the unitary approach to transportation.
5. At least in theory, it is imperative that there be community involvement in decision-making dealing with transportation plans.
6. The federal interstate highways system helps tie the nation together economically and in other ways.
7. The Maryland intrastate primary road system helps tie the State together economically and in other ways.
8. The State's secondary road system provides local travel functions and services to adjacent land uses.
9. The Chesapeake Bay toll bridges and the Baltimore Harbor Tunnel represent major, highly expensive highway projects that pay for themselves.
10. The counties still have an important role in local highways development.
11. The heavy toll taken by highway accidents is both unnecessary and unsolved.
12. Driving a motor vehicle is a privilege, and the State screens those who seek and retain operator's licenses.
13. The point system as a way of screening drivers reflects the State's concern about weeding out unfit operators of motor vehicles.
14. The compulsory motor vehicle insurance law shows that the State is becoming mandatory in its protective measures.
15. The Baltimore-Washington International Airport is a State responsibility.
16. The City of Baltimore was not financially capable of supporting the necessary physical changes to modernize the airport.
17. Airport study and improvement for small towns in Maryland represent unfinished business.
18. The success of the Port of Baltimore is the State's most important single factor in economic growth.
19. Port activities have been revolutionized in recent years.
20. Foreign trade is intimately interwoven in Maryland's progress through the Port of Baltimore.
21. The Port of Baltimore is a good example of how public and private enterprises can operate in the process of controlled capitalism for the common good.
22. Public ownership and management of bus transportation is based on the concept that the State's economy is dependent upon this venture.
23. The rapid transit systems planned for the Baltimore and Washington metropolitan areas give formal substance to the fact that the counties and the big city (in both cases) are economically bound together.
24. We are awakening perhaps too late to the importance of railroads to a State unitary transportation plan.
25. The Secretary of Transportation has great powers in making decisions, though they are open to review.
26. The Public Service Commission is the referee between the needs of the utilities and those of the public.

Questions for Discussion: Take a position.

1. The modal approach to transportation is better than the unitary approach (or the other way around).
2. The federal government should pay nearly all costs for the maintenance of interstate roads as it does now for construction.
3. The State is giving too much attention to primary roads and not enough to secondary highways.

4. The State should build another bridge across the Bay at the northern end of the Chesapeake.
5. The motor vehicle point system is too liberal and should be tightened.
6. Drunken drivers at first offense should have their operators' licenses revoked forever and jailed.
7. The State should subsidize more heavily the development of airports in the small Maryland communities.
8. The Baltimore rapid transit system is just too expensive to be worth it (or it is probably the best thing the metropolitan area has ever done).
9. The State should buy some of the abandoned railroad roadbeds and develop commuter traffic.
10. The Maryland Public Service Commission should have an ombudsman, as well as a people's counsel, associated with the agency.

Chapter 19: Department of Licensing and Regulation

Review Questions

1. Why might the department be considered a consumers' protective agency?
2. What social forces have brought radical changes in laws dealing with women in industry?
3. What are the main tasks of the Division of Labor and Industry?
4. The Division of Labor and Industry has six operating services. Name them and give an illustration of an activity carried out by each service.
5. Show how widespread is the coverage of insurance supervision by the State Insurance Division.
6. What recourse does a policy holder have if he feels he has been mistreated?
7. What are some of the important terms of the Insurance Reparations Reform Bill?
8. What are the "pros" and "cons" of "no-fault" automobile insurance? How is it working in other states?
9. How does the Bank Commissioner check on the fiscal health of State banks? What other activities are carried out by the commissioner?
10. What are the terms of the Maryland Small Loan Act? Why are problems related to sales finance so troublesome? Why was the office changed from Small Loans to Consumer Credit?
11. What are the roles of the Real Estate Commission of Maryland and its hearing board?
12. How do the State-chartered building and loan associations differ from the federally chartered institutions in the same field? Why does Maryland now seem better protected against more scandals in the building and loan field such as occurred some 15 years ago?
13. How is the consumer protected from shoddy or unsatisfactory home-improvement work?
14. Name three Maryland agencies that regulate entertainment or sports. What powers does each have?
15. Name five licensing agencies in the department. Should auto repairmen be licensed?

Generalizations and Concepts. Support with facts.

1. The Department of Licensing and Regulation is a protective agency.
2. The State is likely to see a greater demand for licensing and regulation of more consumer services.
3. The rights of labor, such as collective bargaining, are likely to be expanded and to cover more workers in the future.
4. The need for a Maryland Department of Labor has supporters on the "pro" and "con" sides.
5. Employers under federal and State requirements probably will be required to offer more protective labor measures (such as collective bargaining, minimum wages, and maximum hours) in the future.
6. The employer is held responsible for the safety of his workers.

7. Insurance companies and their practices are being more carefully scrutinized by the State Insurance Division. Reparations reform is in the air.
8. Insurance of bank accounts makes bank runs and failures, such as those of the 1930's, almost impossible.
9. The days of unrestricted interests on small loans are over.
10. The real estate field is just beginning to police its practices.
11. Maryland is now protected against more scandals and bankruptcies in the building and loan field.
12. The consumer now stands protected against shoddy work in home improvement.
13. Maryland regulates many recreational activities that might otherwise be controlled by groups that profit from illegal procedures.
14. The censorship of movies is a very debatable subject, with U.S. Supreme Court decisions as backdrops.
15. Licensing control by workers in the field being licensed is going to be more open to criticism in that it brings about in-bred practices.

Questions for Discussion. Take a position.

1. Auto repairmen should be licensed and repair jobs regulated.
2. All special laws dealing with women in industry should be repealed. Women should be governed by the same labor laws as men.
3. Minimum wage laws tend to keep young people from getting jobs.
4. The State should have permanent safety inspectors at all factories or industrial plants employing more than 100 workers.
5. The State should adopt "no-fault" automobile insurance.
6. The office of the Commissioner of Consumer Credit should be given more powers in credit sales affairs.
7. The Real Estate Commission should have greater power in the control of practices in the field.
8. All home improvements, irrespective of amounts of money involved, should be governed by the Home Improvement Commission.
9. The State Board of Motion Picture Censors should be abolished.
10. At least one-third of all members on boards that license practitioners should be lay persons.

Chapter 20: Workmen's Compensation Commission

Review Questions

1. What are the powers and the responsibilities of the Workmen's Compensation Commission?
2. Describe three ways by which Maryland employers can meet their compensation responsibilities.
3. What is the basic purpose of the compensation system?
4. What are the requirements about filing a claim for compensation?
5. What are the possible compensation claims for temporary partial disability injuries?
6. What are the possible compensation claims for temporary total disability injuries?
7. What are the possible claims for permanent partial disability injuries? For permanent total disability?
8. What death claims are possible?
9. Who are eligible for compensation based on occupational diseases? How have the courts clarified eligibility?
10. What is the composition of the Medical Board of Occupational Diseases and what are its powers?
11. How have compensation laws been liberalized by recent court decisions?
12. How does the right to appeal operate?
13. Give some indication of the number and kinds of compensation cases heard in a typical year.

Basic Generalizations and Concepts. Give supporting facts.

1. Maryland was one of the early states to establish workmen's compensation protections.
2. The concept of compensation grows out of the belief that employers have the responsibility to protect workers.
3. The insurance requirements for employers reflect the belief that private enterprise can be the insurer but if that is not used, government is there with the State Accident Fund to do the job.
4. The requirements in regard to filing claims and collecting compensation insurance reflect the belief that government (the State) should see that the worker is justly compensated but it should also protect society from the malingerer.
5. Compensation awards reflect cost of living, nature of injuries, and loss of pay.
6. Compensation awards are based on the category of injuries. Are they temporary or permanent? Total or partial?
7. The concept of compensation for occupational disease is a comparatively new thought; courts are continually adding new meanings to this protective law.
8. In all compensation cases the right of appeal by employer or worker is of great importance.
9. The greatest number of compensation cases are in the temporary, partially injured category.

Questions for Discussion. Take a position.

1. Compensation rates are much too low in these days of rising prices.
2. Anyone intoxicated while injured should not be eligible for compensation.
3. The requirements for filing claims should be relaxed, particularly the 60-day limit for filing the first claim. Sometimes symptoms appear a long time after an accident.
4. Death claims should be paid in full whether there are wholly dependent survivors eligible or partially dependent survivors. A death is a loss of life either way.
5. Compensation for occupational diseases in its ultimate interpretation could lead to payments for virtually every illness of a worker and every death. For example, many workers are prone to high blood pressure in tense jobs and diabetes in sedentary jobs. Should they be compensated?

Chapter 21: Economic and Community Development

Review Questions

1. Why is it more difficult to identify the tasks of the Department of Economic and Community Development than it is for others?
2. What are the incentives for industrial firms to settle in a particular area?
3. How does the department see its own mission?
4. What is the role of the Board of Review?
5. Name some of the commissions that operate under the department.
6. How has the Office of Business and Industrial Development aided business expansion?
7. How has the federal government assisted in business expansion?
8. How has the Maryland Industrial Development Financing Authority encouraged new enterprises to come to the State?
9. What are some of the concrete contributions made by the Division of Tourism?
10. Why is the Seafood Marketing Authority valuable to the economy of the State?
11. What historical and cultural affairs are promoted through the department?
12. Maryland counties and municipalities have housing agencies (not directly related to the Department of Economic and Community Planning) that handle problems falling into three categories. Describe the categories and give illustrations from Baltimore City.
13. Describe Cambridge's public housing and urban renewal projects.
14. What kinds of data are included in the Community Economic Inventory for each county?

15. Select five different counties in different geographic areas—Eastern Shore, southern, central, and western Maryland, plus one county in the Baltimore or Washington metropolitan area. For each of these five counties (one should be the one you live in) describe industrial advantages, tax incentives (if stated), and other advantages.
16. How are businesses incorporated in Maryland? What are some of the governing rules?

Basic Generalizations and Concepts. Give supporting facts.

1. The role of the Department of Economic and Community Development is not as clear-cut as that of the other cabinet-level secretariats.
2. Perhaps the name of the DECD should be changed to reflect what it does, viz., Department for Maryland's Development.
3. The reasons for new firms settling in Maryland are varied, e.g., tax incentives and labor availability; but these two obvious ones are joined by availability of facilities for educational, recreational, and spiritual growth.
4. The federal government's financial and other incentives have been of great importance in the State's economic growth.
5. Maryland has not capitalized on tourism as an economic factor in the State's development.
6. The State's historic shrines need to be cherished and perpetuated. The past is part of the present; to lose the past is to endanger the present.
7. Cultural and art activities enrich life beyond the material rewards.
8. With federal assistance, Maryland communities are increasingly making certain that there is a floor of standards below which no family should be asked to exist in housing requirements. Public housing is an accepted principle in America.
9. Urban renewal not only furthers the humanitarian and aesthetic goals, it is good for the economy of a city.
10. The concept of enthusiastic business and civic leaders at the county level working with the Department of Economic and Community Development to produce economic incentives for new industrial enterprises is proving effective.
11. Maryland's incorporation laws are clear-cut.

Questions for Discussion. Take a position.

1. Development agencies stress material growth too much and intellectual and cultural progress too little.
2. Development agencies can stress both economic growth and the preservation of ecology and the State's heritage—as the Department of Economic and Community Development seems to favor.
3. Tax incentives for new firms can be unfair to older firms in a community.
4. Maryland has not capitalized on the natural colonial settings in places like Annapolis, while Virginia has brought thousands of tourists to a reconstructed colonial village—Williamsburg.
5. The Baltimore Symphony and other cultural activities should be heavily supported by State funds.
6. Public housing and urban renewal have (have not) proved their worth.
7. Maryland should encourage the further development of science-based industries, particularly with the presence of highly qualified personnel in the Baltimore and Washington areas, as well as the presence of science-centered universities.
8. The Eastern Shore and western Maryland have resources and advantages never really capitalized for industrial growth.

Chapter 22: Department of Personnel

Review Questions

1. What were the factors that moved the country from a principle of patronage to a principle of civil service or merit in government jobs?
2. Why was it easier to introduce civil service reforms at the State level before the county level?

3. How did county home rule help bring civil service to county governments?
4. What rights for workers, beyond getting the job, were introduced by organized labor and other employee groups?
5. How does the State employment policy protect equality in employment?
6. How does job classification help assure fairness in employment?
7. How are fair salary schedules established?
8. How do competitive examinations and eligibility promote fairness in promotion?
9. What is the theory of retirement and how is the government worker in Maryland provided for his older years?
10. Why is the grievance procedure an important right of workers?
11. Describe the workings of three major retirement systems for State government workers.
12. What are the arguments in favor of extending collective bargaining to instructors of State colleges?

Basic Generalizations and Concepts. Give supporting facts.

1. Civil service came into being in the 1880's to create knowledgeable, dedicated public servants for politically motivated appointments. "The best person should get the job."
2. Civil service came first to the federal government, then to the states, and lastly to local governments, with exceptions such as Baltimore City.
3. From job procurement, the rights of government workers were extended to include vacations, collective bargaining, and grievance procedures.
4. From *civil service*, primarily concerned with "who gets the job," the concept of the best person was extended to *merit system*, viz. "who is promoted."
5. From the concept of merit system there evolved the field of *personnel practices* which included vacation pay, illness and pension coverages, and other fringe benefits in employment.
6. The legal requirements of personnel practices are increasingly requiring attention, e.g., minimum wage practices; and fair employment practices as affecting sex, race, ethnic and religious backgrounds, and older Americans.
7. The federal government has led the way in the promotion of fair employment practice laws.
8. Organized labor has recently brought many government workers under its aegis.
9. Even colleges are beginning to be bound by contract requirements between the faculty's organization and management.

Questions for Discussion. Take a position.

1. The various cabinet-level Secretaries should (should not) come under civil service requirements.
2. Preferential appointments and promotions should (or should not) be made in such a way as to bring in more minority representation in each State department where the gaps are significantly below the 18 percent characteristic of the black population of the State.
3. College professors should have the choice of joining the State pension system or the national teachers' pension plan (TIAA).
4. Collective bargaining should be a right for all State governmental workers.
5. The State has too many governmental workers on its personnel rolls.

Chapter 23: Department of State Planning

Review Questions

1. Explain the function of the Department of State Planning as the coordinator of activities by other departments.
2. What is the role of the State Planning Commission?
3. Indicate five major bond authorization bills submitted by the department to the 1972 legislative session.
4. What kinds of review coordination with the federal government are carried out by the State Clearing House in the department?

5. How does the "Early Warning" notification operate?
6. How does the Clearing House improve the State's quality of proposals for federal aid and its chances for getting federal money?
7. How successful is the State in getting federal funds?
8. Which natural resources commissions have been aided by the State Planning Research Programs Division?
9. How does the State Planning model help to forecast future actions by the State and local governmental units?
10. Describe any one of the river basin planning programs and indicate its value.
11. How is the department participating in the North Atlantic Regional Water Resources Study?
12. What is the purpose of the Northeastern United States Water Supply Study?
13. How does the department relate to the 23 county planning agencies and the 55 active municipal planning departments in Maryland? How does it help them get federal money through the "701" application? Give some illustrations of the community technical advisory services. Indicate how the department helps these local planning agencies to fulfill the federal requirements for areawide planning.
14. What is the department's concept about providing alternatives to decision makers in planning? What kinds of resource utilization is the Division of Comprehensive State Planning interested in developing?
15. What are the six factors given prime attention in the Generalized State Land Use Plan published in 1974?
16. How is the Human Resources Plan of the department unique?
17. Show how land-use planning coordination helps to bring about improved living.
18. Give an illustration to show that alternative solutions to the transportation needs of a Maryland area must bring a final decision that is best for most of the people.
19. Show how the Department of State Planning cooperates with other State departments to bring about better water supplies and improved waste management.
20. Why is interstate cooperation imperative when planning Chesapeake Bay and Susquehanna River projects?
21. What recommendations were made by the department in respect to Assateague Island?
22. What role does the department play in helping State and local agencies secure federal housing funds?
23. What are multi-purpose governmental centers? What values do they have?

Basic Generalizations and Concepts. Give supporting facts.

1. Overall State coordination by the Department of State Planning is a crucial requirement if money, resources, time, and efforts are not to be wasted.
2. The coordination, planning, and submittal to the legislature of the State's capital improvements programs and the authorization of the related bonds are the unique responsibilities of the Department of State Planning.
3. The State Clearing House sees State projects, that are supported in whole or in part by federal funds, through all the necessary stages and hurdles.
4. The Clearing House has increased the level of federal grant funding in Maryland.
5. The research division of the department has taken a lot of the guesswork out of the planning of State projects and replaced the pure guesses with scientific and computerized information.
6. The river basin planning commissions and the water supply studies represent considerable success in interstate cooperation.
7. A good deal of the important planning is taking place at the municipal, county, and regional levels with the assistance of the Department of Planning.
8. Comprehensive State planning gives the State and its public and private agencies a clear direction of where Maryland should be going.
9. Human, as well as land, resources are to be comprehensively planned.
10. If Transportation is to operate at the unitary level then there must be much planning within that department and between Transportation and other departments.

11. Environmental quality and open-space usage can be assured by planning.
12. Assateague Island should be developed as a State and federal park.
13. Multi-purpose government centers will prove their worth to the public.

Questions for Discussion. Take a position.

1. All State departments should report their planning desires to the Department of State Planning at the very first stages of development.
2. The DSP should have the absolute power of veto over any State project.
3. Capital improvement bond issues for State projects should require voter approval much as is required for municipal projects by the City of Baltimore.
4. All municipal, county, and State requests for federal construction funds should be screened by DSP before they are sent to Washington.
5. State Planning models which seek to forecast economic-environmental impacts on employment, income and population flow are subject to so many variable factors that they have limited value.
6. Areawide and regional planning are hindered by narrow county feelings.
7. Comprehensive State Planning destroys the initiative of many public and private agencies in that it eliminates alternatives and competition.
8. No land at Assateague should be for private development.
9. The Department of State Planning has too much power over local and State agencies now—to give it more would be injurious.

Chapter 24: Department of General Services

Review Questions

1. Name some of the State's buildings in Annapolis. In Baltimore.
2. Show that the State is a big real estate developer.
3. Show how the maintenance and repair of State governmental structures are gigantic tasks.
4. What sensitivities are involved in the central purchasing and storage of supplies and equipment? In the selection and appointment of architects and engineers for State capital projects?
5. Which former independent agencies are, since 1970, under the aegis of the Secretary of General Services?
6. Indicate the power of the Secretary of General Services.
7. What is the composition of the Board of Architectural Review and what is its role?
8. What is the role of the Commission on Artistic Property?
9. What is the task of the War Memorial Commission?
10. Indicate five operations carried out by the office of the Director of Engineering and Construction.
11. What is the importance of central State purchasing? Central management of printing and publications?
12. Why should there be a Hall of Records and a State Archivist?
13. Trace the steps and the agencies with which one must touch base if a capital project is to be completed.

Basic Generalizations and Concepts. Give supporting facts.

1. The State is a big real estate developer and land owner.
2. Authorizations for capital bond issues in any single year run into hundreds of millions of dollars.
3. The Department of General Services is the real estate agent and the custodian of property for the State.
4. Central purchasing of supplies and equipment for all State functions saves Maryland much money and assures good quality.
5. The Secretary of the department has wide powers such as the selection and appointment of architects and engineers, which, though subject to the approval of the Board of Public Works, is fraught with sensitivities.
6. There is board review of architectural design and artistic elements.

7. Clear-cut standards and specifications are established and in use for all major building projects.
8. The public school construction division operates a program involving a quarter billion of authorized bond issues yearly.
9. Maryland has an official Hall of Records which gives documentary support to past happenings.
10. There are formal steps that are required for the progress of a capital improvement—each step is a protective measure in the use of State money.

Questions for Discussion. Take a position.

1. All State governmental buildings of importance, especially the ones in Baltimore and Friendship, should be moved to Annapolis or its suburbs, e.g. Parole.
2. The State central purchasing agency should also operate for county and municipal groups, thus increasing quantities and lowering unit costs.
3. Engineers and architects should be selected through closed bidding procedures.
4. Authorities outside the State of Maryland should serve on the Board of Architectural Review.
5. Land purchases for future State governmental complexes should be bought 20 or 50 years in advance of usage.
6. The time between the incubation of an idea dealing with a new building and its fulfillment needs to be shortened.

Chapter 25: Department of Budget and Fiscal Planning

Review Questions

1. Why have the demands for governmental services increased so sharply in recent years?
2. Show how State budgets have increased sharply in recent years.
3. How have county budgets followed the trend?
4. Show that the Maryland Constitution sets forth much of the required budgetary procedure and the requirements for authorizations of bond issues.
5. What are the tasks of the State Comptroller and the Treasurer? How do they get their jobs?
6. How does the Constitutional requirement for a "balanced budget" affect budgeting procedures?
7. What is meant by State general funds being non-earmarked money?
8. Give illustrations to show that the federal government is a large contributor to the revenues received by Maryland.
9. Illustrate that special funds that come to the State revenue are earmarked for special uses.
10. Describe the rates and the amount of revenue brought into the State by any five of the State taxes discussed in this chapter.
11. What are the roles of the Lottery Commission and the director of the lottery?
12. How do the lottery fund and the winnings operate? What portion of the State's profits could go to aid the elderly?
13. Show that more than 50 percent of the State's revenue was appropriated to civil divisions—county and municipal governments. Indicate some of the programs receiving such aid.
14. Show that county tax rates vary sharply.
15. Show that the State and federal governments supply counties (including Baltimore City) with much more than one-half the revenue they need.
16. How do assessments of property determine a county's (or Baltimore City's) property tax rate? What reforms are being initiated in assessments of property?
17. Show that municipal taxes vary in Maryland.
18. How are bond sales handled?
19. Indicate the steps in the preparation and the passage of the State budget.
20. Who are the members of the Board of Revenue Estimates and why is their work so important? How related to the budget?

21. Why is the Board of Public Works probably the most important State board? Who are its members?
22. What is meant by the statement that the budget is the Governor's responsibility?
23. Describe the operations of the various divisions of the Department of Budget and Fiscal Planning.

Basic Generalizations and Concepts. Give supporting facts.

1. The public demands more and more services from government.
2. The cost of State and local government in Maryland has risen sharply in recent years.
3. The Maryland Constitution describes the duties of the key budgetary officers and the procedures in passing the annual State budget. It also describes State loan authorizations and procedures for paying debt service.
4. General funds are revenues that are not earmarked and can be spent for any authorized purpose.
5. Federal funds are increasingly becoming a more important source of State revenue. Most federal funds are earmarked for specific purposes, e.g., education and social services.
6. Special funds are monies collected for a special or earmarked purpose such as highways.
7. The State property tax is earmarked for payment of debt services on capital building programs.
8. The State graduated income tax on individuals is the greatest tax source of revenue for the State.
9. The counties (including Baltimore City) receive a 50 percent (with a few below that figure) piggy-back income tax which individuals pay in addition to the State tax.
10. The State sales and use tax is the second highest tax source of revenue.
11. A number of the revenues from taxes are shared by State and counties (and Baltimore City), e.g., the tobacco tax, the alcoholic beverages excise tax, and the tax on horse racing.
12. The State Lottery required a Constitutional amendment to legalize it in Maryland in 1973 and it is likely to be part of the State's financing structure for all of the foreseeable future.
13. Of all the State's profits from the lottery, 25 percent might go to the support of aid to the elderly.
14. More than one-half of all the revenue collected by the State is turned back to county and municipal governments.
15. State and federal funds are the sources of most of the typical Maryland county's revenue. The remainder of the revenues come largely from local property taxes.
16. In general, the higher the assessment (or the greater the assessment is of the total value), the lower the tax rate.
17. The problem of equalizing assessments in Maryland has presented many pitfalls. Annual assessments administered by State assessors seem to be the most equitable plan.
18. The more a political unit borrows for capital improvement the greater the debt service portion of the budget.
19. Fiscal years start July 1st and end the following June 30th. The State and all of its political units operate their budgets on fiscal years.
20. The budget procedure for any one year is a long-drawn-out process that virtually involves a State institution in continual budget-making.
21. Maryland's Constitution provides for an executive budget system.
22. The State budget must be balanced—there can be no deficit spending.
23. Taxes are increased in rates or new ones established as needs are evaluated in terms of the required general fund monies and the necessary monies.
24. The Board of Revenue Estimates studies the expected revenues that make up the general fund, federal fund, and special fund. Though the board's estimates are based on well-established principles, some of the work is based on good guesses.

25. The Board of Public Works has more responsibility for spending State money than any other State agency.
26. The Department of Budget and Fiscal Planning is responsible for the preparation of the budget and does its work through long- and short-term planning.
27. The budget reflects the philosophy of the Governor and the State administration.

Questions for Discussion. Take a position.

1. The public expects too much from government—then gripes about paying the bill.
2. State taxes can be cut down in this way . . . or the $2.7 billion budget for fiscal 1975 is just about right.
3. The Treasurer should be a Statewide elected officer.
4. There are too many special or earmarked funds in the budget. Studies should be made to place some of these monies in the general fund to simplify distribution.
5. Instead of borrowing money for needed capital costs, some of the buildings might be paid for on a "pay as you go" basis, getting the money from the current operating budget, thus saving interest payments.
6. The State property tax should be eliminated since Marylanders pay county (or Baltimore City) property taxes.
7. Since the State sales tax is a regressive tax, it should be abandoned and the income tax rates hiked to make up for lost revenue.
8. Off-track betting should be established in Maryland as in New York State, with profits going to the State.
9. At least 25 percent of all the State's profit on the lottery should go towards support of education.
10. The piggy-back tax revenues which go to county governments should be kept by the State and used to establish full State funding of all public elementary and secondary education in Maryland.
11. County and municipal governments in Maryland depend too much on property taxes—other forms of taxation should be used.
12. Uniform, annual assessment of property by the State will solve the problem of disparities in taxes paid by homeowners in different counties.
13. There should be a Constitutional or statutory limit of 15 years on all State and local bond issues.
14. The budget procedures are too drawn out—they can be streamlined.
15. The Board of Revenue Estimates should have outside consultants work with it in estimating revenues.
16. The Board of Public Works should not need to review or approve purchases of less than $5,000. It should give that authority to the Secretary of the department involved.
17. The Department of Budget and Fiscal Planning should recommend to a department Secretary how much money needs to be cut from his proposed budget; but let the Secretary decide where he will make the cut.
18. The Department of Budget and Fiscal Planning should insist that each department submitting a budget have it accompanied by 5-, 10-, 15-, and 20-year long-range plans.

INDEX

Note: There are important threads that run through many chapters of the book. It might be well to follow some of these threads by turning to the pages listed in the Index. For example, one thread is the role of the federal government in practically all State affairs. To summarize this point read the pages listed under U.S. Constitution, U.S. Supreme Court, U.S. Congress and federal aid. To follow the influence of the Constitution of Maryland read pages noted under heading. Other threads deal with the Courts of Maryland, the General Assembly and the Md. Attorney-General. A hurried reading of page references under a particular county listing offers a summary of its accomplishments and problems.